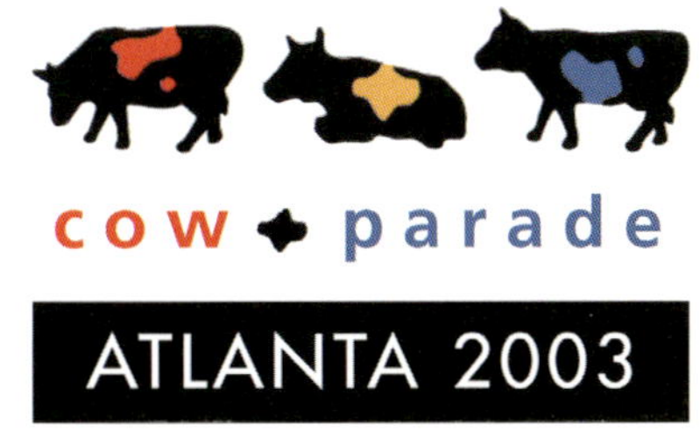
cow parade
ATLANTA 2003
www.cowparade.net

CowParade Atlanta

Celebrating the Art and Culture of the Olympic City

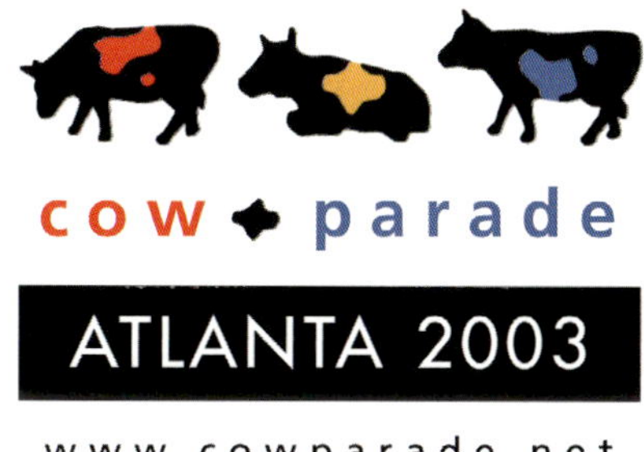

CowParade Holdings Corporation

ORANGE FRAZER *PRESS*
Wilmington, Ohio

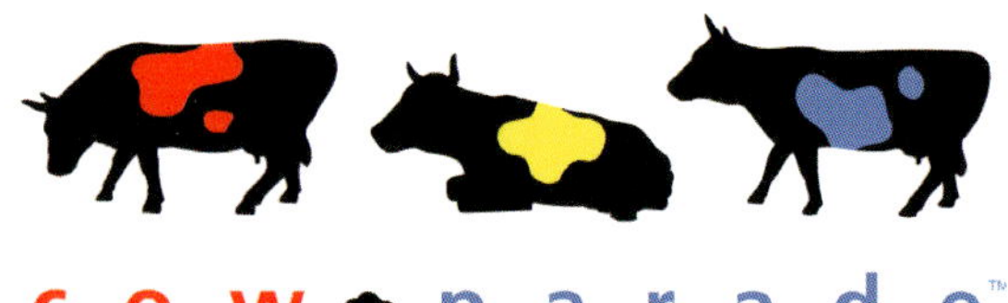

ISBN 1-882203-28-3

Text: Evelyn Ashley, Ronald Fox, Mary L. Sorrel
Cow photography: Matt Baxter
Cover photography: Charlie McCullers
Cover cow: *Freedom Cow* by Stan Mullins and *Atlanta Skyline* by Ashley Mack
Cow silhouettes: Heather Harris, IDIO Technology Studios, Inc.
Book and cover design: Tim Fauley, Orange Frazer Press
Art direction: Marcy Hawley, Orange Frazer Press
Image on page 6, 7, 82, 93 © Lucia Duncan
Image on page 8 © Promotions Marketing, Inc.
Image on page 12 © Delta Air Lines
Image on page 16 © Laura Nix
Image on page 40 © Gary Tilt
Images on page 110, 111 © Jim Carter
Images on page 38 © John Coley
Image on page 67, 139, 140, 169 © Alan B. McKeon
Image on page 142, 143 © Paul Flack
Images on page 184 © Brent A. Thale

Visit the CowParade website at www.cowparade.net

Printed in Canada

Additional copies of *CowParade Atlanta: Celebrating the Art and Culture of the Olympic City* may be ordered directly from:
Orange Frazer Press
P.O. Box 214
Wilmington OH 45177

Telephone 1.800.852.9332 for price and shipping information
Website: www.orangefrazer.com

Library of Congress Cataloging-in-Publication Data

CowParade Atlanta (2003)
Cowparade Atlanta 2003 / CowParade Holdings Corporation ; [cow photography, Matt Baxter].
p. cm.
Catalog of CowParade Atlanta, an exhibition of 150 cow sculptures painted by the artists of Atlanta, Ga., held May 2003-Nov. 2003.
Includes index.
ISBN 1-882203-28-3
1. Cows in art--Exhibitions. 2. Community arts projects--Georgia--Atlanta--Exhibitions.
3. Public sculpture--Georgia--Atlanta--History--21st century--Exhibitions. 4. Cows--Anecdotes. I. Baxter, Matt. II. Title.

N7668.C68C68 2003b
731'.83296422'09758231--dc22

2003061175

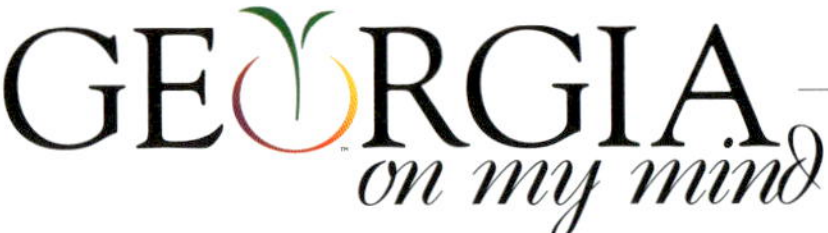

Janis Cannon
Deputy Commissioner of Tourism, State of Georgia

Dear Fellow Lovers of Cows and The Great State of Georgia,

On behalf of the State of Georgia, thank you for your support of CowParade Atlanta! This wonderful, magical exhibit came to our City for the summer of 2003, and along the way, brought smiles to millions of people. It showed, once again, what terrific, community-minded, corporate citizens we have, and raised significant money for very worthy charitable organizations, as well.

We are proud to be the first State in the Southeast to host the cows and to help set the bar for business support and artistic creativity. A private citizen, Evelyn Ashley, and her tireless efforts to promote the city and give back to the community, are the reason the cows came home.

Through this book, we invite you to enjoy the fabulous art of CowParade Atlanta, the story of how it came to be, and it's overwhelming success. Enjoy the effective and moving art that is the cows. And thank you again for your support of this once-in-a-lifetime event.

Have a Great Georgia Day!

Janis Cannon
Deputy Commissioner of Tourism, State of Georgia

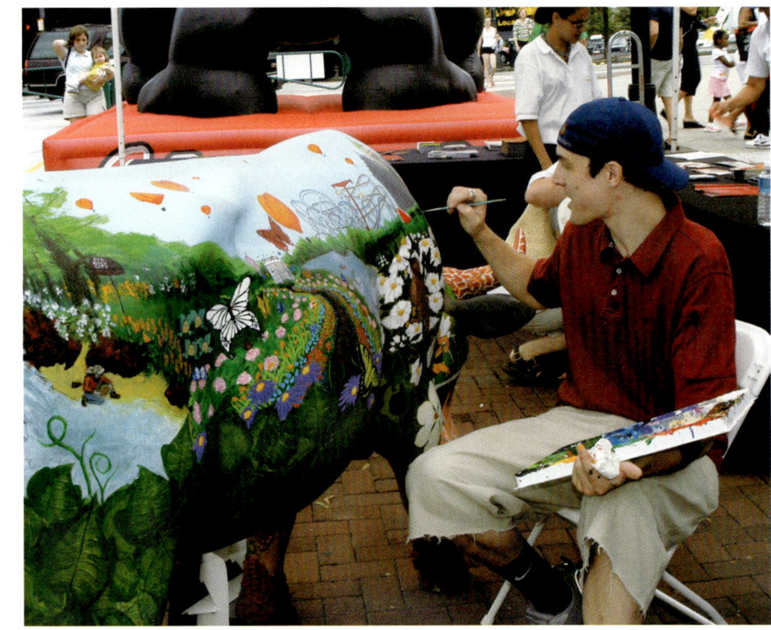

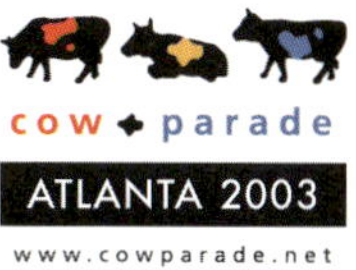

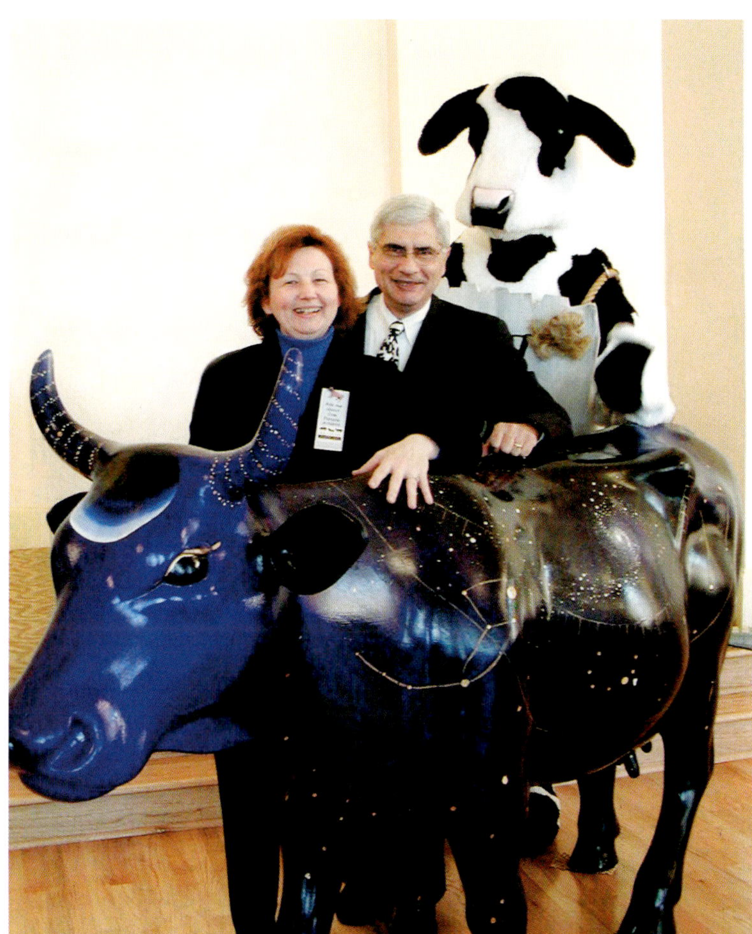

Jerry Elbaum
President, CowParade

WELCOME TO ATLANTA. WHAT YOU WILL SEE on the following pages are the spectacular creations of the artists who participated in this memorable event. Some of these are the works of preeminent artists; others the labors of aspiring artists. Altogether, approximately 130 original works of art were created for exhibition in a variety of public and private venues.

I thank all the artists who participated in this undertaking and the many corporate, business, and individual patrons whose sponsorships helped underwrite the cost of the exhibit. Nothing would have been possible without the leadership of Evelyn Ashley and Alan McKeon, the sponsorship support of Chick-fil-A, McKenna Long & Aldridge, the Southeast United Dairy Industry Association, Inc. and the rest of the CowParade Atlanta team.

Finally, thank you to the people of Atlanta and the state of Georgia for welcoming the cows with open arms and putting their own, unique stamp on CowParade.

Sincerely,

Jerry Elbaum
President, CowParade

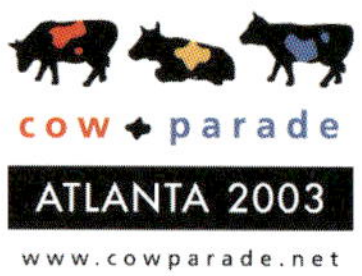

Evelyn Ashley
Chairman, CowParade Atlanta

Dear Friends,

Inside this book you'll find the fabulous story of how a group of volunteers with an amazing amount of support from businesses with vision—and a sense of community—joined together to create, launch and make a success of CowParade Atlanta.

The process of putting this event together has been overwhelming and amazing and fantastic all at once. Many people ask me how you go about doing something like this and I tell them that being Chairman of this event was like starting a business on steroids. When we started working in the fall of 2002, we had no start-up capital and yet we knew we had a hard deadline of getting the event opened by the end of June 2003. The key to every successful business is getting the right people around you. I have been lucky to have a group of people that got on board from the beginning and have helped me bring this event to life. Without their hard work, intensity, introductions, and support there would be no CowParade Atlanta!

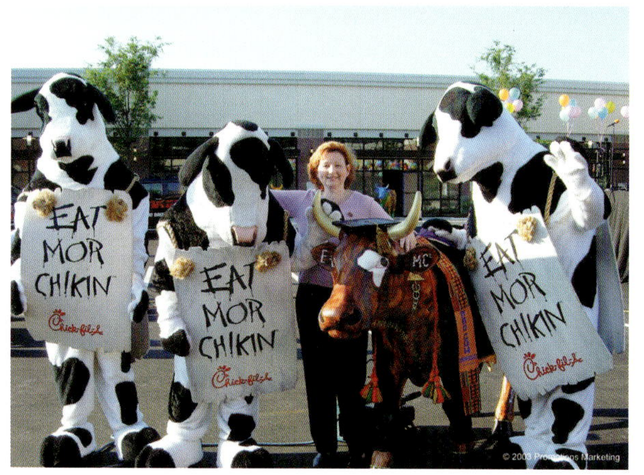

Had anyone told me a year ago that we would have support from over 50 sponsors to produce over 150 cows selected from designs submitted by over 700 artists, I would have laughed. In December of 2002, when we had only one cow sponsored, this looked like an insurmountable challenge. Yet here we are, with cows all over the streets, painted by unbelievably talented artists, with fantastic response from the sponsors—and a fabulous CowParade.

My husband, Alan McKeon, played a major part in the creation of CowParade Atlanta. We live by the rule that when an idea gives you butterflies in the stomach (whether due to fear, excitement or some other feeling!) it is probably important enough to act on it. We did, with the help of so many others. Here is a "dream to reality" product. Who knows what child, what artist, what entrepreneur CowParade Atlanta might inspire?

Moo!

Evelyn Ashley

Chairman
CowParade Atlanta

Moo'ving Art Around The World

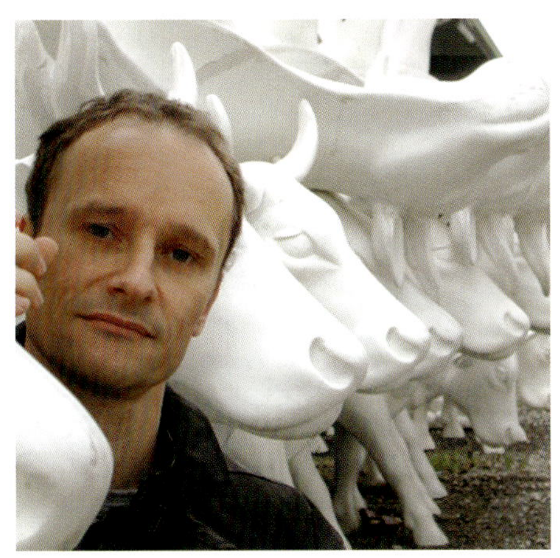

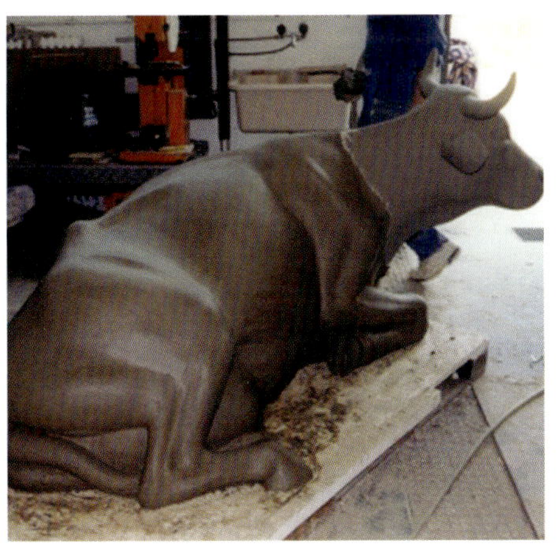

CowParade is the world's largest and premier public art event. From Chicago and New York in 1999 to London, Sydney, and Auckland, CowParade continues to evolve, not just in size, but also in quality and creativity. While the basic cow sculptures remain the same, each city's artists are challenged by the creations from past events, inspired by the culture and history of their respective cities, and moved by their own interpretation of the cow as an object of or canvas for art. No two works of art are the same.

The essence of CowParade is the artistic creativity it generates and the wonderful smiles it brings to the faces of children and adults alike who are touched by the delightful creations. As a bonus, the events ultimately benefit charity through the auction of the cows at the conclusion of the event. CowParade events have raised millions for charities worldwide.

Why Cows?

Simply, they make people smile and have the added benefit of making a great canvas for art. The beloved CowParade sculptures were created by Pascal Knapp, a Swiss-born artist who resides in New York. Pascal's father, Walter Knapp, an artist himself and a Zurich businessman, conceived of the cow-art concept and asked Pascal to create the first cow sculpture—the standing cow for an event titled 'Land Ahoy, Off to Zurich' in 1998. Pascal enthusiastically accepted the assignment and went to work.

The process entailed first creating a wooden armature around which he sculpted the cow out of clay. He used roughly one ton of clay to create the cow sculpture. His sculpture was so well received by the Zurich Retailer's Association he was immediately asked to do two more models. He then created the grazing and the reclining cows. Each cow sculpture provides the artist with a broad canvas and unique curves and angles, making them ideally suited to all forms of art. They have now been reinterpreted, altered, and morphed into over 2500 one-of-a-kind works of art, capturing the hearts and imaginations of over 100 million people worldwide.

Chicago, New York and Beyond. Peter Hanig, a Chicago shoe retailer, saw the exhibit in Zurich in the summer of 1998 and immediately felt the event should be brought to the Windy City. Three hundred cows and millions of visitors later, CowParade Chicago 1999 was regarded as the single largest and most successful event in the history of the city. CowParades conclude with an auction of the cows benefitting local non-profit organizations. CowParade Chicago's auction netted an incredible $2 million plus for local non-profits, averaging over $15,000 per cow.

From Chicago, CowParade moved to New York City in the summer of 2000, where five hundred cows grazed Central Park, Rockefeller Center, Park Avenue, and other world famous locations, capturing the hearts and imaginations of New Yorkers and its 10 million plus visitors. It was the first and only event staged simultaneously in all five New York City boroughs and was regarded by Mayor Guiliani as the Big Apple's top event of the millennium year.

In 2001 CowParade moved south to Kansas City, Missouri and Houston, Texas. CowParade Houston, the first event with a single charitable beneficiary, raised over $1 million for the Texas Children's Hospital. In 2002 and 2003, the cows truly spanned the globe, with events in Portland, London, Sydney, Las Vegas, San Antonio, Auckland, Dublin, and Brussels, proving that the cow is truly a universally beloved animal. In September 2003, the "cows come home" to West Hartford, Connecticut, the hometown of CowParade, while Tokyo hosts the first CowParade in Asia. Stay tuned to www.cowparade.net for events in 2004 as the CowParade canvas continues to diversify with events in cities in South Africa, Sweden, and England.

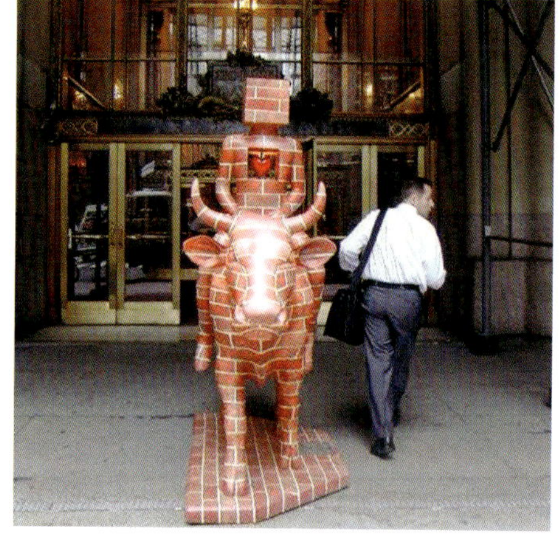

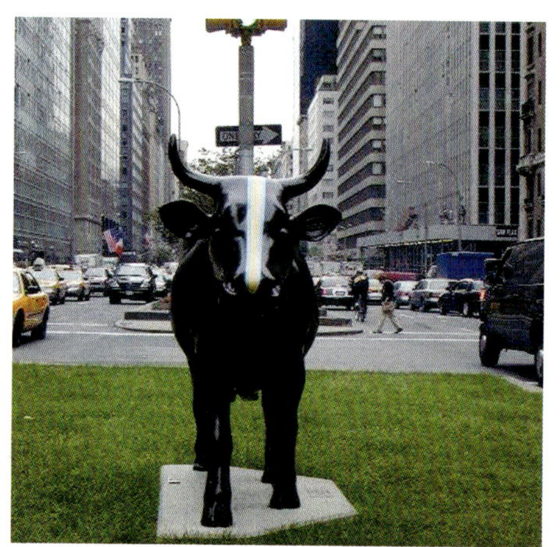

Atlanta—Cows in History

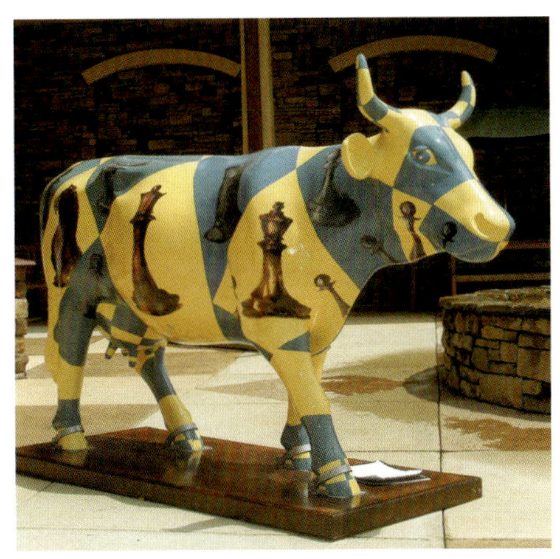

It is only fitting that the CowParade cows should ultimately come to Atlanta. Many of the roads that now weave through this magnificent southern metropolis got their start as cow trails, where farmers and merchants traveled the same paths as the cows to begin what would grow to be a major metropolitan center. To this day, pastureland surrounds the City and cows still graze on the edges of one of America's most vibrant business communities.

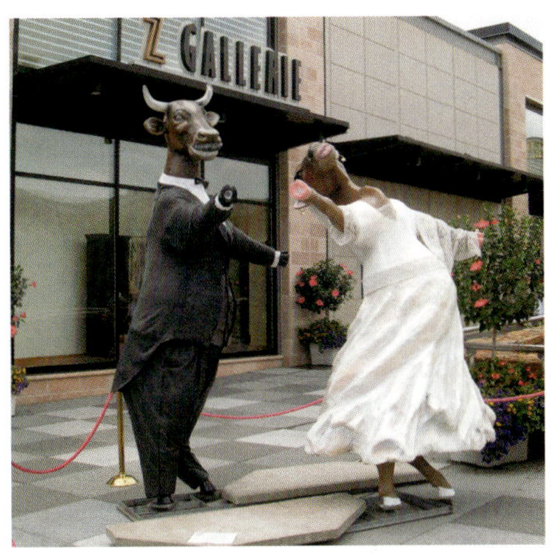

Maybe it's because of that history with cows that the people of Atlanta embraced CowParade and enthusiastically created their own. CowParade Atlanta wrote its own page in the ever-evolving history of the City. Volunteers turned out in droves to support the infrastructure an event of this magnitude requires; artists took a chance and found that transferring their style from canvas to udders was fun (and gave them new perspectives on their craft); and Atlantans and visitors photographed one another, on and around cows, in "herds" of their own.

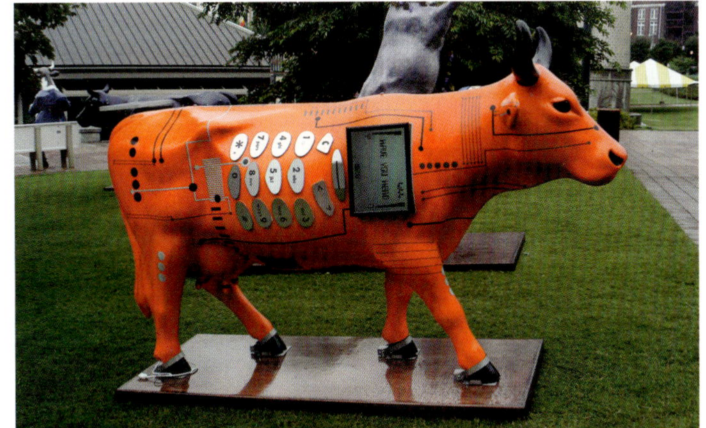

The Making of CowParade Atlanta

How did CowParade make its way South? It started when Evelyn Ashley and her husband, Alan McKeon, took a trip to New York in the summer of 2000.

Like everyone who happens upon a CowParade and its herds of cows on streets or in building lobbies, seeing the cows made them ask, "What on Earth is this?" While they were among New York's herds, they spent time looking at the creative art and talking with others about the cows being there. When they returned home to Atlanta they remained intrigued.

A year and a half later, Alan, in his annual quest for just the "right" Christmas gift, entered the Houston CowParade's on-line auction and bought Evelyn a cow. On Christmas morning, she unwrapped Cosmic Cow, a blue cow that twinkles with the stars of the galaxy (created by former astronaut, Cynthia Scott-Johnson), and went from being intrigued by the cows to decorating a room around one.

Everyone who saw Cosmic asked, "Why have they never been to Atlanta?" Curious about that herself, and eager to see a CowParade in Atlanta, Evelyn emailed CowParade Holdings in Connecticut for information. Six weeks later she met with CowParade Holdings CEO Jerry Elbaum, who persuaded Evelyn, a partner at McKenna Long & Aldridge, that she was the ideal person to make an event like this happen. In turn, McKenna Long & Aldridge recognized the community and charity impact of CowParade and agreed to sign on as host sponsor, and to donate Evelyn, a support team, and office space to the event.

Even Cosmic Cow got into the act, serving as an ambassador for those who'd never seen a CowParade and couldn't imagine life-sized cows as art. Now Cosmic is back in Evelyn and Alan's living room, and Evelyn curiously awaits Alan's next gift—and, perhaps, the next adventure it will take them on.

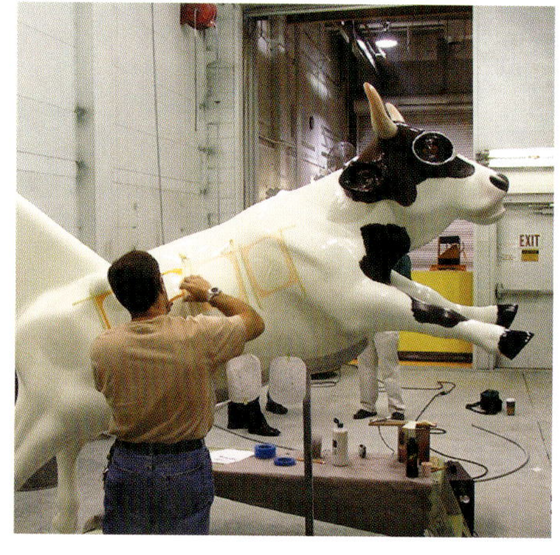

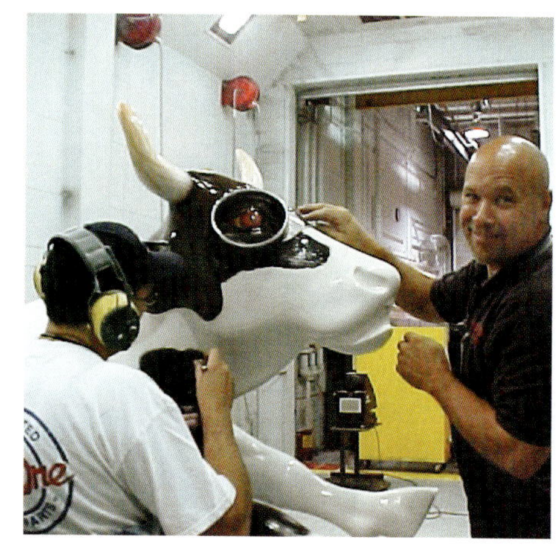

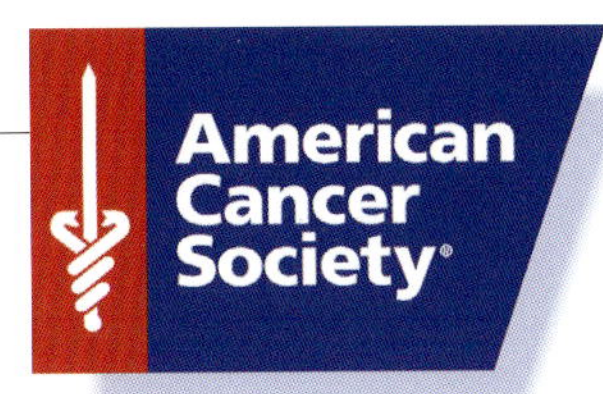

Jack Shipkowski
Executive Director, Southeast Regional Office of
American Cancer Society

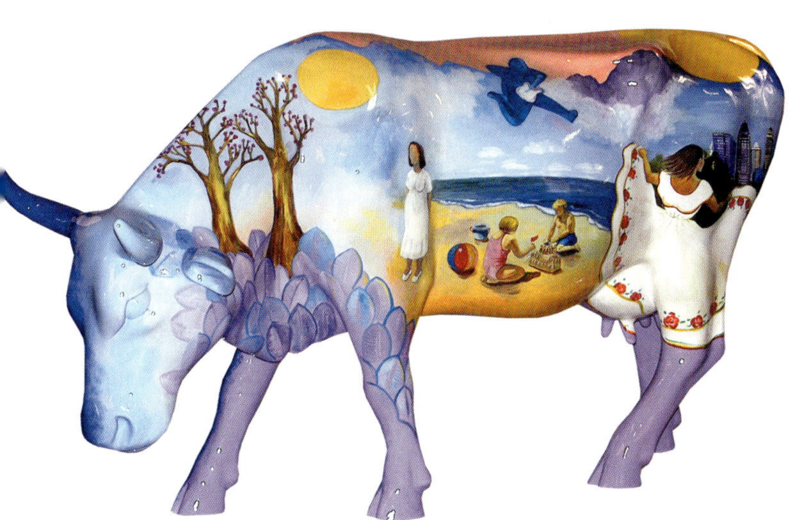

The American Cancer Society's Southeast Division is proud to be one of the beneficiaries of CowParade Atlanta. The fight against cancer requires the support of concerned individuals, corporations and organizations. The American Cancer Society thanks you for your generosity.

Proceeds from CowParade Atlanta were donated through the Cattle Barons' Ball—a Cancer Society fundraiser that has become a national phenomenon and, coincidentally also made its debut in Atlanta in 2003. The western-style event, which takes place in 50 cities, offers an exciting evening of fun, entertainment and fund-raising.

Dollars raised through CowParade Atlanta, the Cattle Barons' Ball, and other American Cancer Society fund-raising events, support the Society's efforts in research, education, advocacy and service.

Jack Shipkowski

Executive Director, Southeast Regional Office of
American Cancer Society

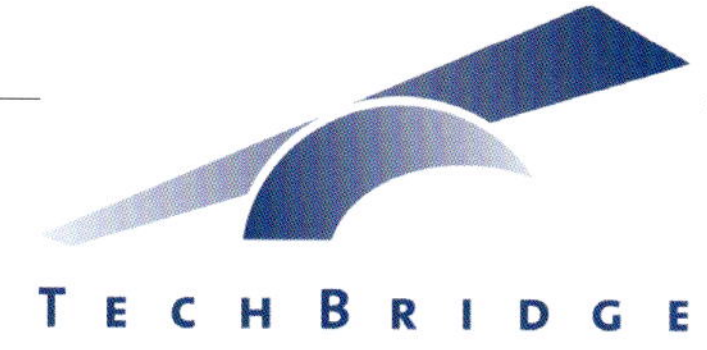

Jack McMillan
Chief Executive Officer, TechBridge

TechBridge is an Atlanta-based nonprofit organization that helps other nonprofits use technology to better serve the community. TechBridge provides professional, affordable technology consulting services, innovative technology solutions and access to the financial, technical and human resources that nonprofits need to be successful with technology. We were pleased to be chosen as a CowParade Atlanta beneficiary and welcomed the opportunity to spread awareness of TechBridge and our mission.

When nonprofits better integrate technology into their daily operations, they can deliver their services more effectively and reach their full potential. TechBridge helps greater Atlanta's nonprofits reach that potential.

In 2002 alone, TechBridge delivered over 7,000 hours of professional technology services and programming for more than 40 nonprofits in the Atlanta area, and as an affiliate of the national NPower network, we donated over $500,000 in free software.

We were so excited to be involved in CowParade Atlanta that we signed on to sponsor a cow, too. Our cow, Chip, created by Georgia artist Mary Engle, truly represents TechBridge and the work we do. She is made out of 15.5 lbs of SIMMS, 12 lbs of Circuit Boards / Finger Cards and 25.83 lbs of CPUs all donated by FREE BYTES, a nonprofit organization that reuses and recycles computer equipment. When we unveiled her at our May 2003 Digital Ball fund-raiser, we weren't sure how much she weighed, but we knew she was a heavy hitter—and a hit!

Best Regards,

Jack McMillan
Chief Executive Officer
TechBridge

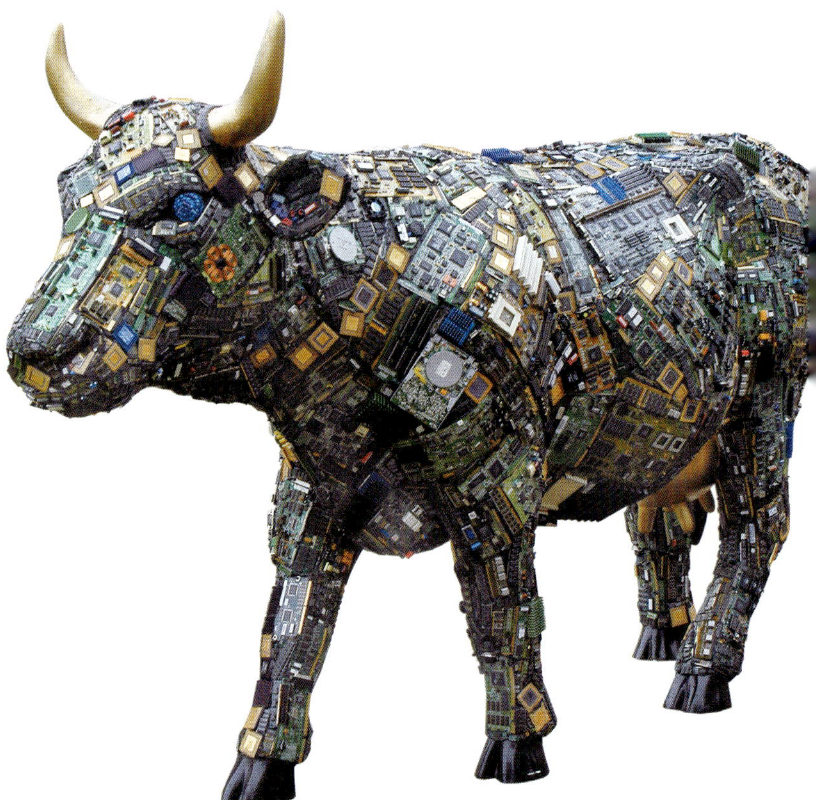

CowParade Atlanta Presenting Sponsor Chick-fil-A

WITH A RALLYING CRY OF "Welkum Brutherz, Join the Fite," Chick-fil-A's famous Cows welcomed their CowParade brethren to Atlanta, and Chick-fil-A—one of the nation's largest privately-held restaurant chains—signed on as presenting sponsor of CowParade Atlanta. The marriage was a natural partnership, as Chick-fil-A is well-known for its award-winning "Eat Mor Chikin®" advertising campaign that features renegade Cows urging consumers to choose chicken over beef. Chick-fil-A's 100-plus Atlanta-area operators joined forces with CowParade to create an enjoyable and memorable event for the city and its visitors.

Chick-fil-A and their "Eat Mor Chikin" Cows lent their creativity and support to CowParade from the start. The clever Cows carried "Welkum" signs and painted CowParade cows during the kick-off press conference; played key roles in all of CowParade's events and promotional activities; and even sent a bovine contingent to Centennial Olympic Park to wish the CowParade cows well as they took their places on Atlanta's streets.

In addition to helping raise money for CowParade Atlanta's beneficiaries, Chick-fil-A chose to auction some of the herd it received as presenting sponsor to benefit WinShape Homes®, a long-term foster care program established by Chick-fil-A founder S. Truett Cathy.

Credited with introducing the original boneless breast of chicken sandwich and pioneering in-mall fast food, Atlanta-based Chick-fil-A, with 1100+ restaurants in 36 states, is the third-largest quick-service chicken restaurant chain in the nation, based on annual sales.

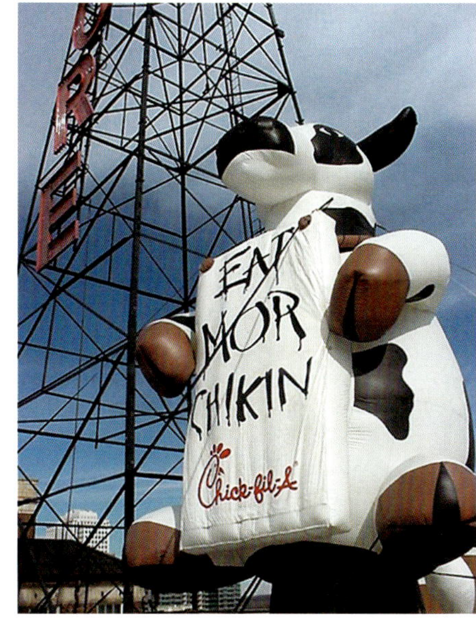

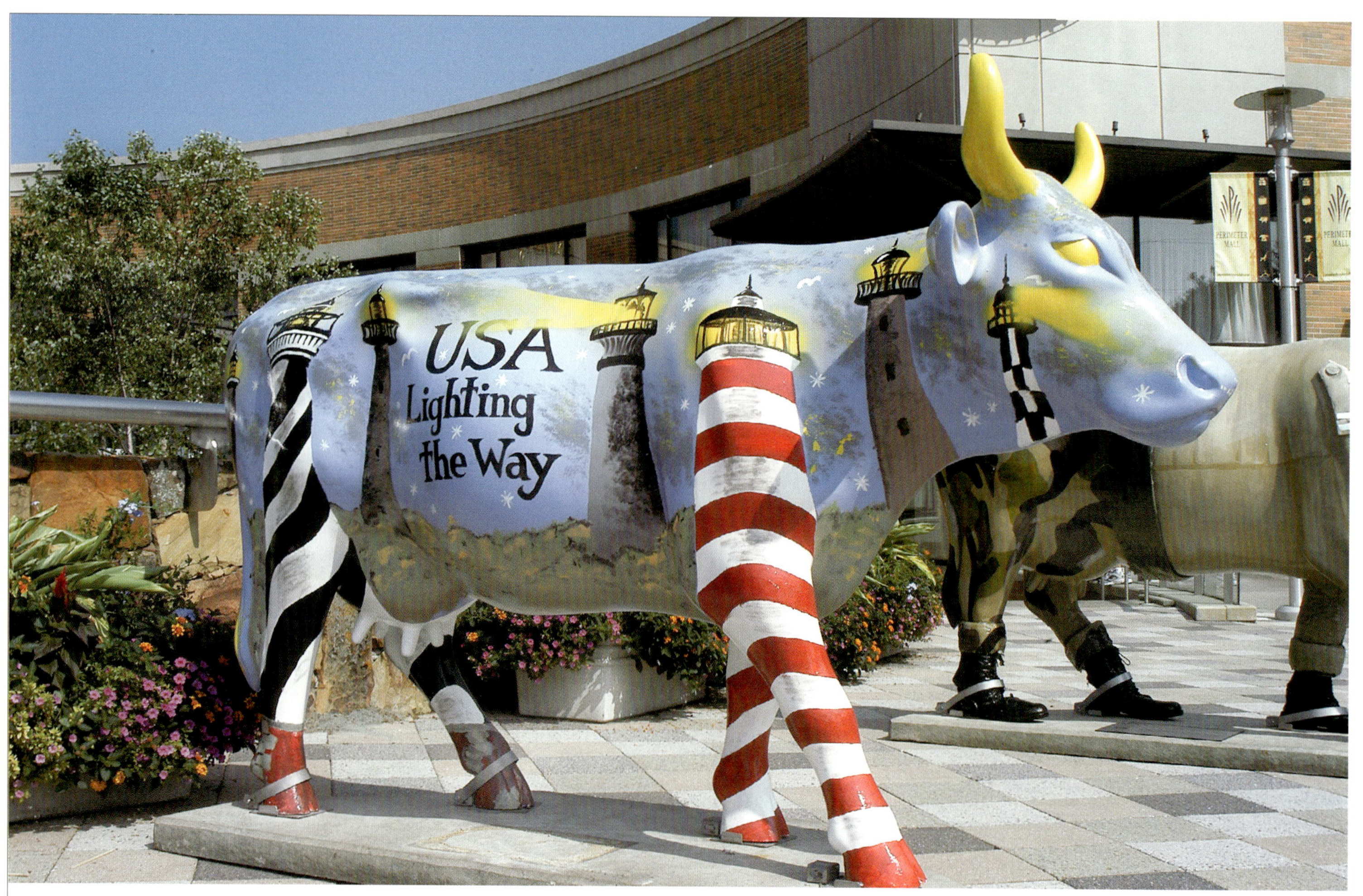

Lighting the Way USA
Zachary Cambria & Justin Winslow
Chick-fil-A

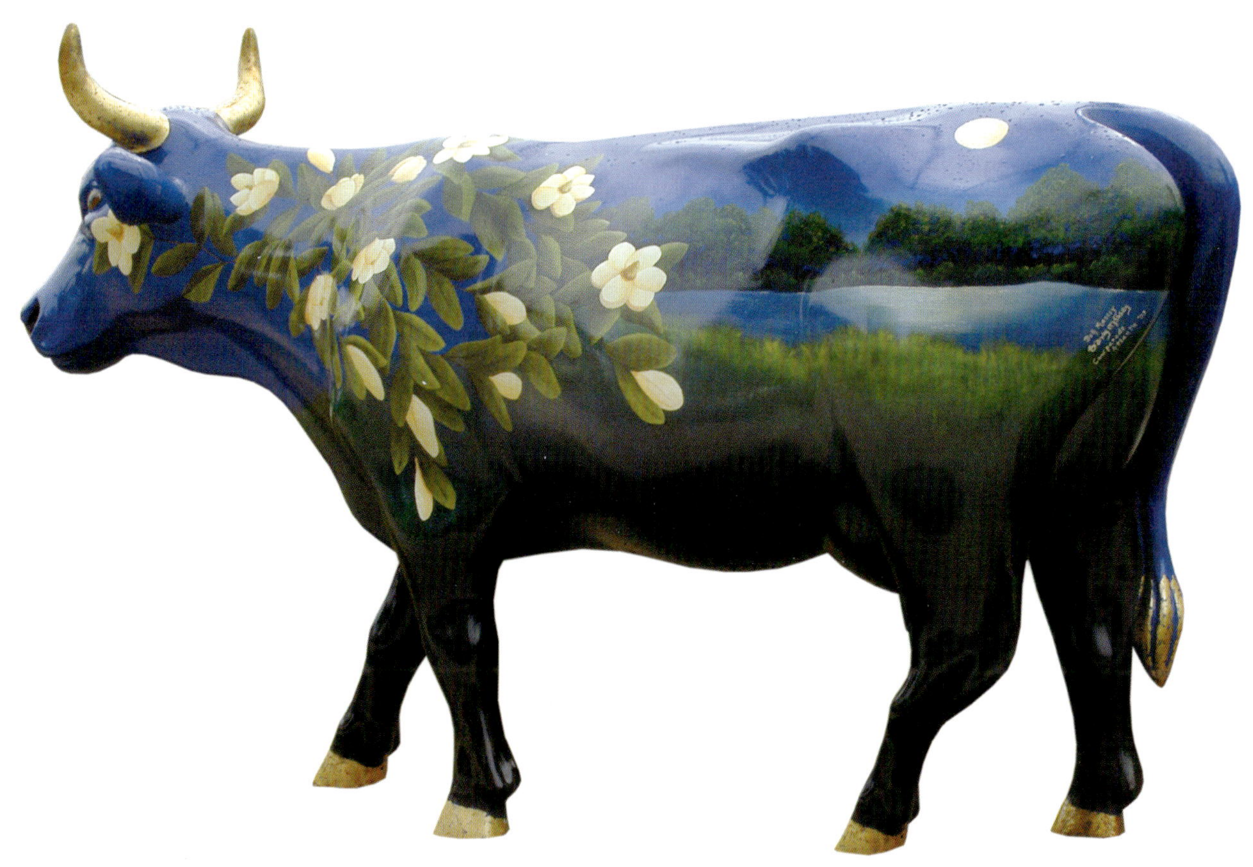

Moo-on Light and Magnolias
Dell Massey
Chick-fil-A

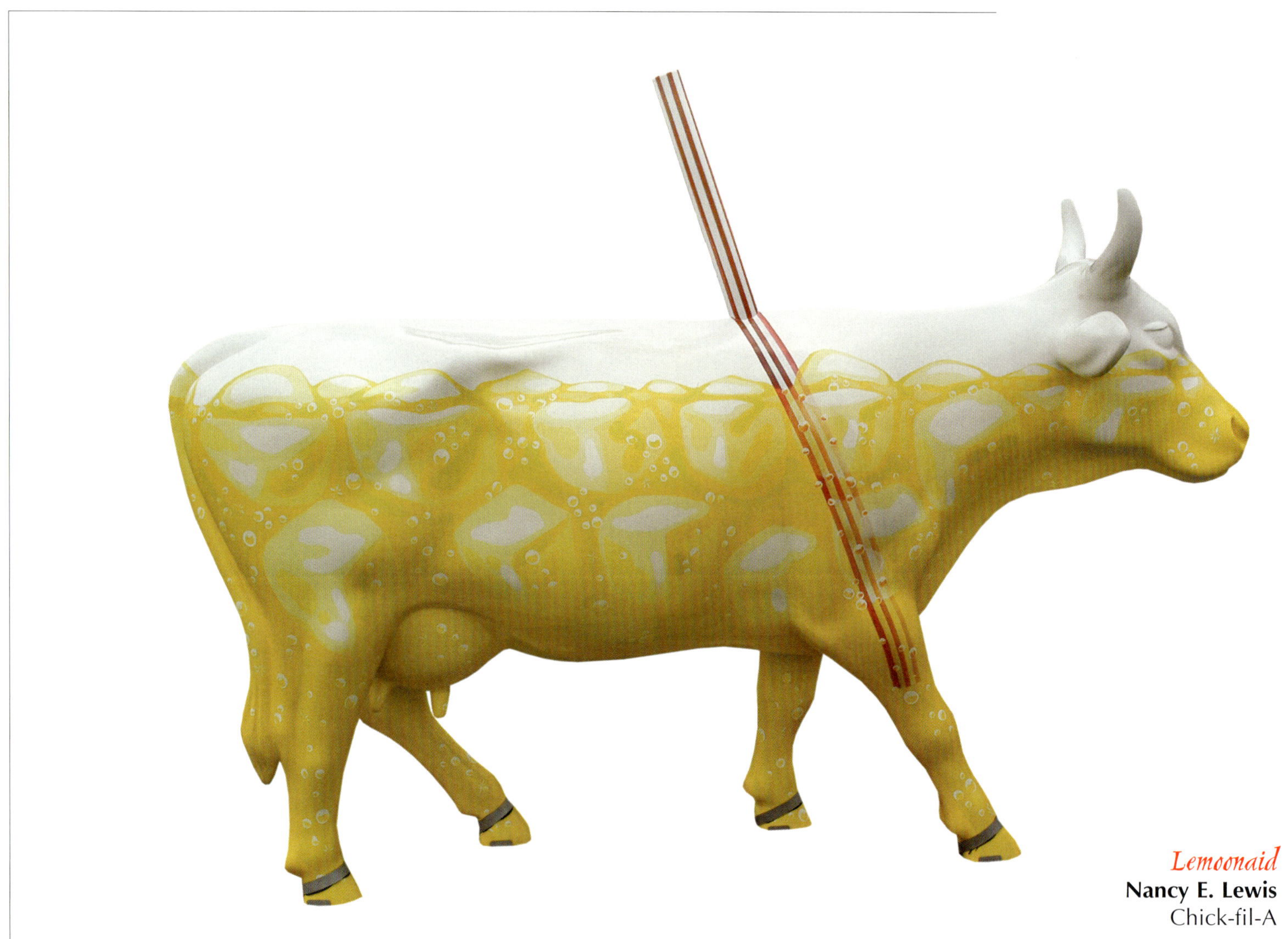

Lemoonaid
Nancy E. Lewis
Chick-fil-A

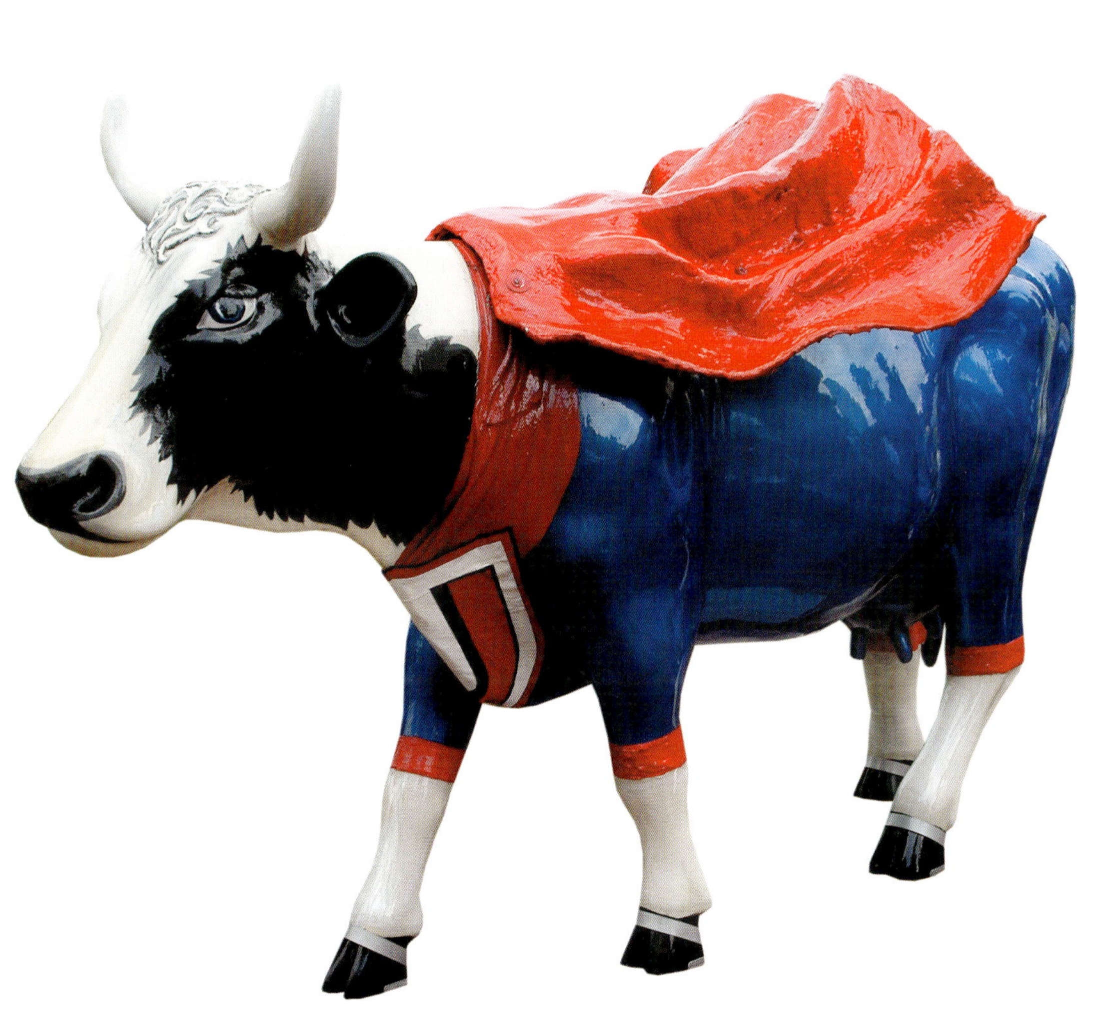

Untippable
Chris Warner
Chick-fil-A

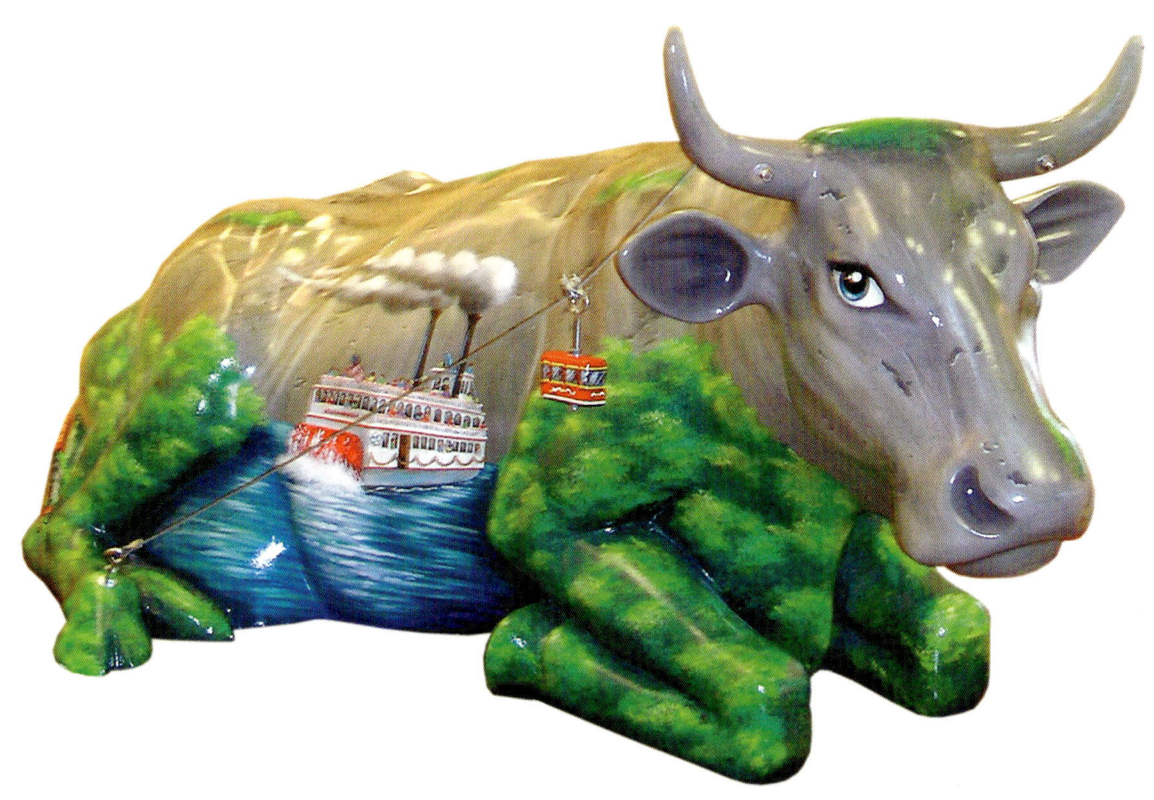

Steern Moontain
Nancy E. Lewis
Chick-fil-A

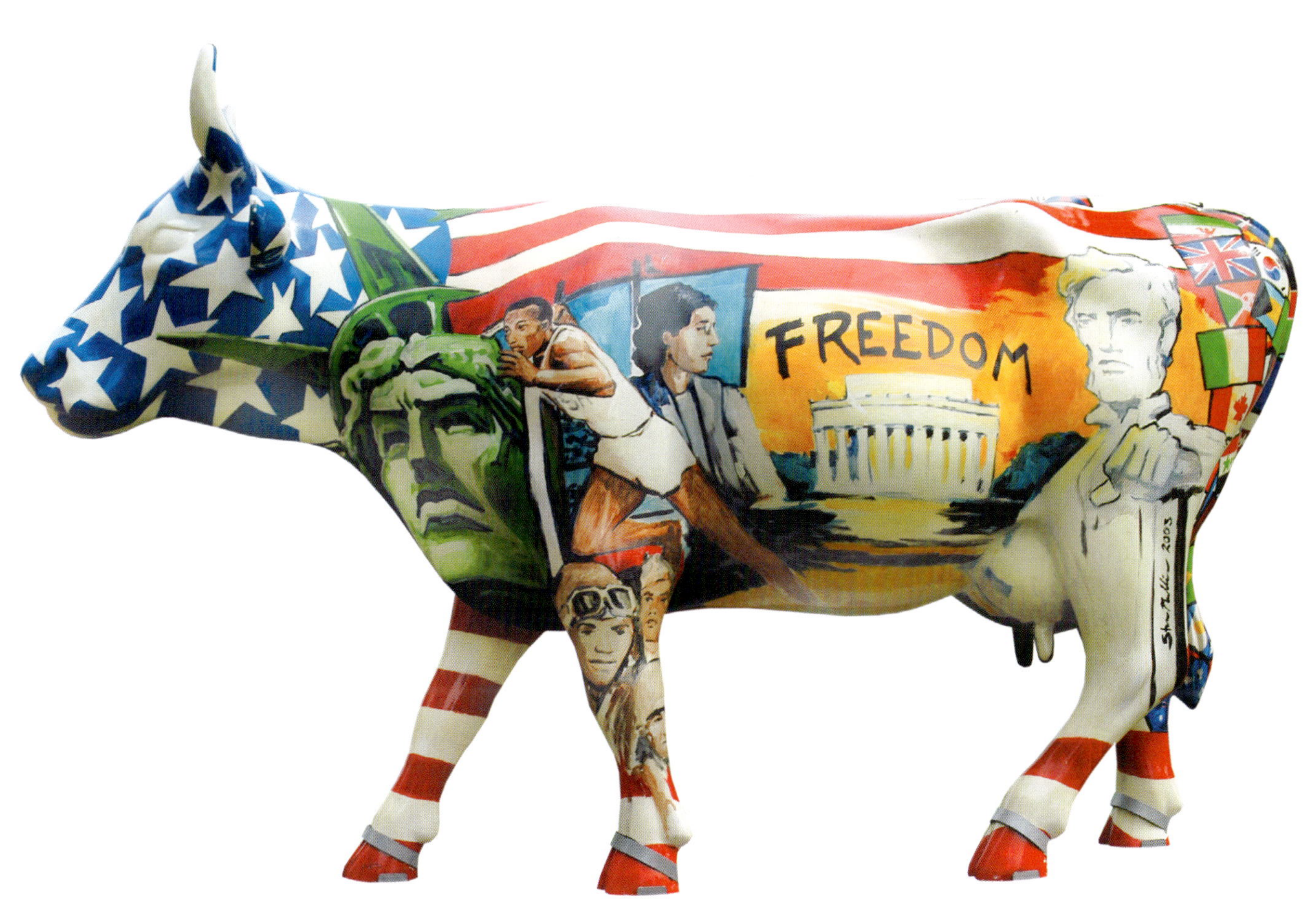

Freedom Cow
Stan Mullins
Chick-fil-A

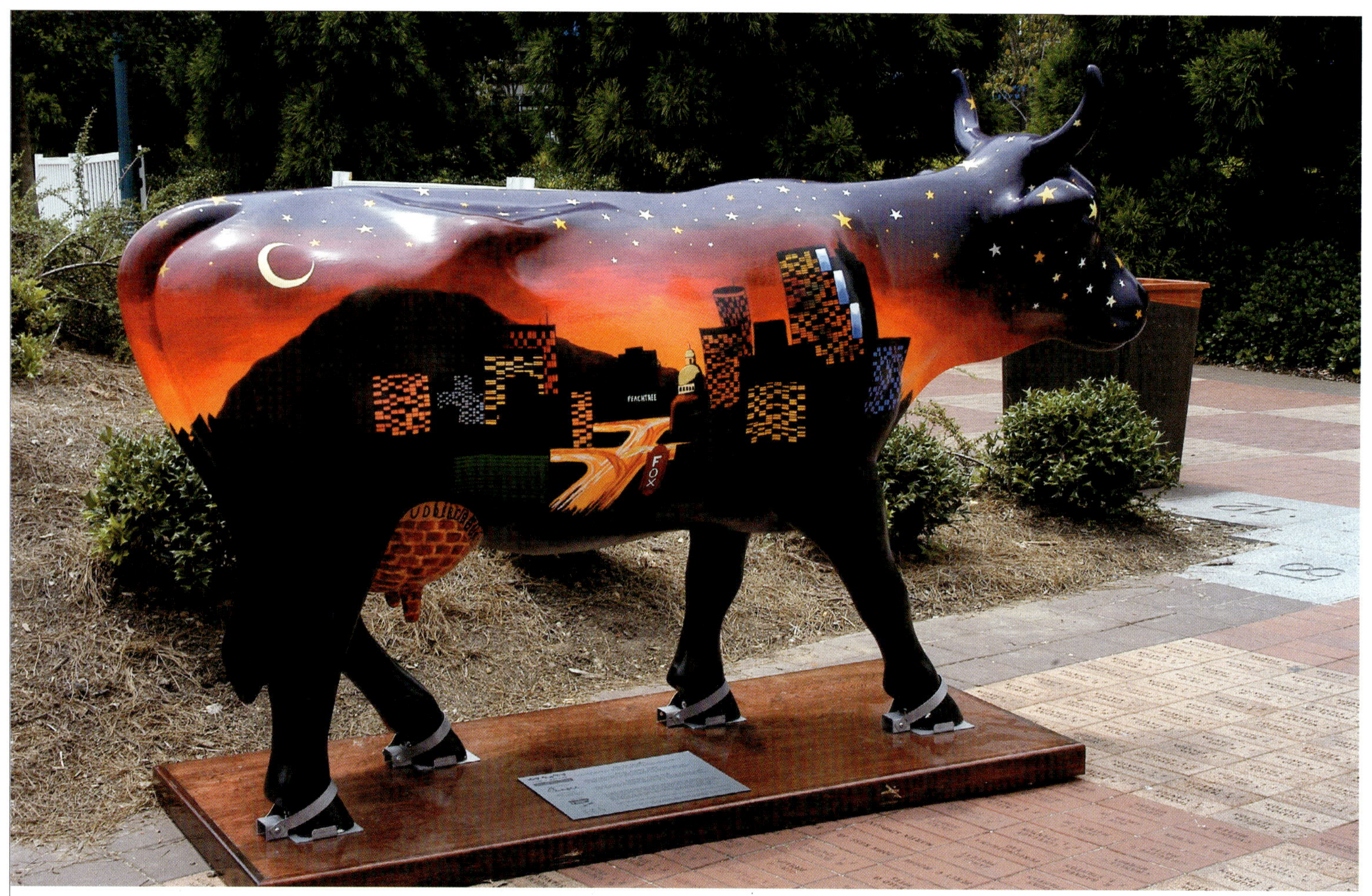

Atlanta Skyline
Ashley Mack
Chick-fil-A

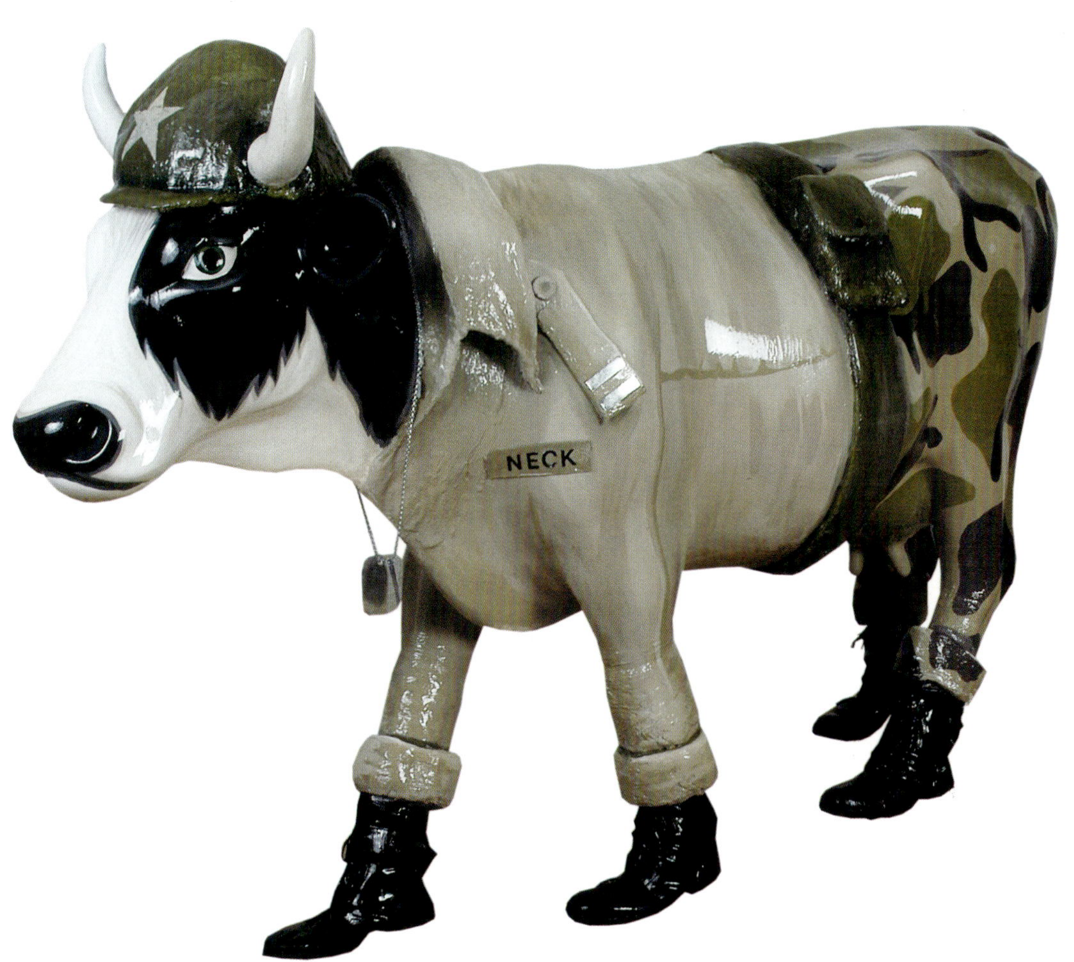

LeatherNeck
Chris Warner
Chick-fil-A

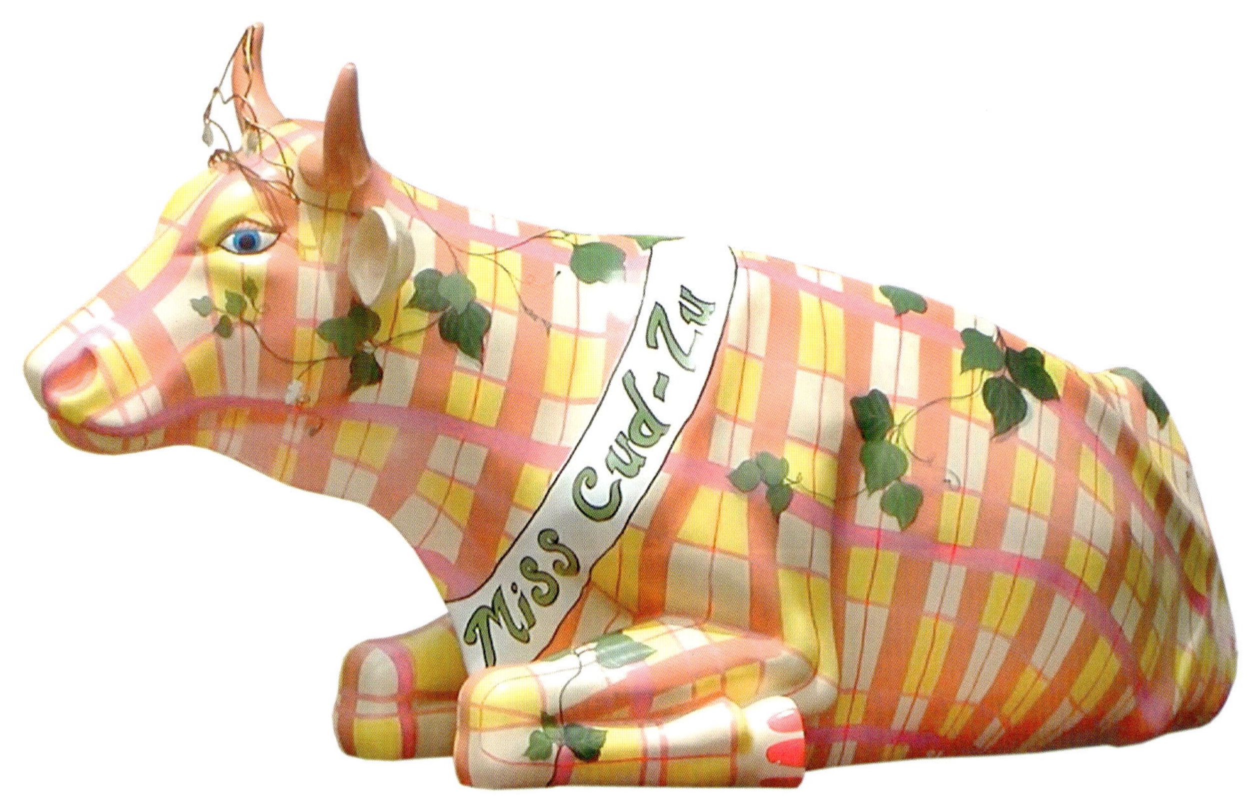

Miss Cud-Zu
Mary Jane Kenary
Chick-fil-A

McKenna Long & Aldridge

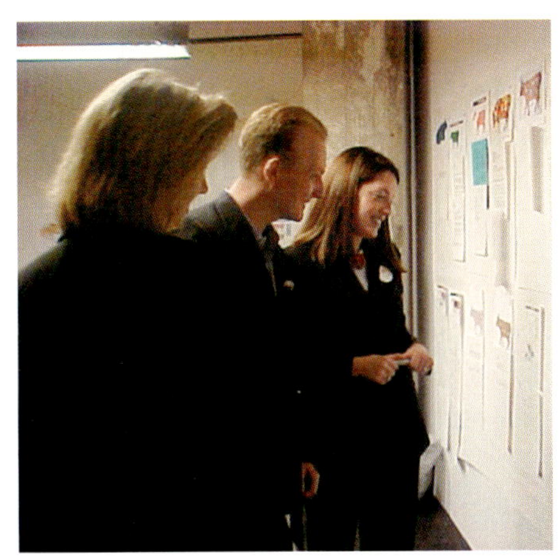

Many might be surprised that a law firm would be integral in bringing a CowParade to any city—or that it would donate the resources and facilities to the event to the extent that McKenna Long & Aldridge did in Atlanta. McKenna Long & Aldridge is no ordinary firm. When partner Evelyn Ashley presented her "big idea" for a 2003 business development project to John Aldridge, he rallied their partners behind CowParade. The Firm donated Evelyn and Event Coordinator, Michelle Isom, as well as the office space and many other office services to CowParade Atlanta. Their assistance didn't stop there. The Firm's Government Affairs practice was critical in getting the City of Atlanta herded together and loving the cows!

Two of the Firm's twelve sponsored cows were set aside to be designed and painted by the winners of an inter-office (across nine of the Firm's U.S. offices) challenge. To the Firm's pleasant surprise, "Grand Prize Winner" Adine Le's design of "Material Cow" not only passed the CowParade Design Selection Committee's high standards, but was immediately usurped by fellow sponsor Star 94 to be the first of five music-related cows to be chosen by the radio station. Winner Linda Clay submitted "Making Time Cownt," which asks viewers the question: "Are we making time count or just counting time?"—probing issues central to time-based law. The design team of Sharon Brooks, Monica Murak, Deborah Rosenfeldt, and Susan Rosmarin submitted the cooperative "Volunsteer Cowncil" where they brought children of Firm members together to pass on the Firm's "spirit of teamwork."

Six of the Firm's cows were set aside for a School Program. The schools were chosen from designs generally submitted by the art students and their teachers and produced some of the most fascinating and well loved cows of the event.

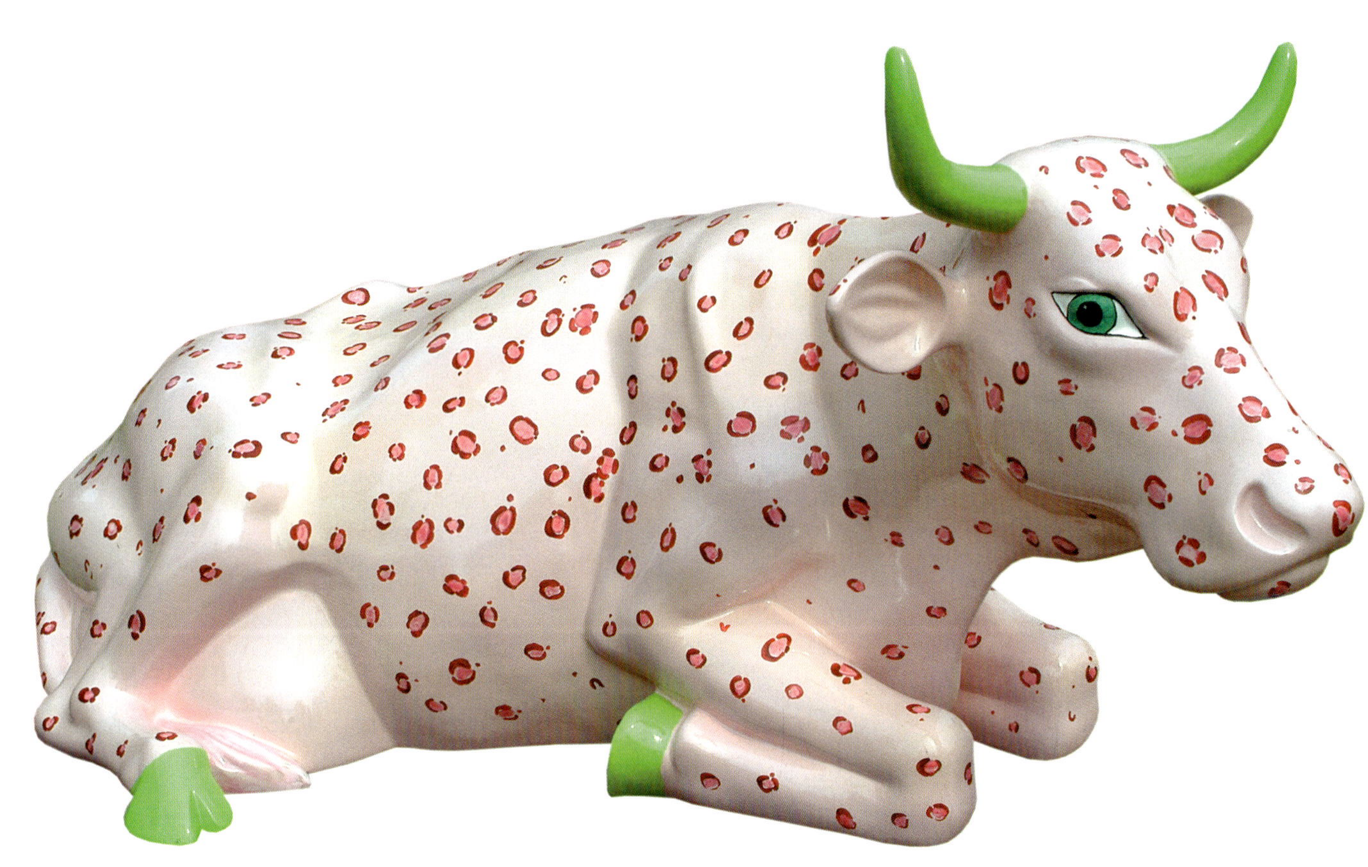

Moo-nique
Katie Stapleton & Adaptive Arts Students
McKenna Long & Aldridge LLP

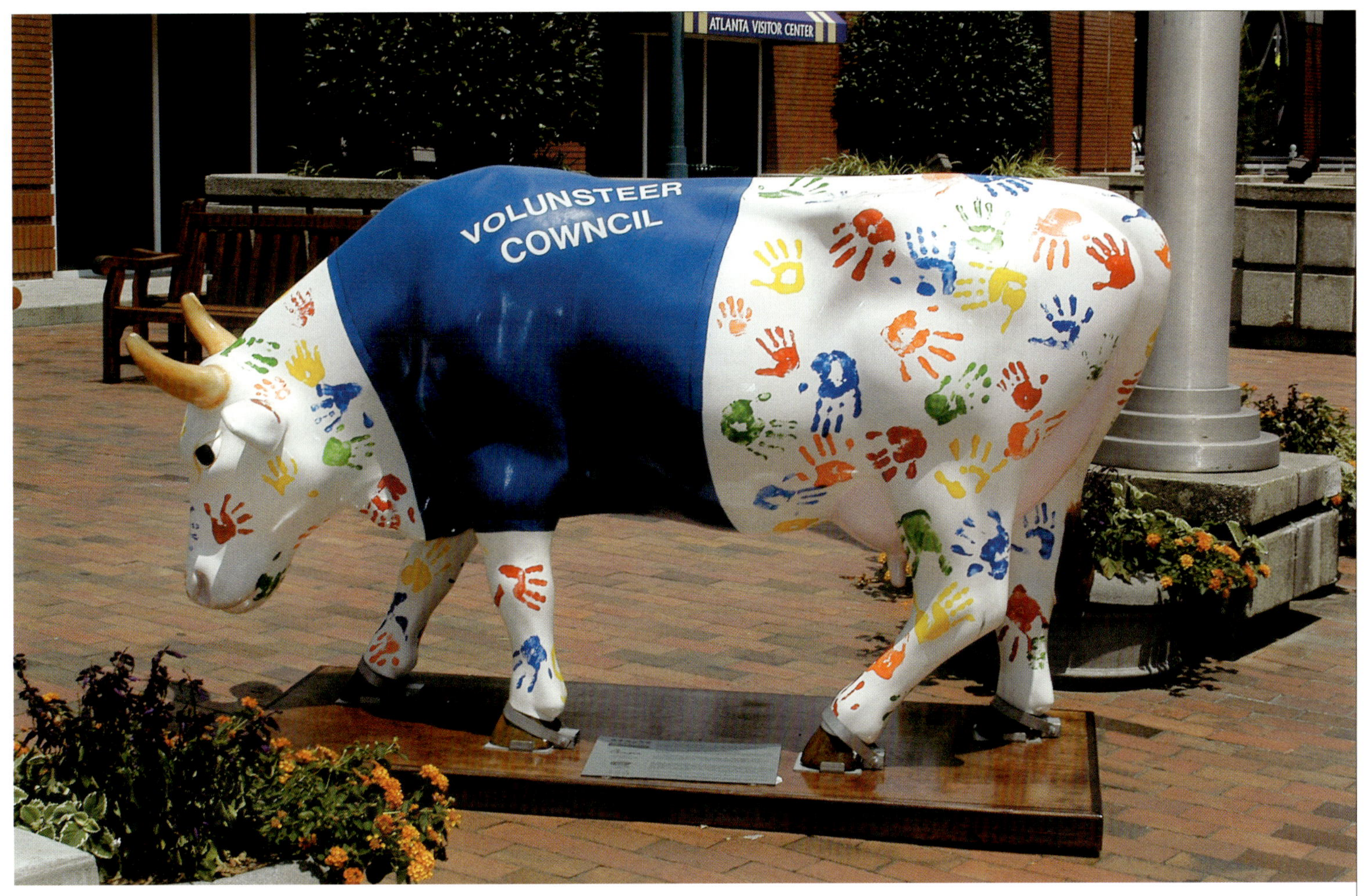

Helping Hands—Volunsteer Cowncil
Sharon Brooks
McKenna Long & Aldridge LLP

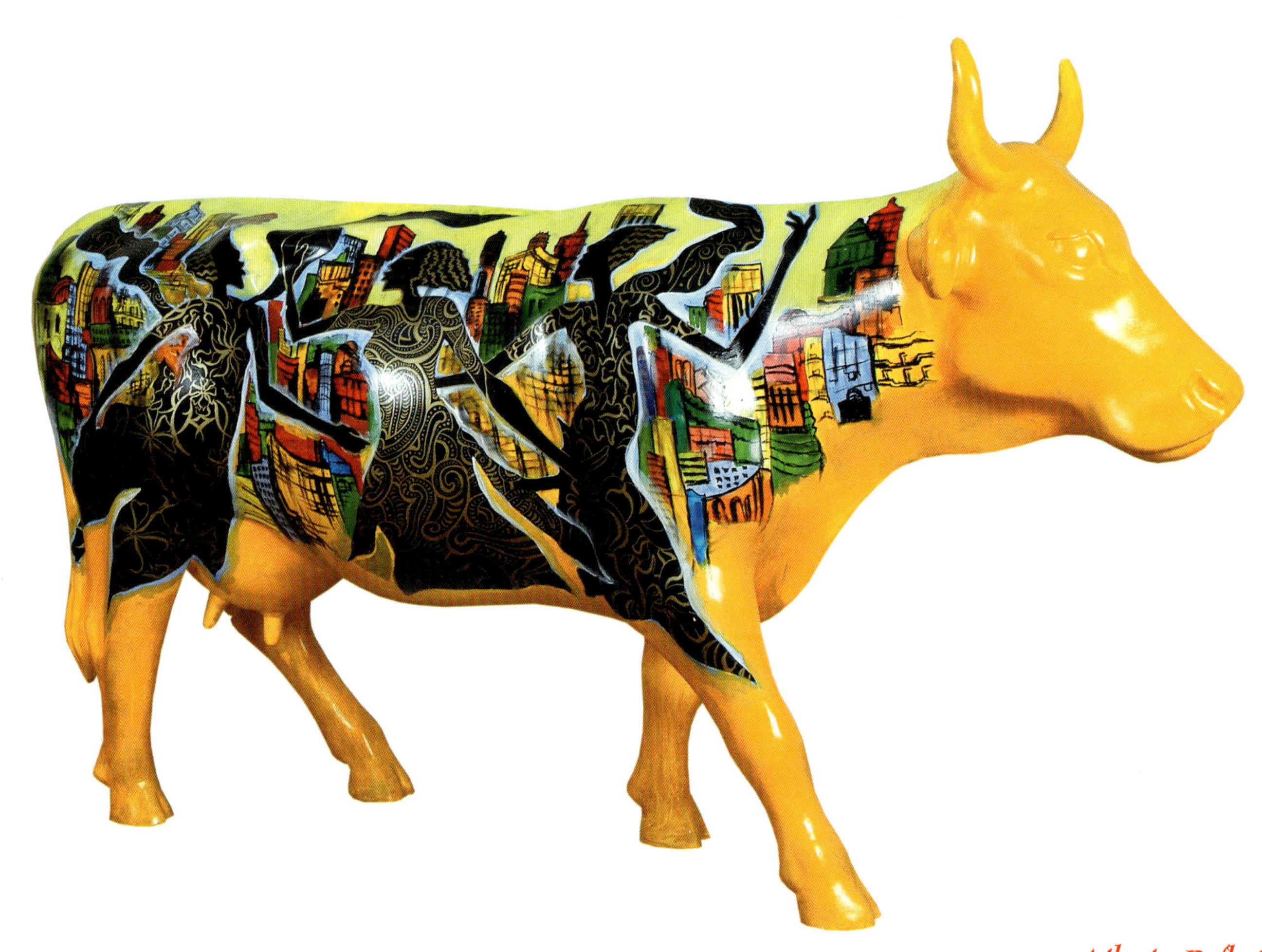

Atlanta Reflections
Corey Barksdale
McKenna Long & Aldridge LLP

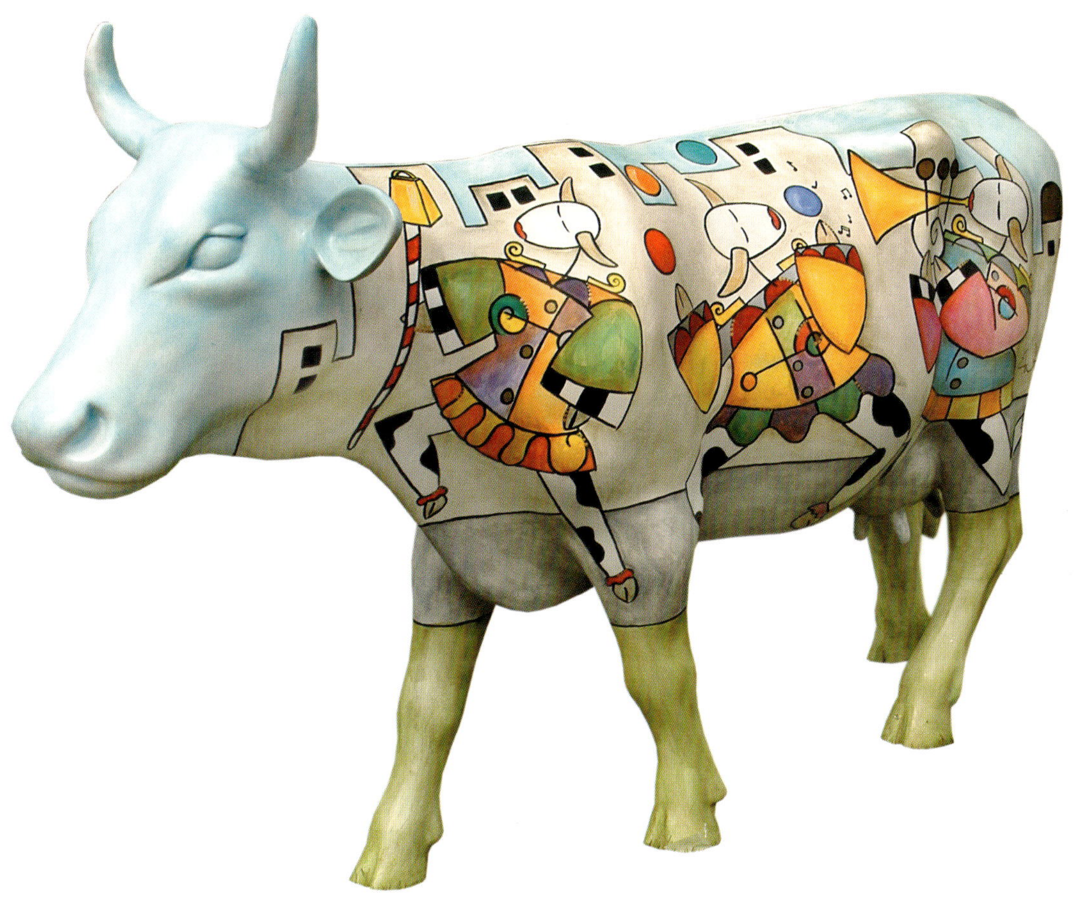

CowParading Cow
Eric Waugh
McKenna Long & Aldridge LLP

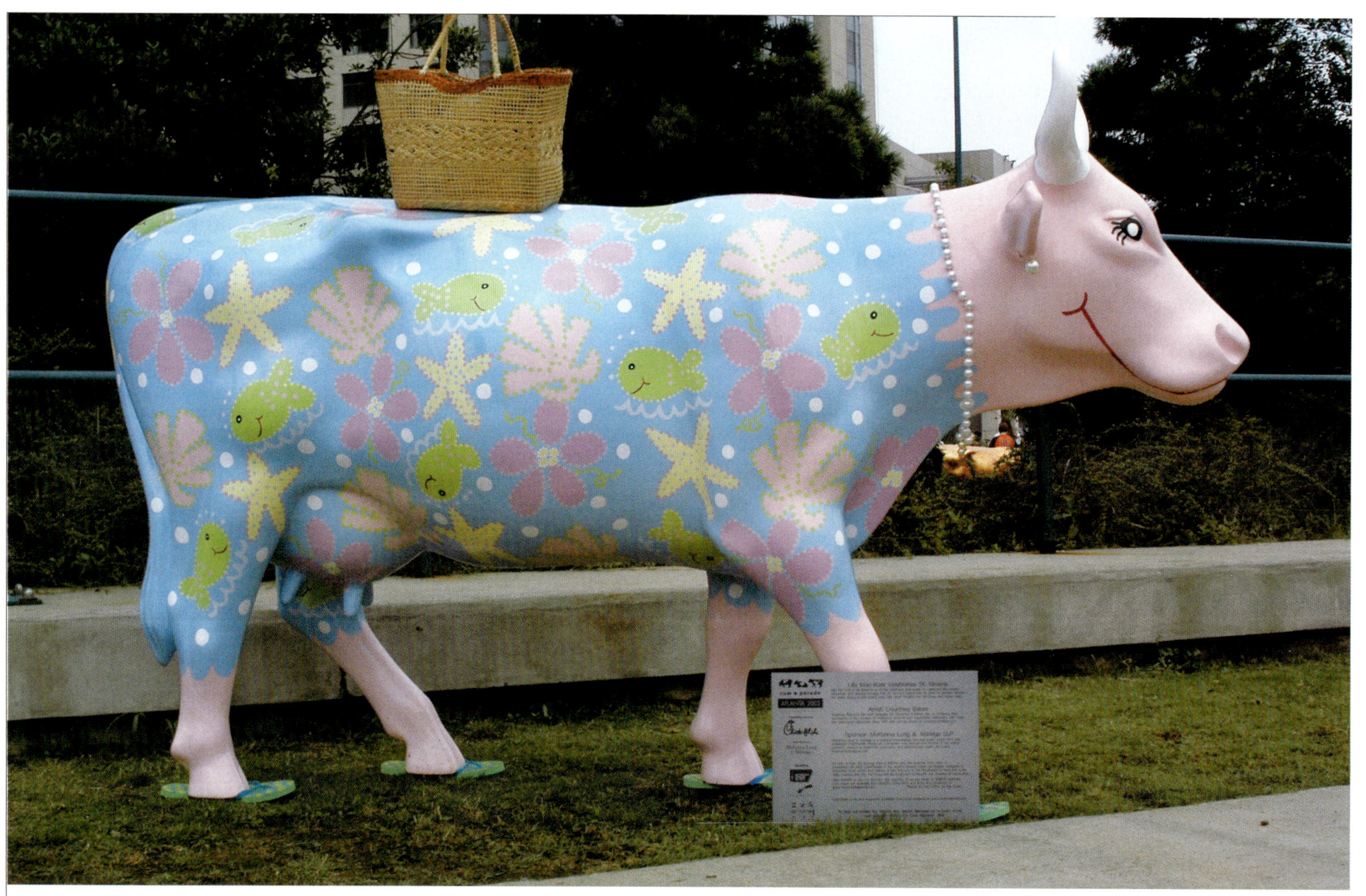

Lilly Moo-litzer Celebrates St. Simons
Courtney Baum
McKenna Long & Aldridge LLP

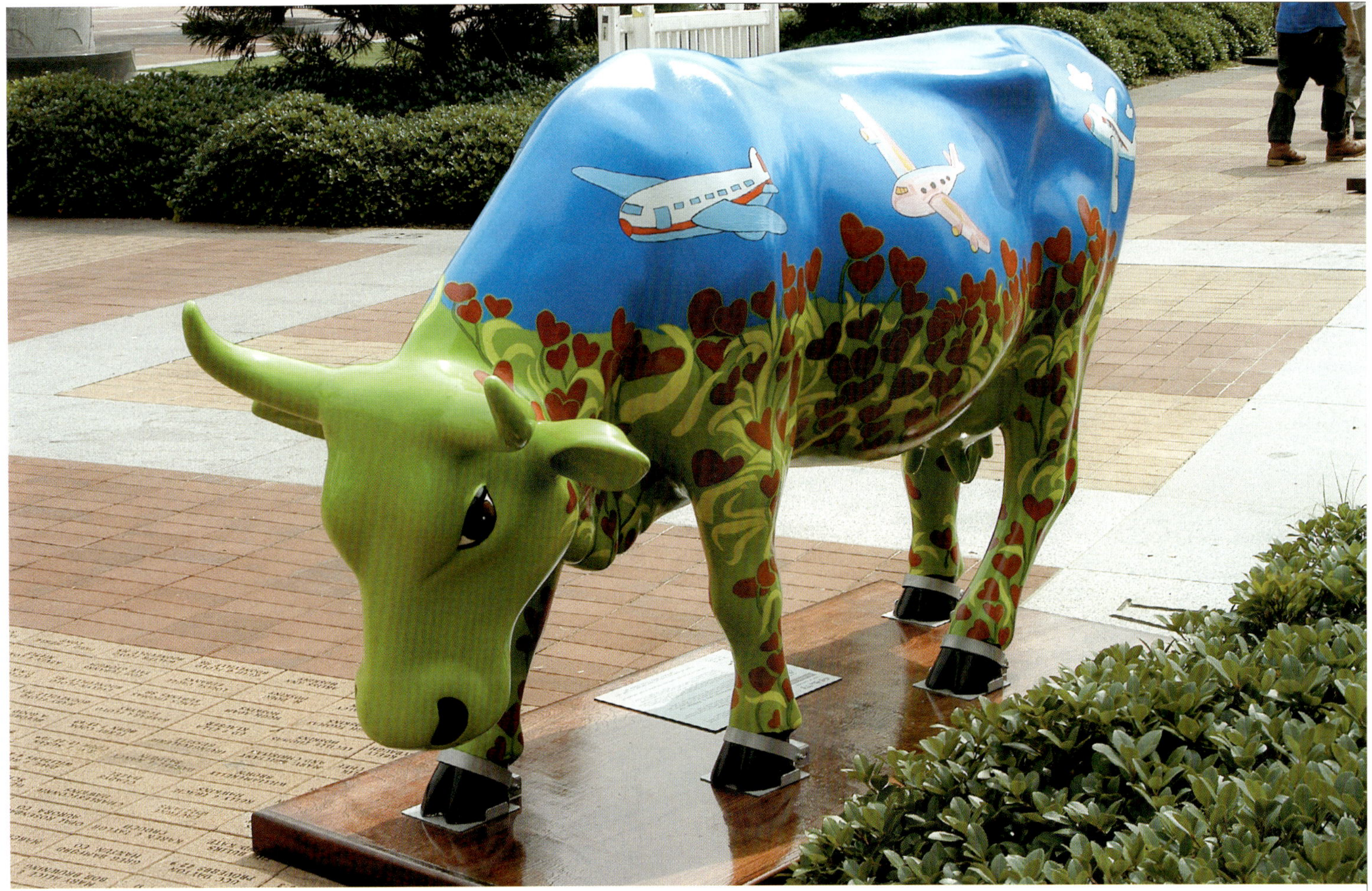

HeartsField

Elaine Baran

McKenna Long & Aldridge LLP, dedicated to its client, Delta Air Lines, Inc.

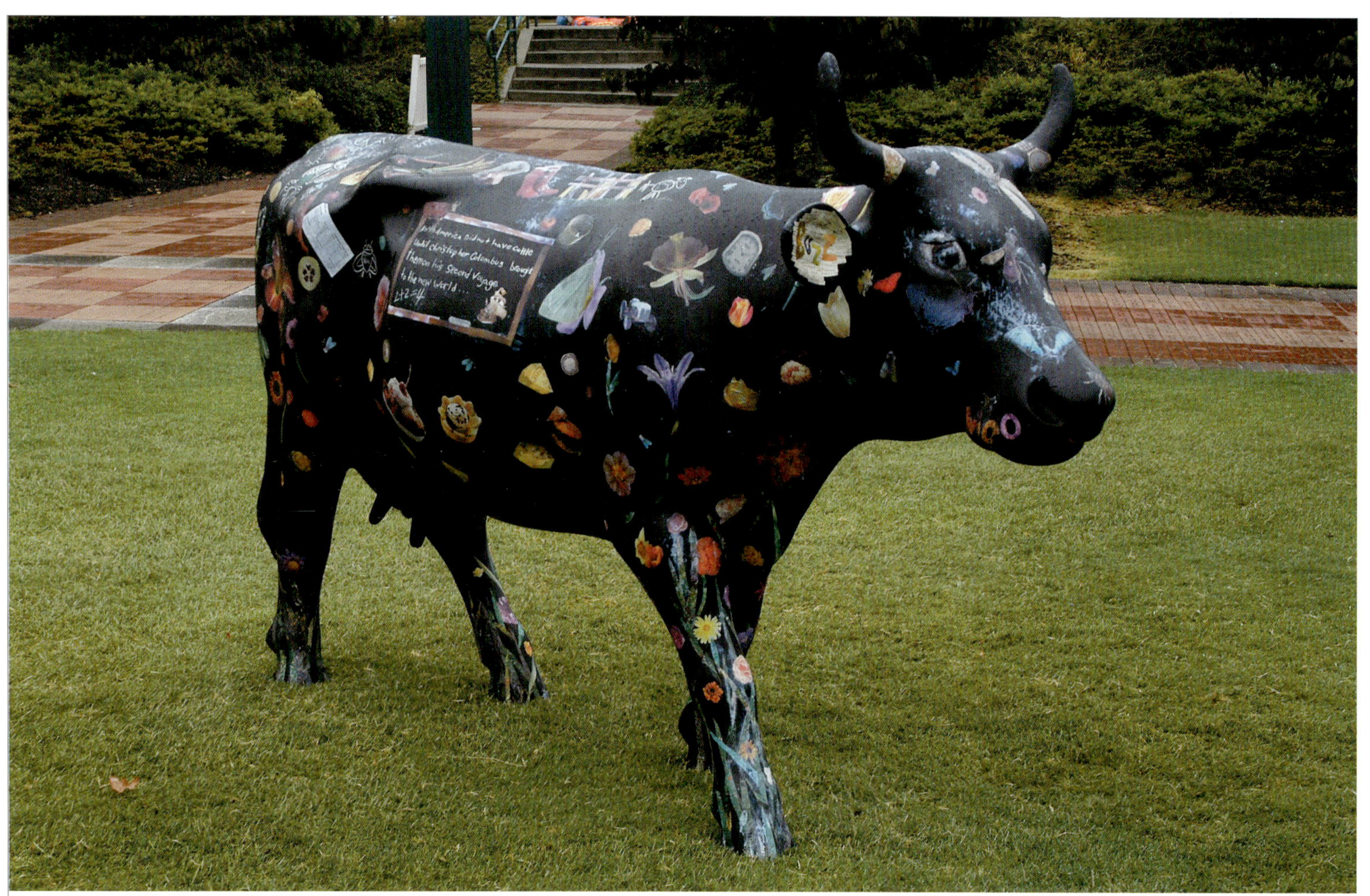

Hillside How Now Cow

Daniel Troppy

McKenna Long & Aldridge LLP

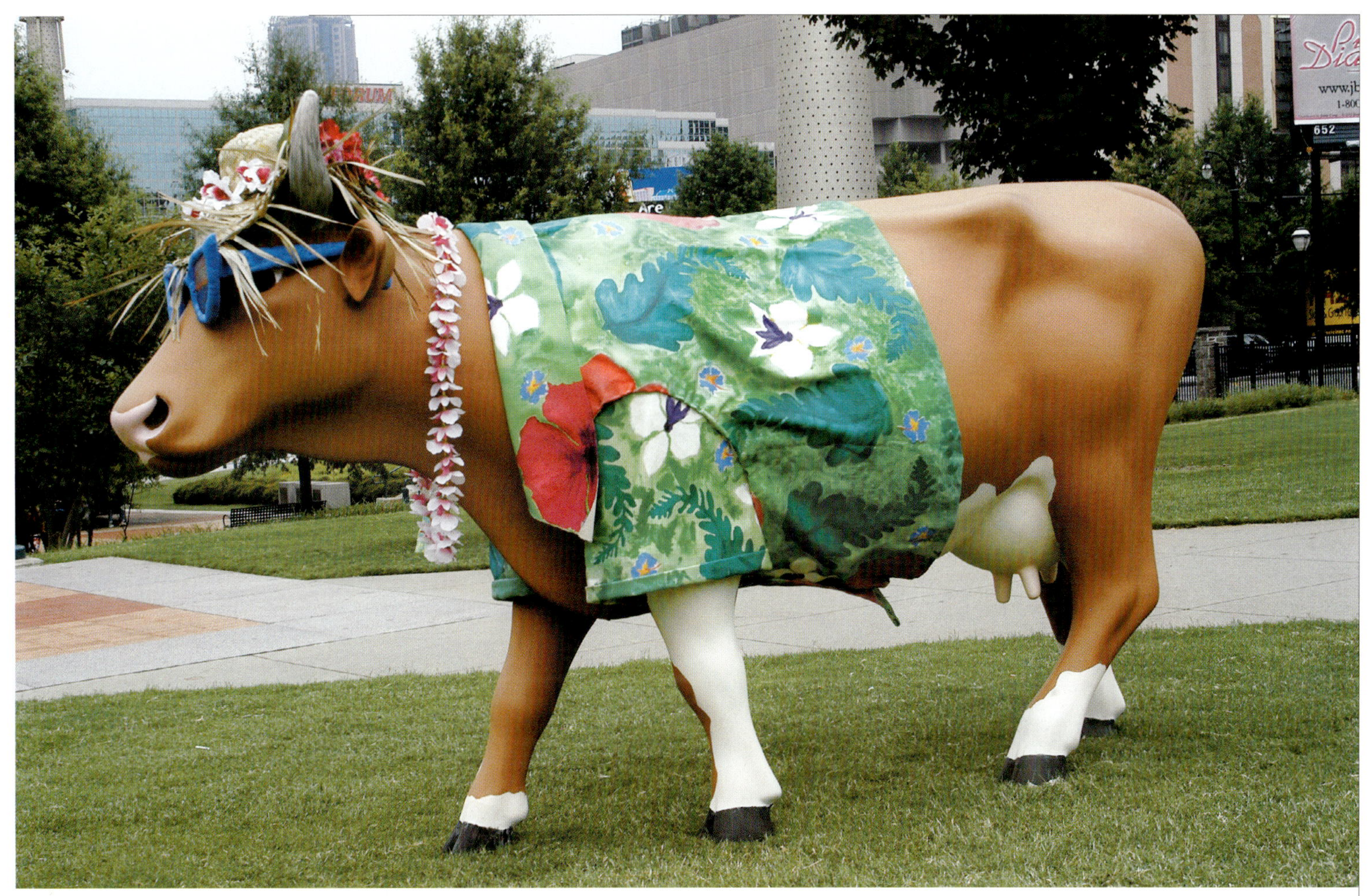

Maui Cowi

Cynthia Dersch & Galloway School

McKenna Long & Aldridge LLP

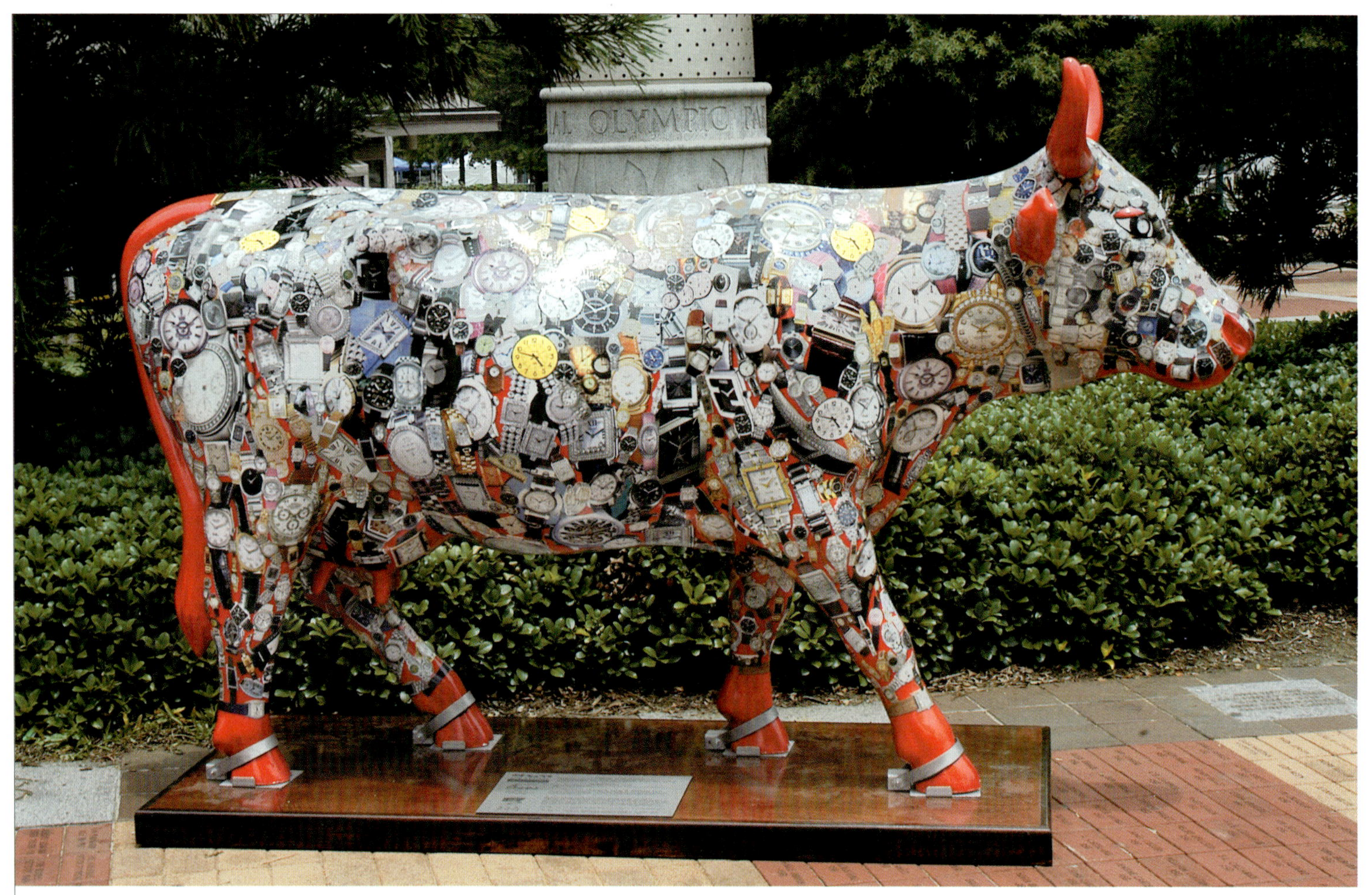

Making Time Cownt

Linda Clay

McKenna Long & Aldridge LLP

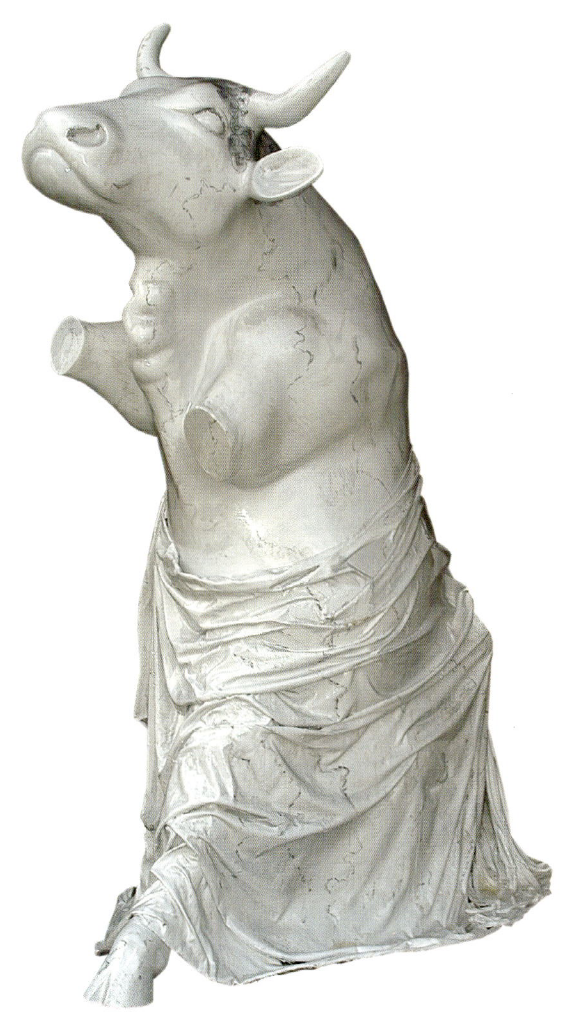

Venus de-Moolo
Pam Carsillo & Students
McKenna Long & Aldridge LLP

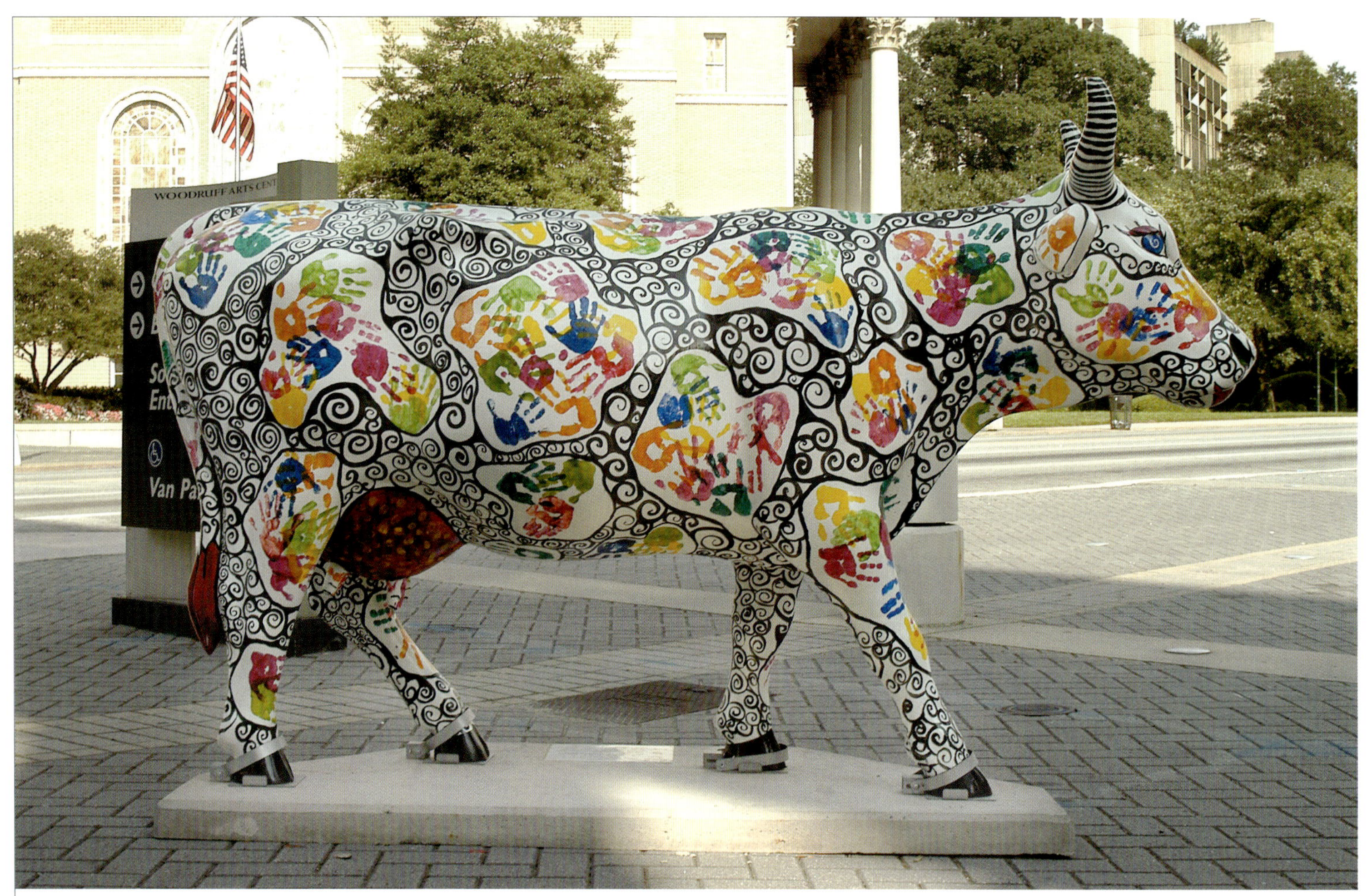

High Five
Joyce O'Brien & Atlanta International School
McKenna Long & Aldridge LLP

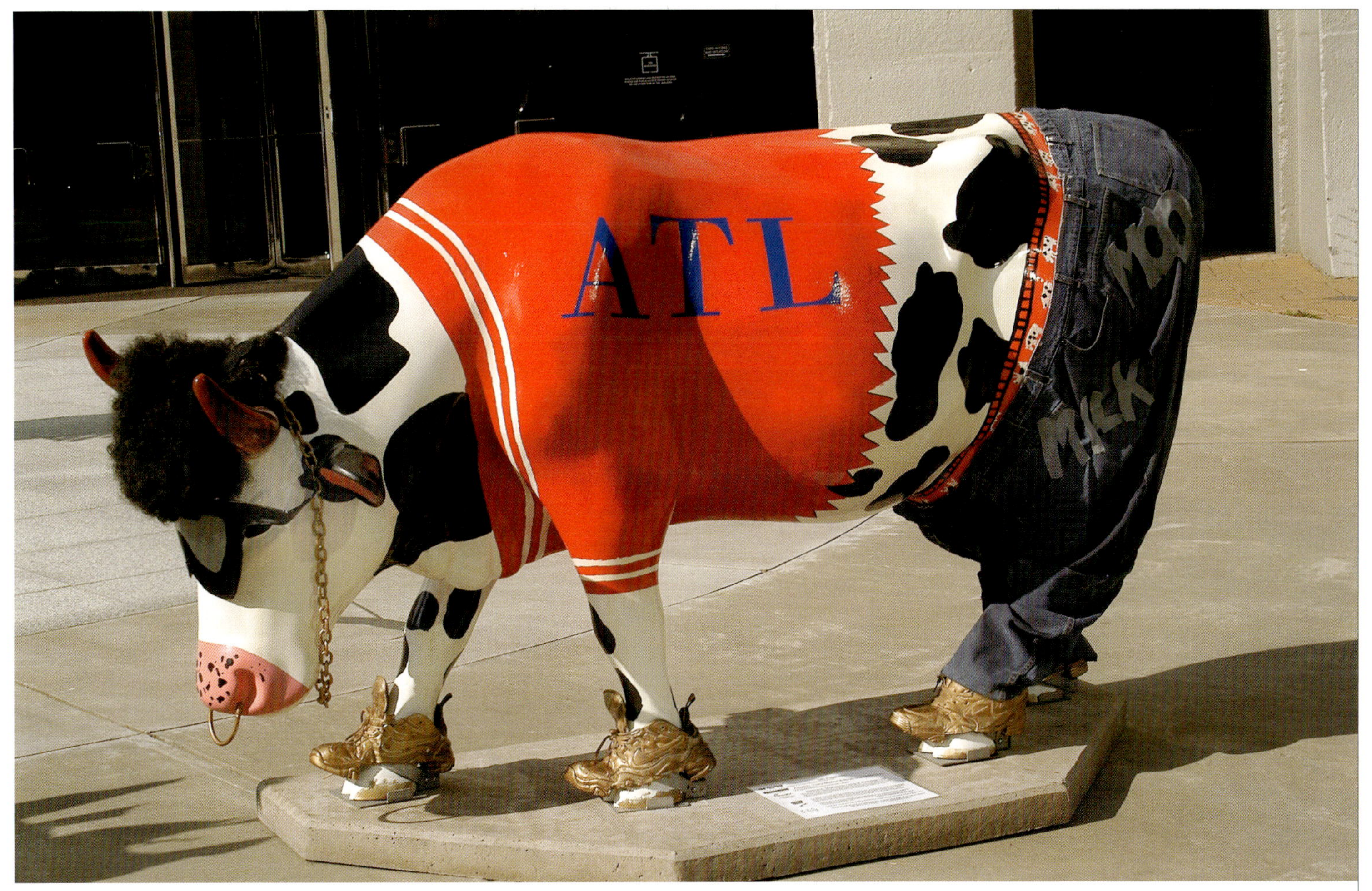

MC Fresh Milk
Tracy Marino & Boys and Girls Club of Metro Atlanta
McKenna Long & Aldridge LLP

Southeast United Dairy Association

What product has to be the official beverage of CowParade? Milk, of course! The Southeast United Dairy Association and the "got milk?®" campaign, funded by dairy farmers, knew the CowParade was a natural for promoting nature's most perfect food.

Southeast United Dairy Association proudly sponsored four udderly moo-velous cows. "Circus Cown" juggling milk, cheese and yogurt, represents the dairy industries new "3-A-Day of Dairy for Stronger Bones" program. "Say Cheese" cow displays Atlantans with that American icon—the milk mustache—along with famous celebrities. "Curly-Q-Cow" cow, with its beautiful latticework design, represents dairy farmers care for their animals and the environment and "Fresh Milk" with its milk bottles says it all about these fabulous animals!

CowParade offered Southeast United Dairy Association a unique and fun opportunity to reinforce American's need for three dairy products a day for good health.

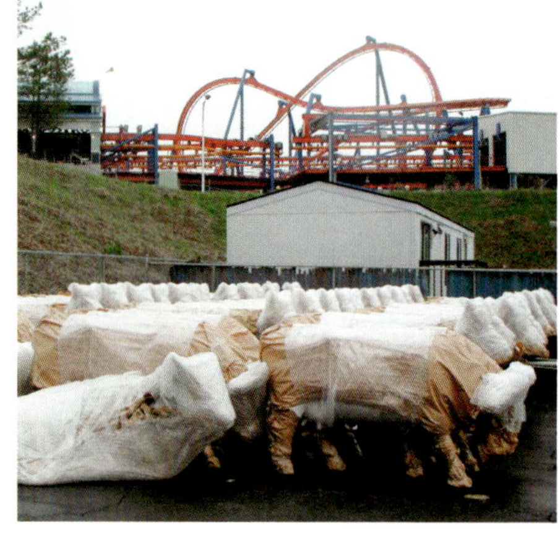

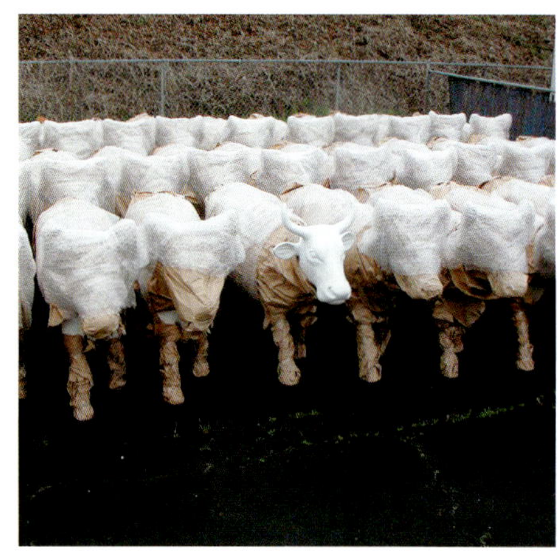

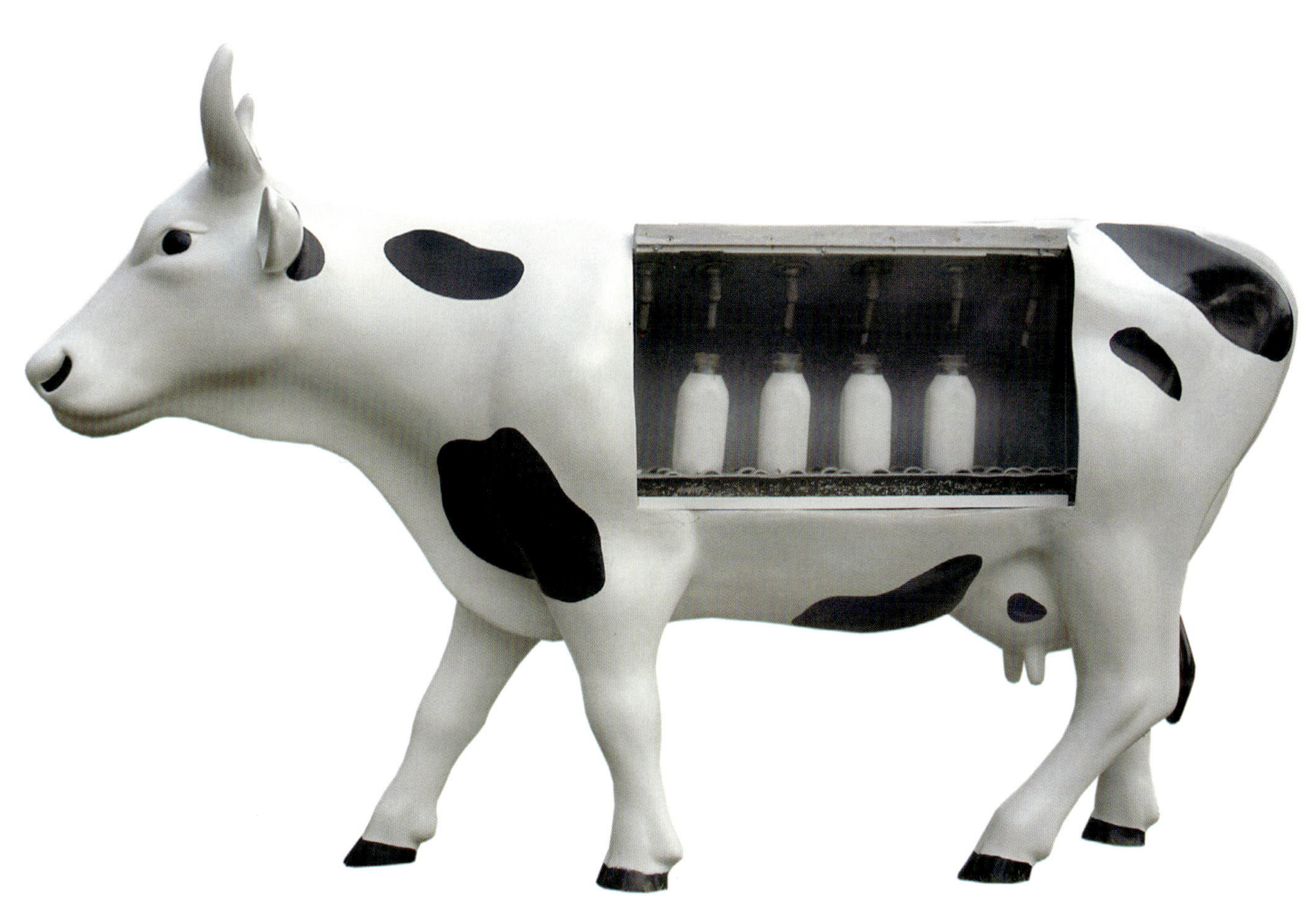

Fresh Milk
Steven Dana
Southeast United Dairy Association

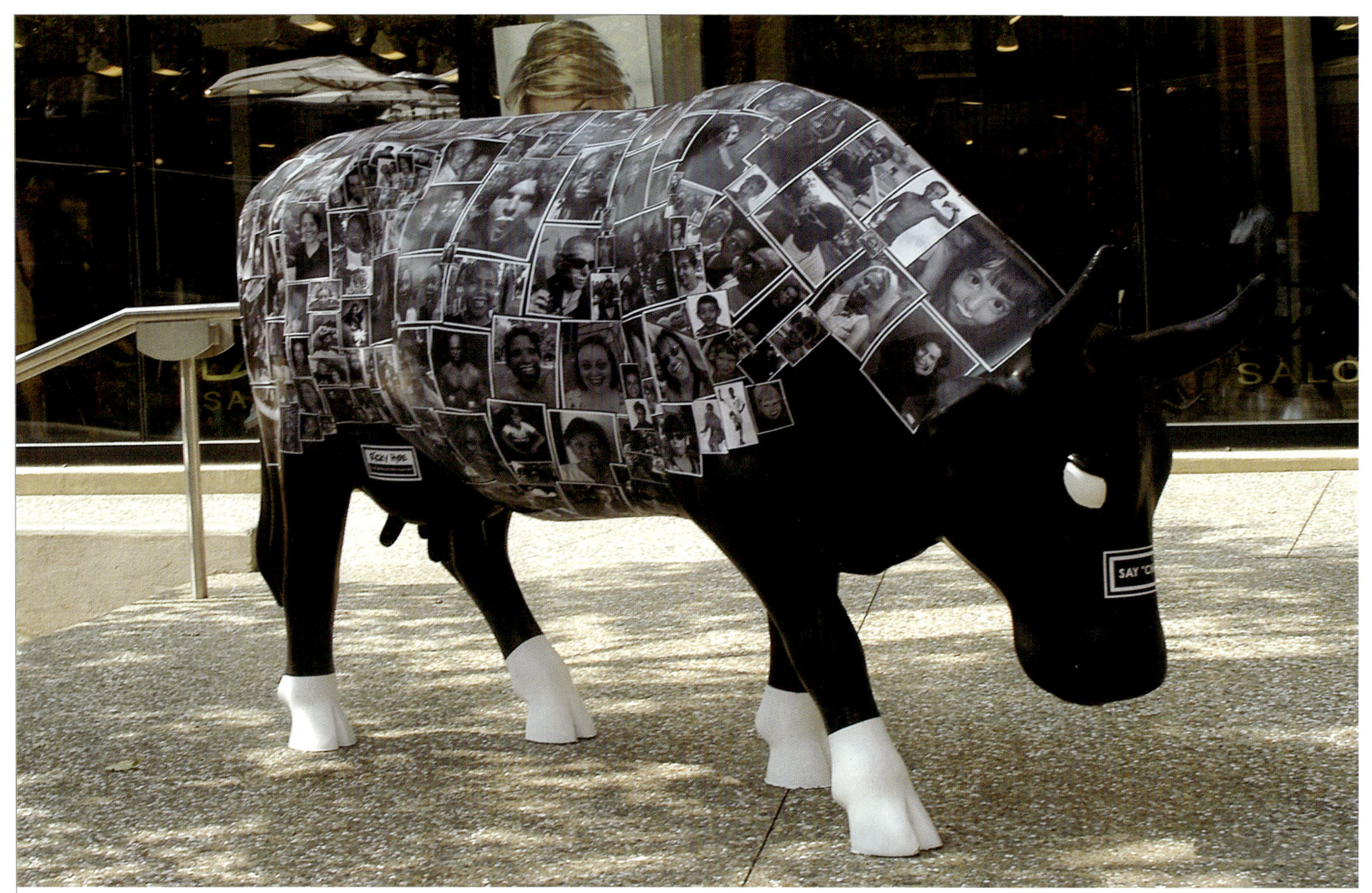

Say Cheese
Ricky Hyde
Southeast United Dairy Association

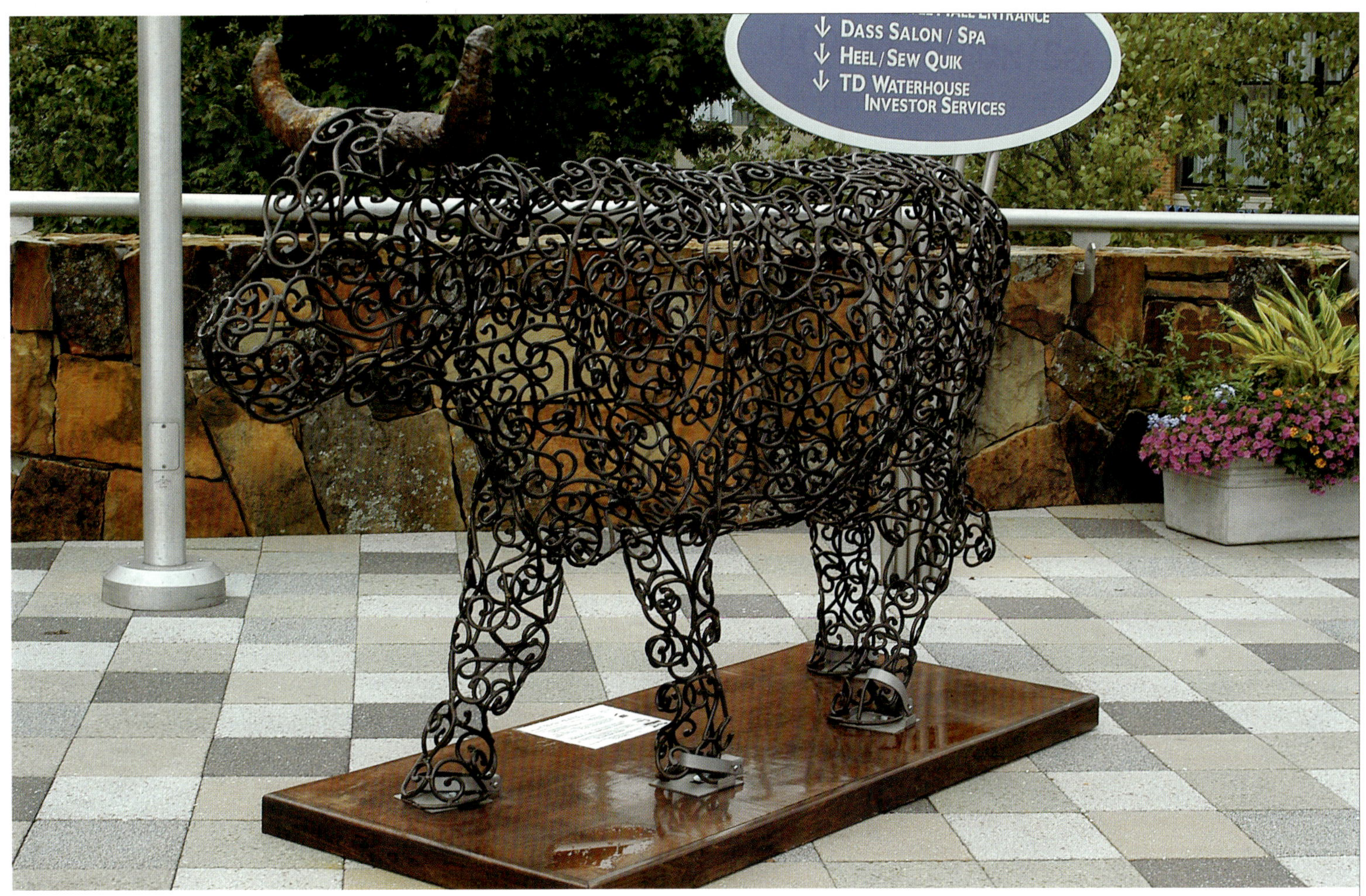

Curly-Q-Cow
Michael Puzio
Southeast United Dairy Association

Media Partners

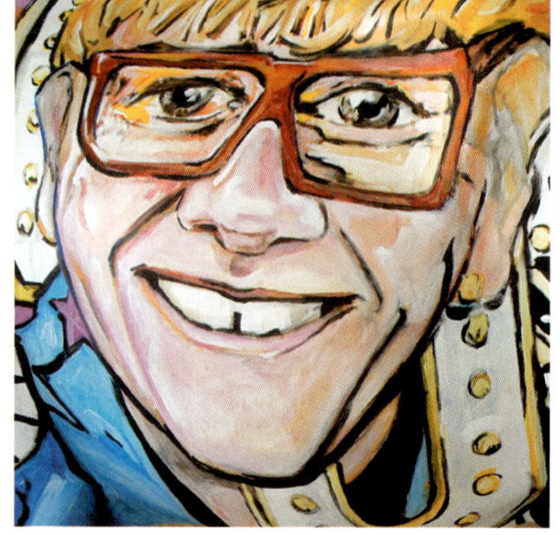

MEDIA PARTNERS CAME OUT IN strength to support CowParade Atlanta. Popular Top 40 Radio station Star 94 signed on first and helped solicit sponsors, let artists paint cows in their lobby, and provided loads of advertising support and on-air promotion. As an added plus, Star 94 DJ Vickie Locke coordinated the approval for artist Stan Mullins to paint "Don't Let the Sun Go Down on Moo," a tribute to Atlanta part-time resident, Elton John.

The *Atlanta Journal-Constitution* newspaper also provided significant advertising support, letting people know how to sponsor cows, where to find cows, and how to buy cows at the auction. The paper's on-line entertainment news service, accessAtlanta.com, ran a fun "Bum Steer" contest where people could "vote off" their least favorite cows. When a cow was voted off, it was "tipped" and its picture ran upside down.

Yahoo.com sent their computerized icon cow, which was created for CowParade New York, to Atlanta to provide interactive fun at Perimeter Mall and later in the Cow Hospital at Underground Atlanta. As the Internet Communications Partner with CowParade Atlanta, Yahoo! helped to publicize the live and Internet auctions—and provided the platform for the Internet auction of the CowParade Atlanta cows.

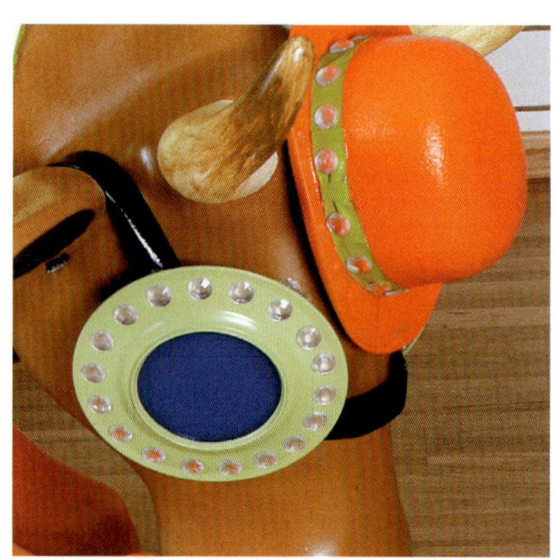

Peach Cowbler

Claire Dunaway

Star 94

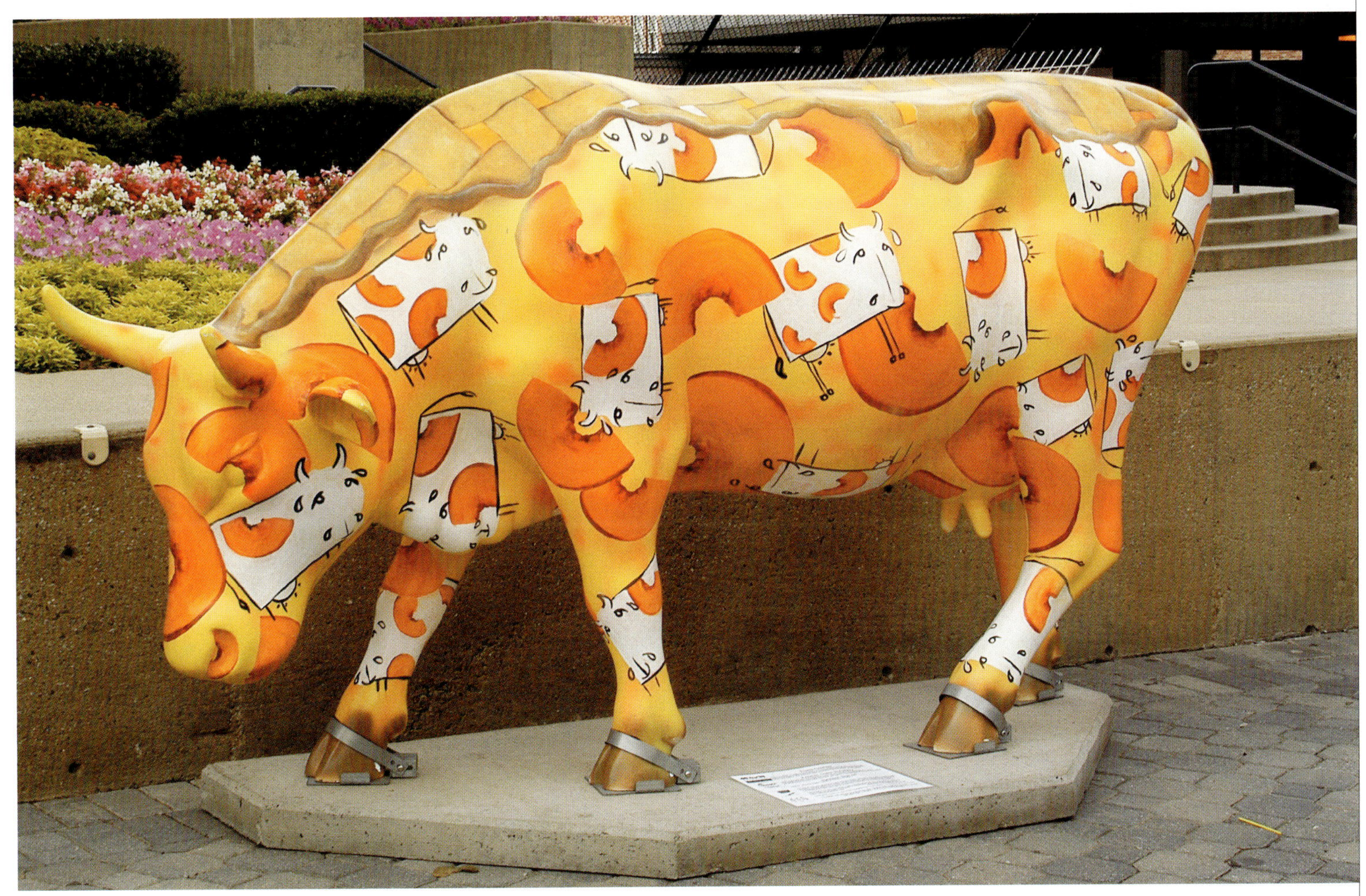

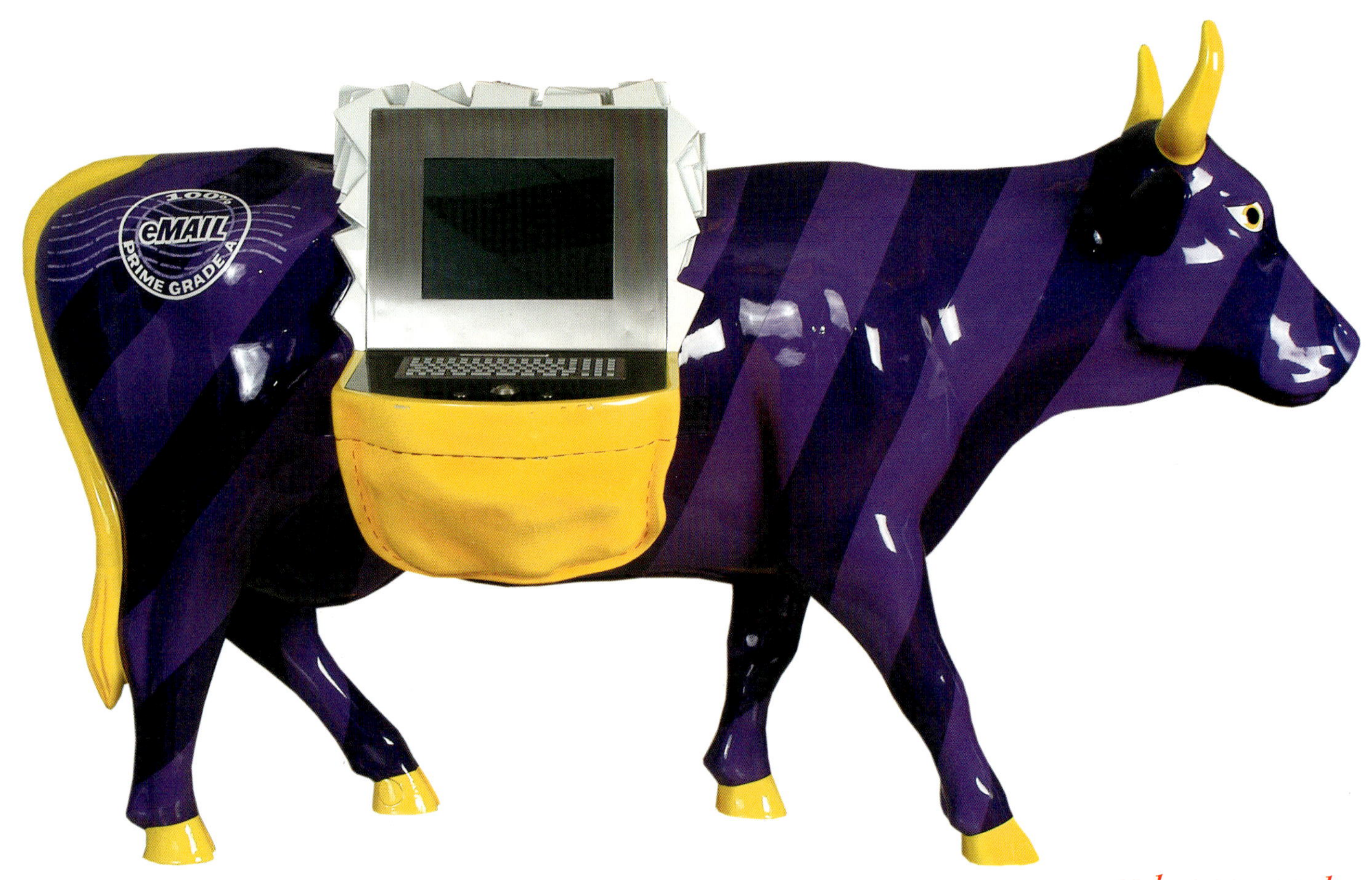

Yahoo! Moo Mail
Amy Armock
Yahoo!

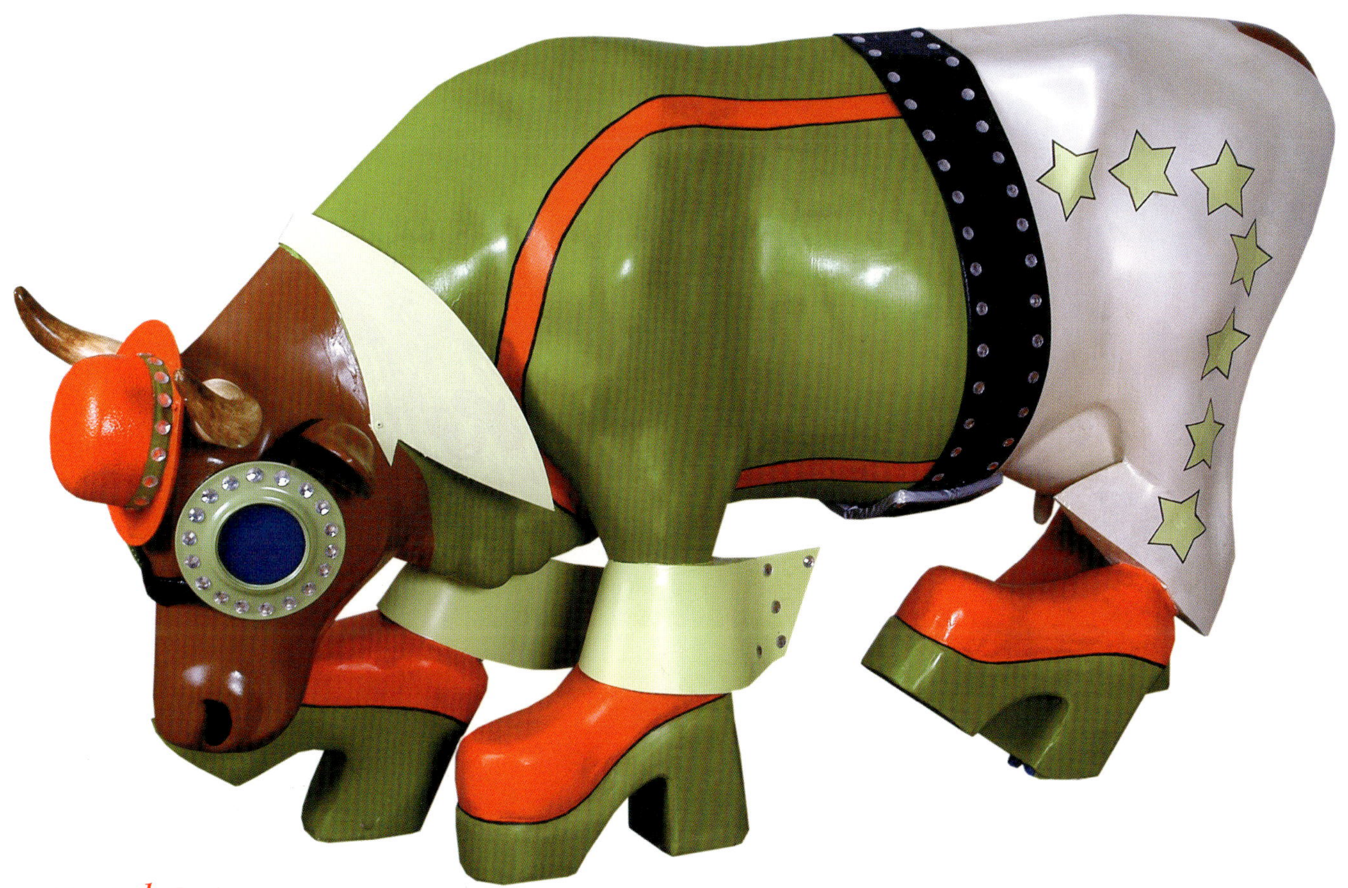

Moosical Genius
Carol Armitage, Kristin Stern, Scott Feldman
accessAtlanta.com

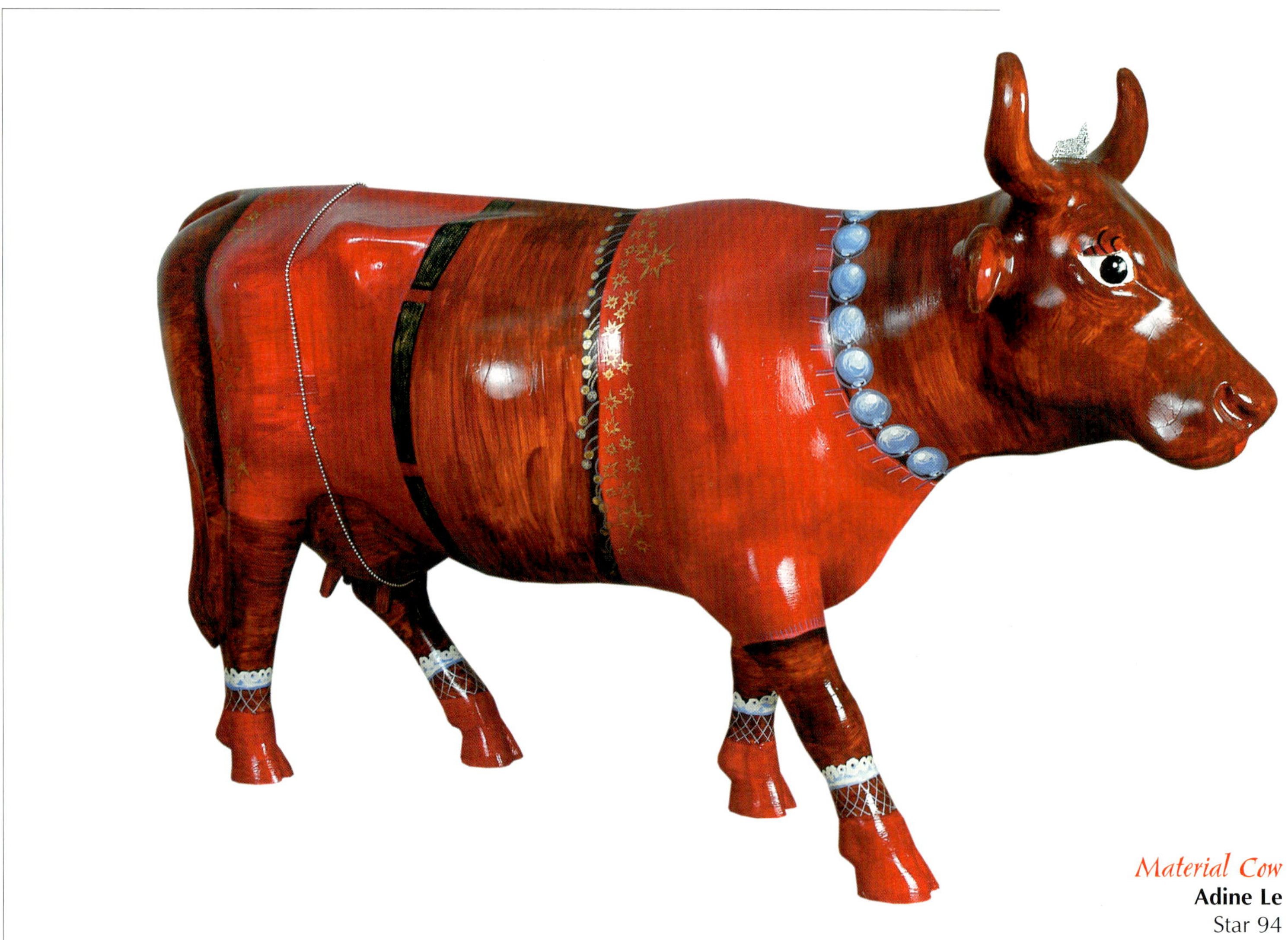

Material Cow
Adine Le
Star 94

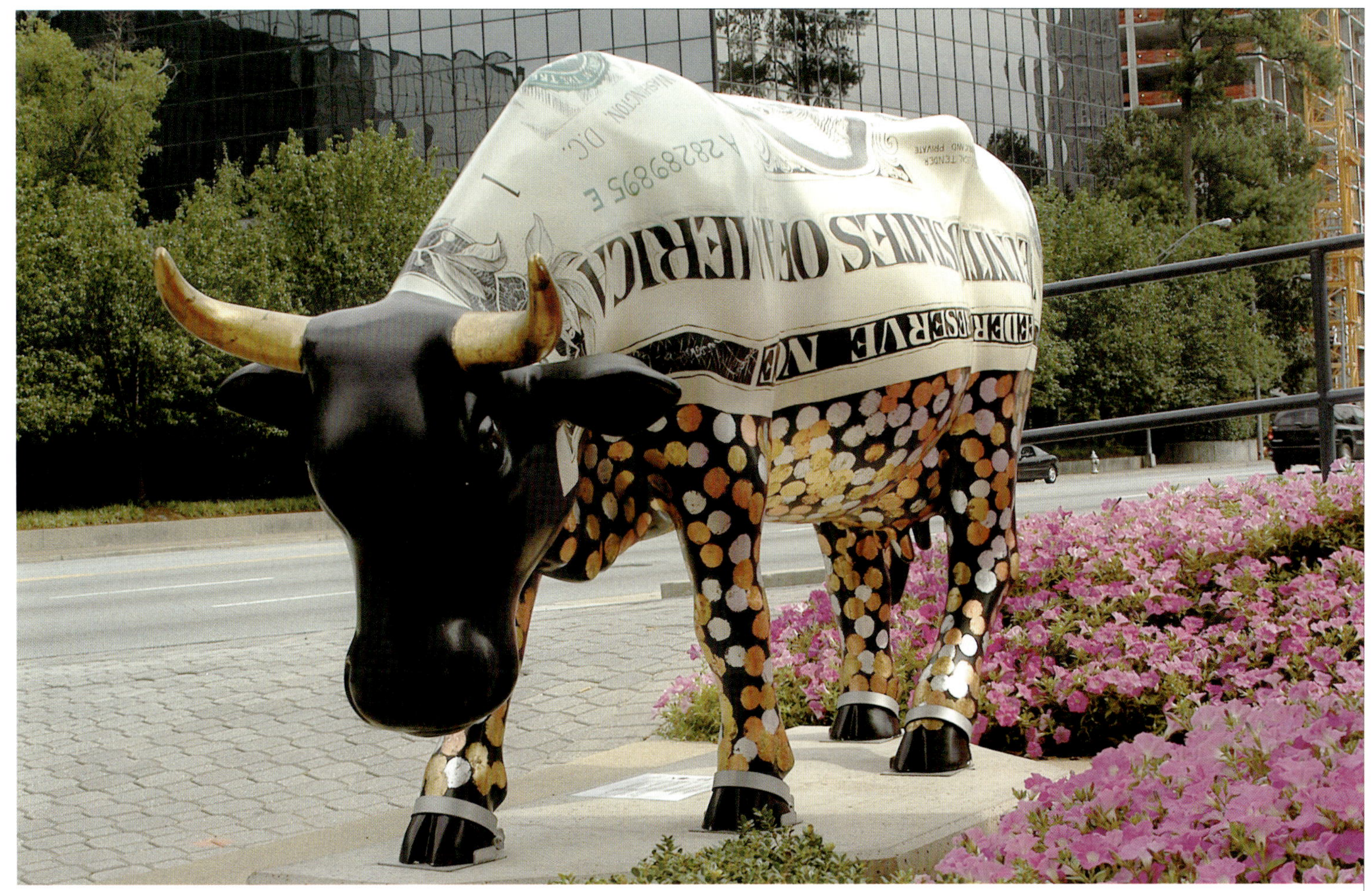

Cash Cow (Milk Money)
Cheryl Linn Myrbo
Star 94

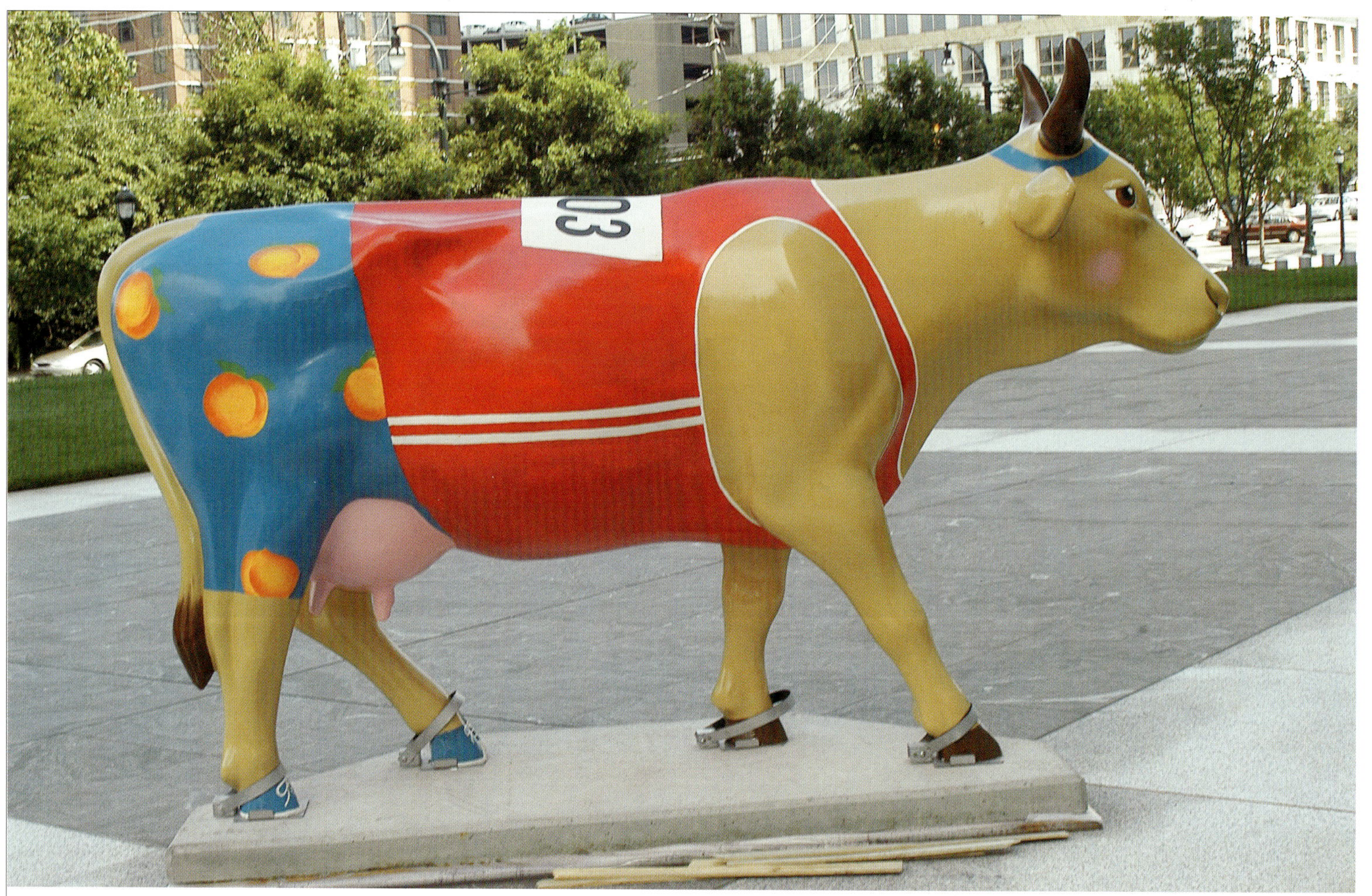

Hoofin' Down Peachtree
Deb Rauschenberg & Lucinda Maberry
Atlanta Journal-Constitution

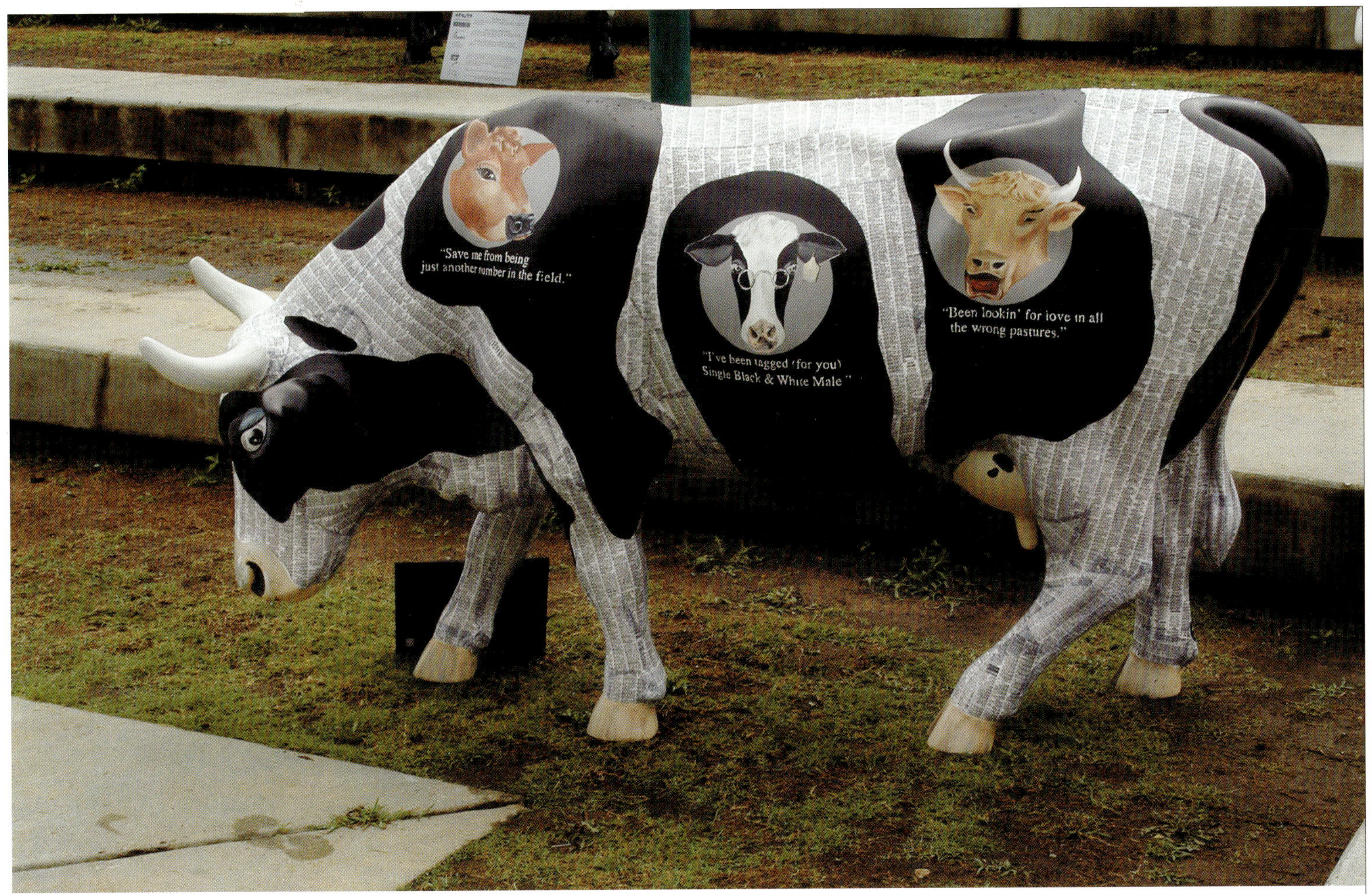

Udder Love
Kristi Kent
ajcpersonals.com

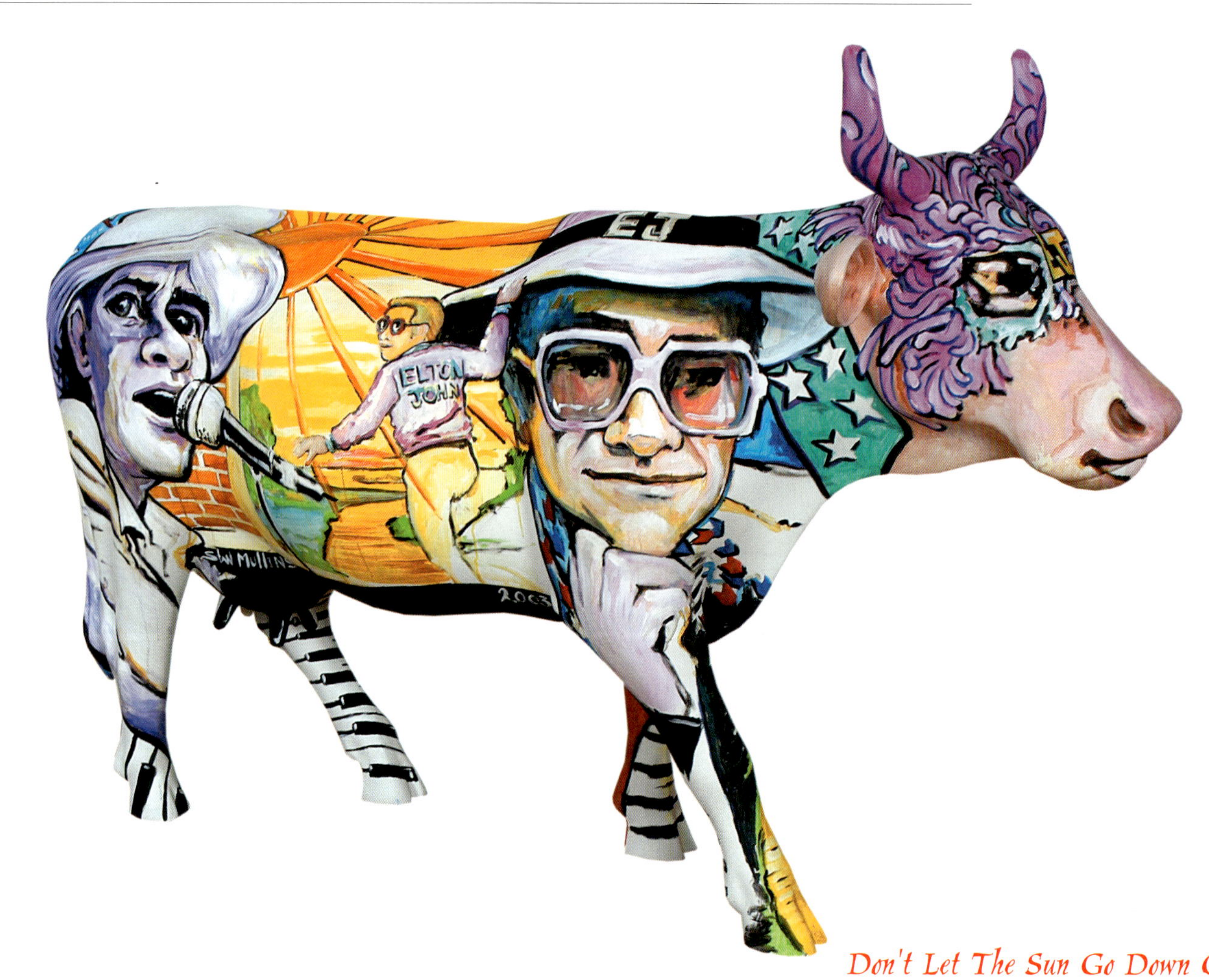

Don't Let The Sun Go Down On Moo
Stan Mullins
Star 94

"Our cows, up or down."

—Stephen De-Cow-ter

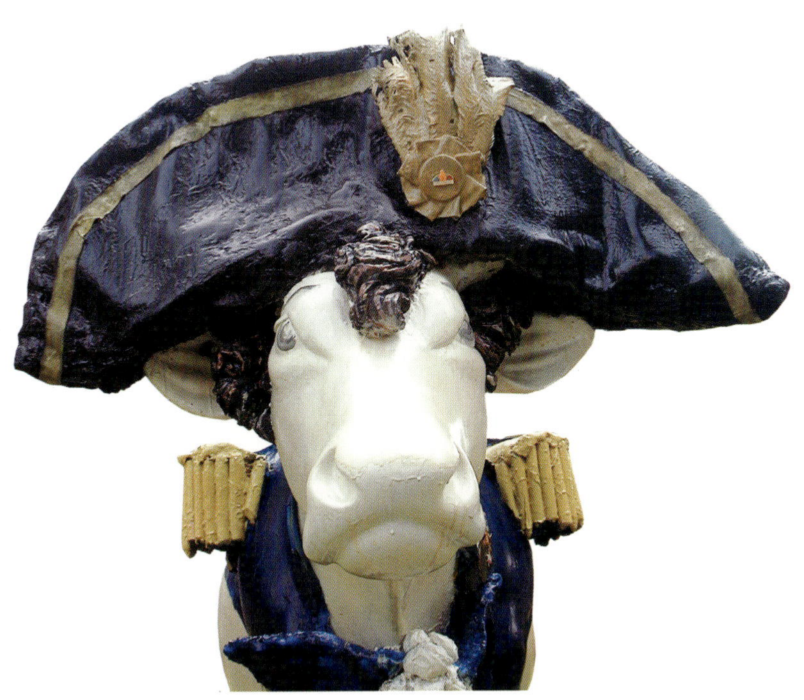

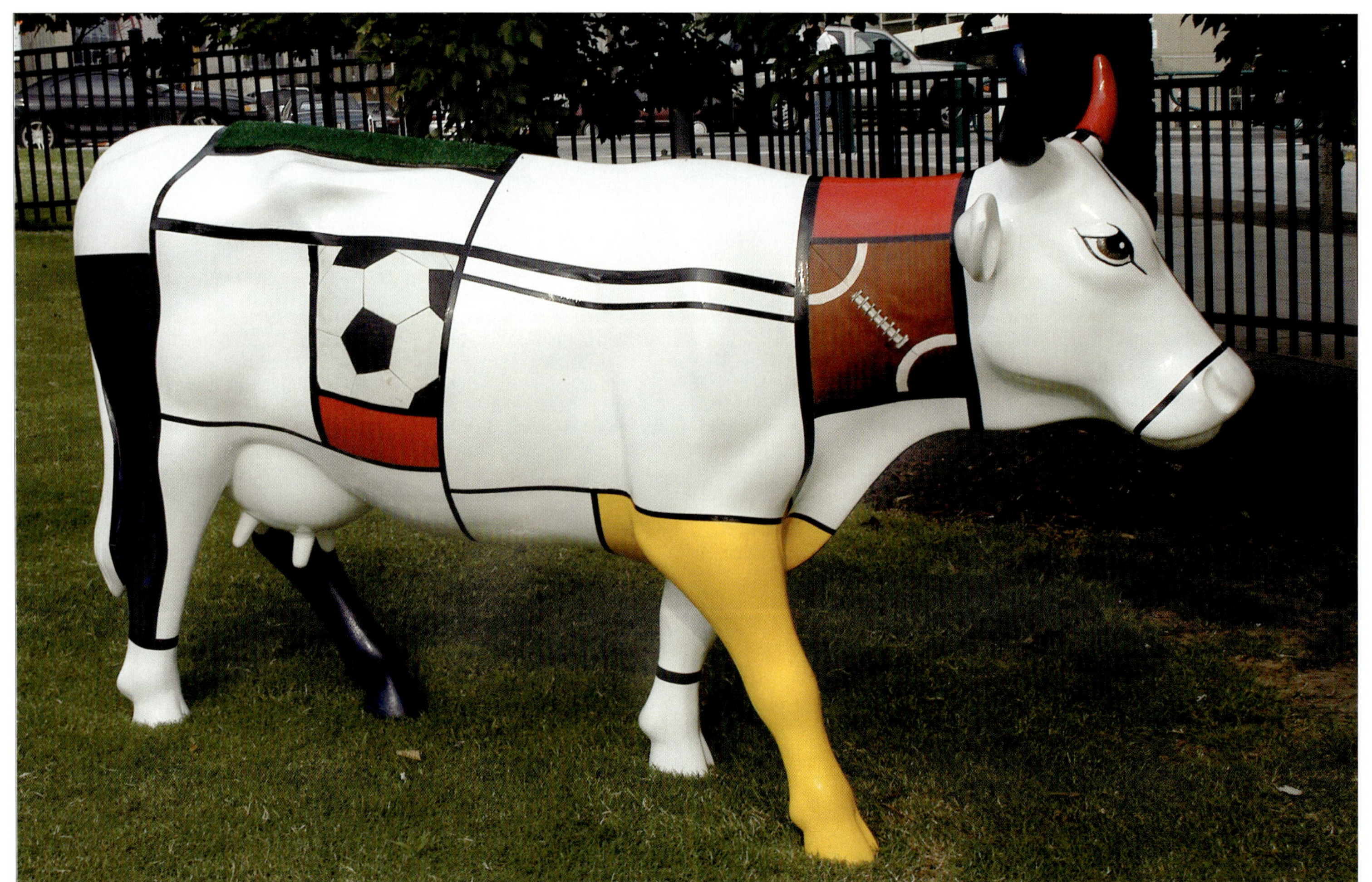

Moondrian Sports Period
Peggy Wilson
CowParade Atlanta

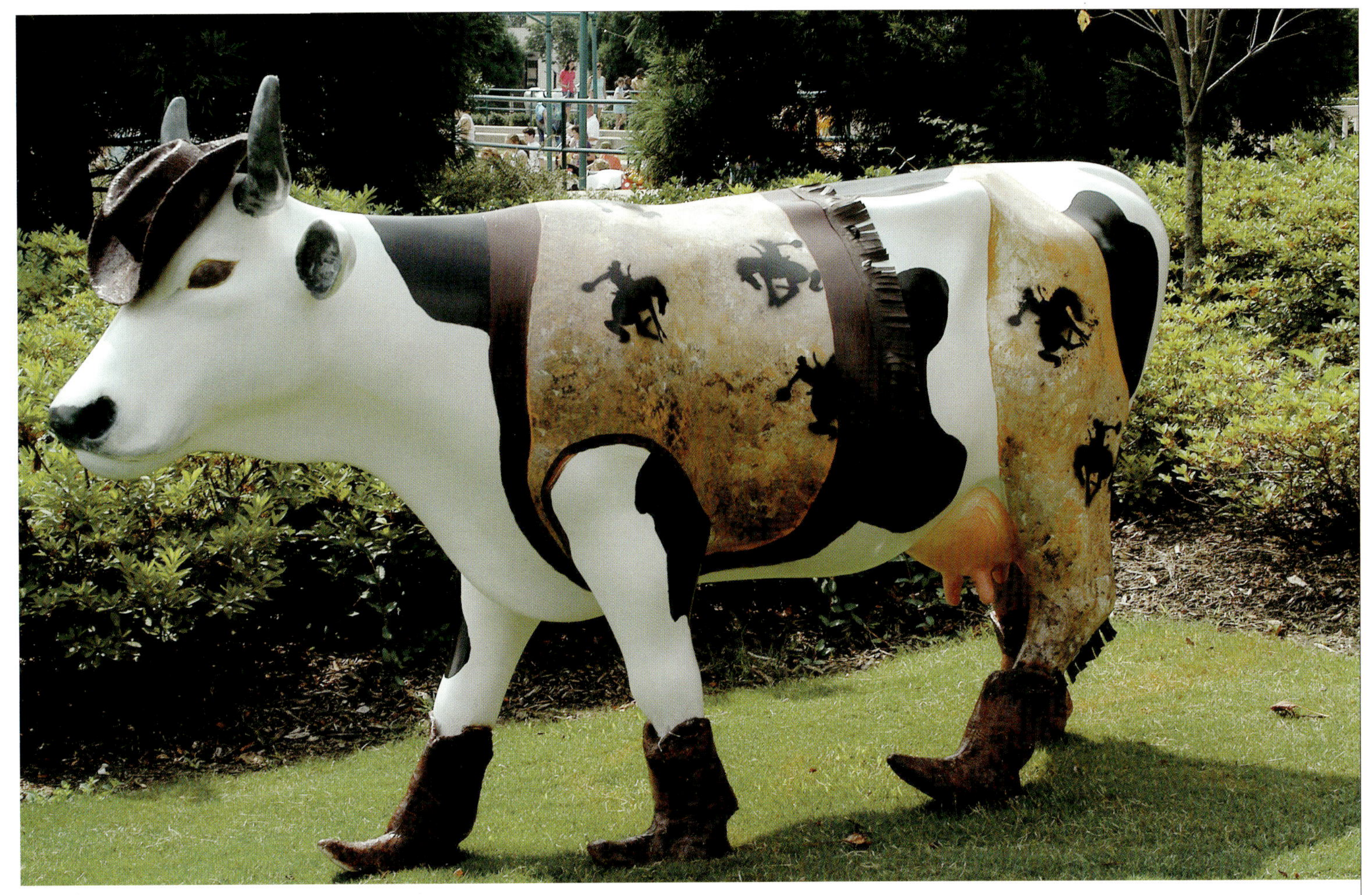

Cowboy Cow
Nan Milam & Eagles Landing National Art Honor Society
Andretti Speed Lab

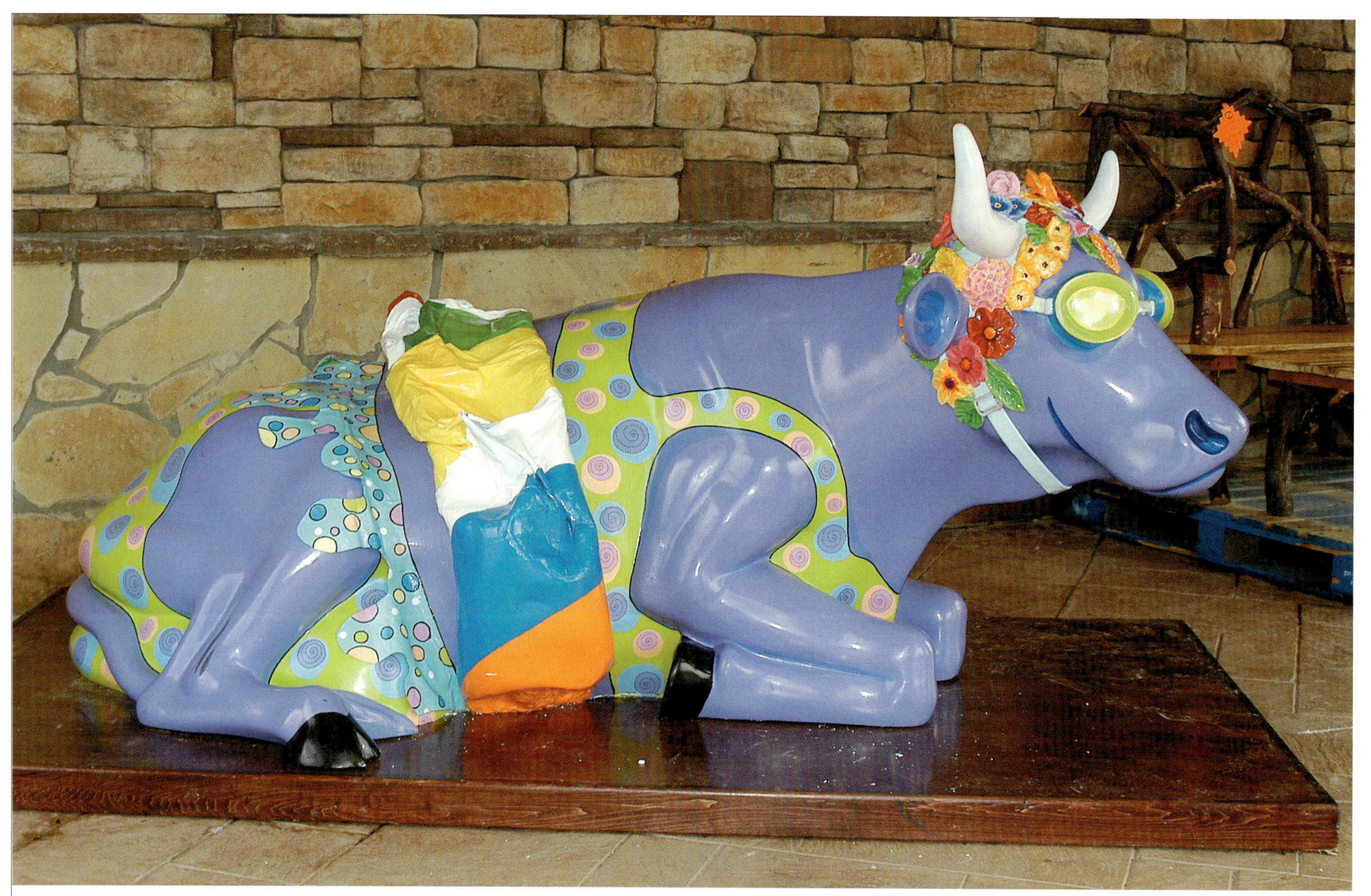

Betty the Beach Baby Bovine
Jean Ann Jedwabny
Harry Norman

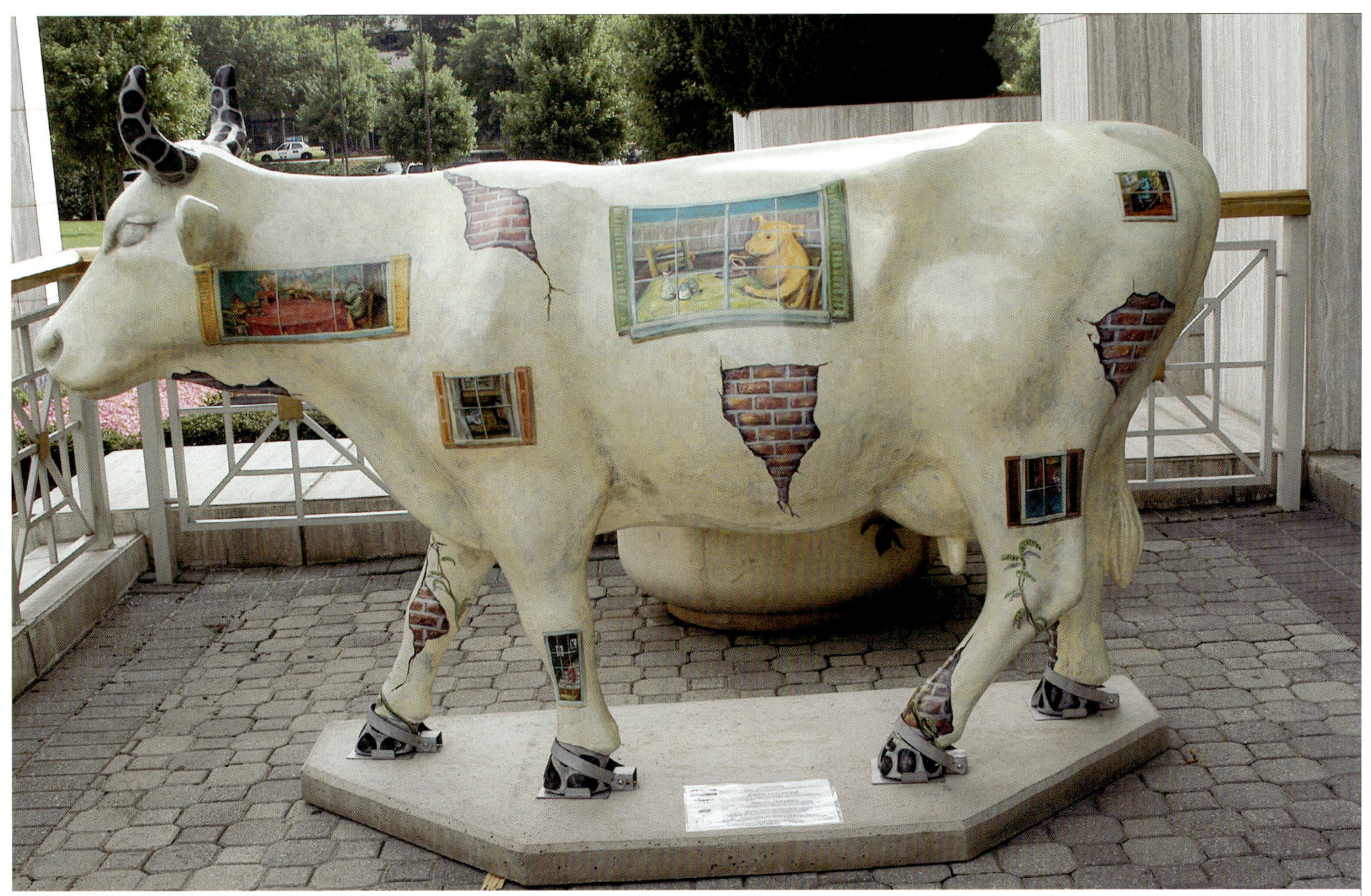

Little Lives
Linda Mitchell
HomeBanc

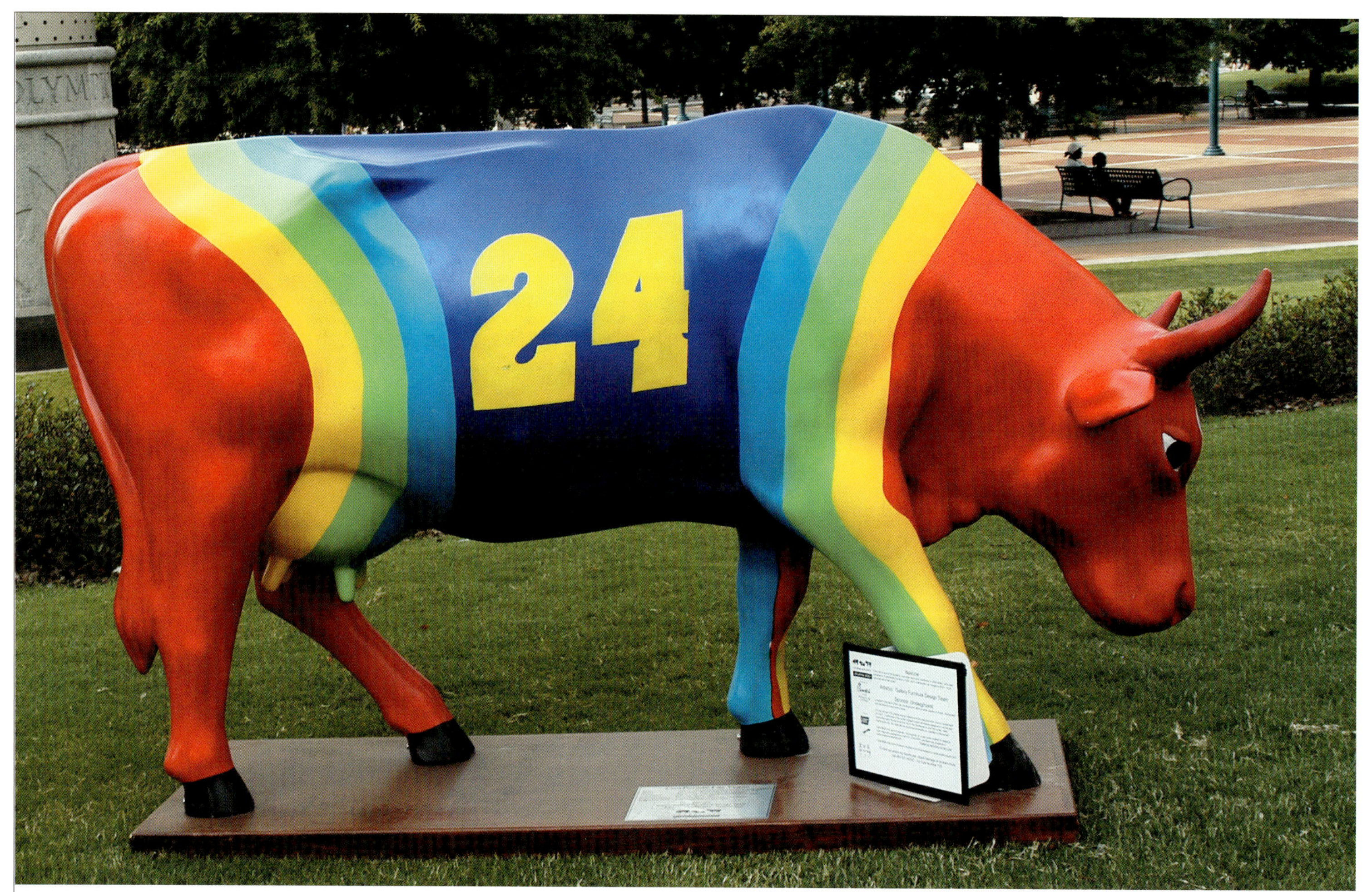

Nascow
Gallery Furniture Design Team
Underground

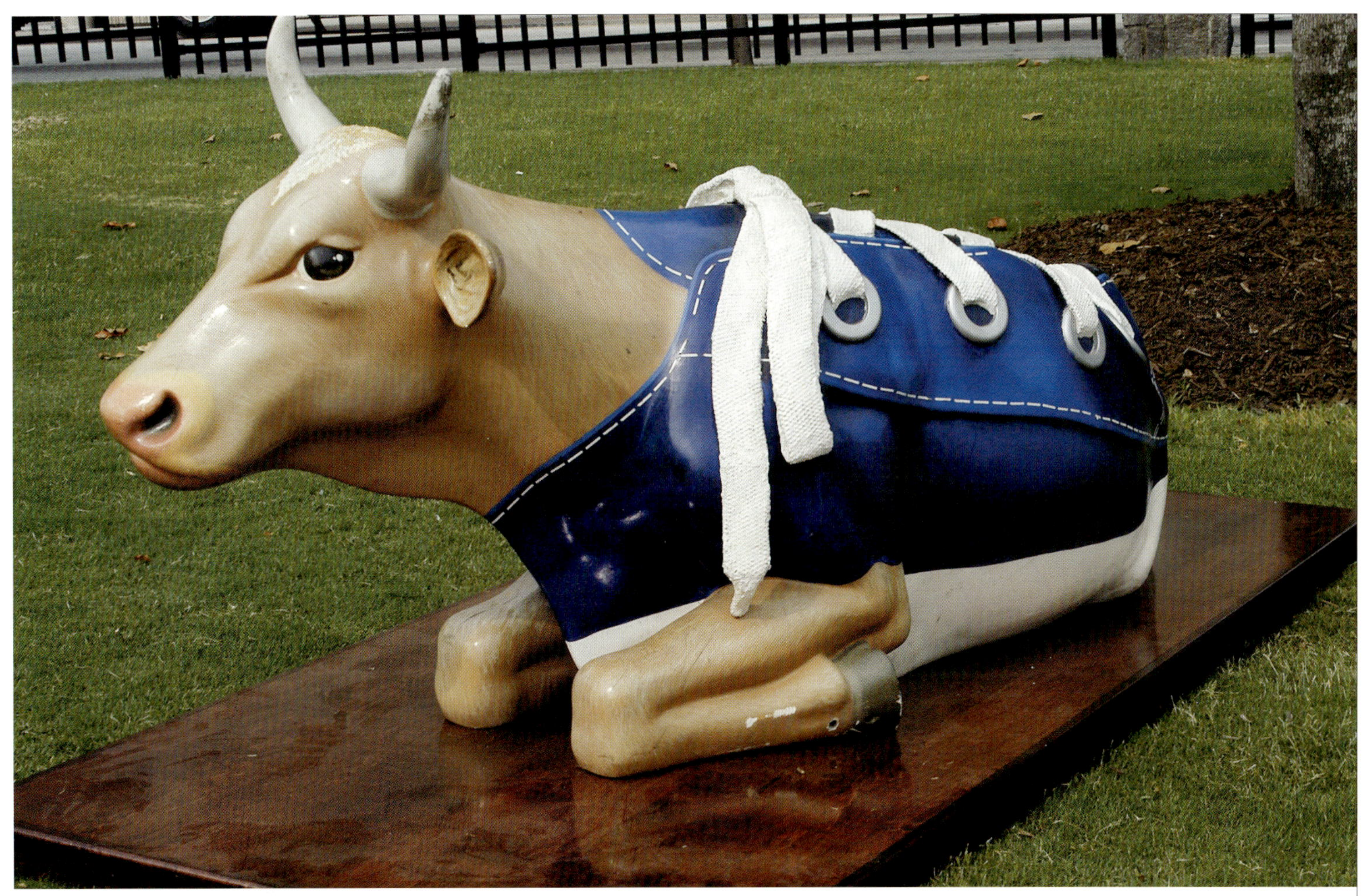

Moo-Shoe
Iris Rosenberg
CowParade Atlanta

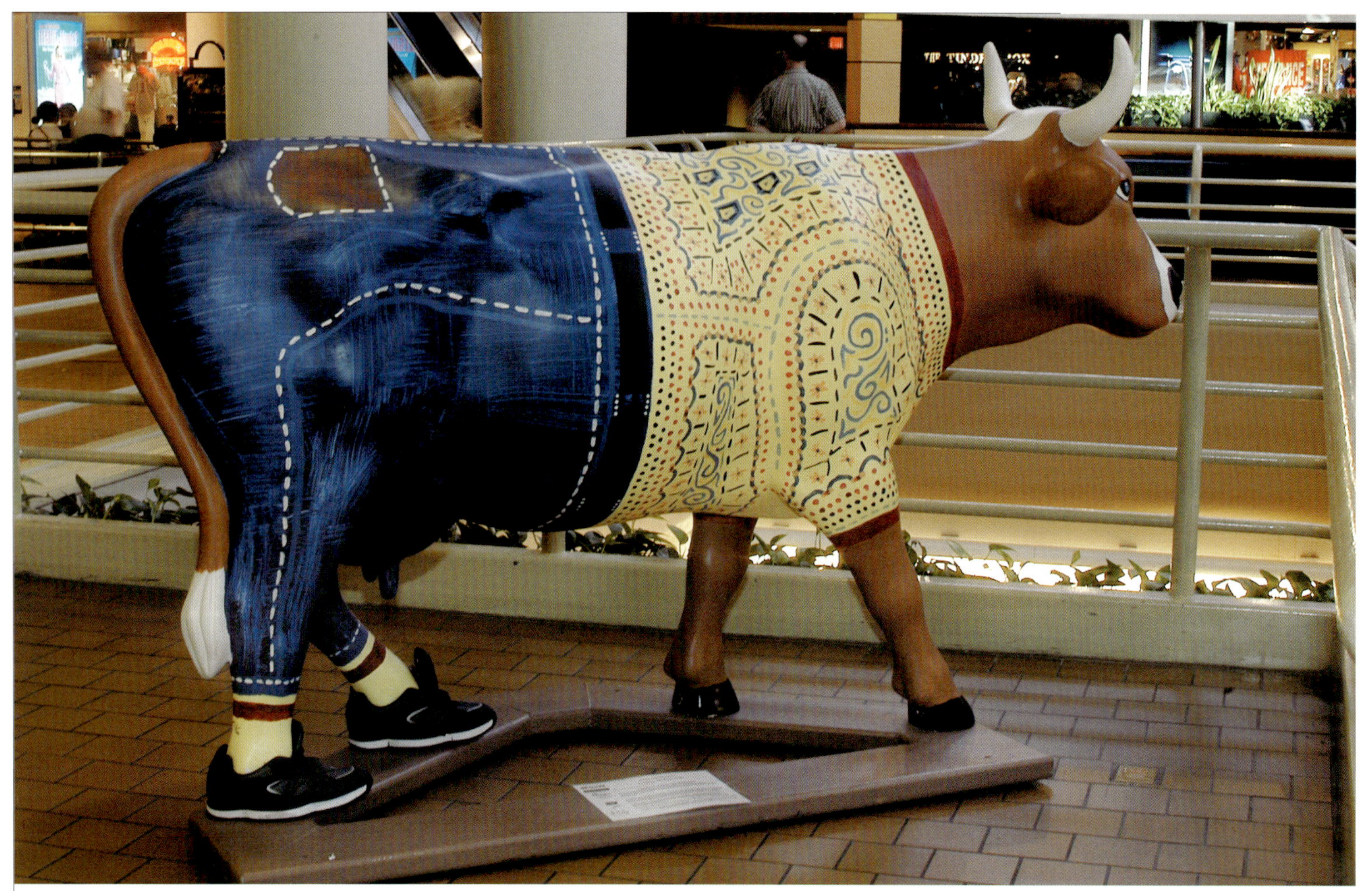

Keep GA Mootiful
Michael Weil
Keep GA Beautiful

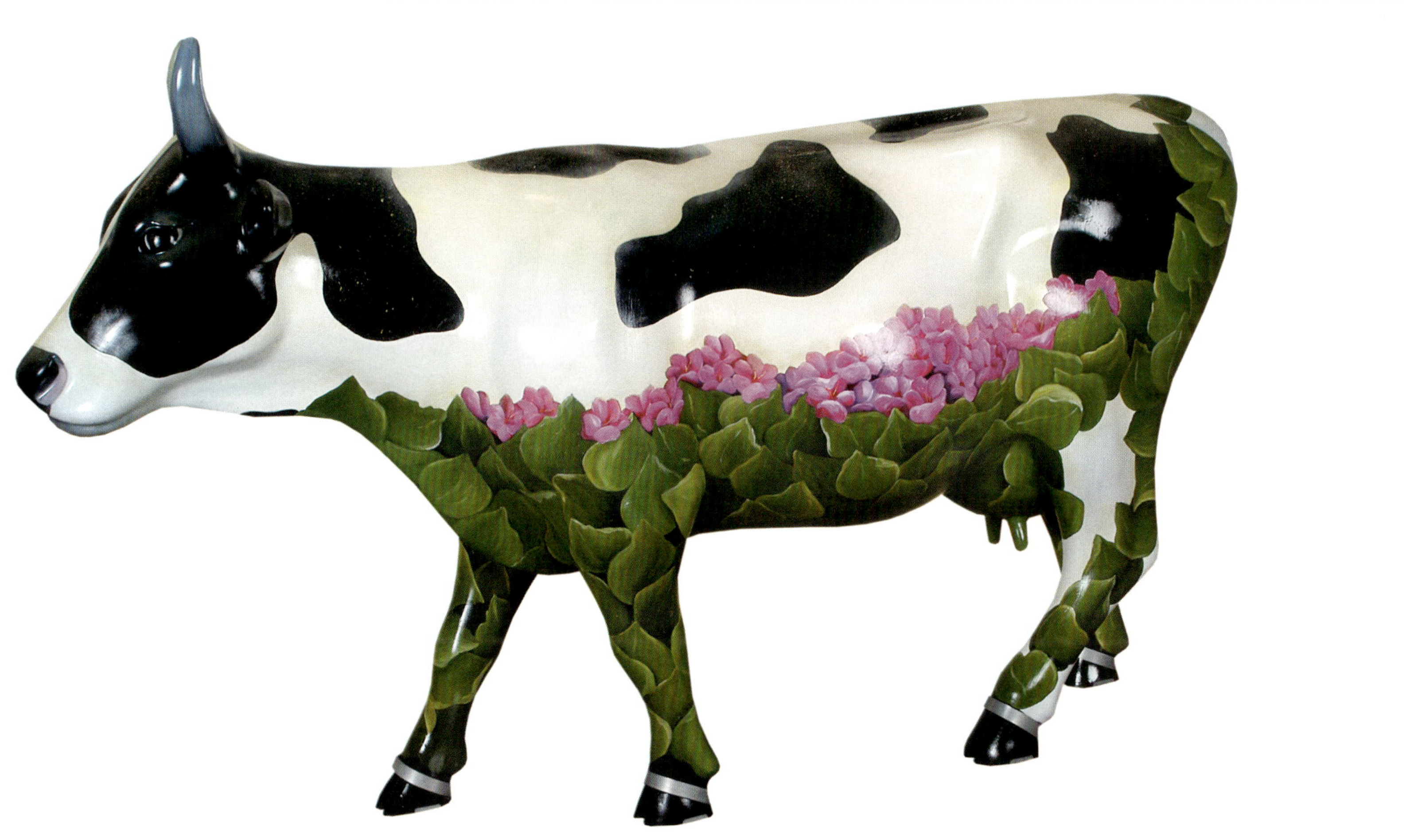

The Pollen Cownt
Jordan Mastrodonato
CowParade Atlanta

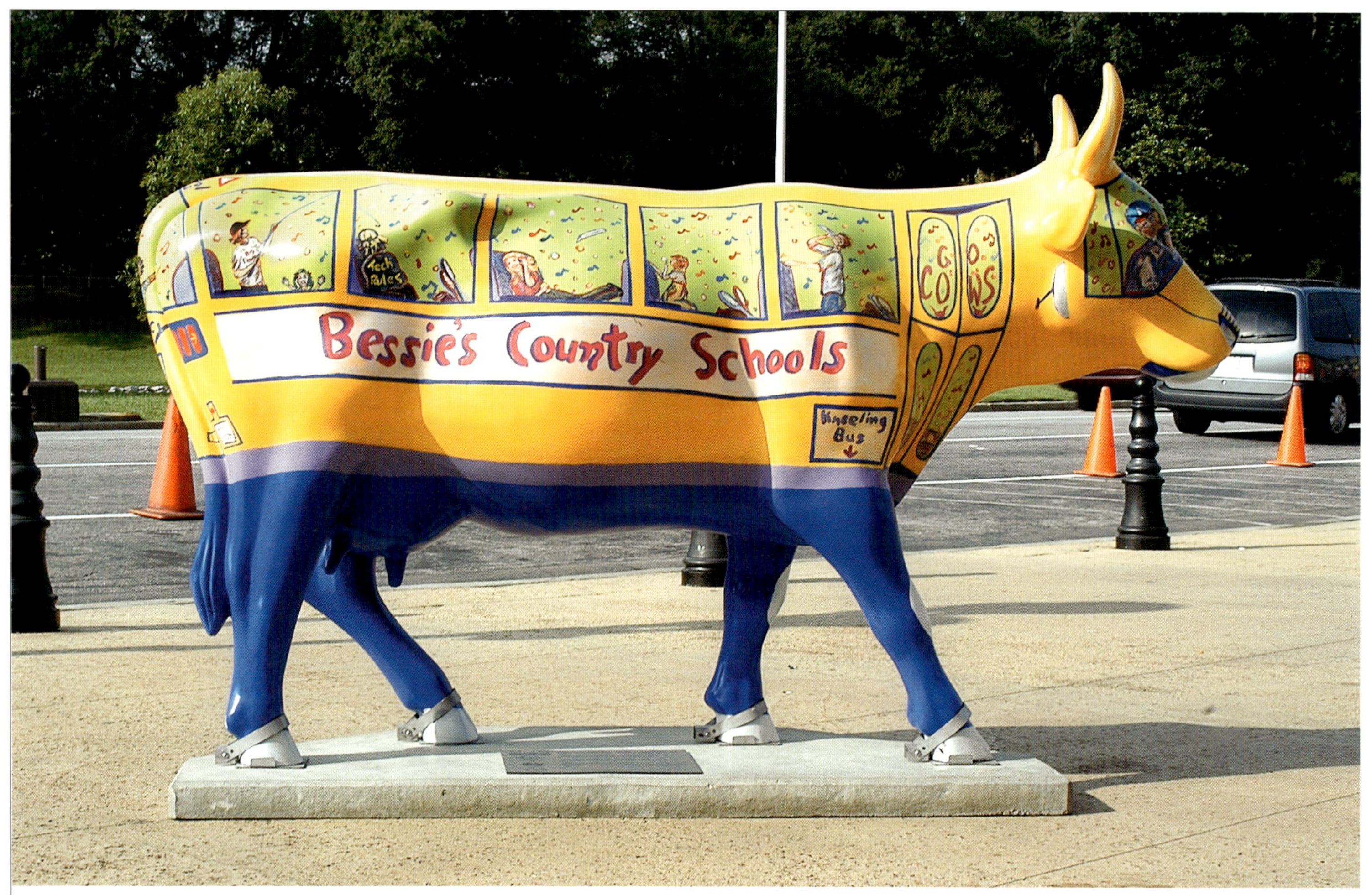

Bessie's Bus
Anita Stewart
Southern A&E

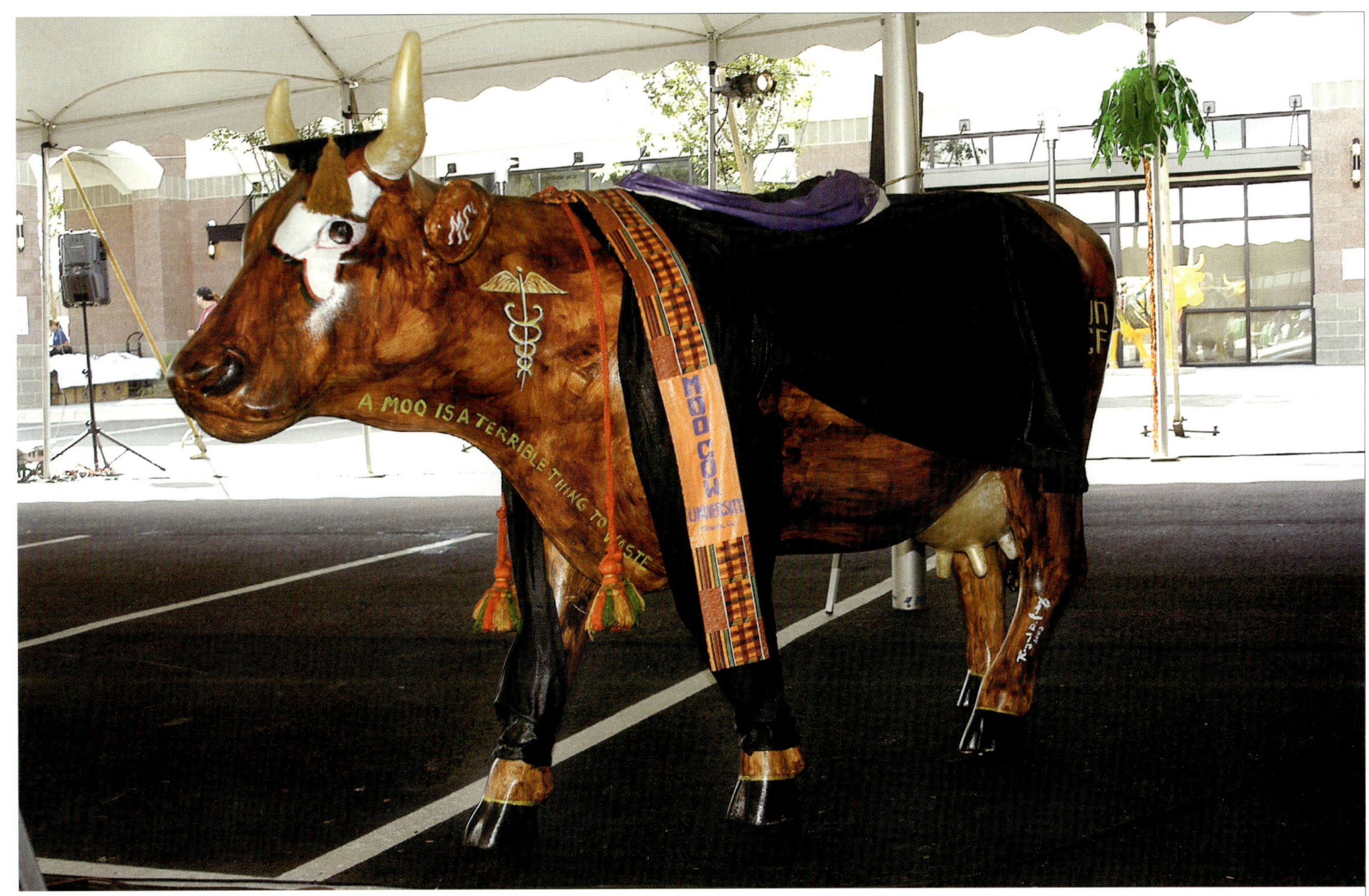

Smart Cow
Raymond Cody
Camp Creek MarketPlace and North American Properties

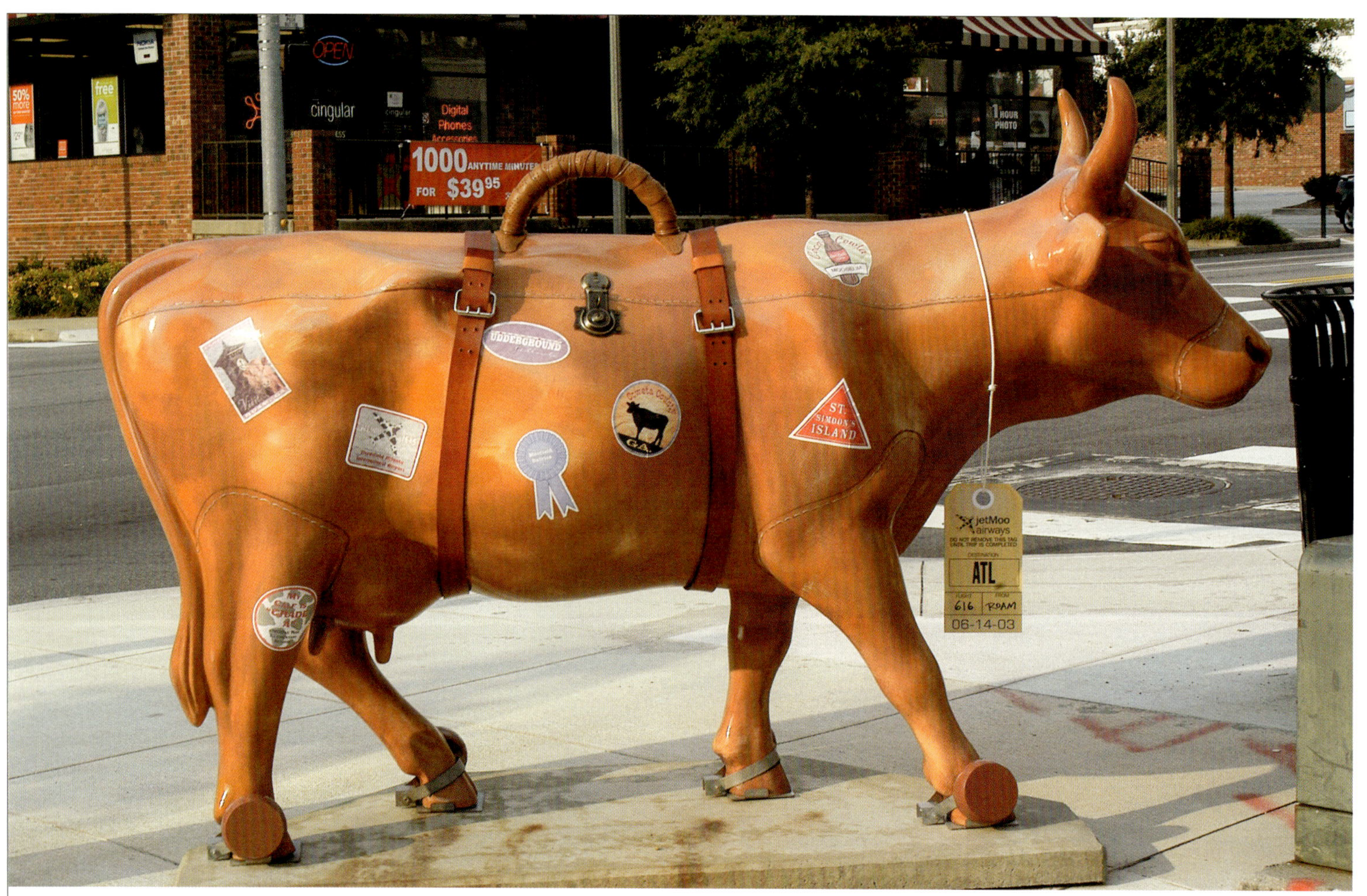

Mooey Vuitton
Ann Clayton
ajc.com/travel

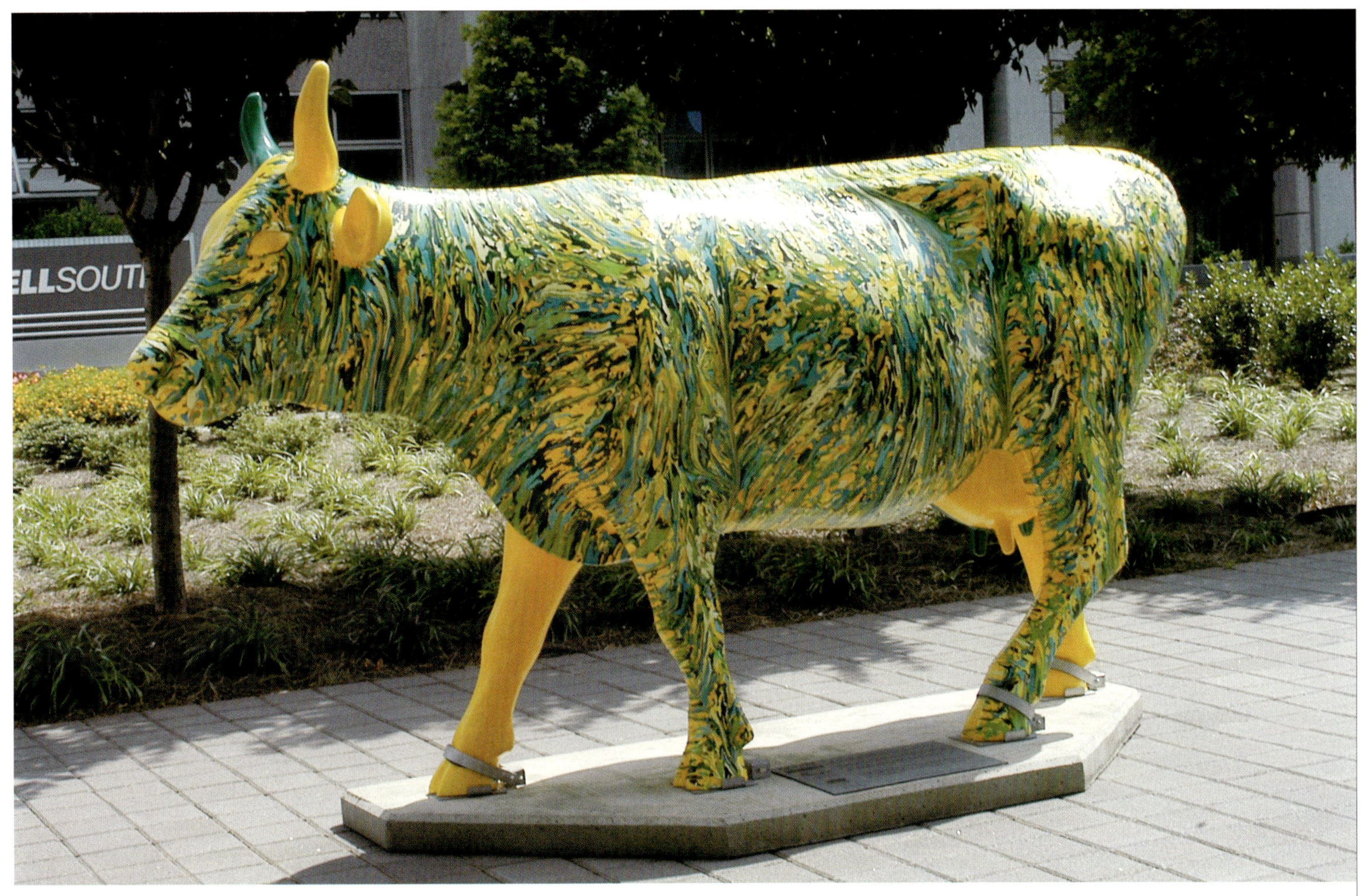

Greener Pastures
Cecil James Cumberland
Evelyn Ashley & Alan McKeon

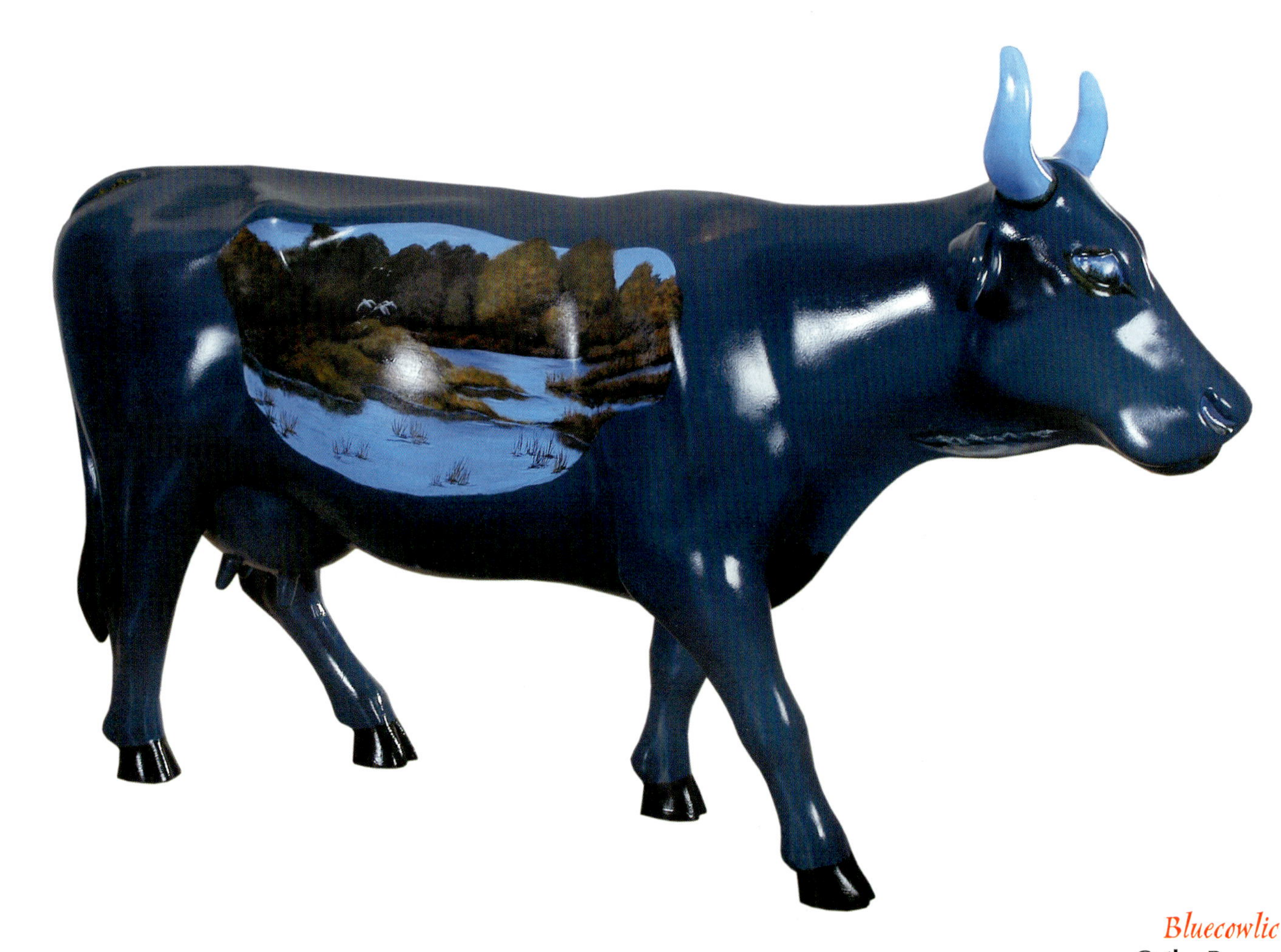

Bluecowlic
Cathy Brown
CowParade Atlanta

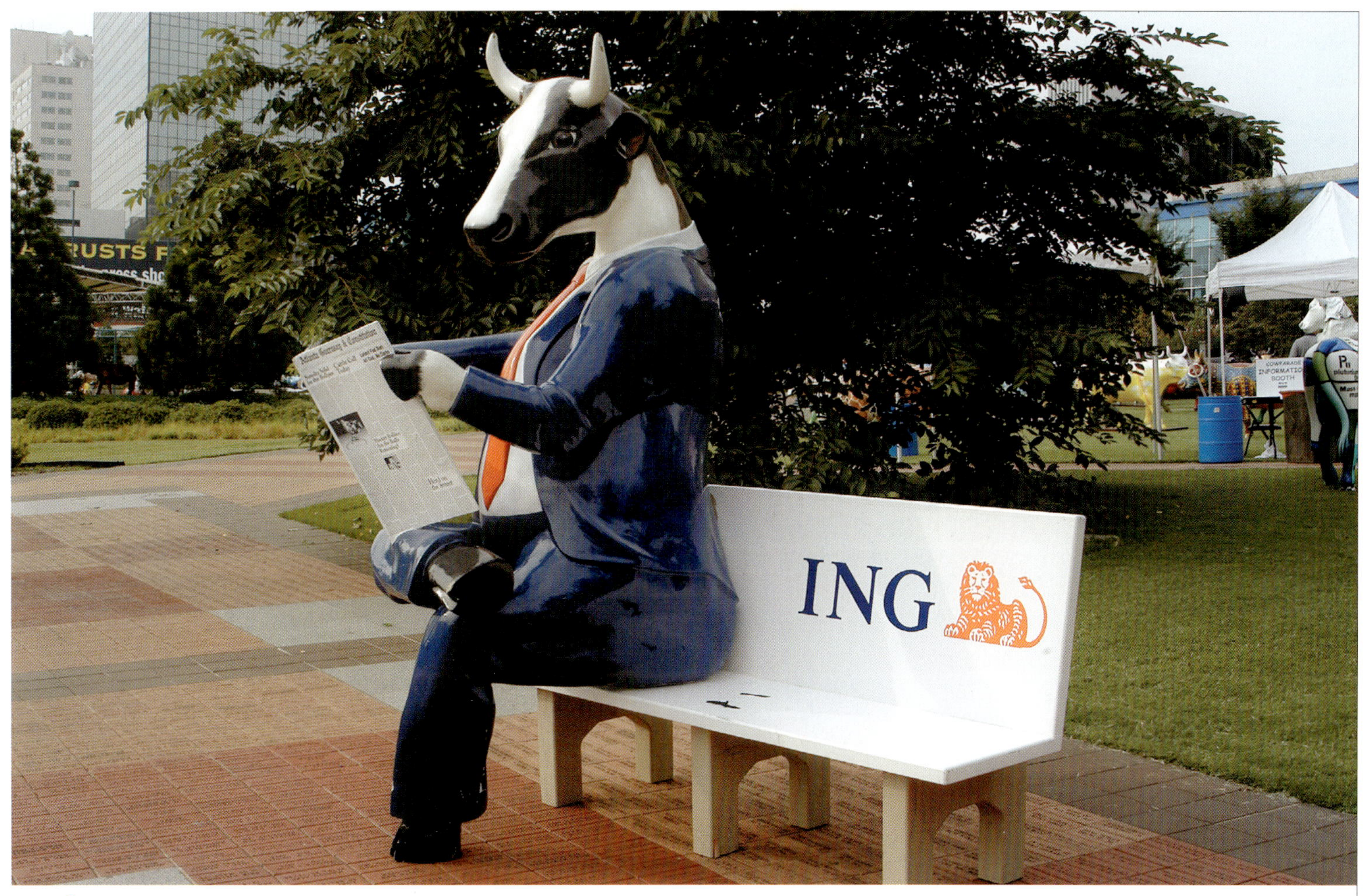

Bench Cow
Scott Tao LaBossiere
ING

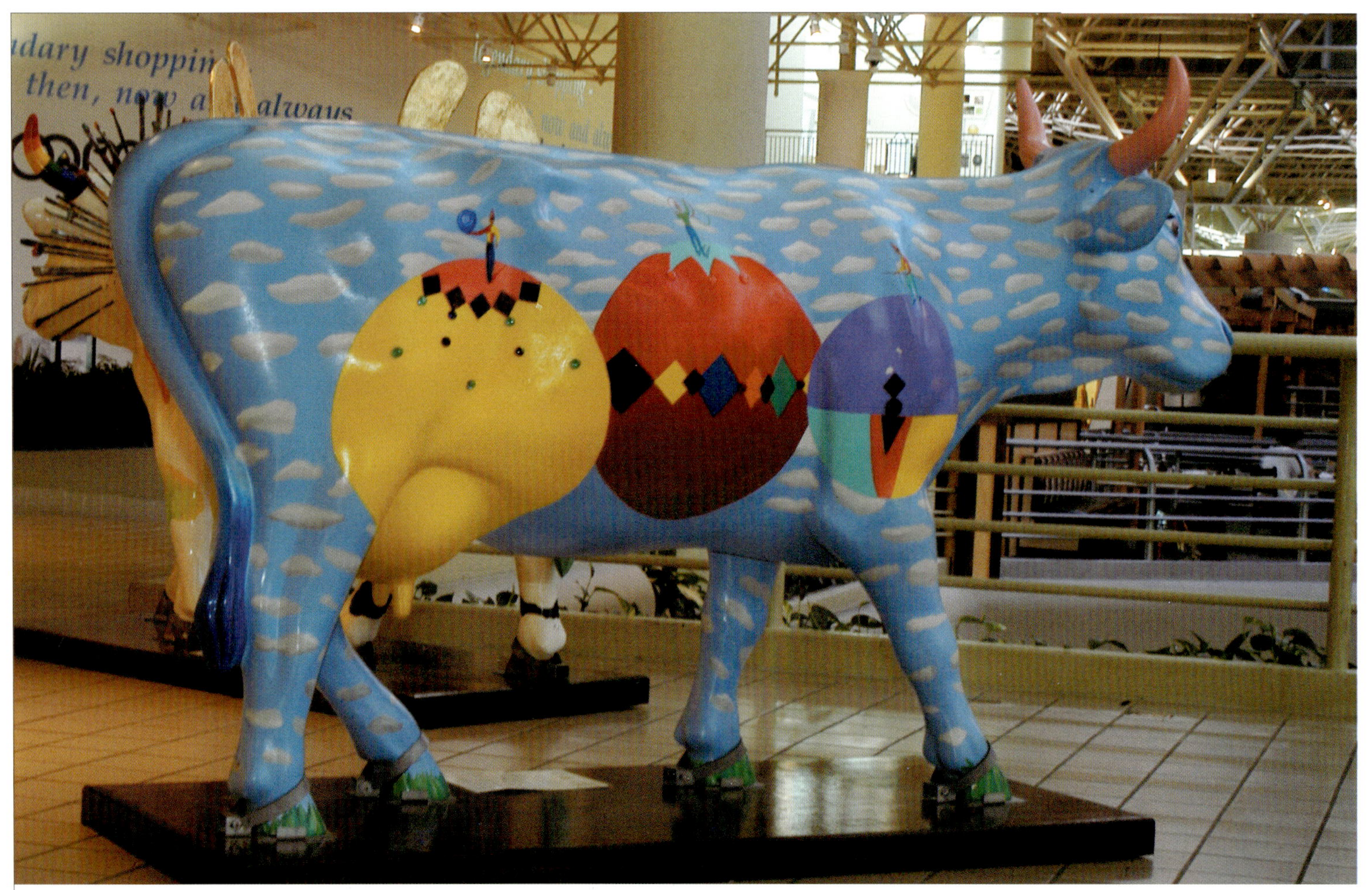

Bovine Balloonacy
Anthony Ardavin
Reliance Financial Corporation

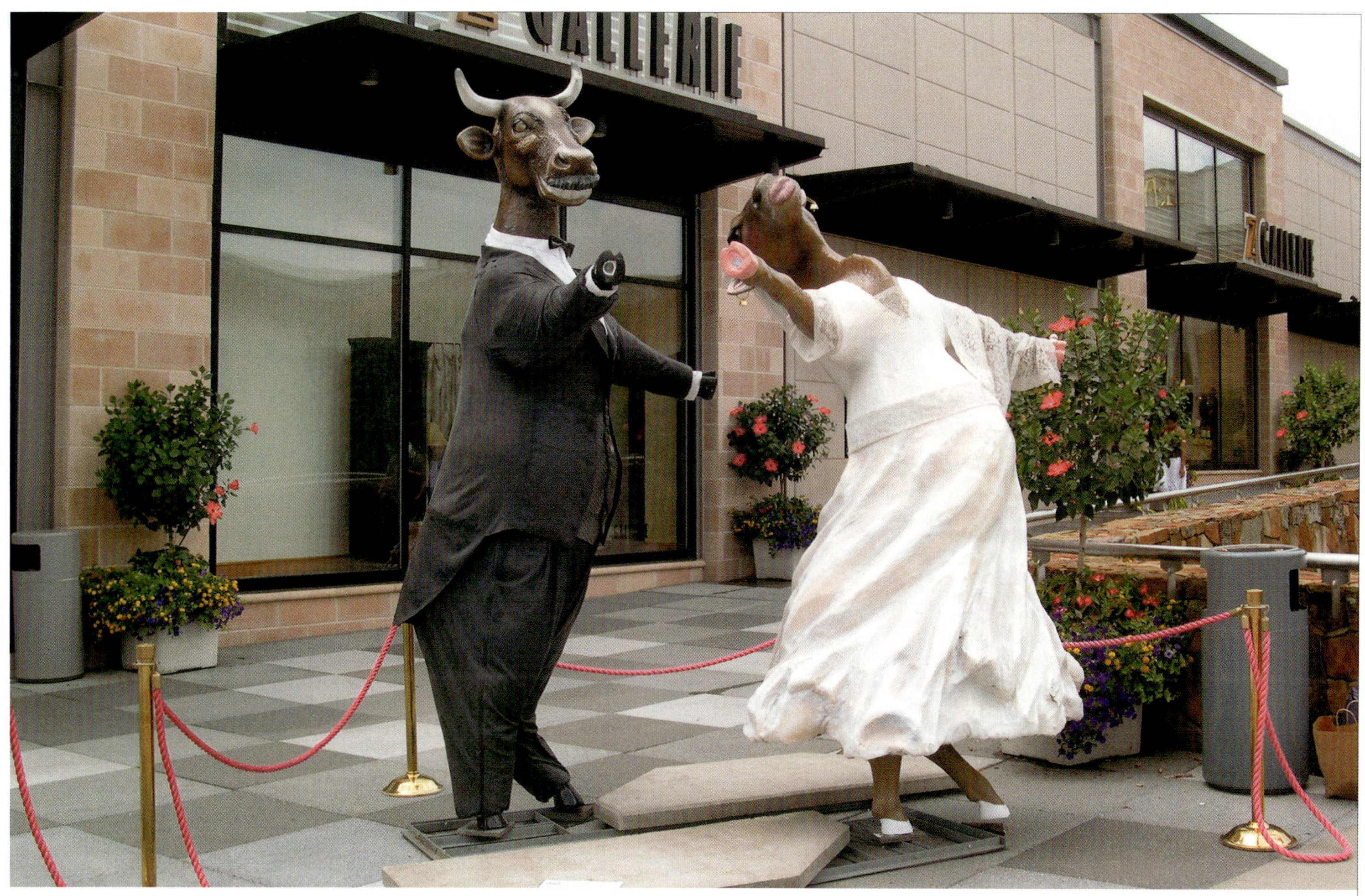

Moolyweds
Eileen Desterno
After Hours Formal Wear

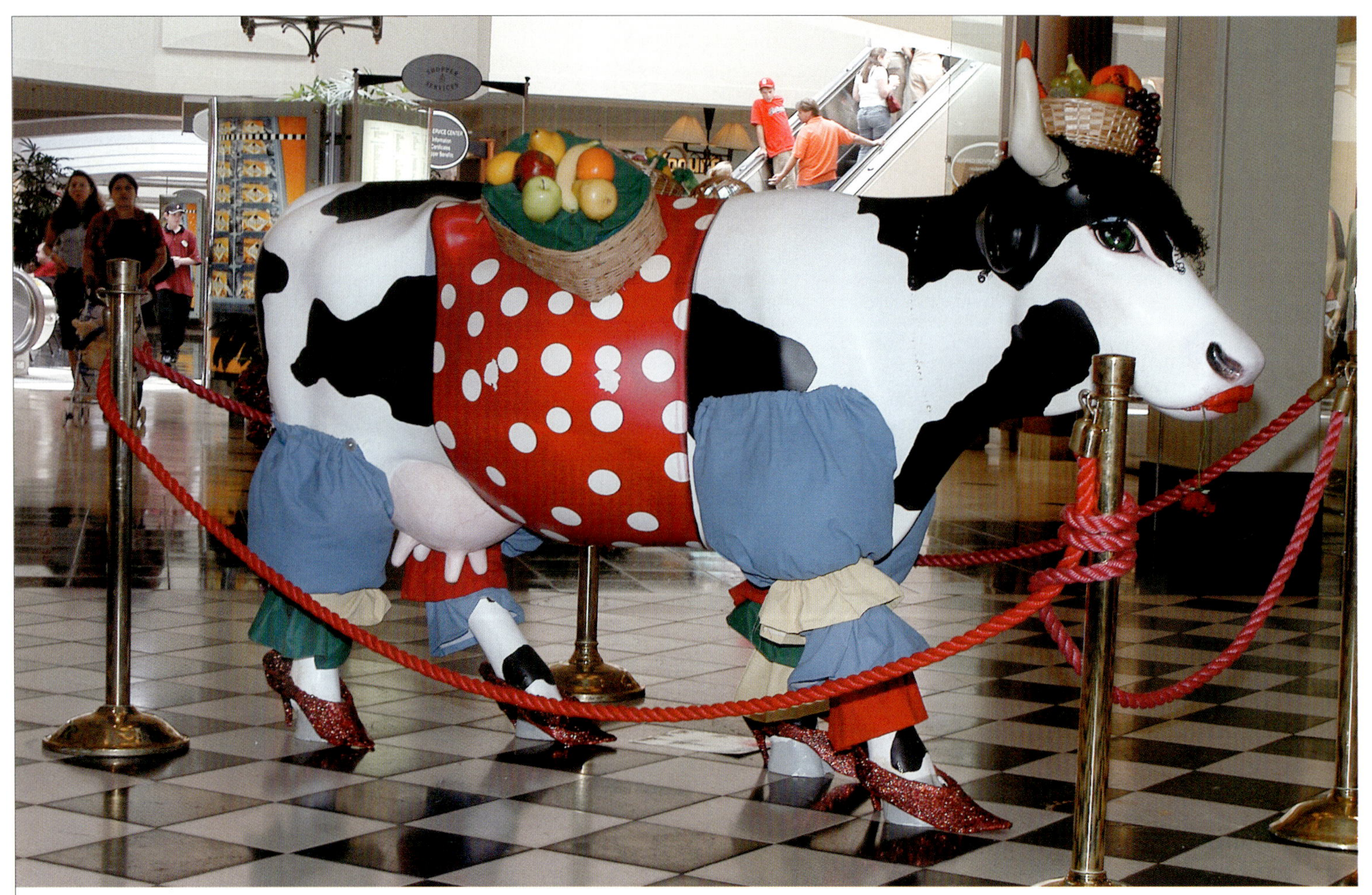

Tropicowl

Jaime Valero, Victoria Martin-Gilly, Waldo Vinces, Maria Lucia Sarmiento

Perimeter Mall

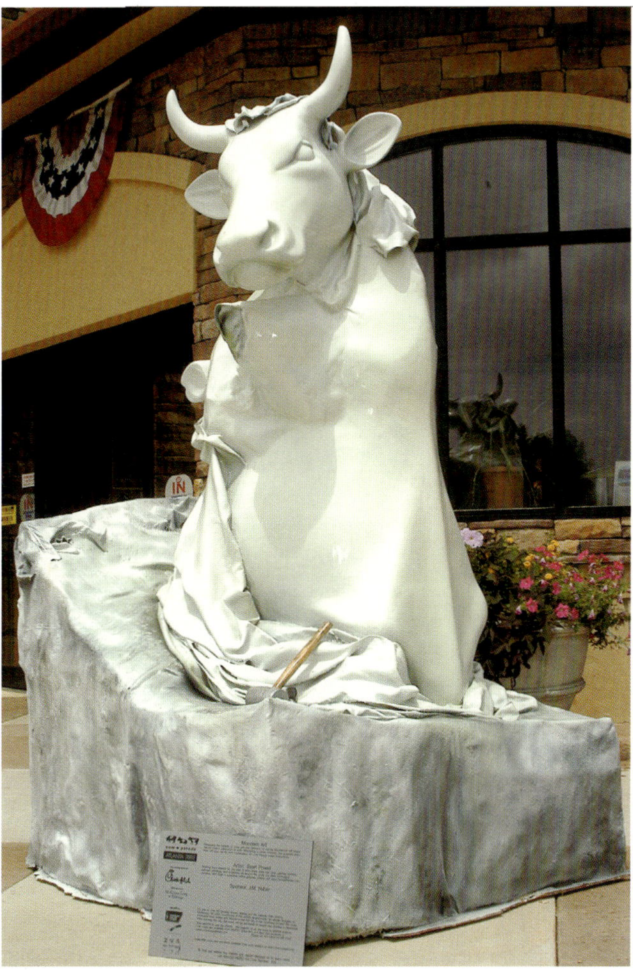

Moodern Art
Sean Powell
J.M. Huber

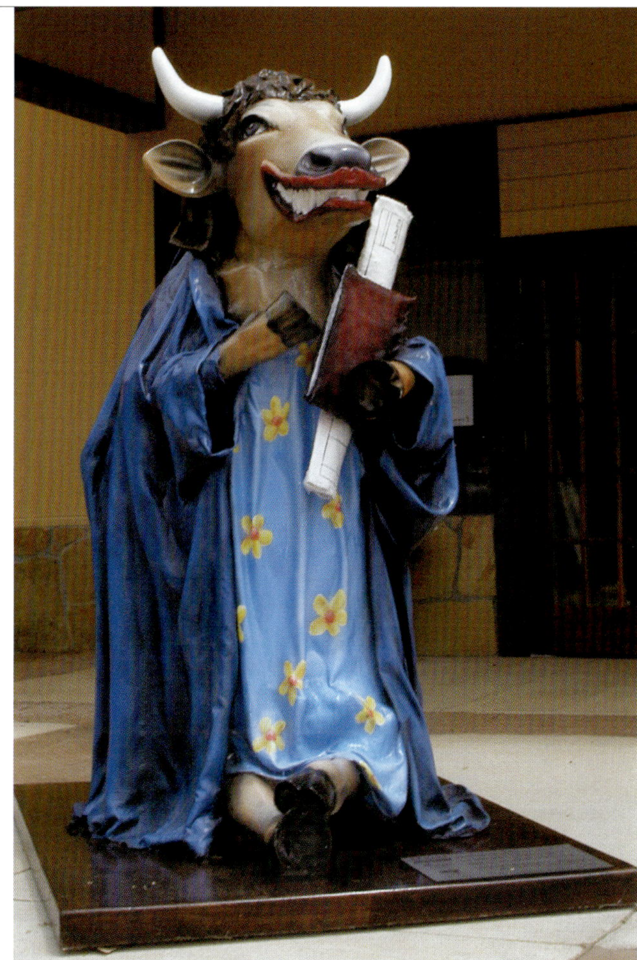

ELE
Sean Powell
Elements, A Home Design Studio, Inc.

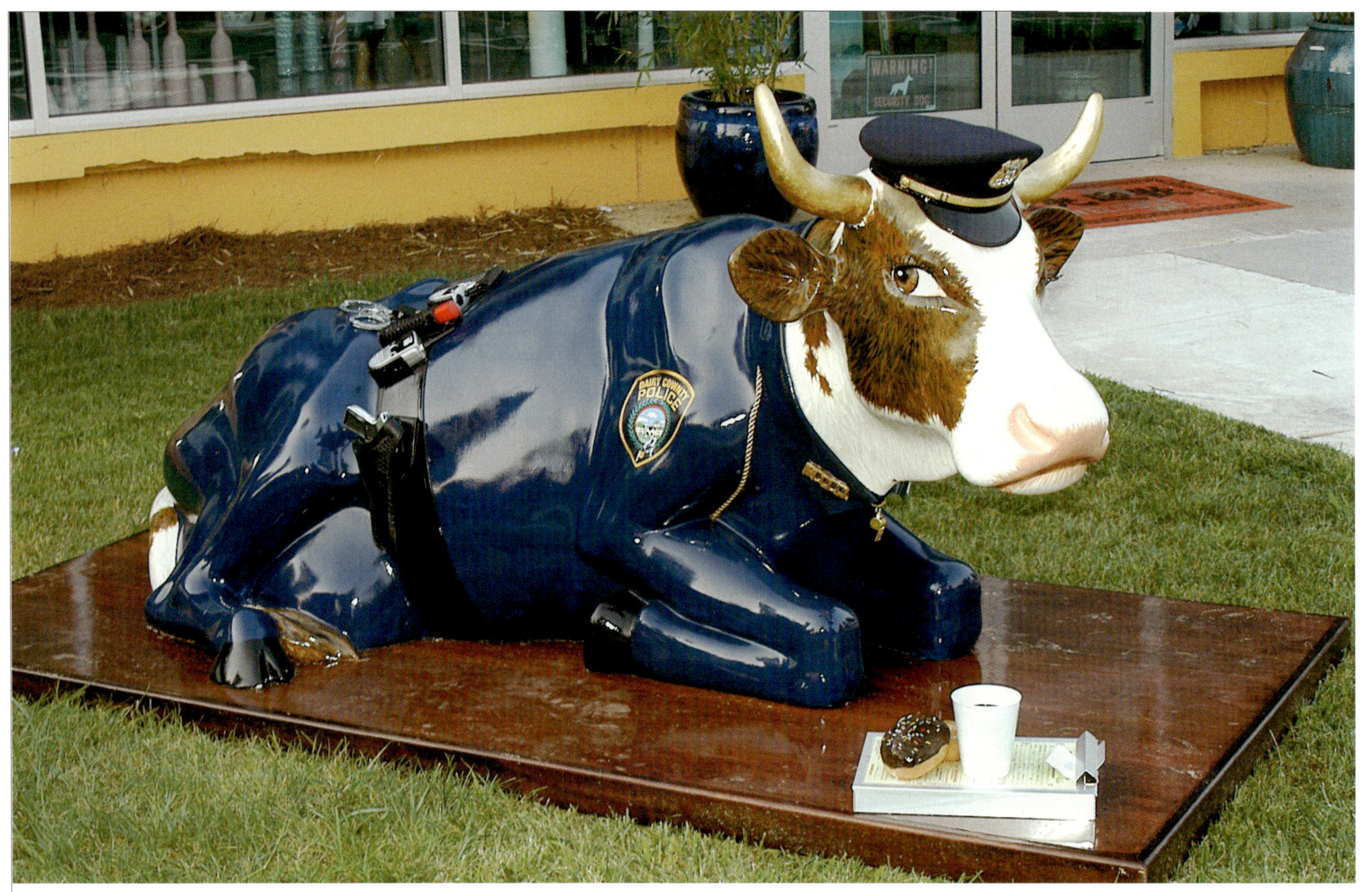

Steak Out!
Barry Imhoff and Wendy Meyer
Cartel Properties

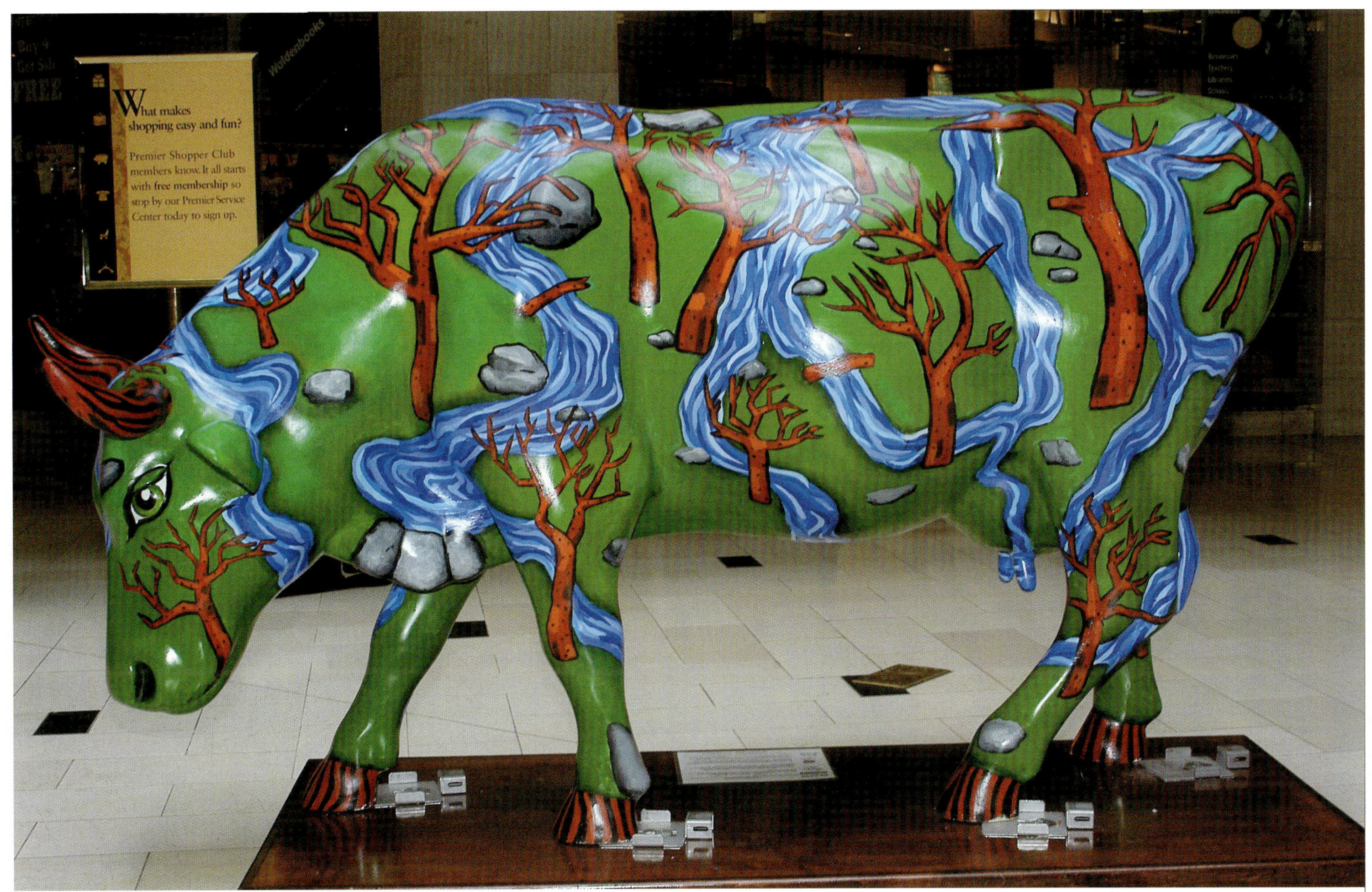

Chattamoochee
Shannon Brickey
LongHorn Steakhouse

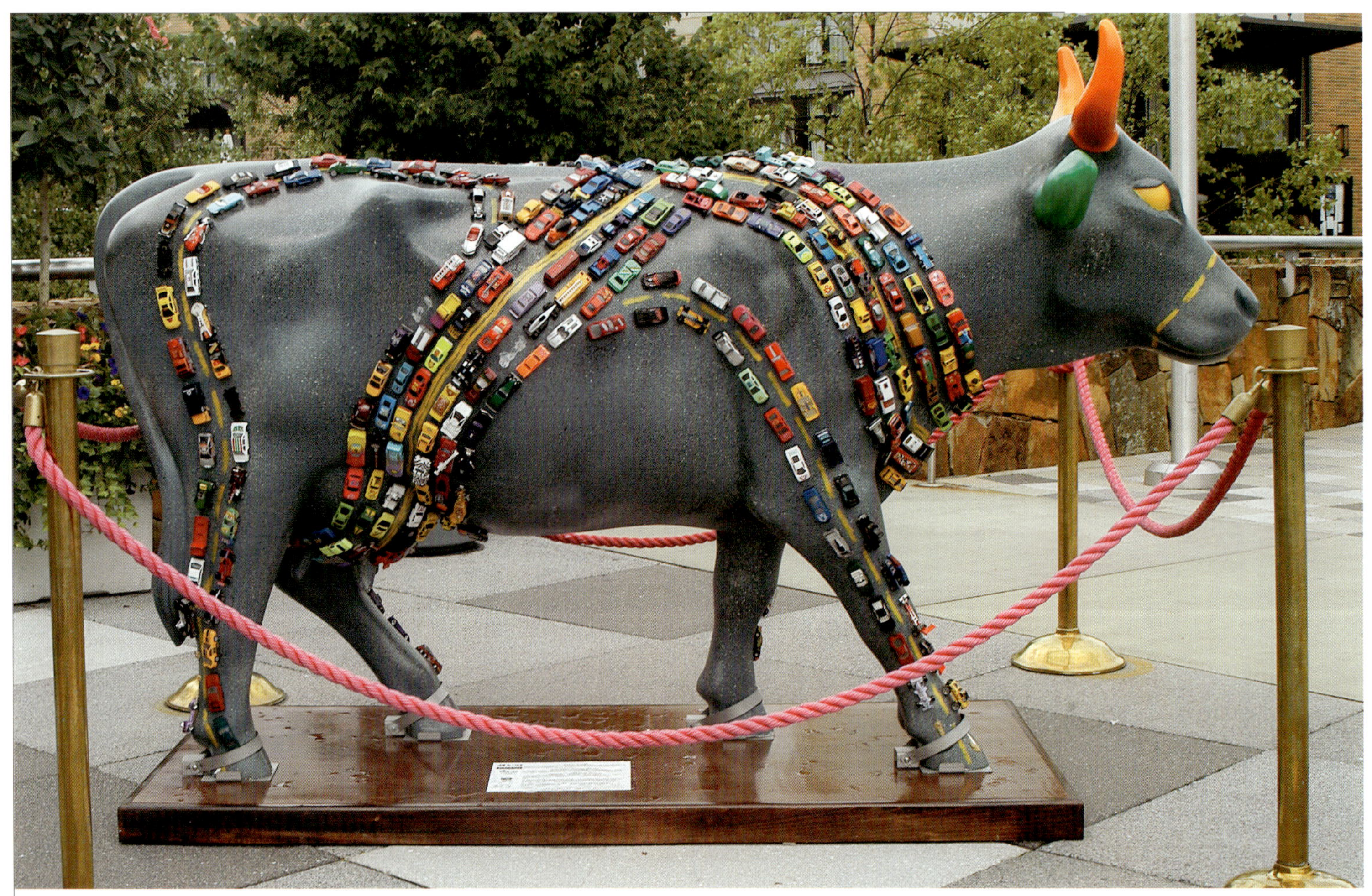

Steer Clear
Gregg Bauer
Hayslett Sorrel

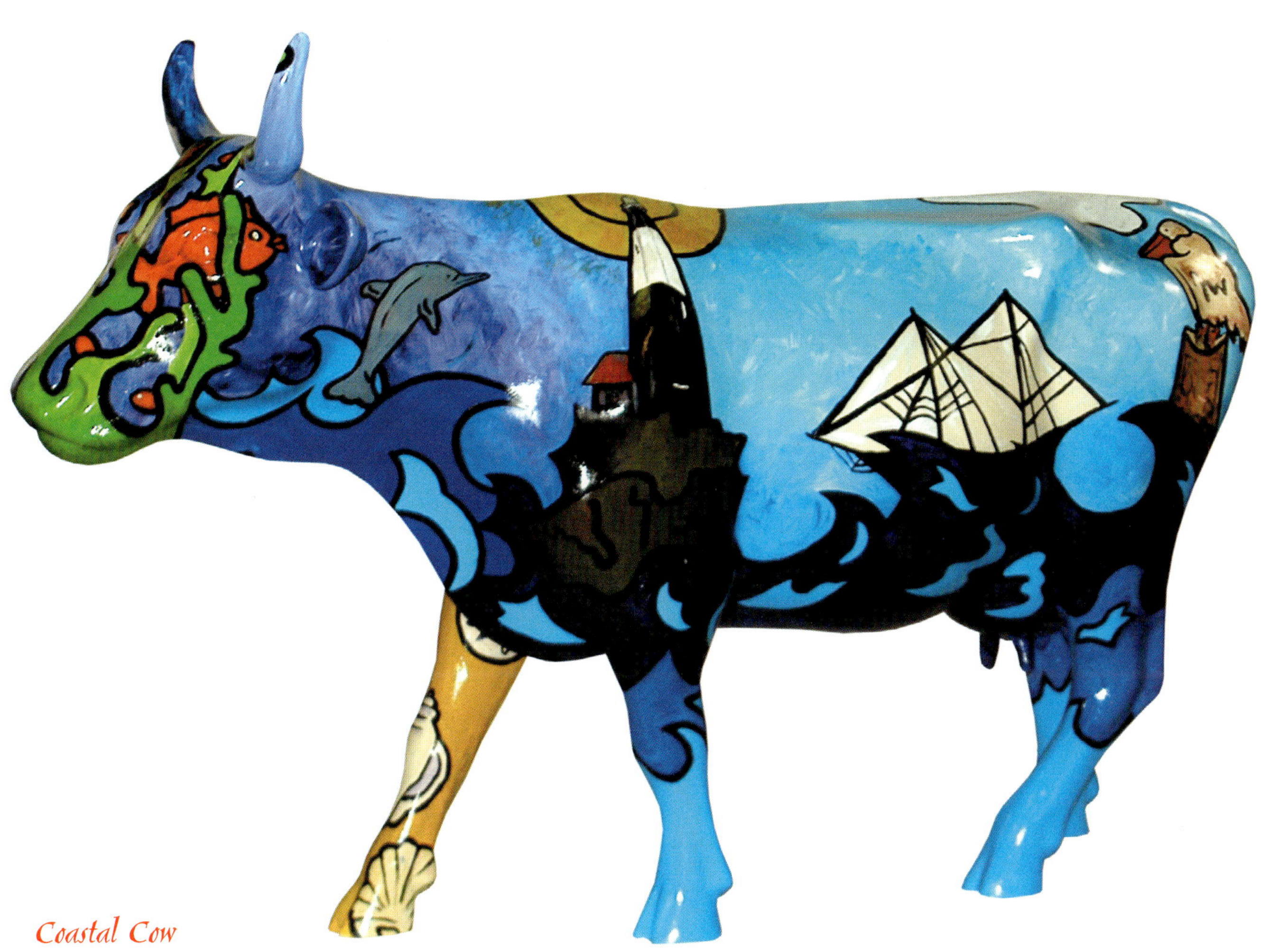

Coastal Cow
Katrine Trantham
CowParade Atlanta

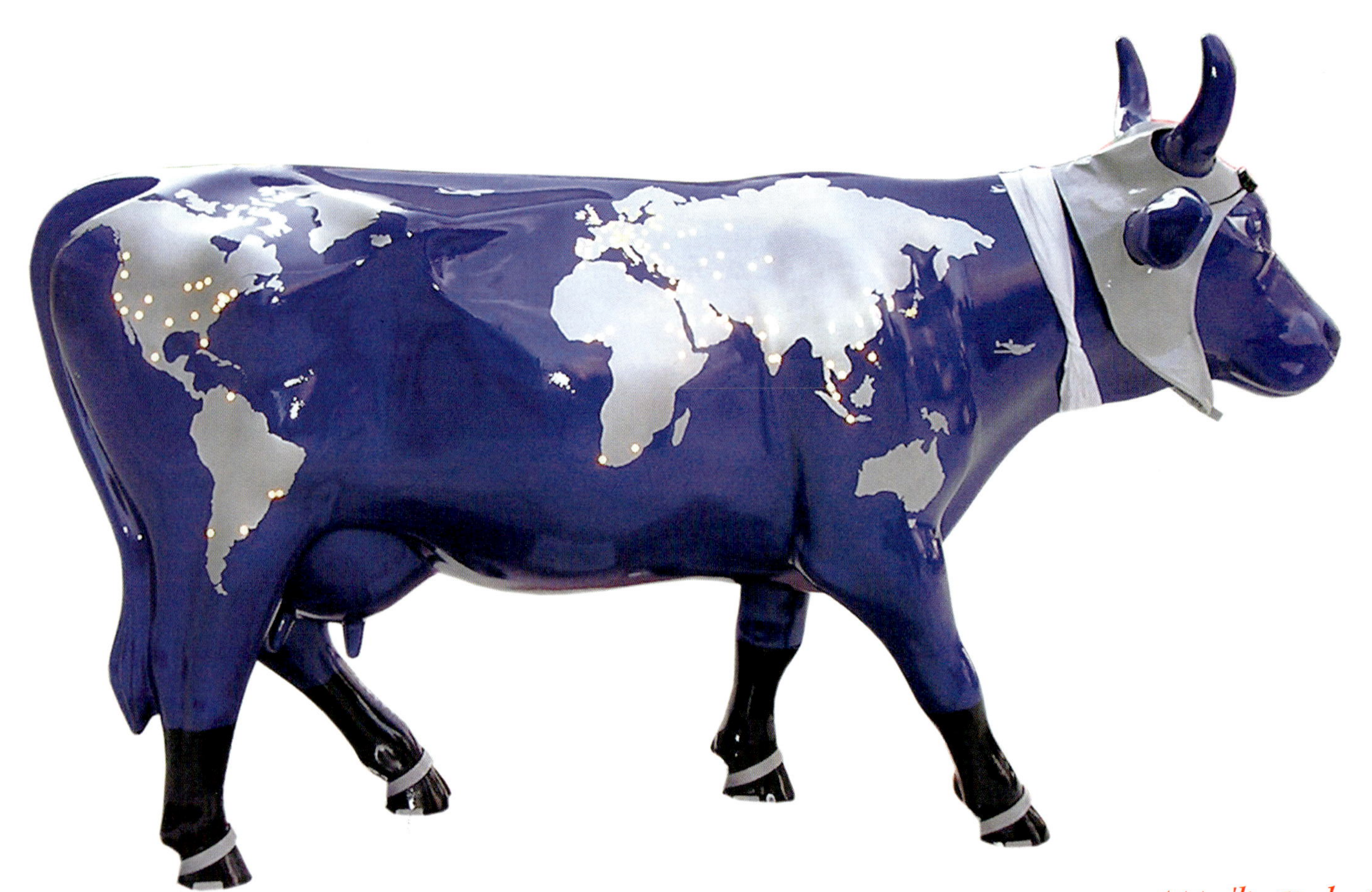

AMoo'lia Earhart
Wulf Kuehmstedt & Filipp Zyryanov
Lufthansa

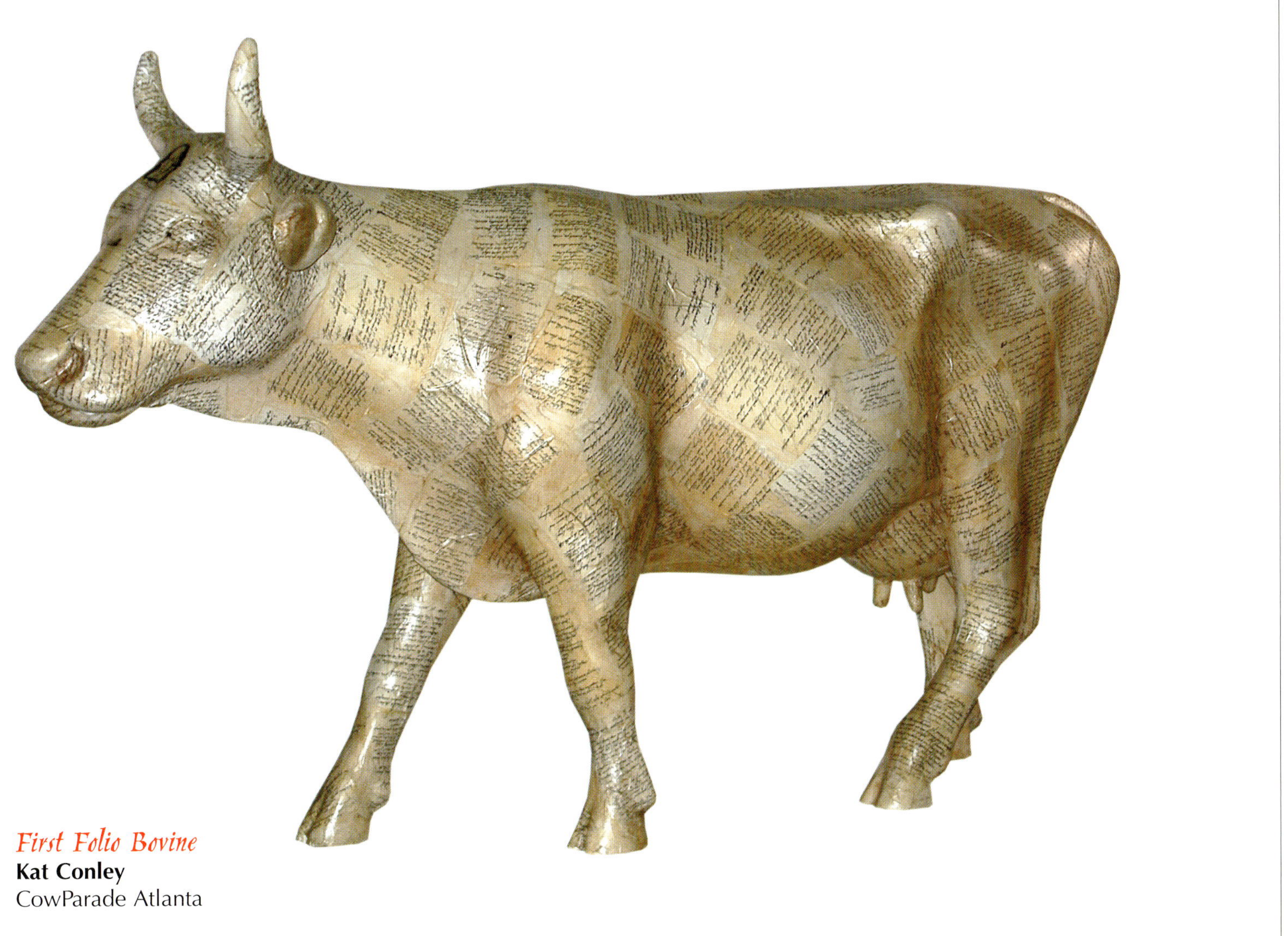

First Folio Bovine
Kat Conley
CowParade Atlanta

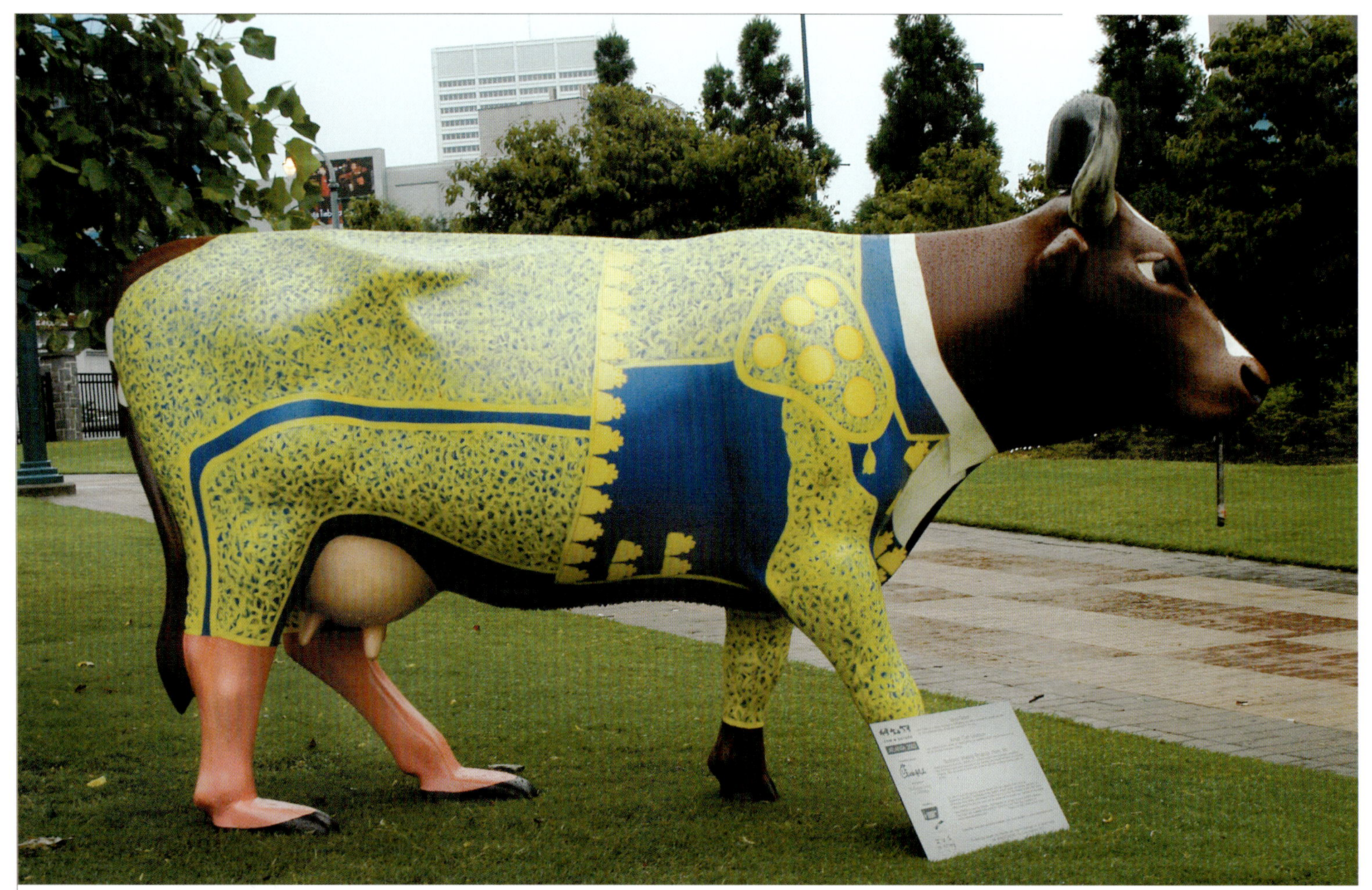

Moo-Tador
Carl Linstrum
Making Projects Work, Inc.

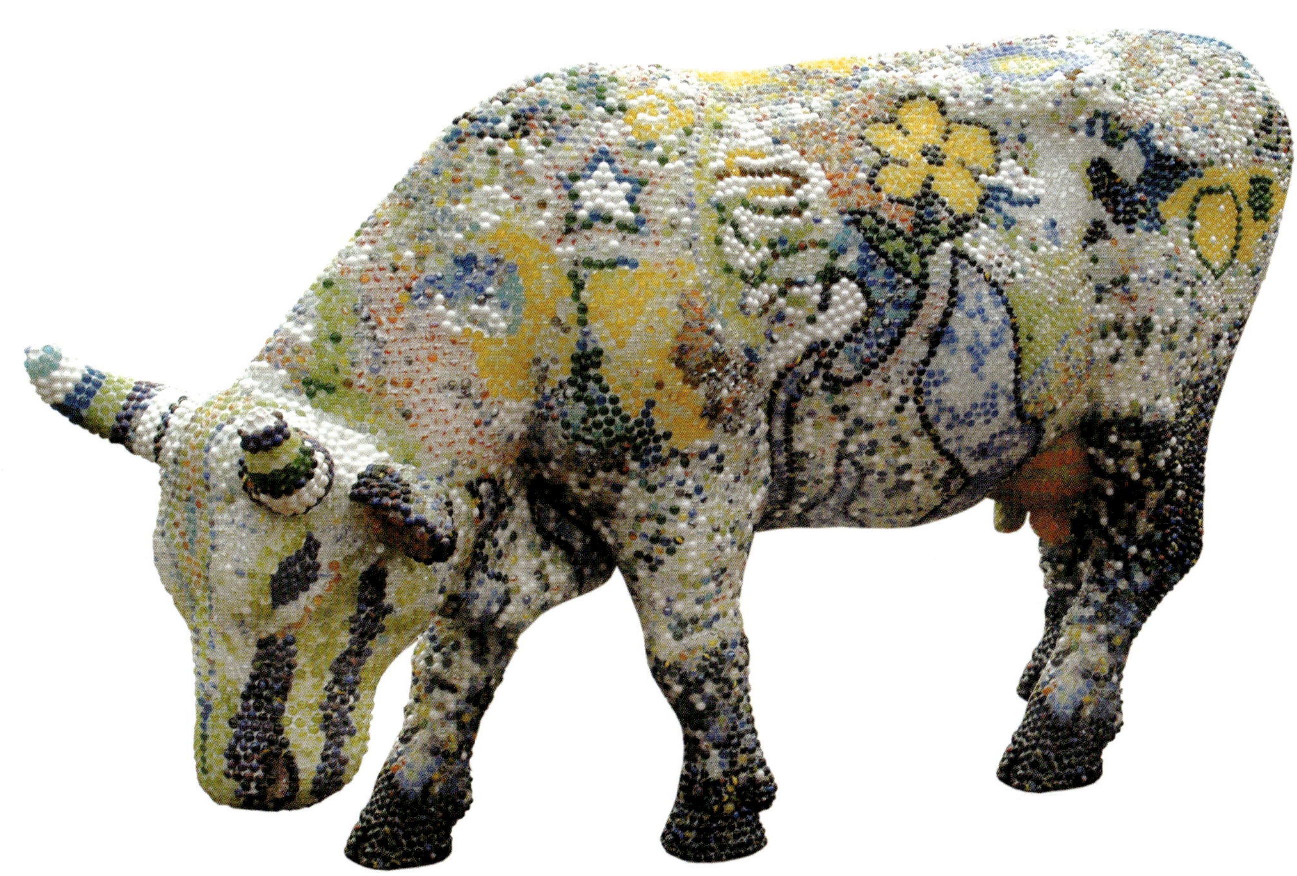

Mar-Bull-Ized Cow
Thomas Swanston
Accenture & Microsoft

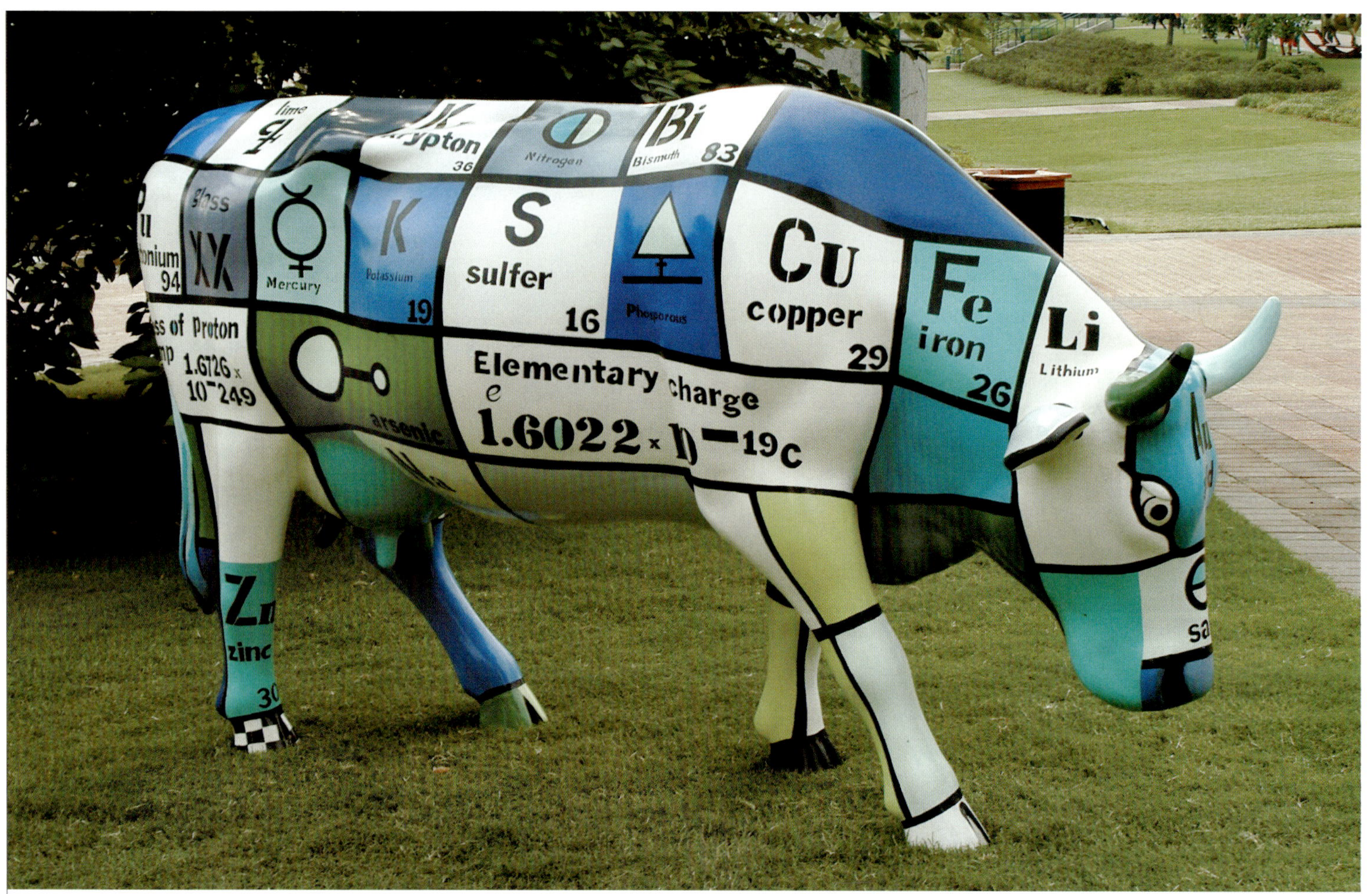

Cow Science
Colin Carew and Jennie Booth
CowParade Atlanta

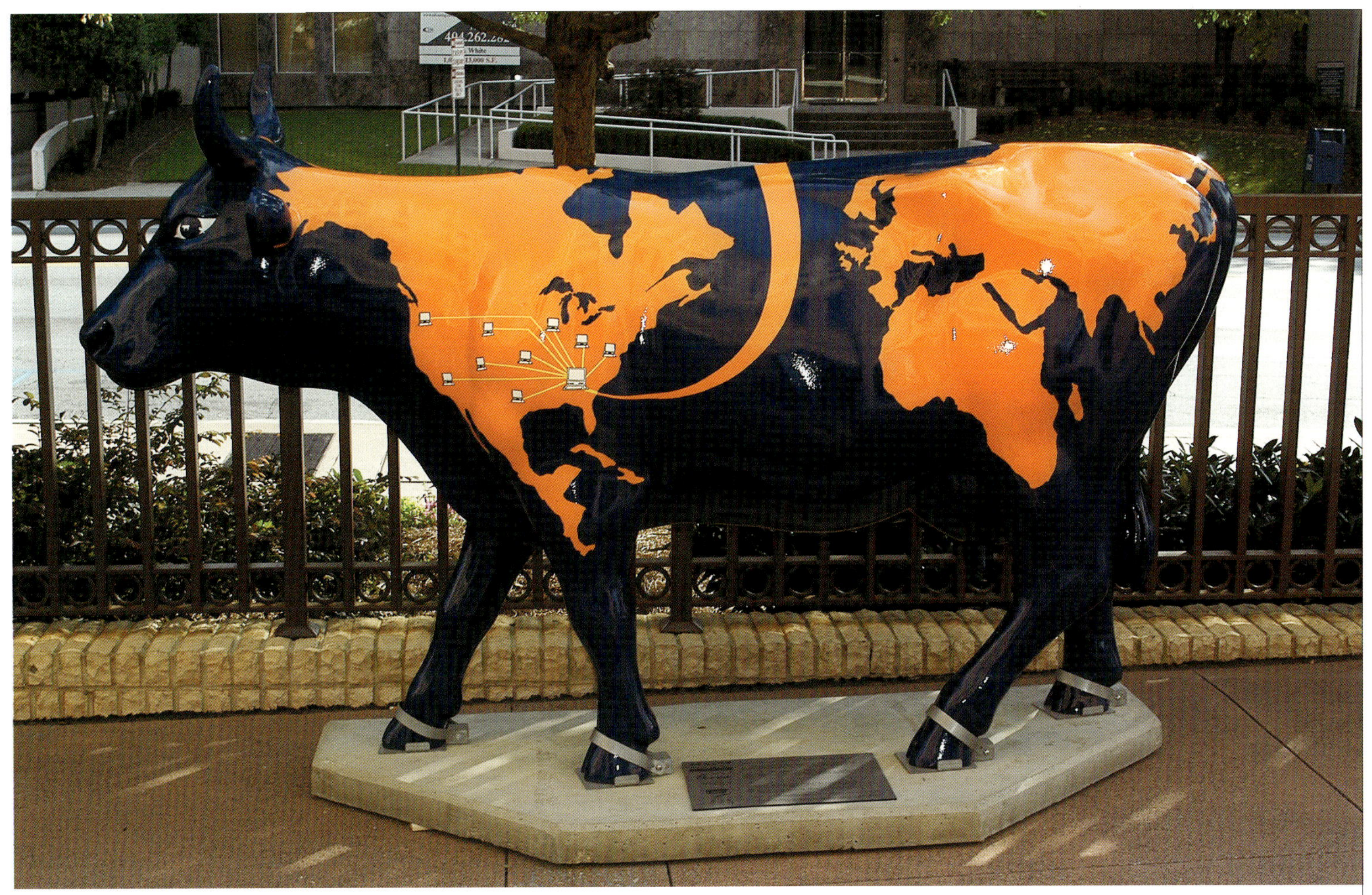

Mooove to EarthLink

Wulf Kuehmstedt & Filipp Zyryanov

EarthLink, Inc.

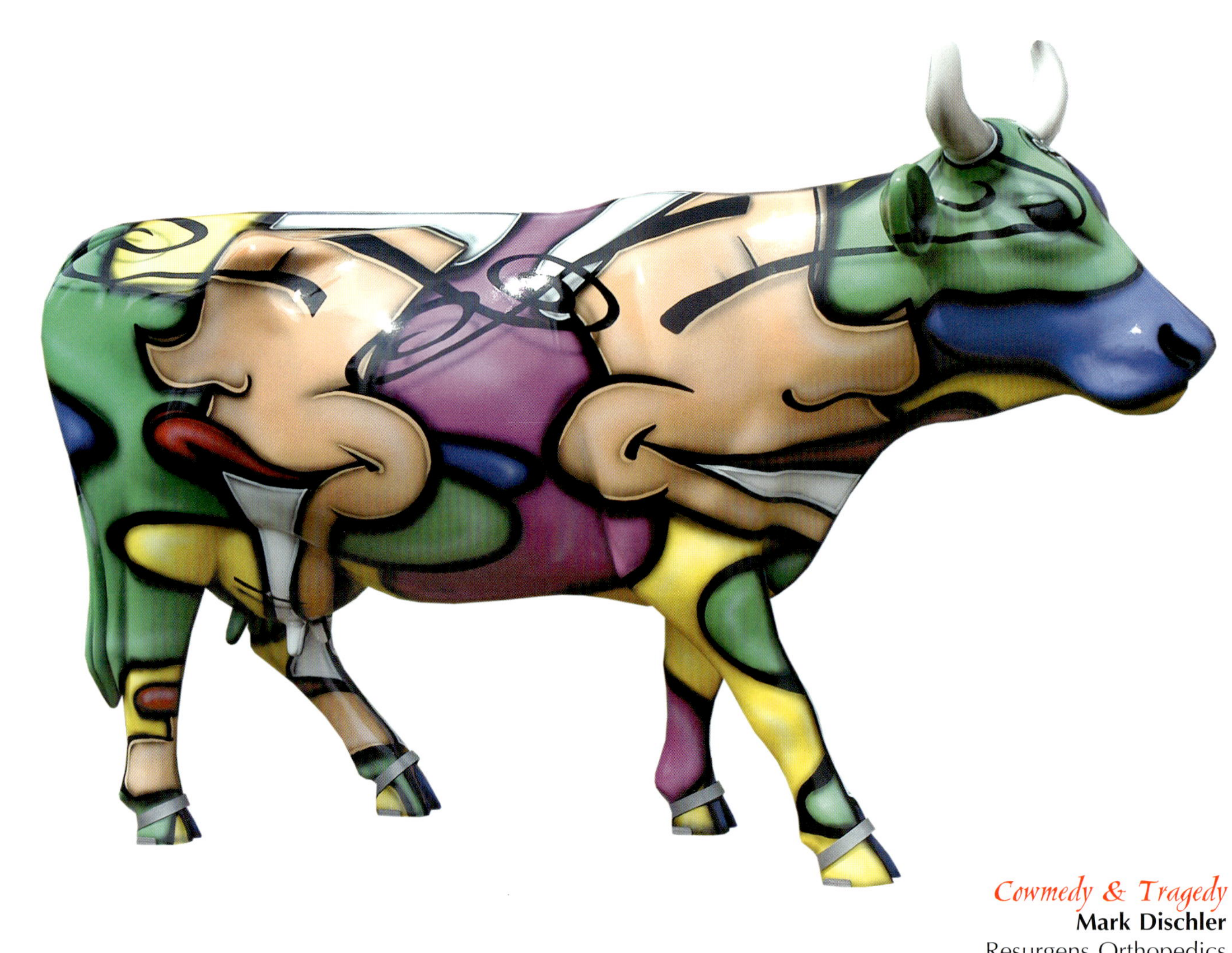

Cowmedy & Tragedy
Mark Dischler
Resurgens Orthopedics

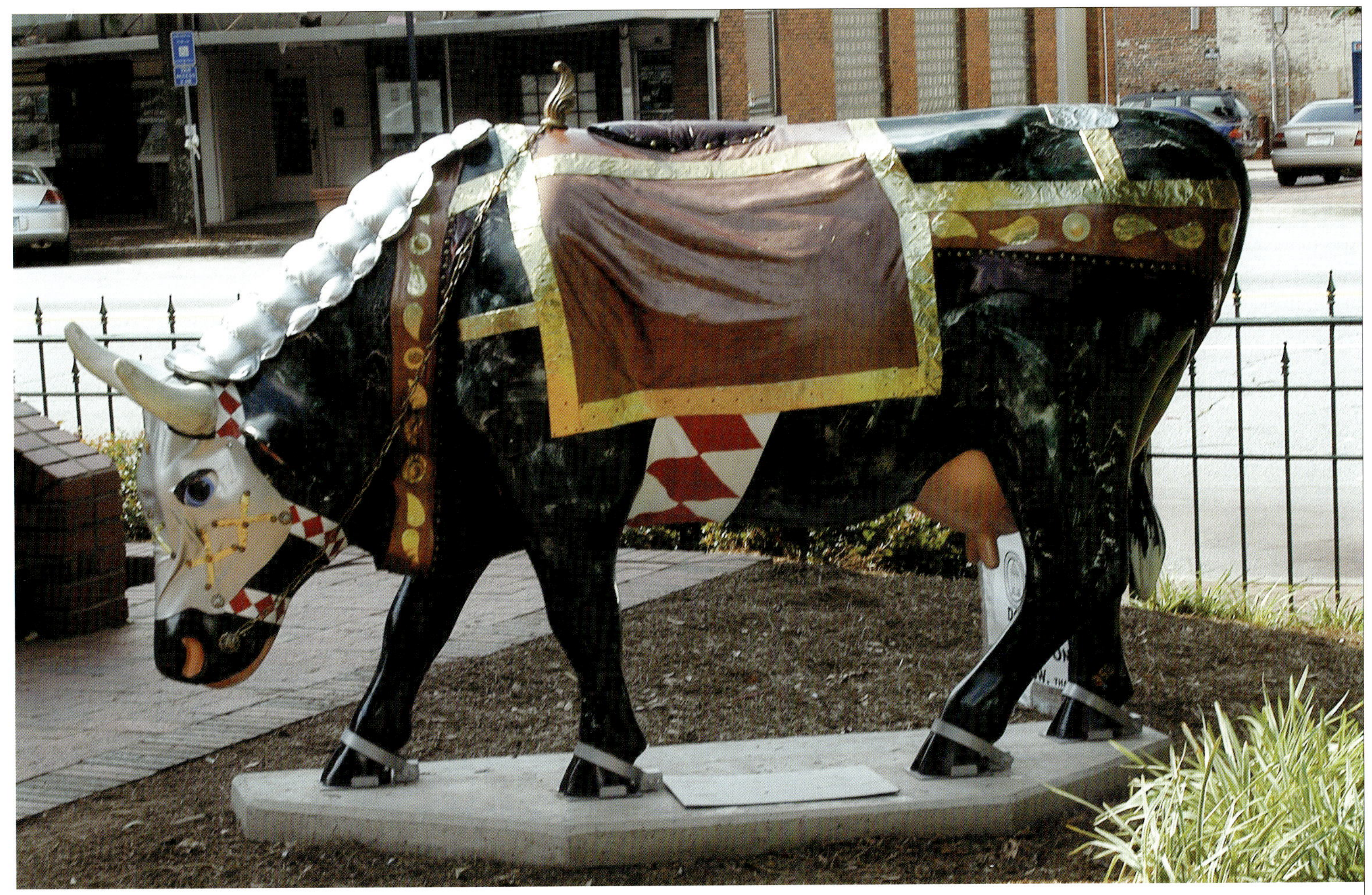

The Noble Steer
Felicite Smith Verren
Marietta Development Authority

Georgia Tourism's Cow-lossal Support / Georgia on Moo Mind

In May 2003, CowParade Atlanta joined the Georgia Department of Industry, Trade, & Tourism (GDITT) to celebrate National Tourism Week with a Media Day at the Ringgold, Georgia Visitor's Center. The press event in the northernmost corner of the State also celebrated the many reasons to visit Georgia in the summer of 2003, including CowParade Atlanta. The event also featured a display of cows, and artist Robert DeLoach doing a public painting of "Georgia on Moo Mind," the GDITT-sponsored cow. During the summer of 2003, GDITT hosted cows at six of its heaviest-traveled visitor's centers, provided CowParade maps to hundreds of thousands of travelers and provided great kid activities at the CowParade Kickoff Family Fun Day at Centennial Olympic Park.

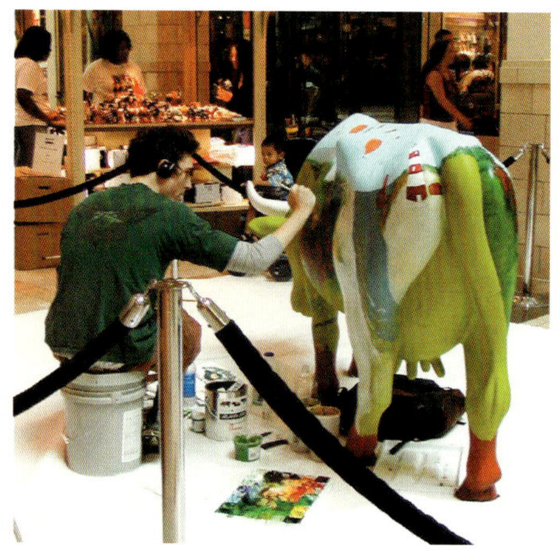

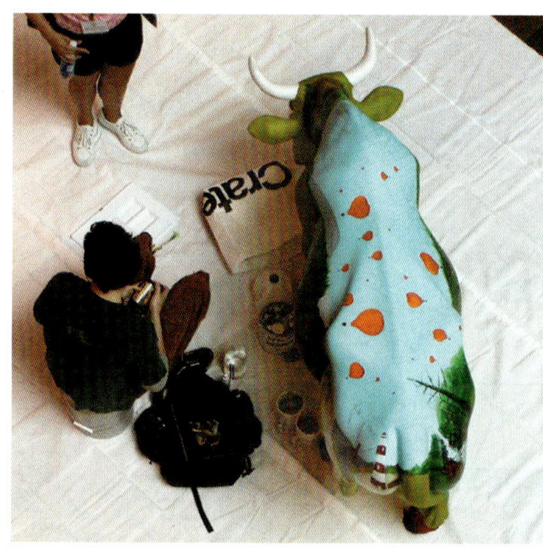

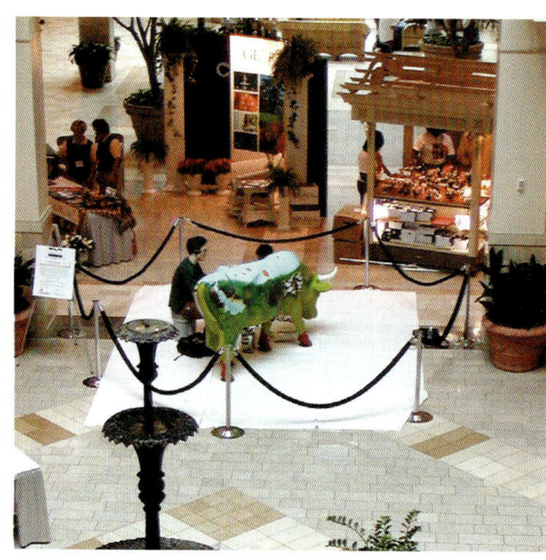

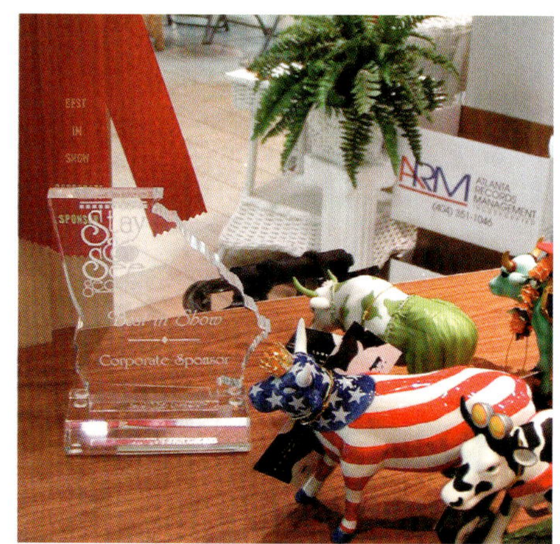

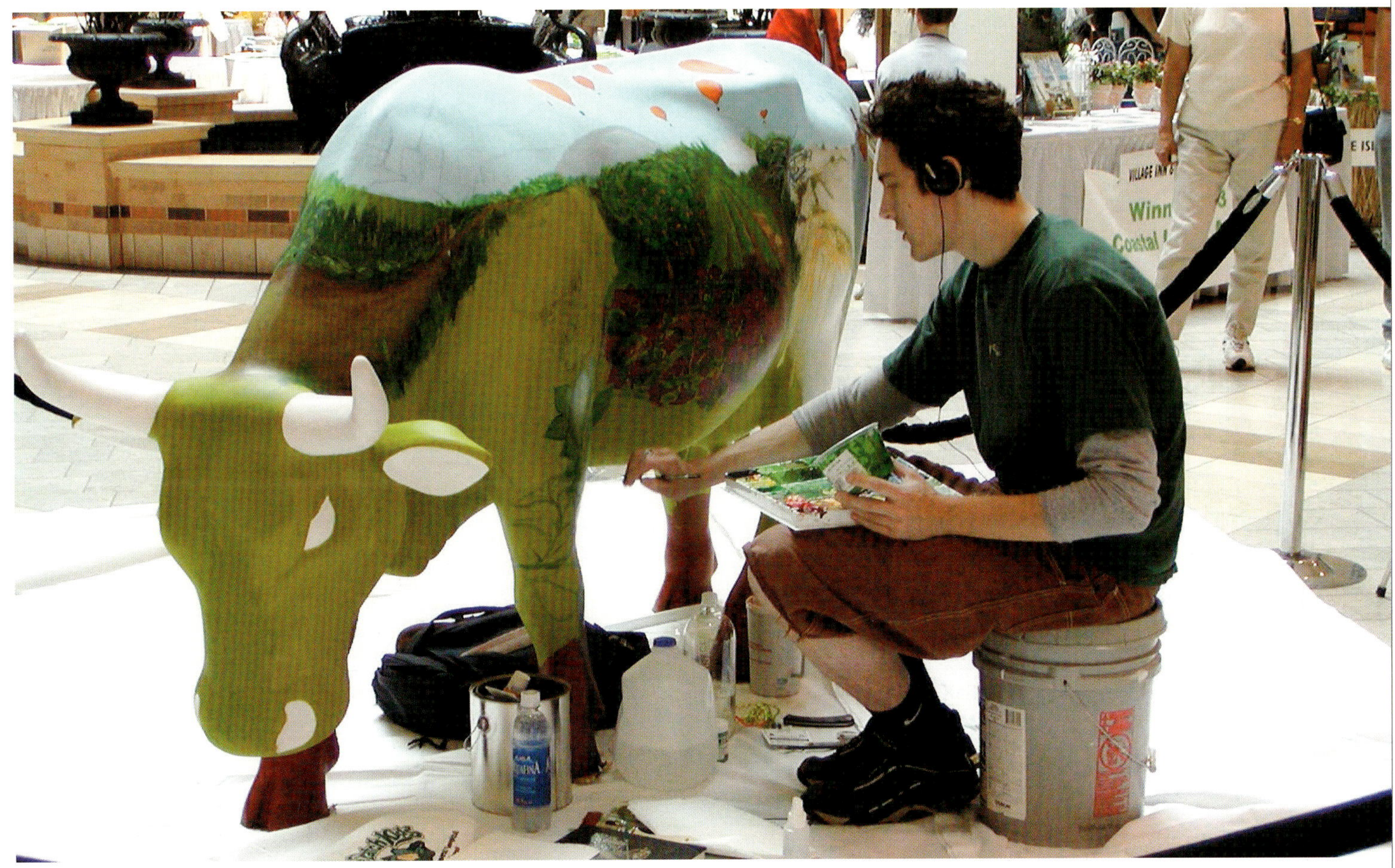

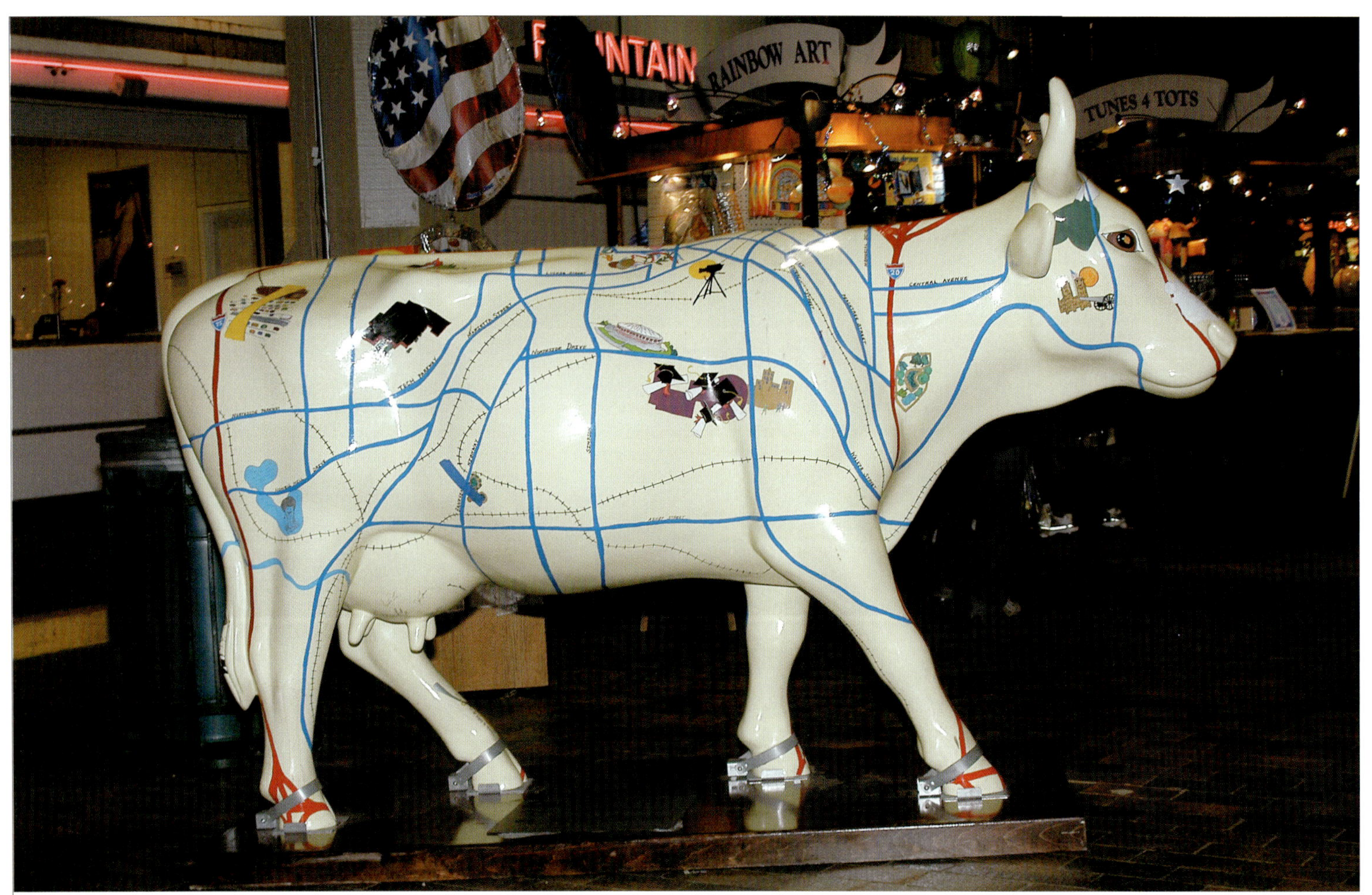

Atlanta Downtown Cow-nnector
Sally Hall
Accenture

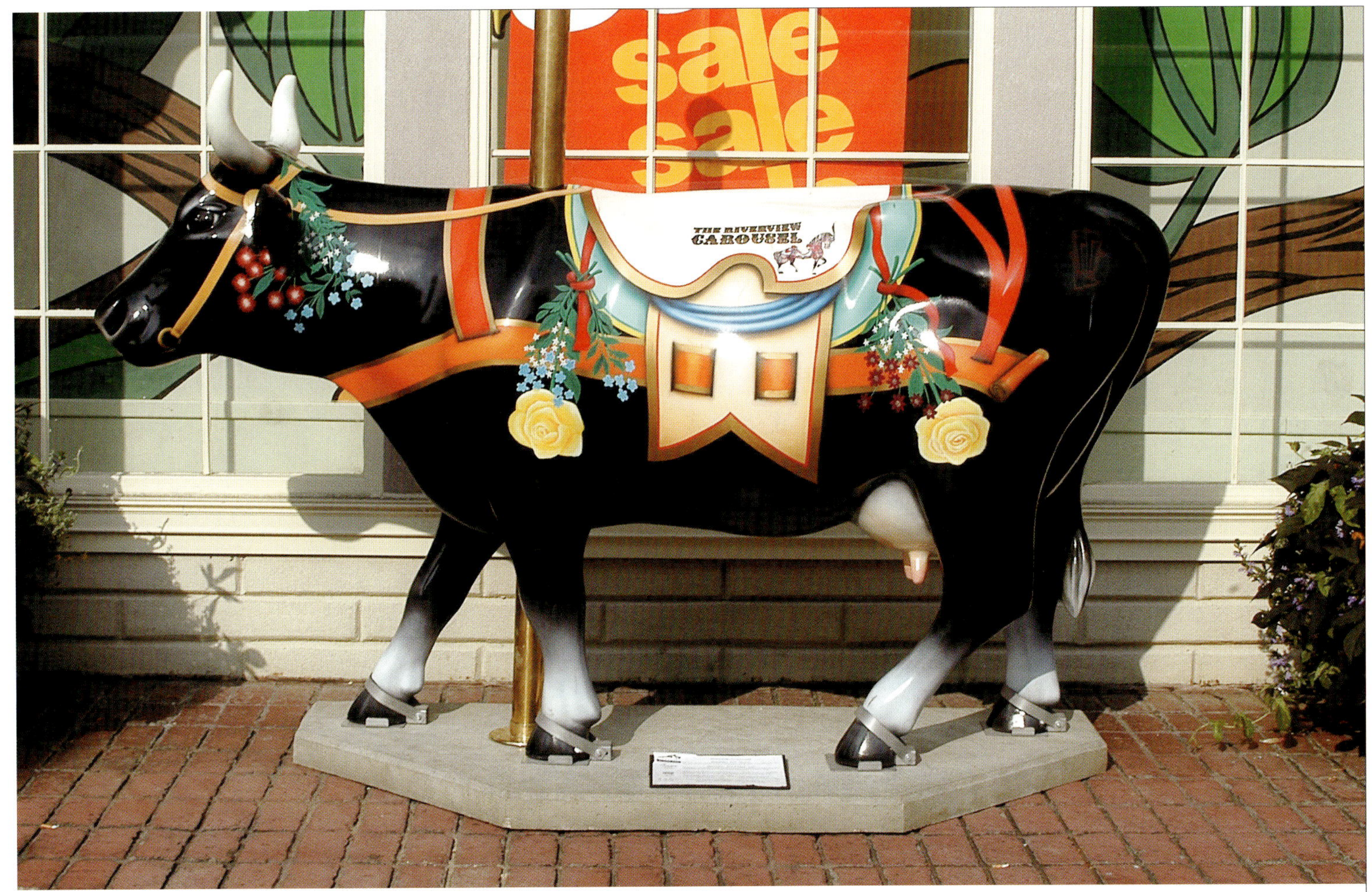

Riverside Cowousel
Tim Quinn
Six Flags, Inc.

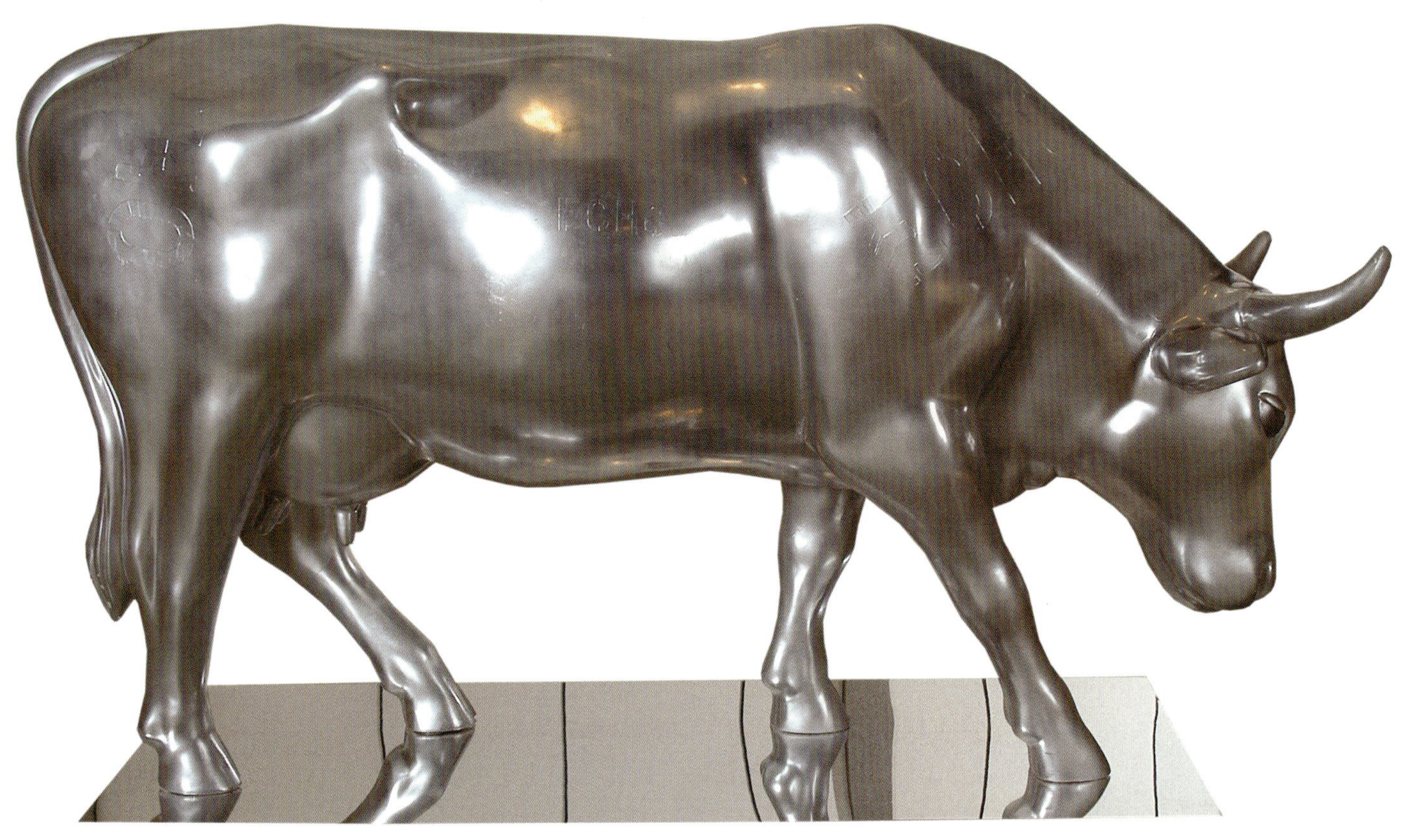

Narcissus and Echo
Sidney Smith
CowParade Atlanta

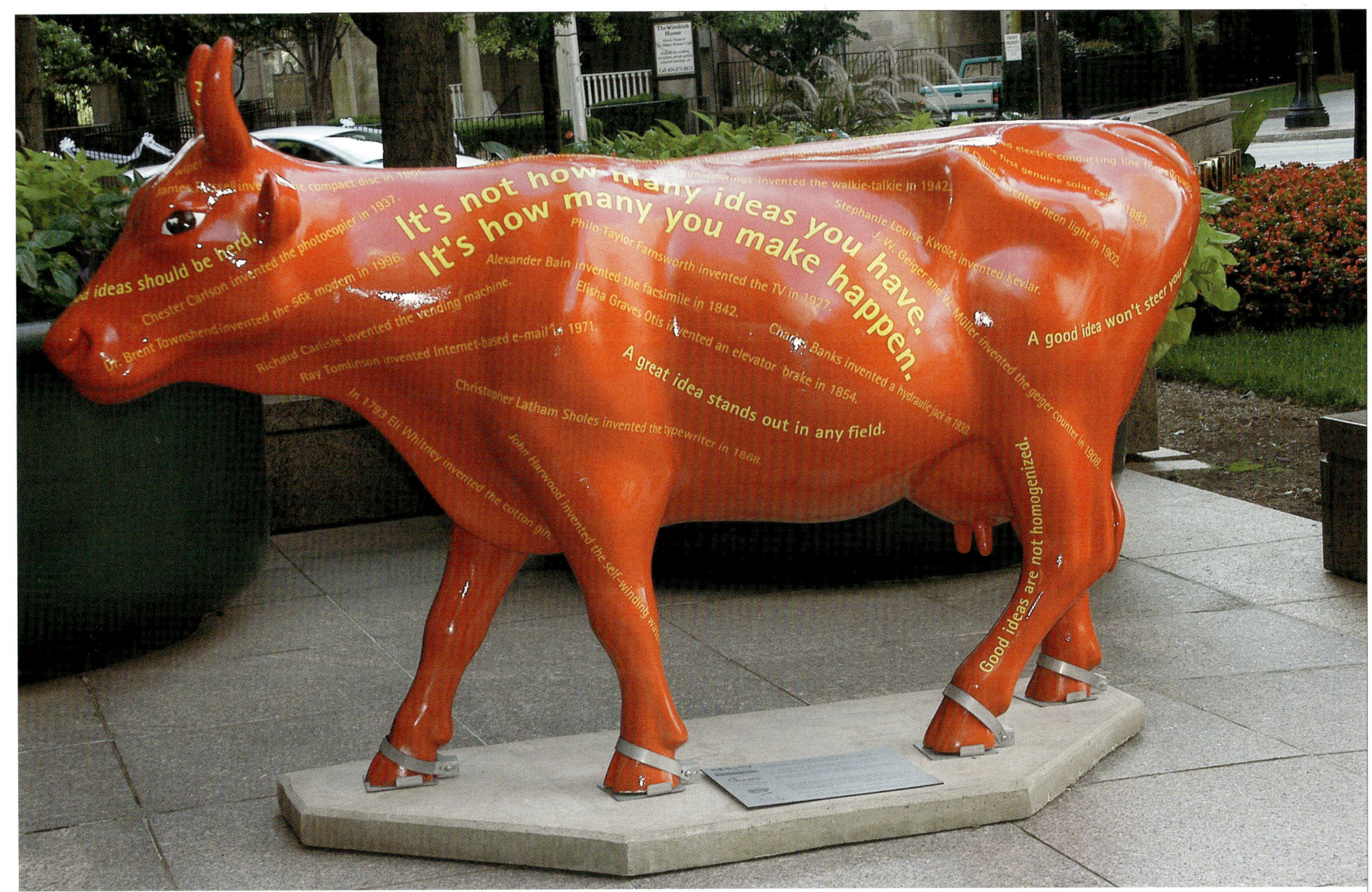

Moother of Innovation
Wulf Kuehmstedt and EAI Atlanta
Accenture

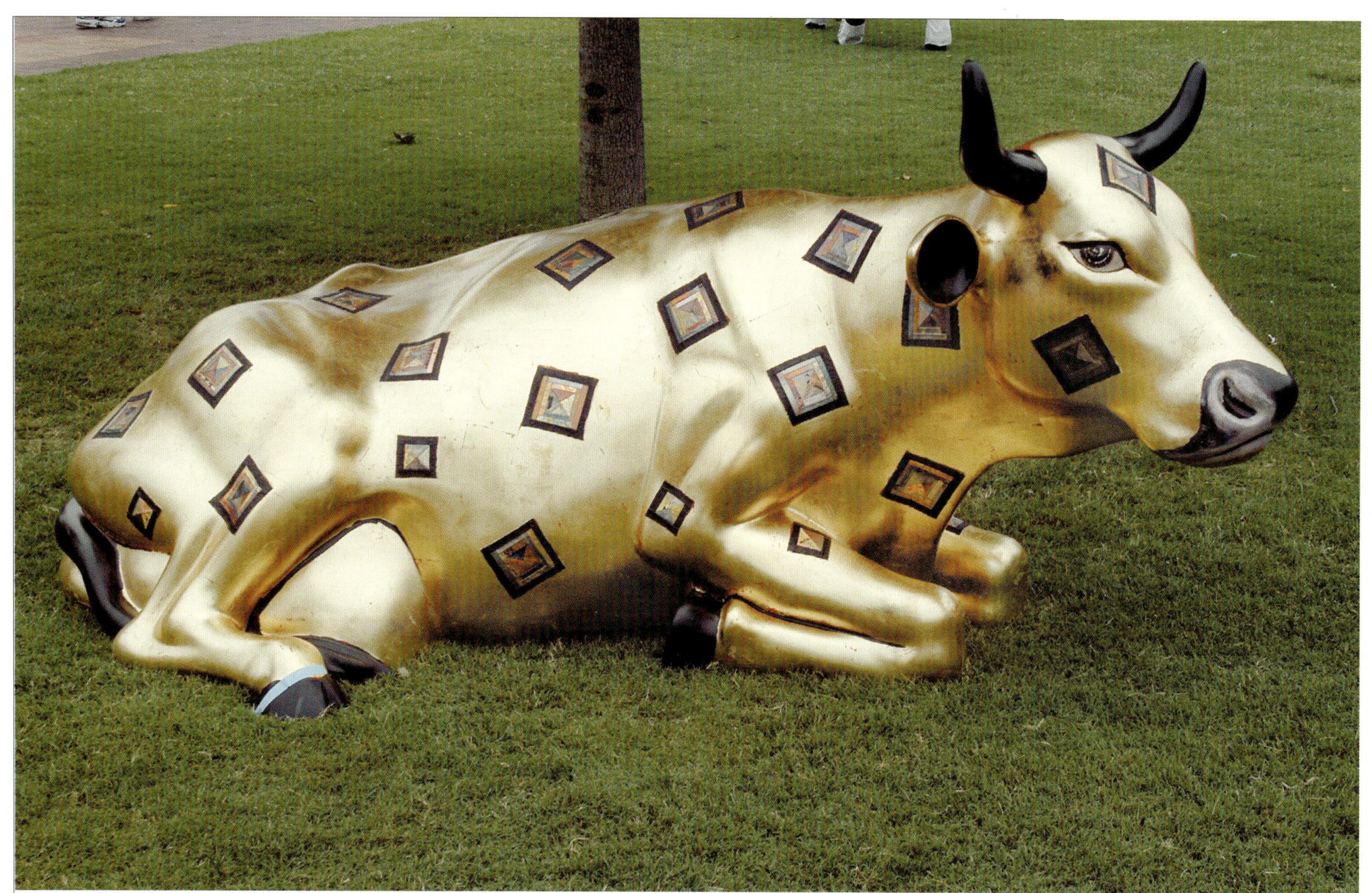

Gold Peace Work Cow
Lucinda Carlstrom
Kilpatrick Stockton LLP

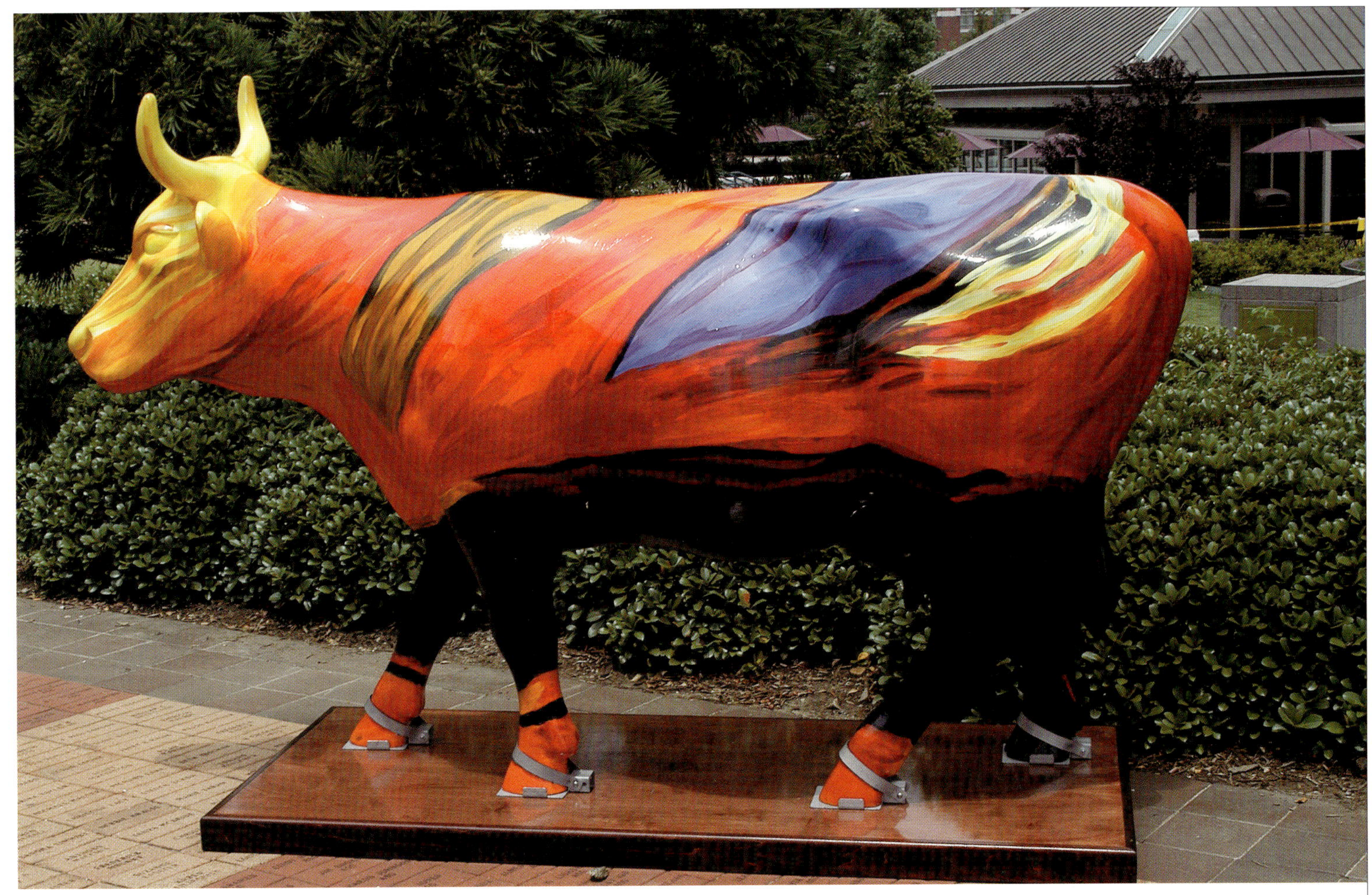

ChromaCow
Deanna Sirlin
Cartel Properties

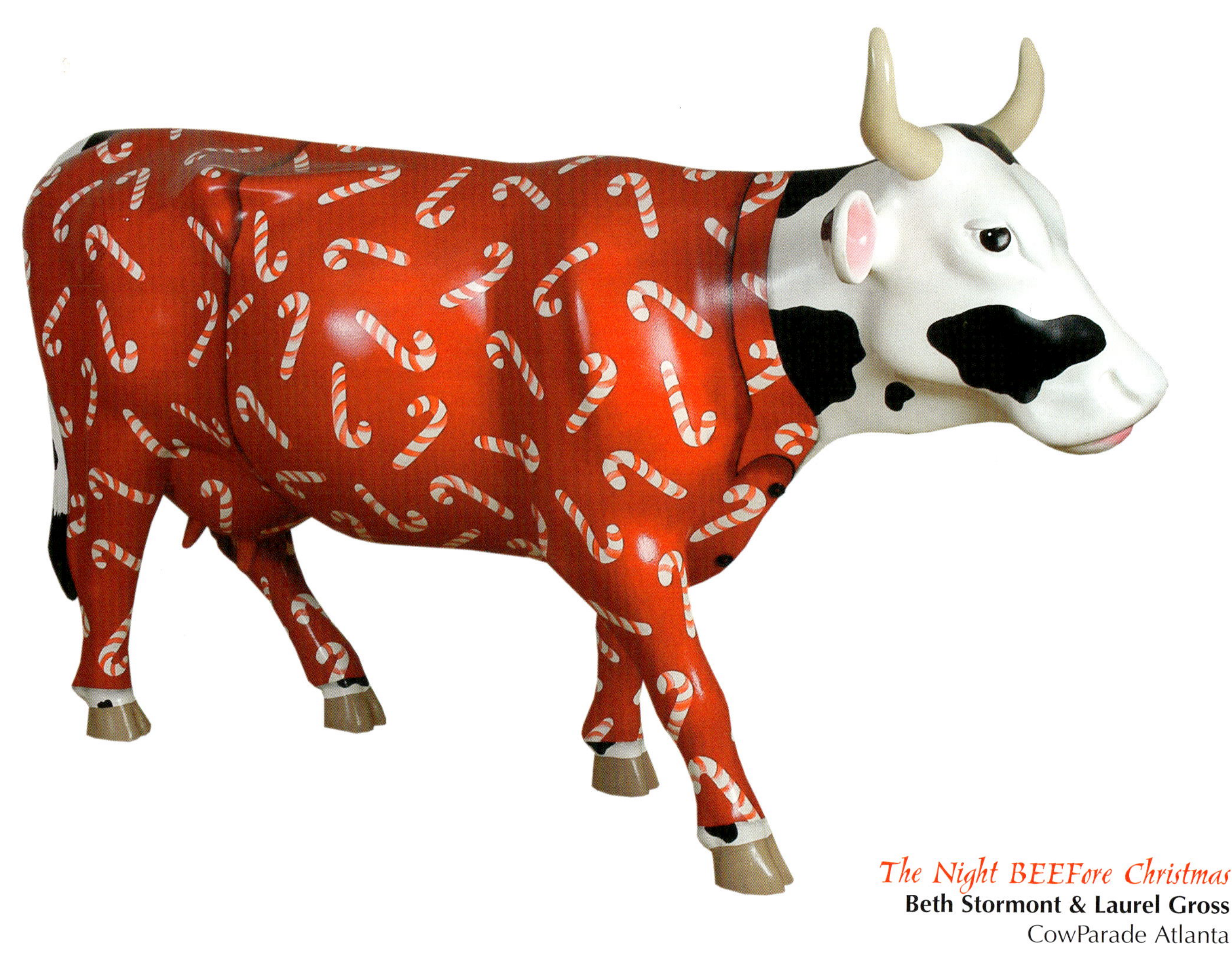

The Night BEEFore Christmas
Beth Stormont & Laurel Gross
CowParade Atlanta

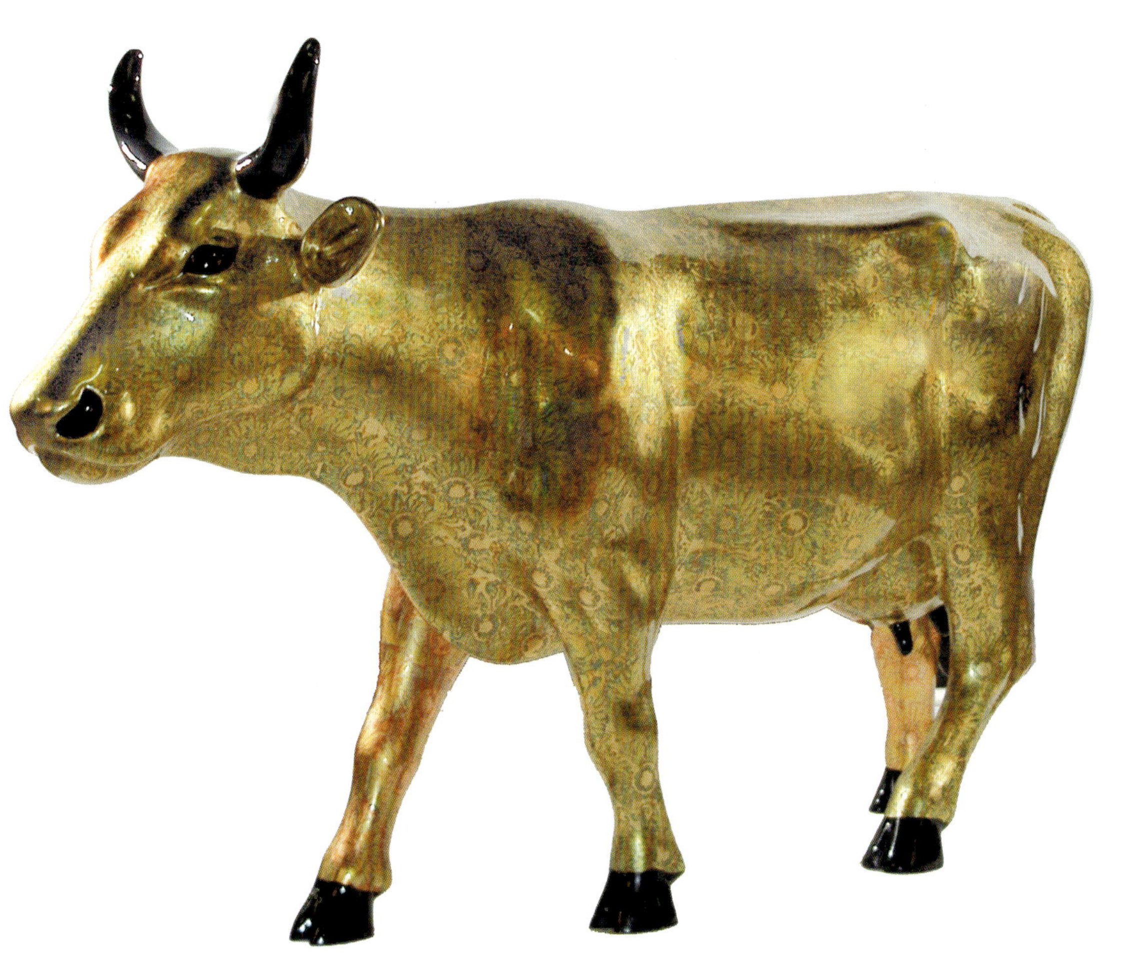

Cowleidoscope
Garry Grant
Parisian

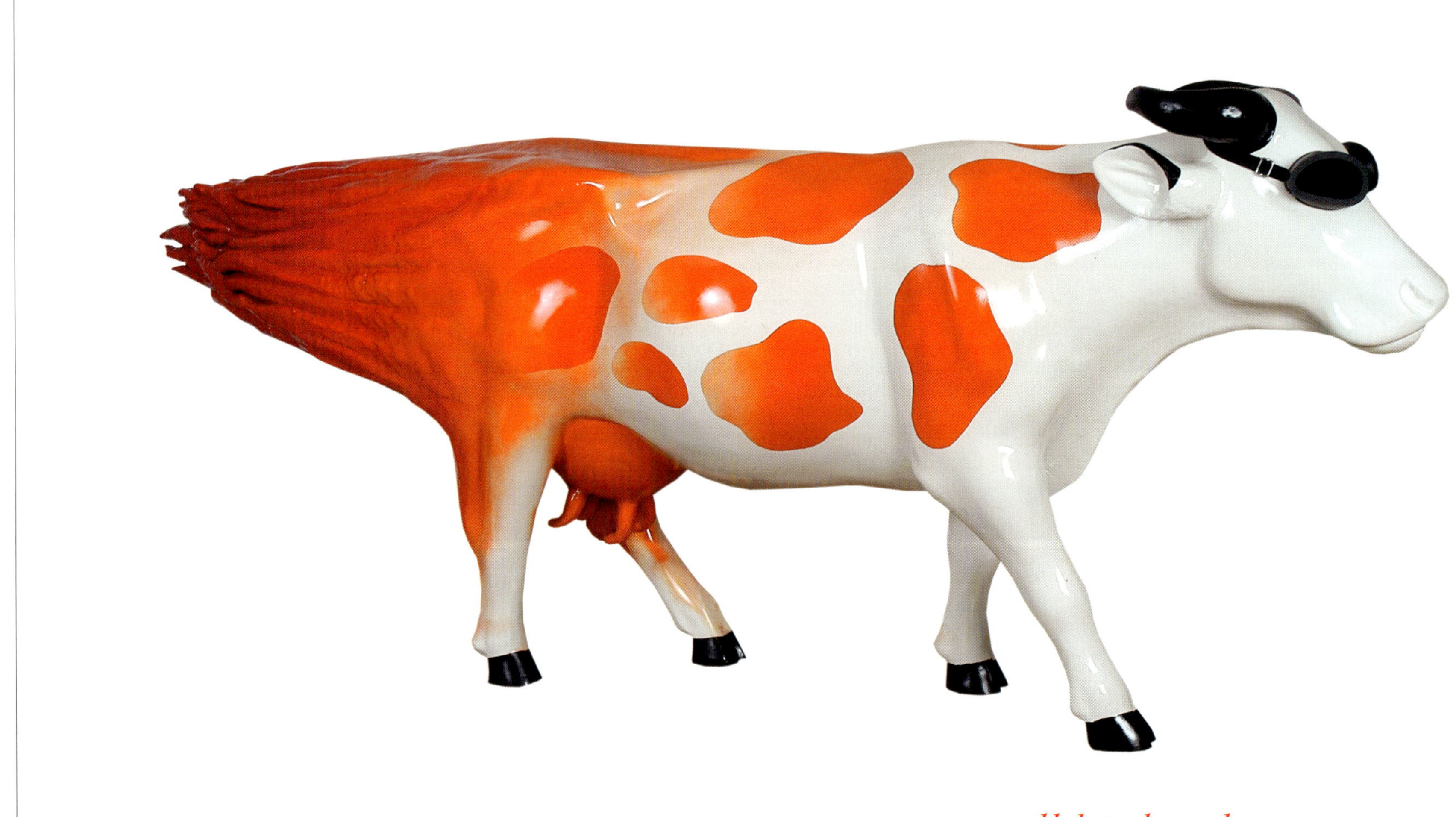

Udderly High-Speed Cow
Thomas Royal
EarthLink, Inc.

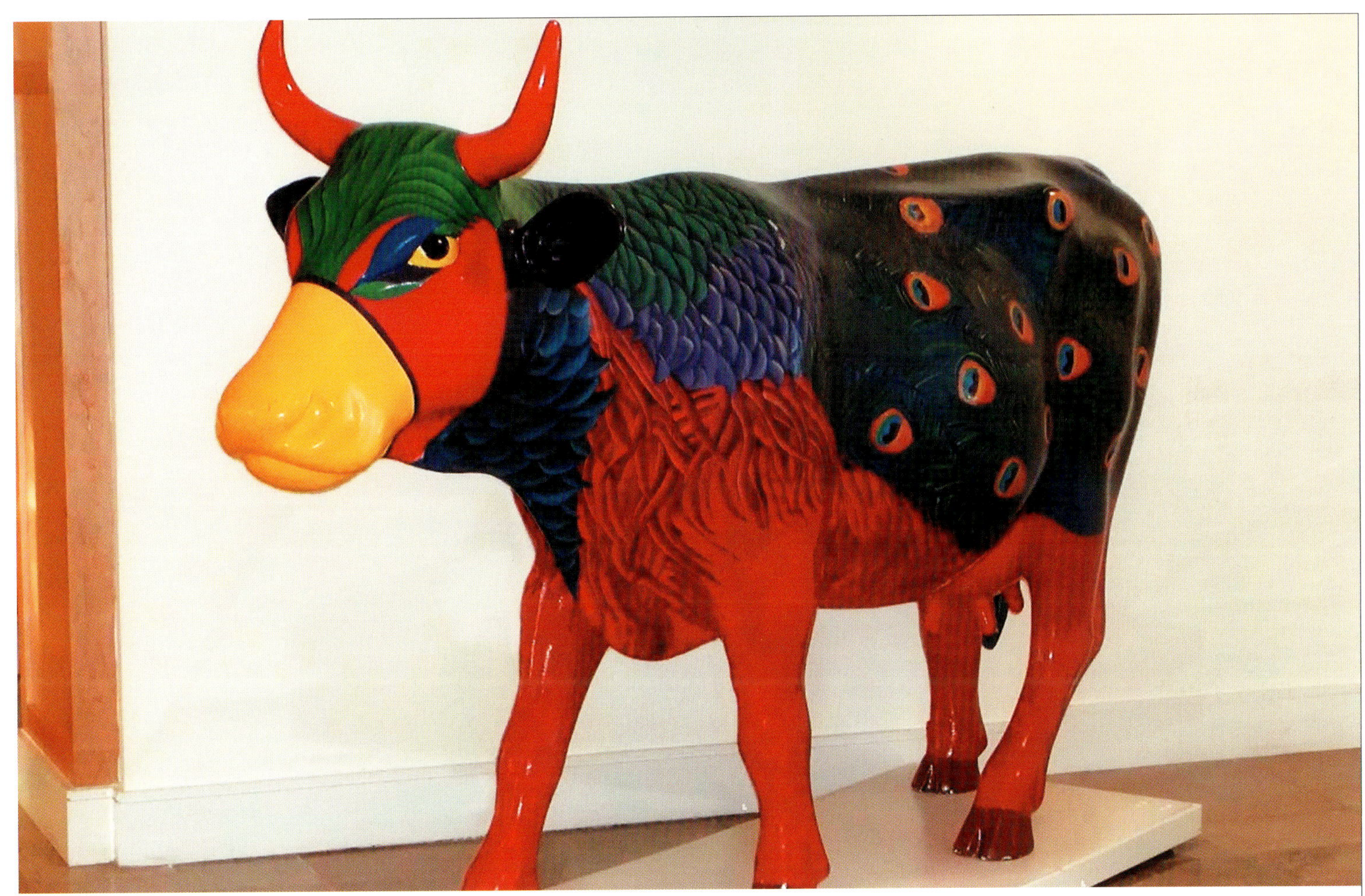

Peacock
Eve Hadley
CowParade Atlanta

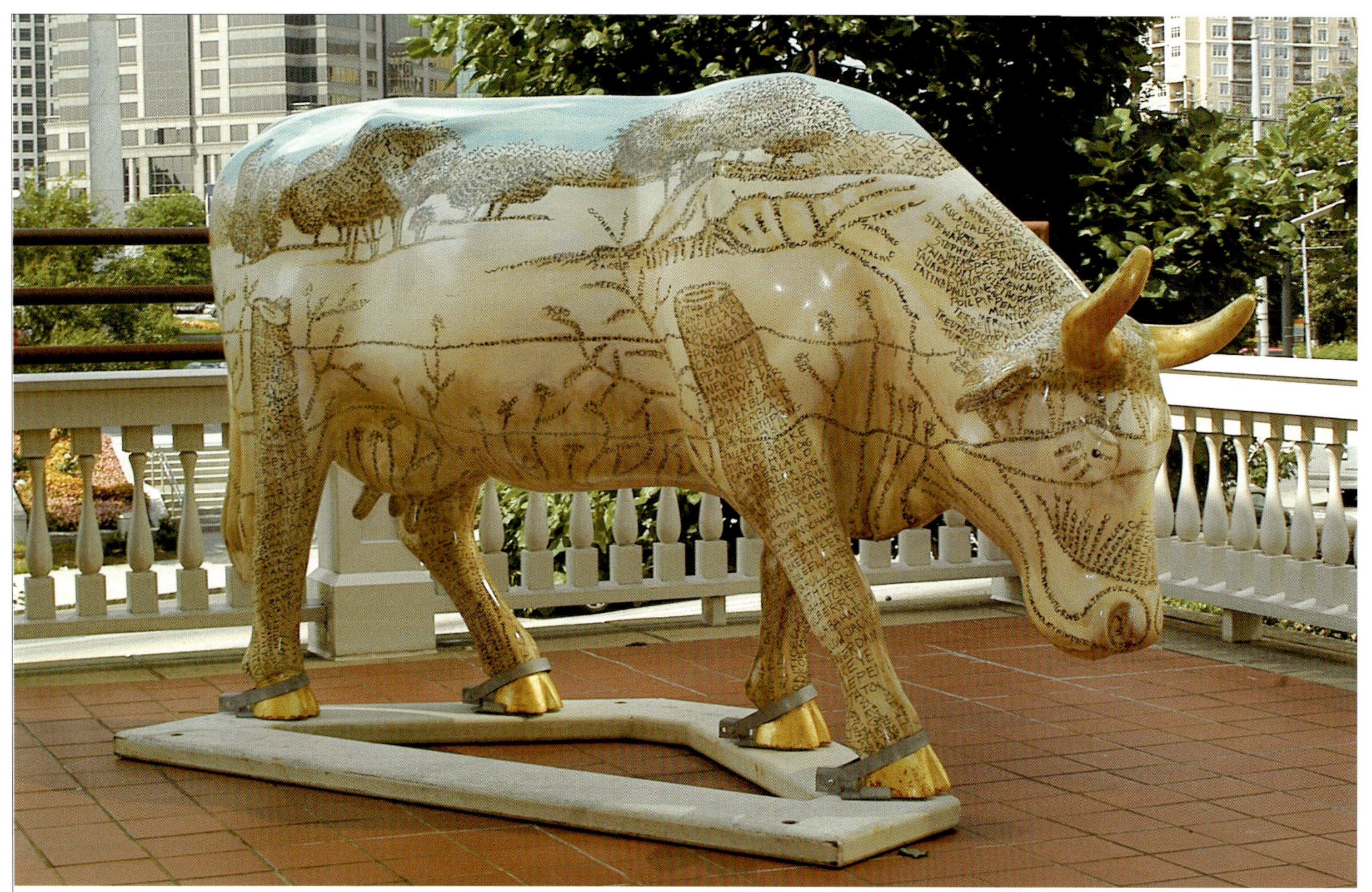

Cow with Pastoral
Randy Taylor
The Biltmore

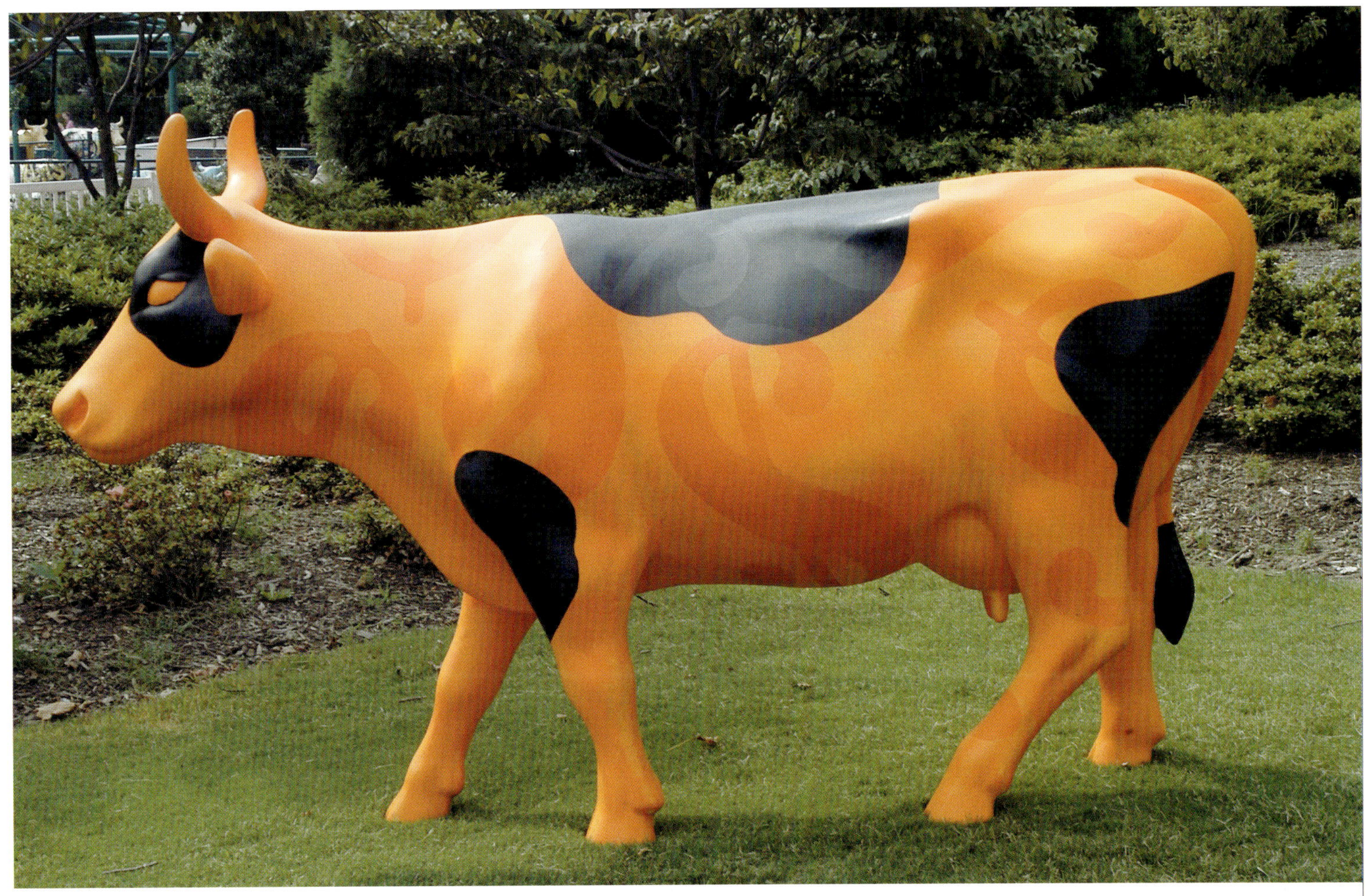

Cash Cow
Bill Mayer
ING

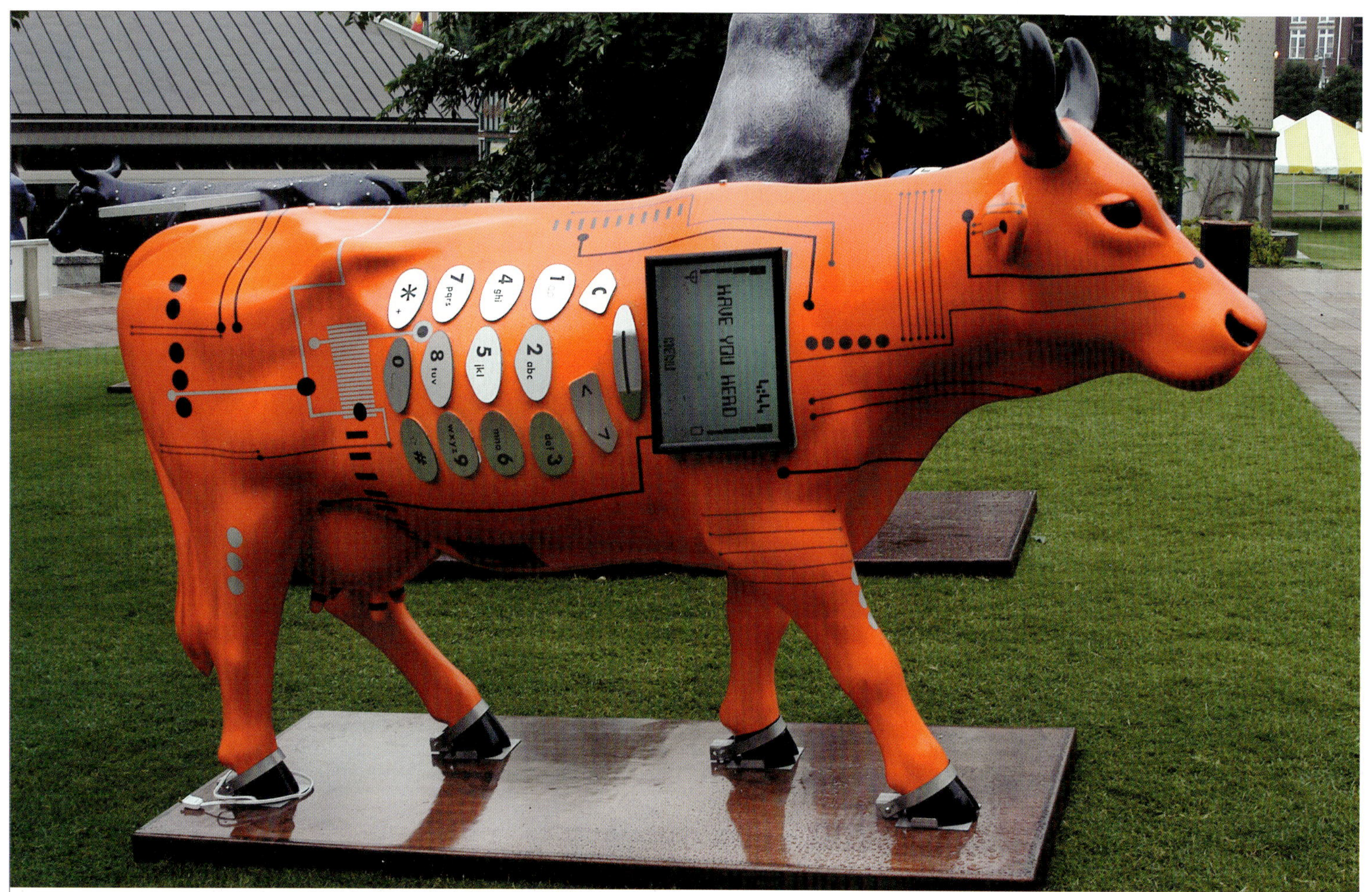

Cattle Call
Dave Gyatt
Cingular Wireless

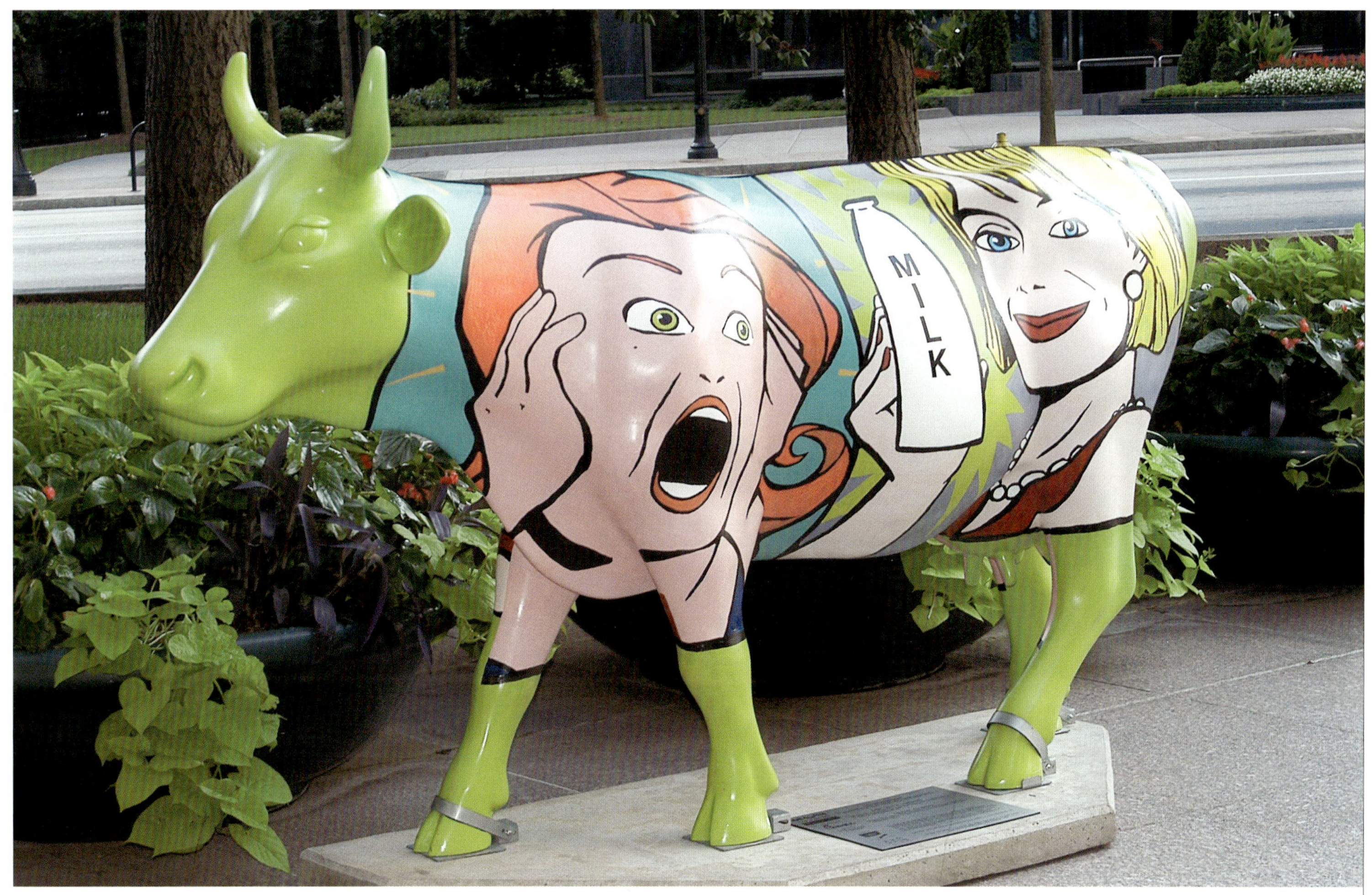

Lactose Intolerabull
Mark A. Husbands
Accenture

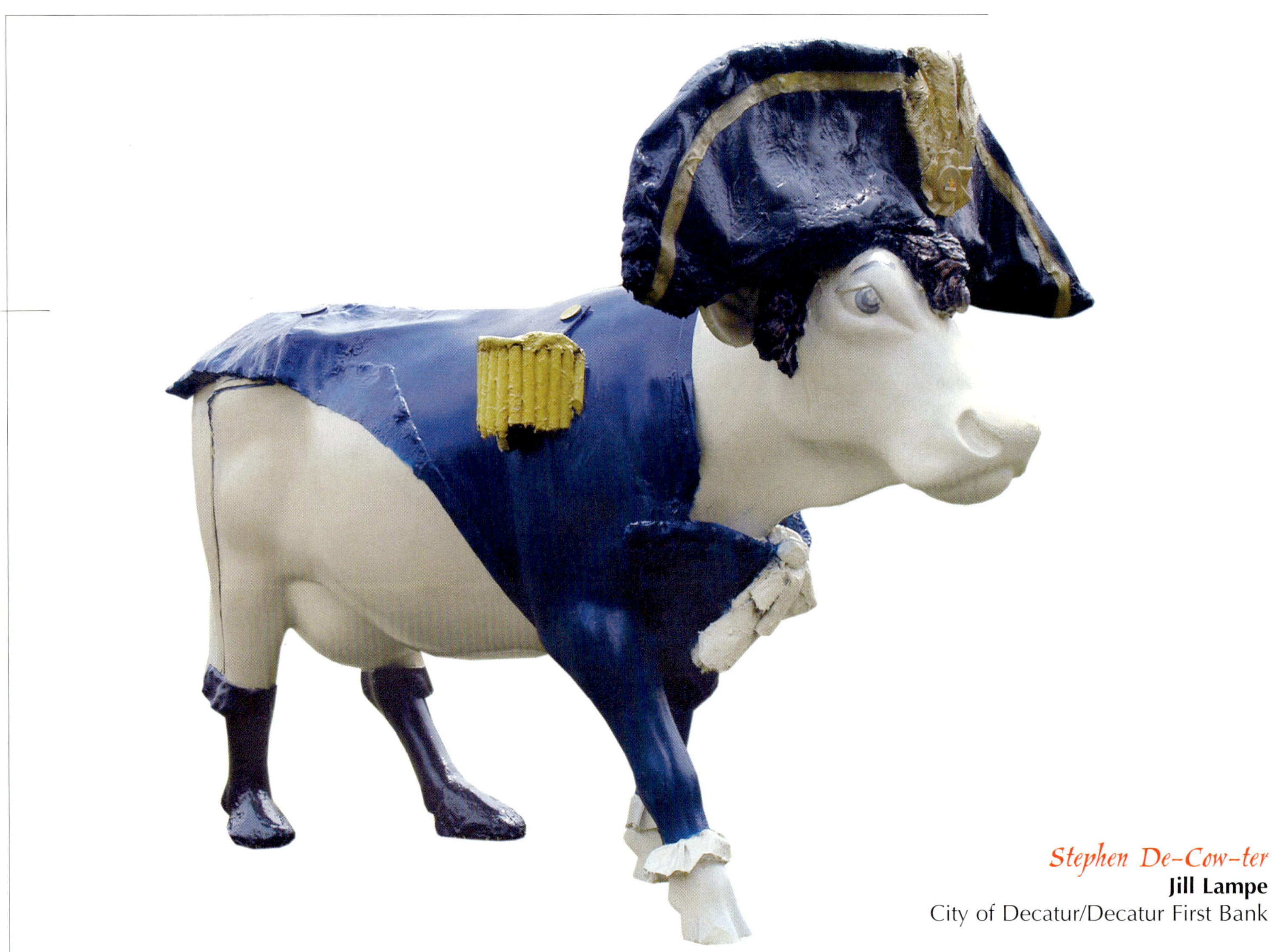

Stephen De-Cow-ter
Jill Lampe
City of Decatur/Decatur First Bank

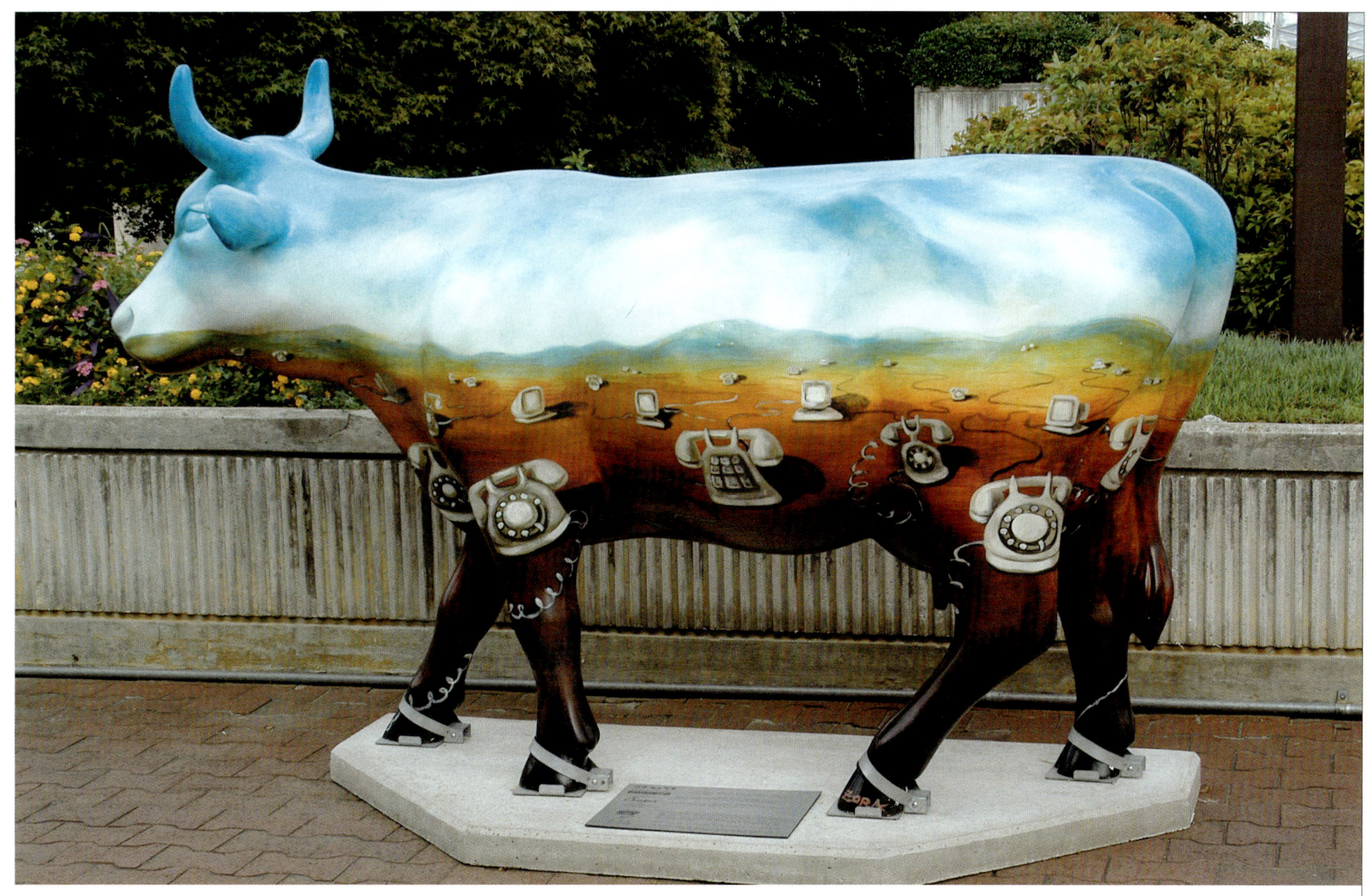

For Whom The CowBell Tolls
Zora Janosova
BellSouth

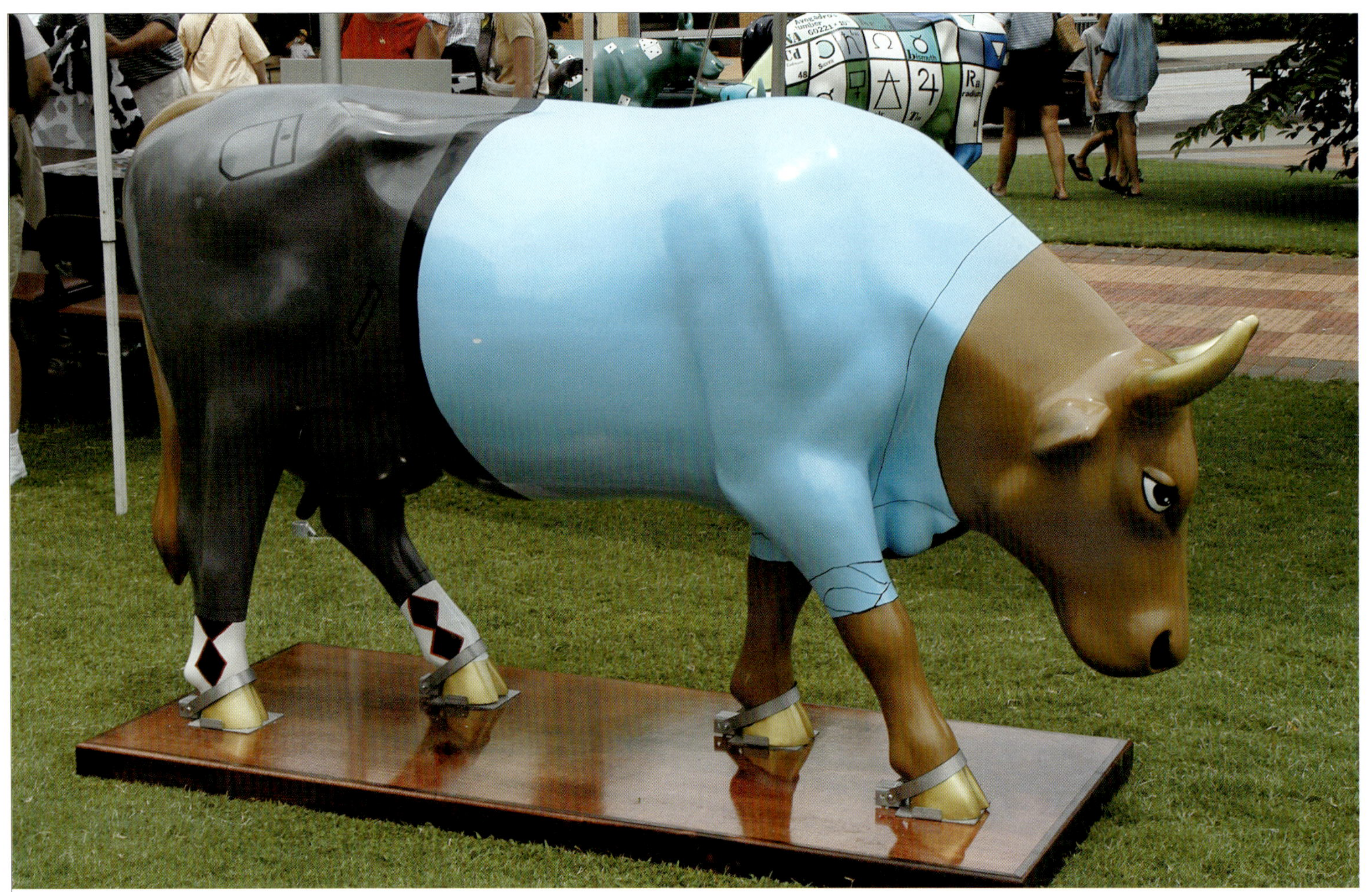

White Cowllar Moobility
Hudi Sandgren
Jubilee Cultural Arts Alliance

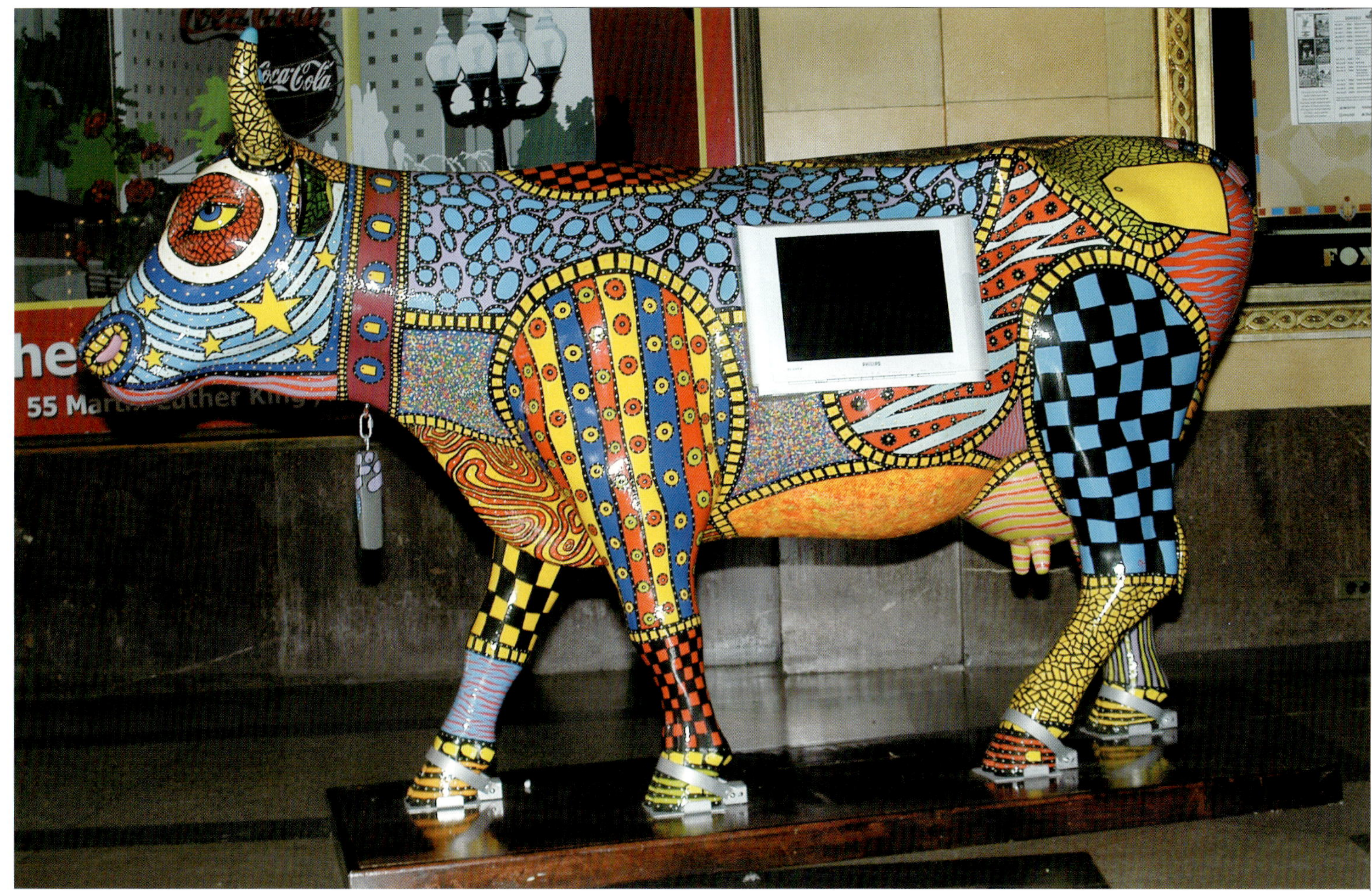

Technology on the Moove
Glenn Fox
Best Buy

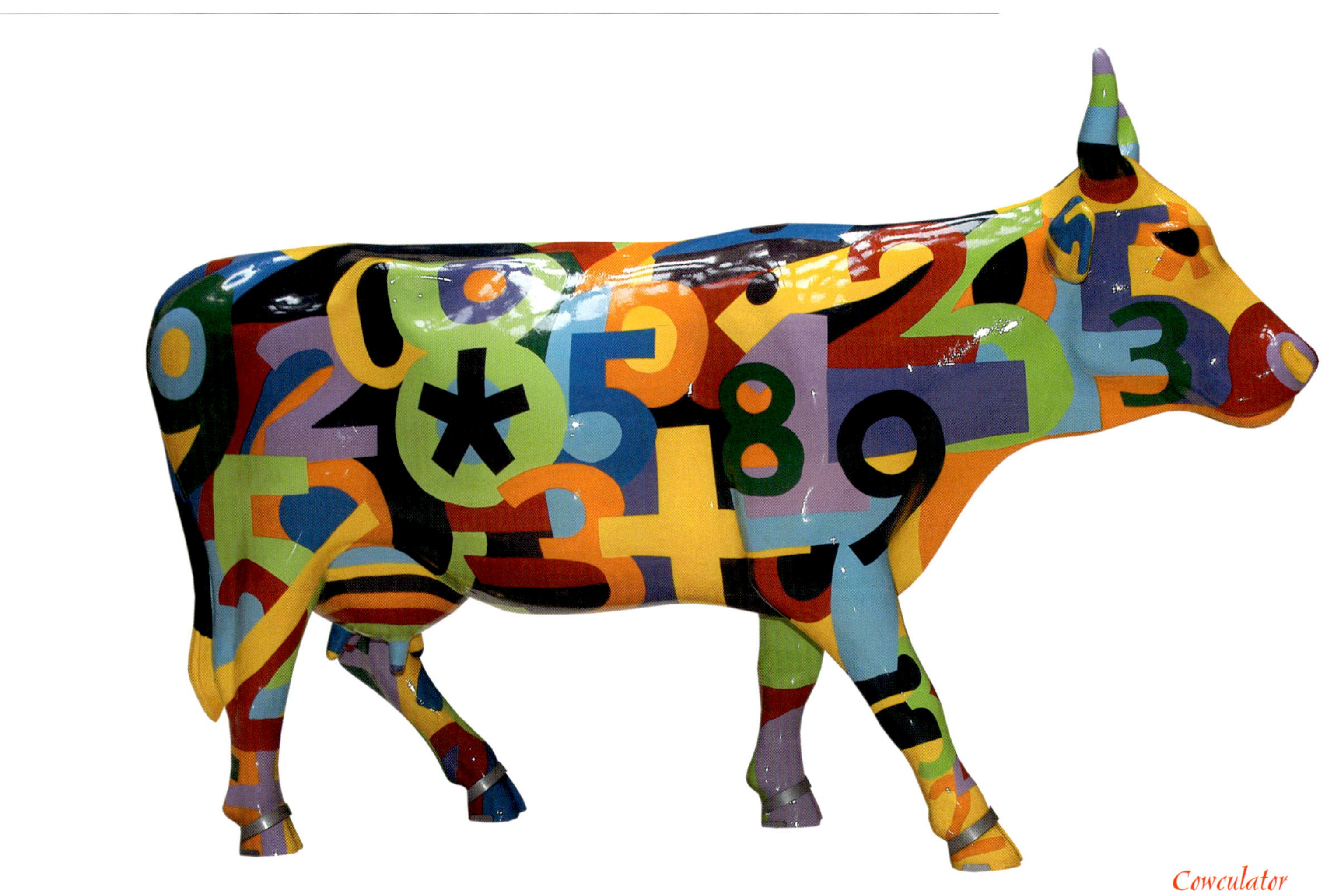

Cowculator
Bonnie Collins
Georgia Society of Certified Public Accountants

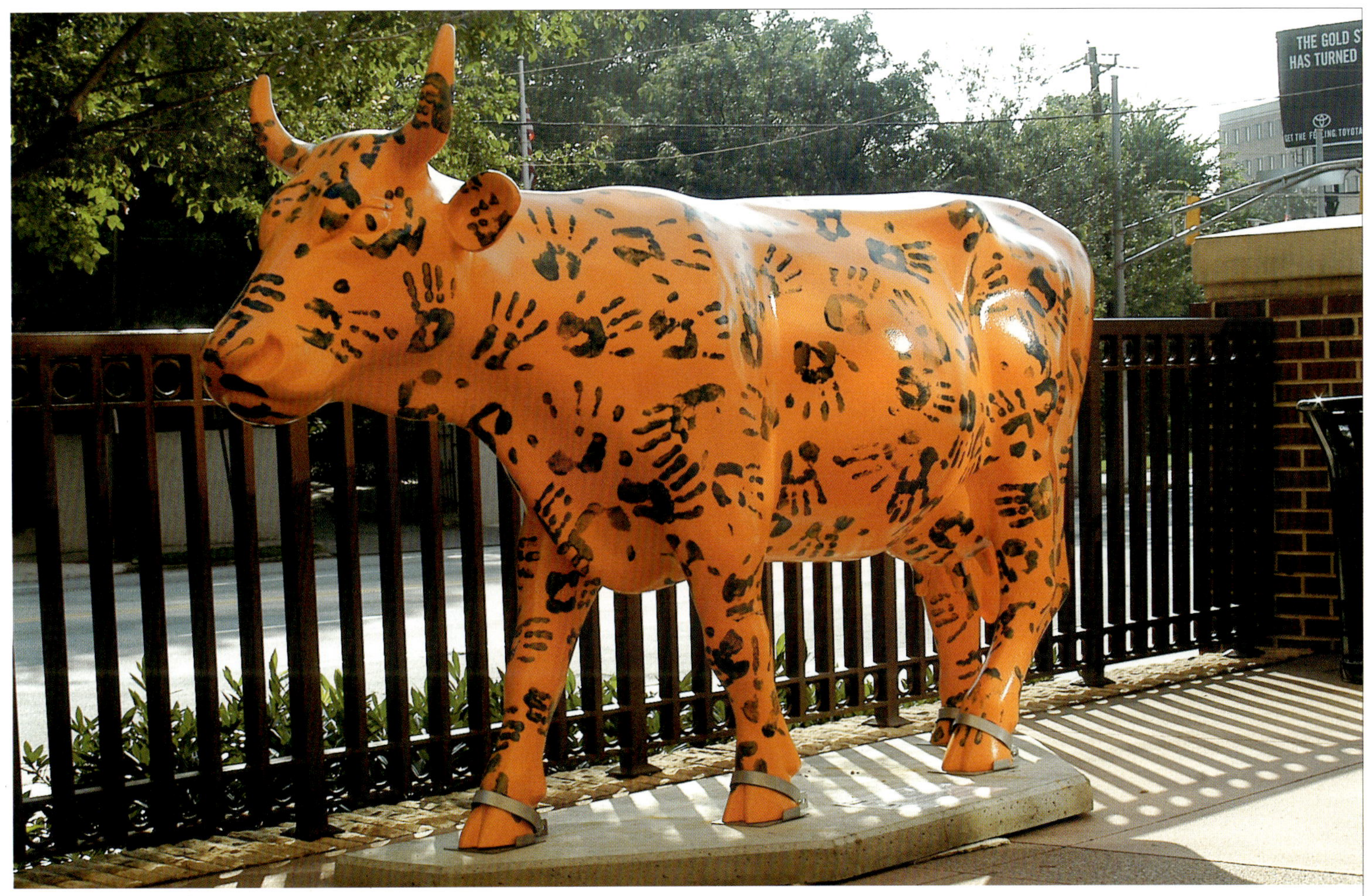

Cowlossally Great Customer Service
Sharon Brooks and Lynn Gay
EarthLink, Inc.

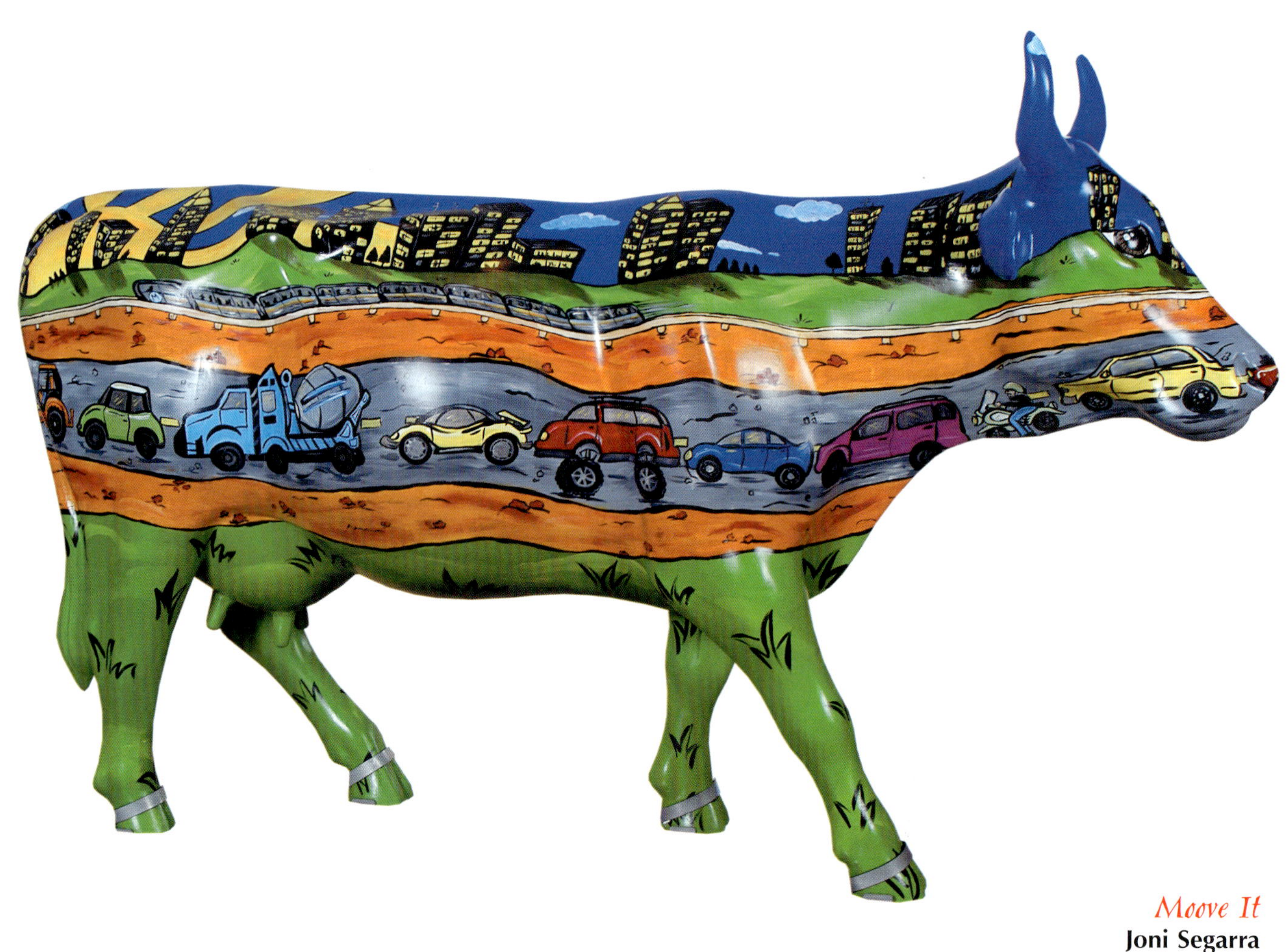

Moove It
Joni Segarra
CowParade Atlanta

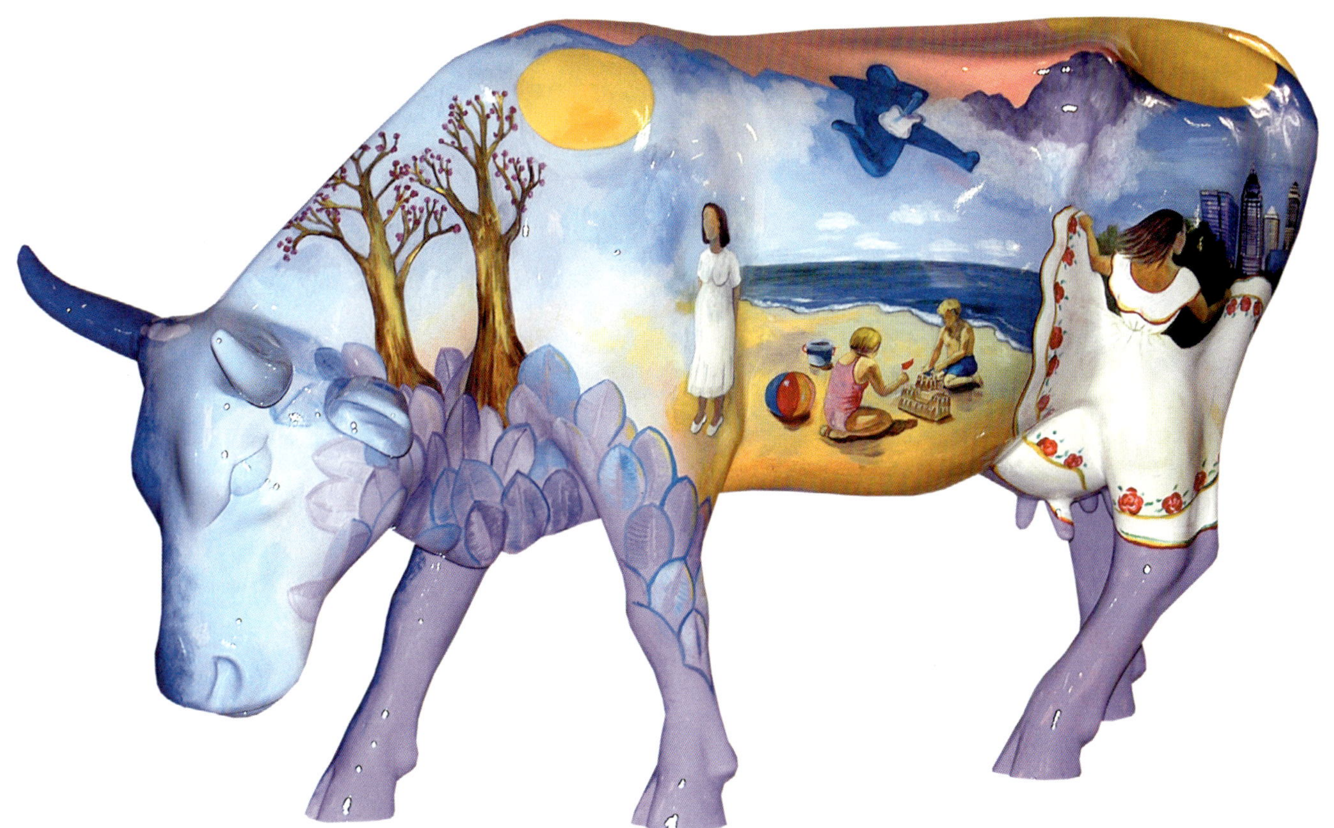

Matilda
Monika Ruiz
CowParade Atlanta

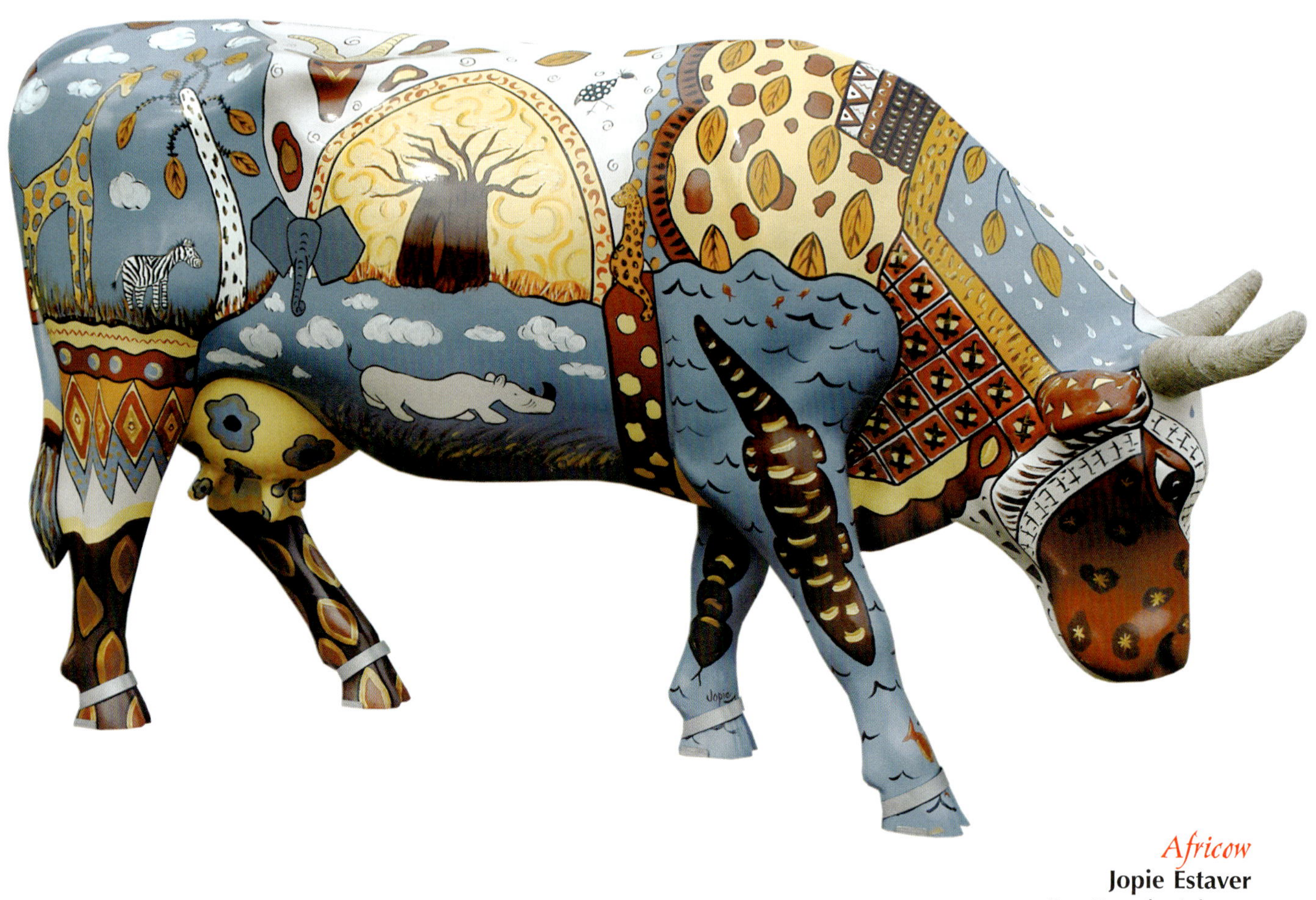

Africow
Jopie Estaver
CowParade Atlanta

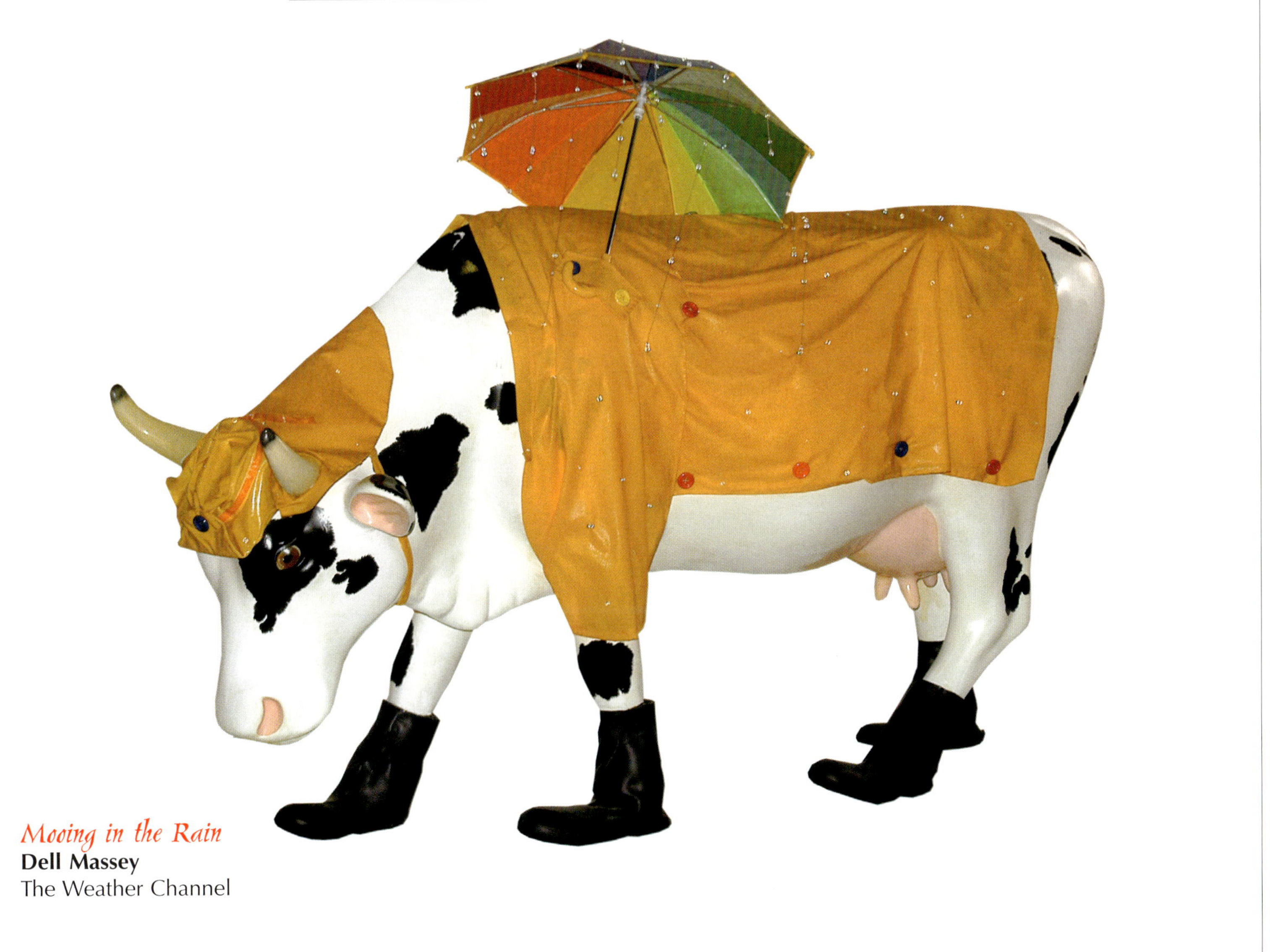

Mooing in the Rain
Dell Massey
The Weather Channel

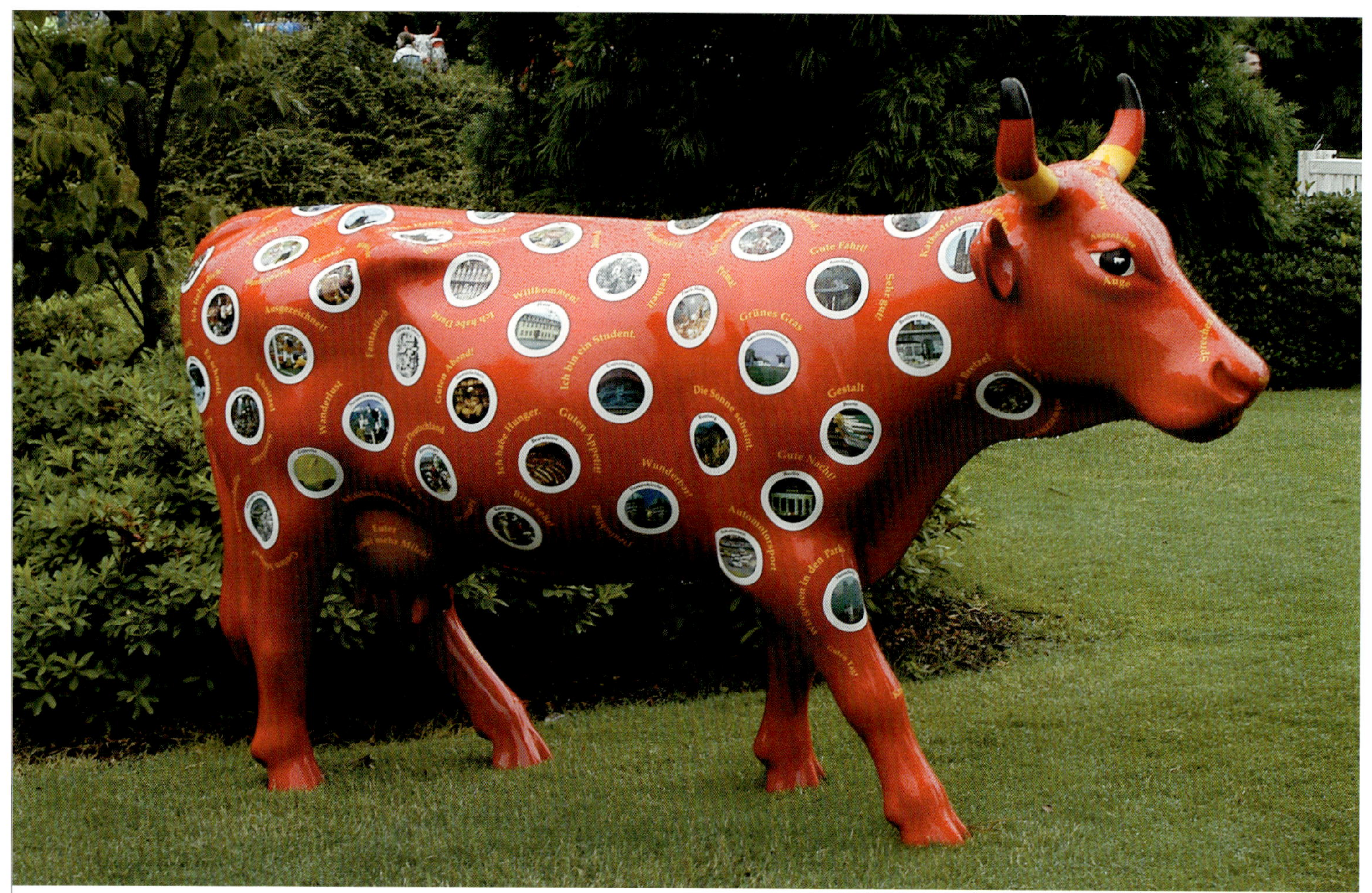

Moo-Koo
Wulf Kuehmstedt
Goethe Institute

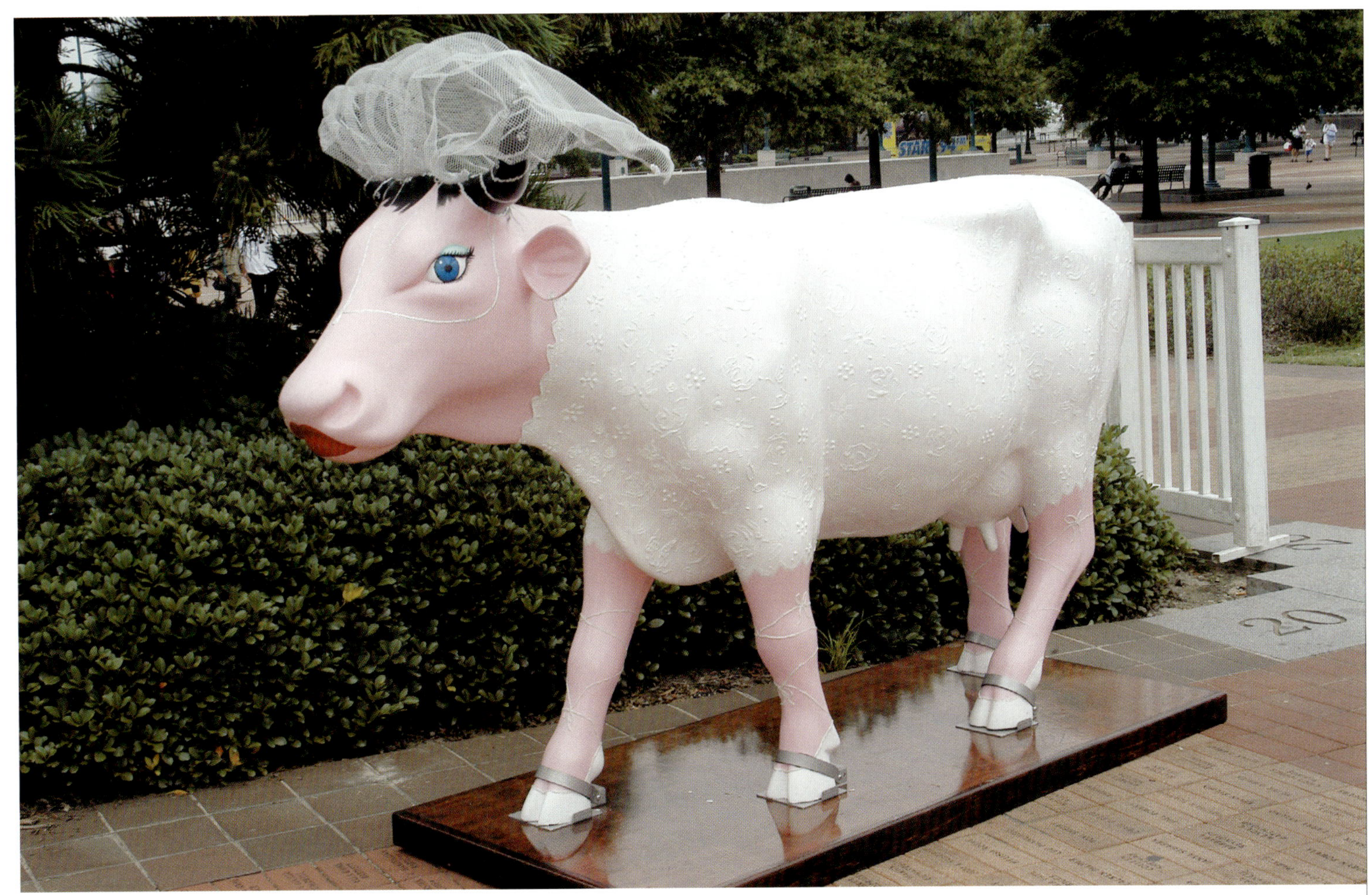

Bridal Cow
Bojana Joksimovic-Ginn
CowParade Atlanta

Eric Waugh & The Parade of Cows

Eric Waugh, from Montreal, Canada, is the world's best-selling artist of original works and a leading contributor to charities. Waugh painted his cow live in front of Atlanta audiences over three days in April 2003. Waugh believes in the concept of public art. By painting live, he offers the public an opportunity to experience the evolution of his artistic process from start to finish. Waugh is self-taught, and works primarily with acrylics. Whether painting in his studio or in live painting performances creating art inspired by music, Waugh showcases his distinctive style. His cow features "Cows on Parade" with his trademark vibrant colors; his lively sense of movement; and his whimsical figures, this time cows. Waugh's cows juggle, play instruments, and delight children as they parade an urban landscape representative of Atlanta. Waugh's artistic style mimics his own positive outlook and his celebration of life's joyous occasions, such as parades. Eric's cow expresses his artistic exploration of color, movement, and energy, and reveals the beat of his heartfelt passion for the arts, his creative process and life.

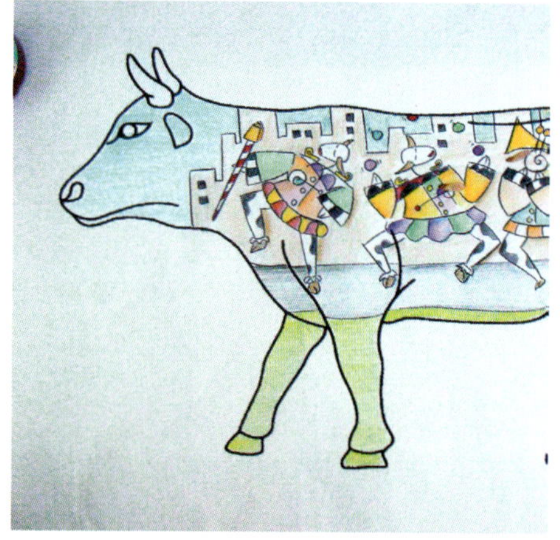

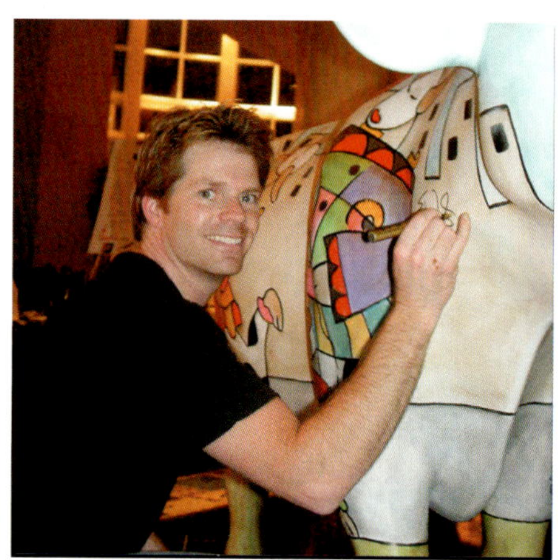

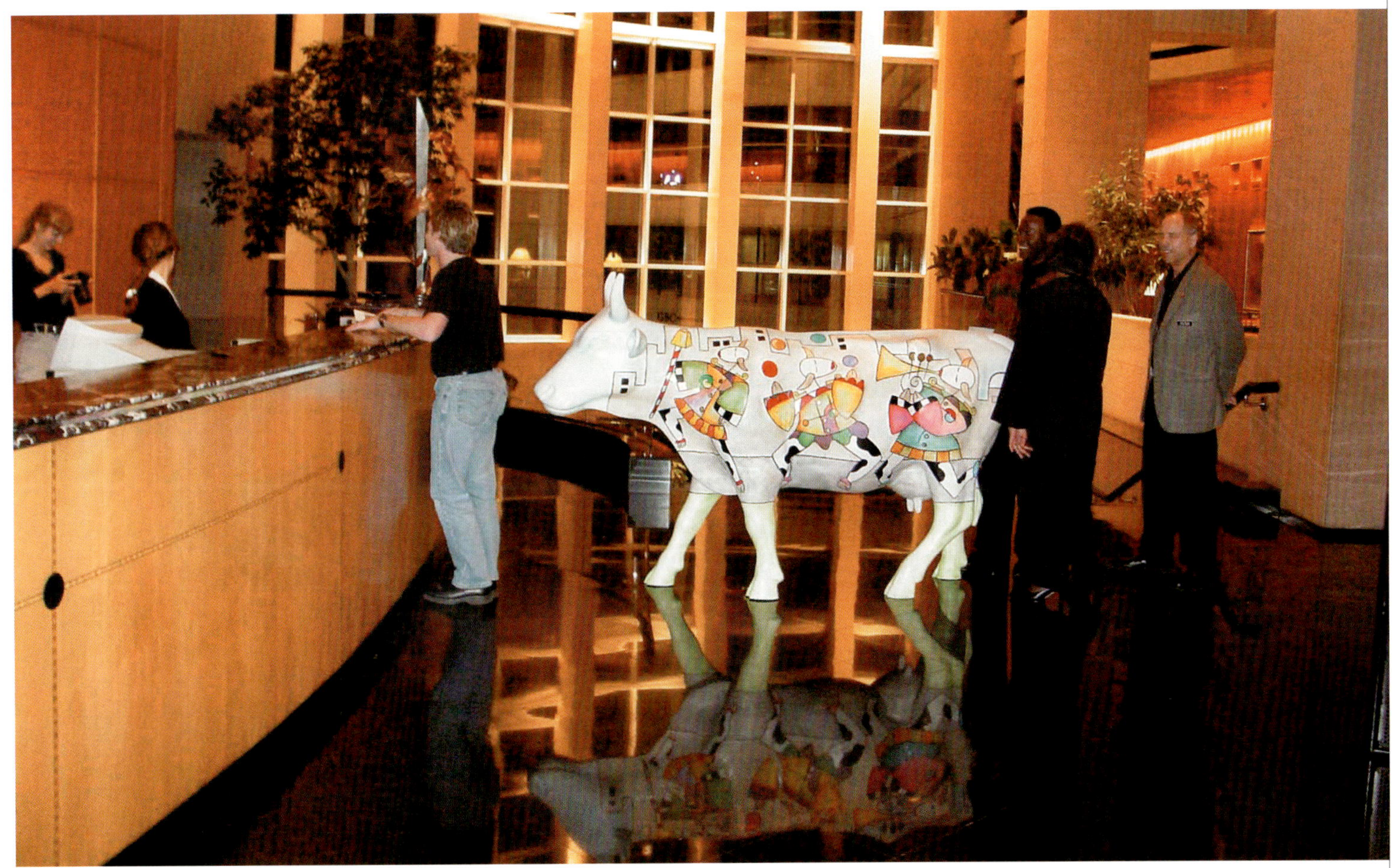

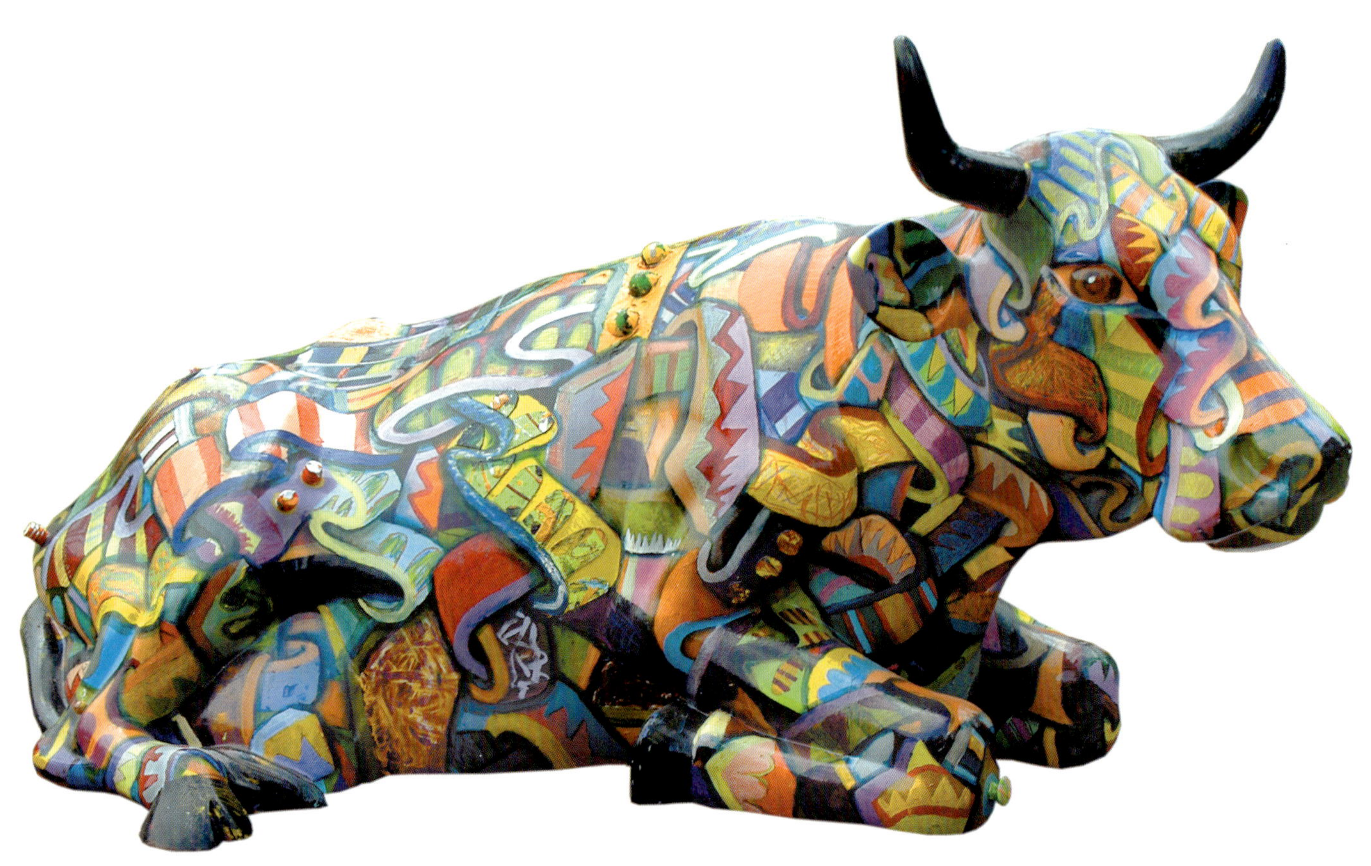

Got Soul Tribute to Marvin
Kevin Cole
Evelyn Ashley & Alan McKeon

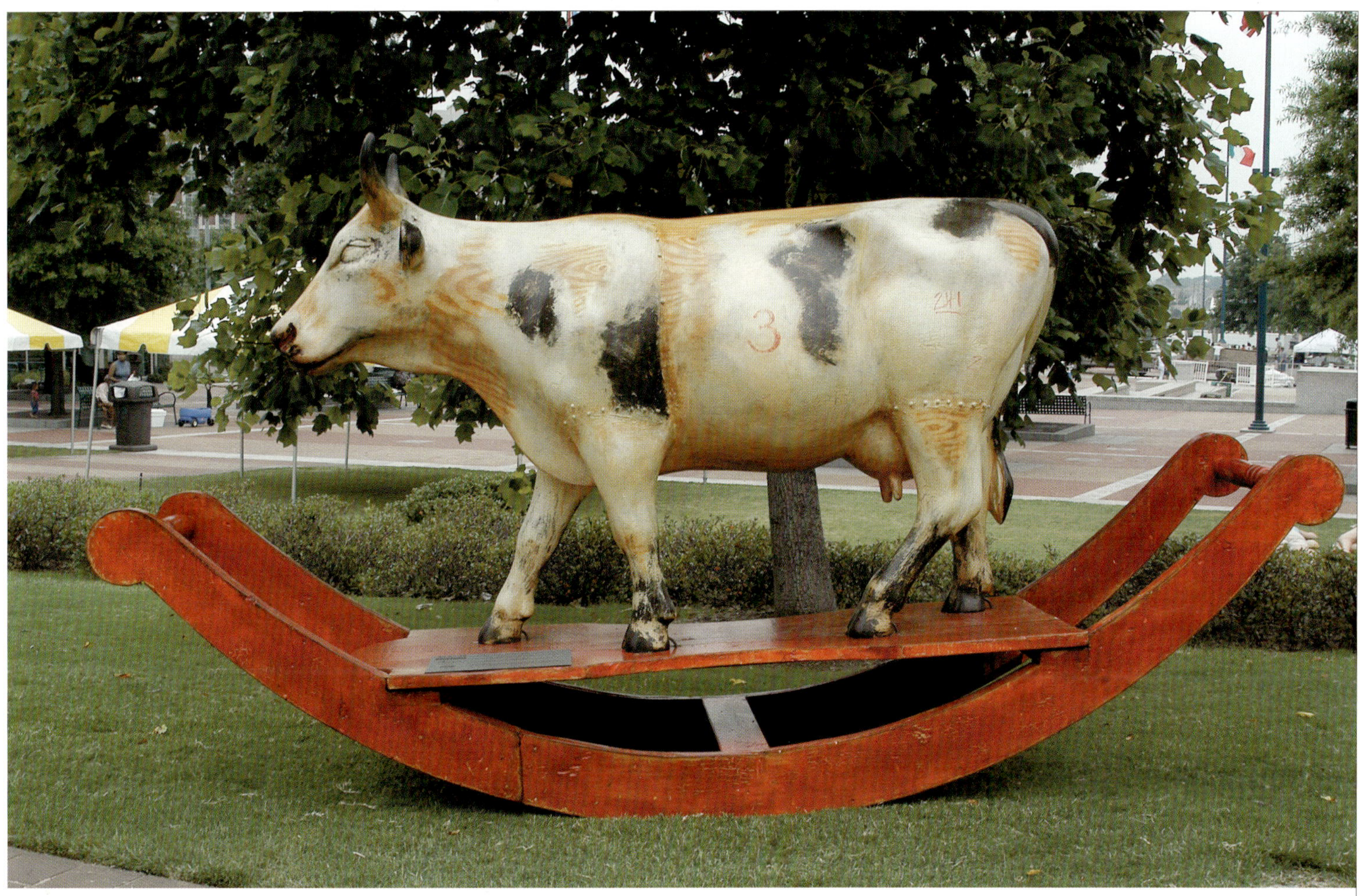

Rocking Cow
James Way
MCI

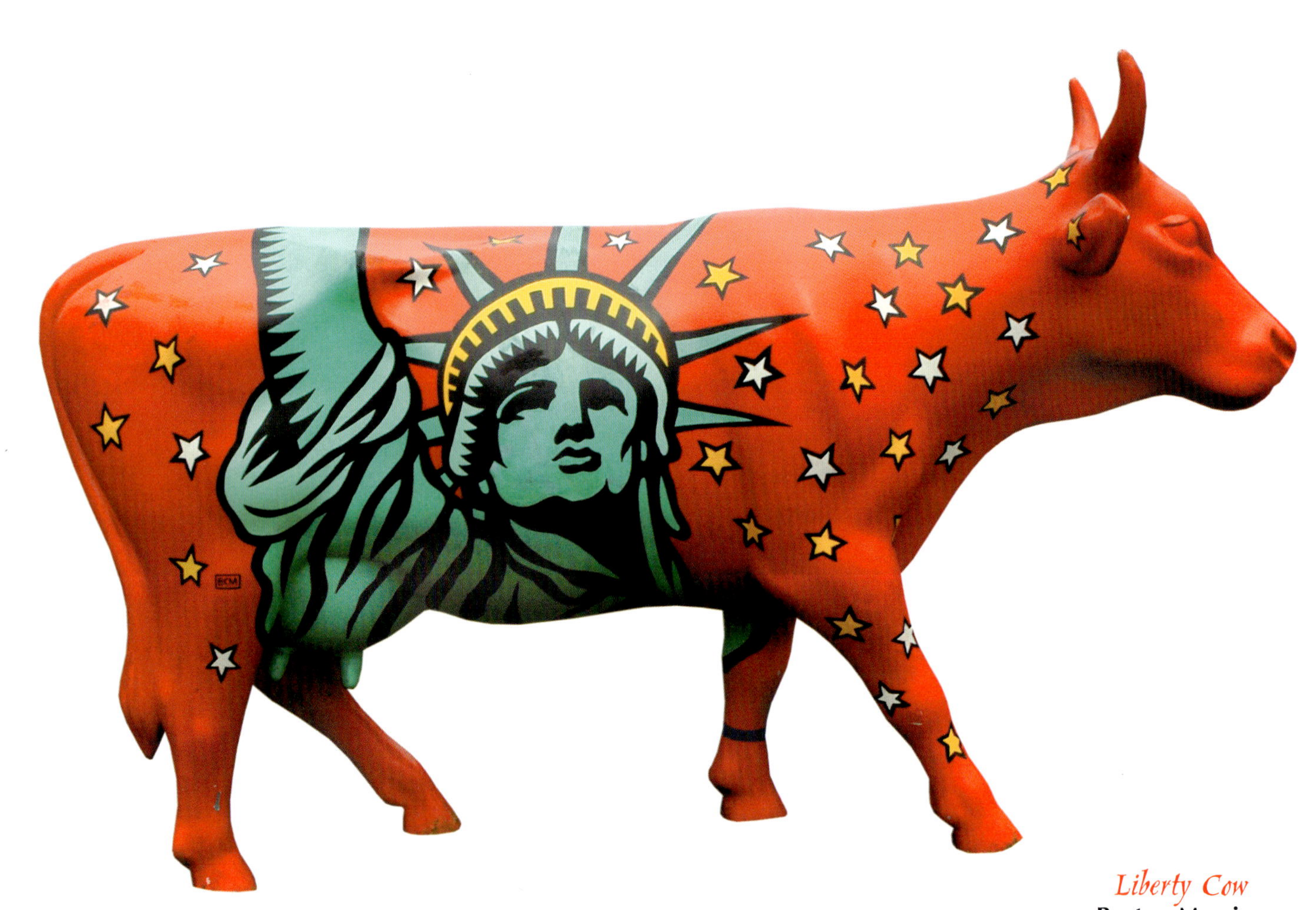

Liberty Cow
Burton Morris
CowParade Atlanta

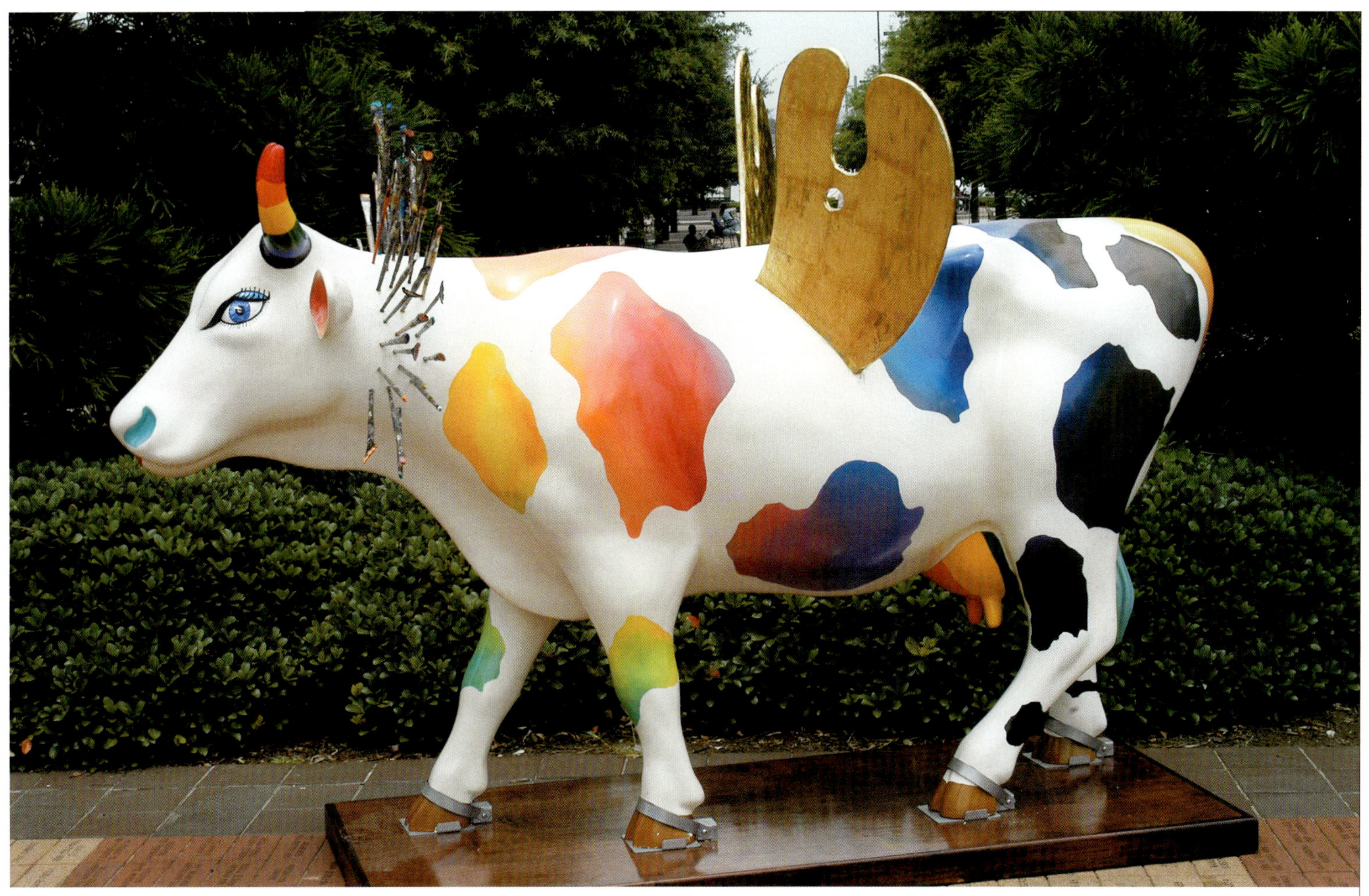

Mythic Art Cow Goddess
Larry Jens Anderson
Entertainment Design Group

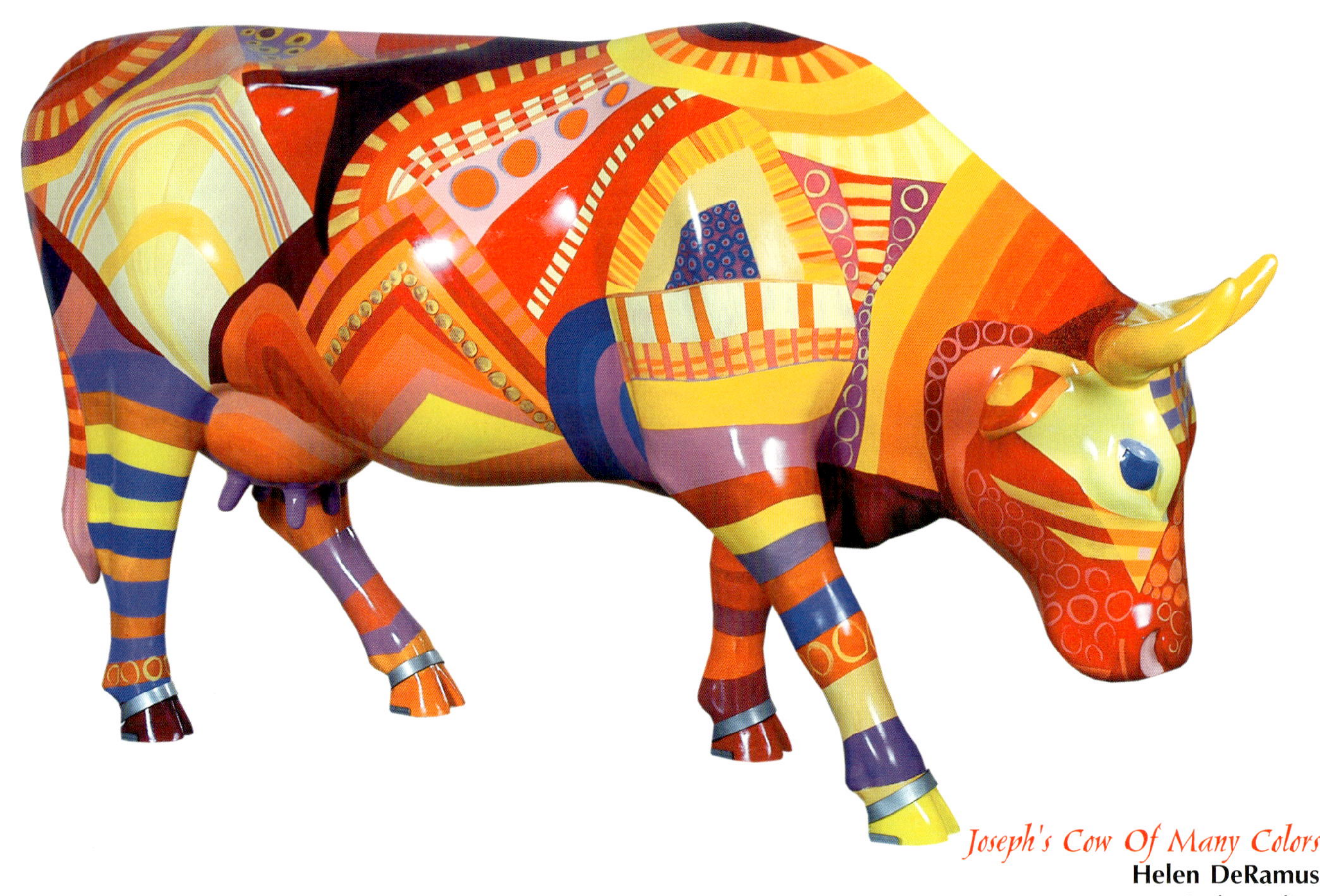

Joseph's Cow Of Many Colors
Helen DeRamus
Resurgens Orthopedics

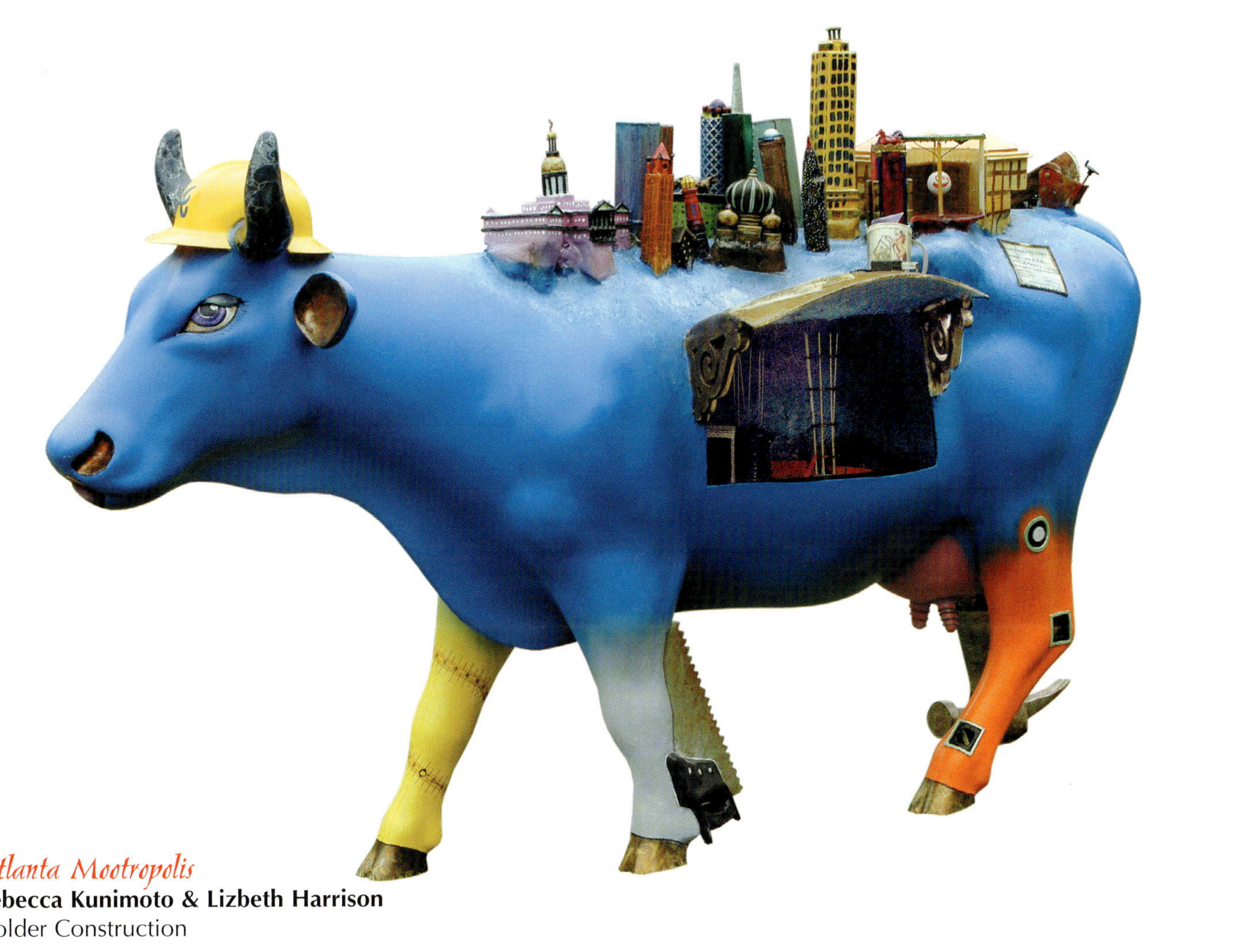

Atlanta Mootropolis
Rebecca Kunimoto & Lizbeth Harrison
Holder Construction

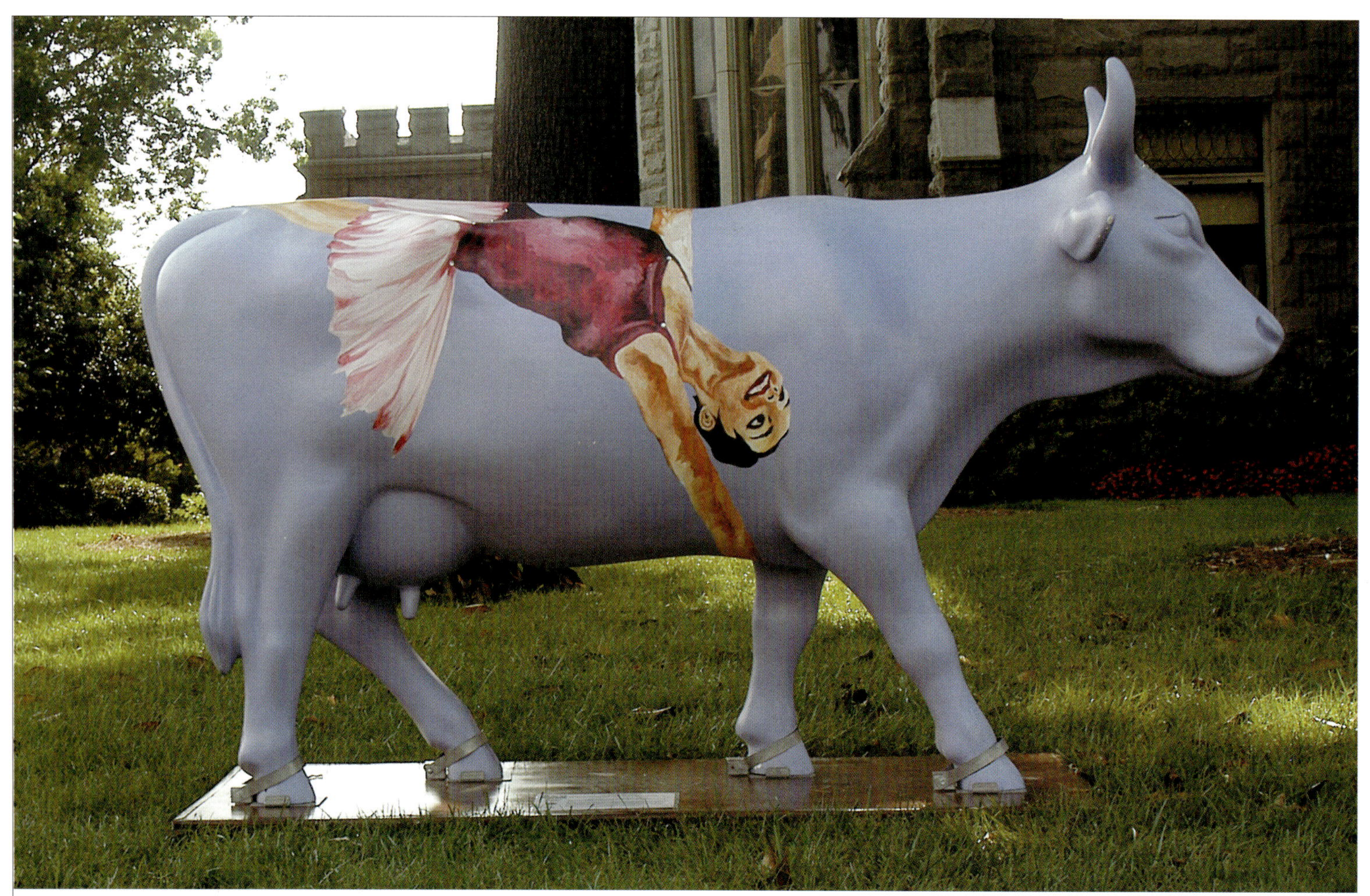

Grazeful Mooves
The Arts Factory
CowParade Atlanta

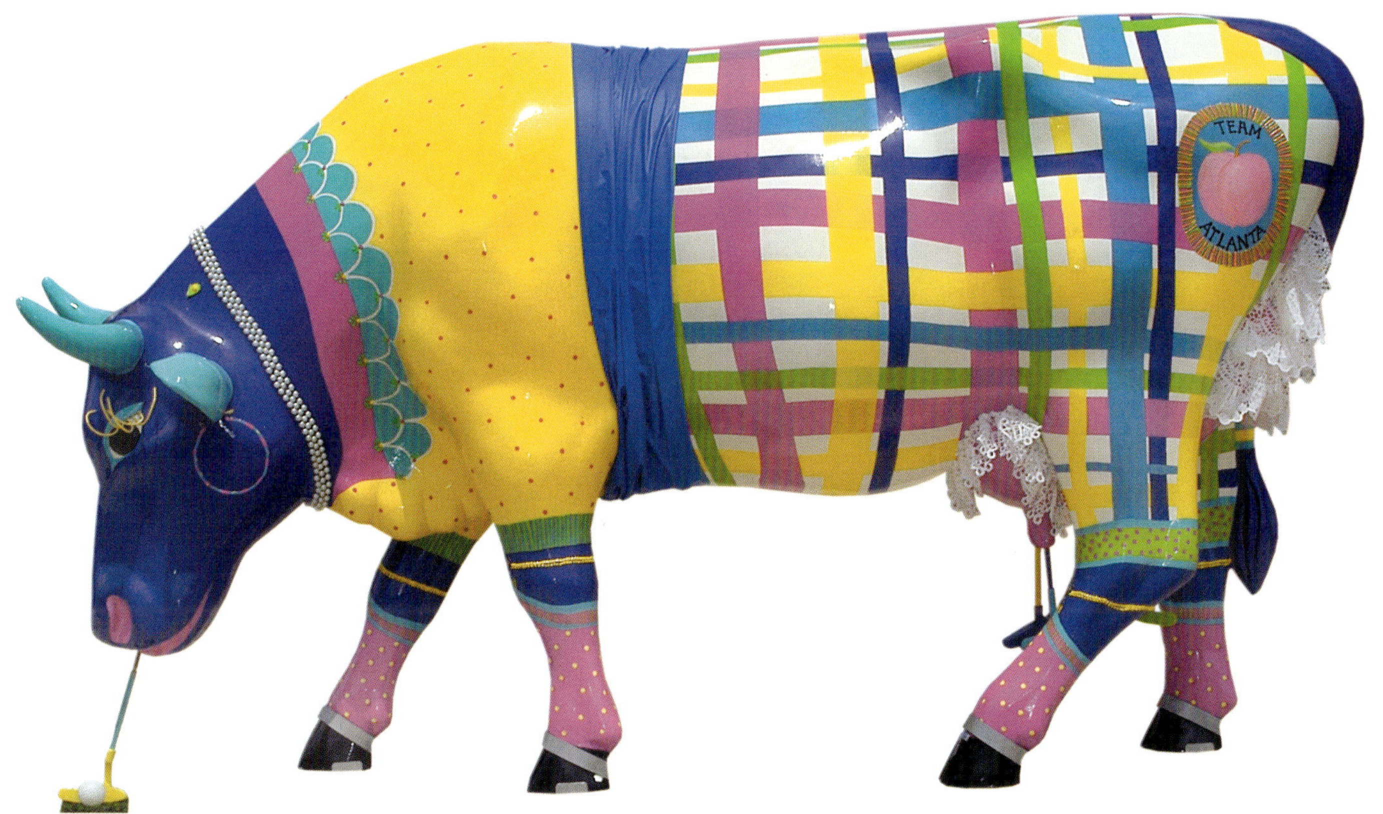

Miss Udder Putter
Lynn Weisbach
IGA Foothills Big Canoe

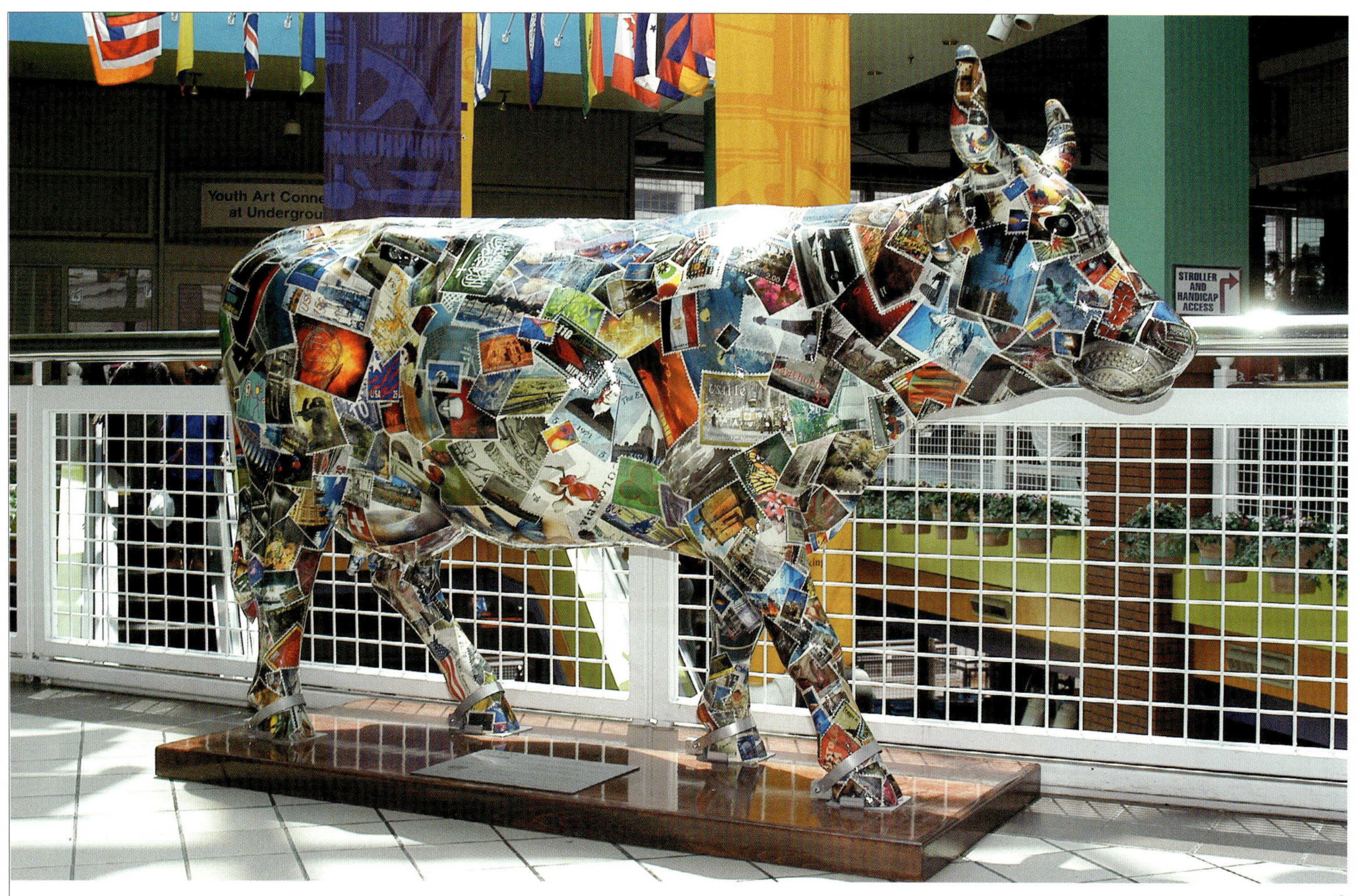

Stampede
Stephanie Eaker
Accenture

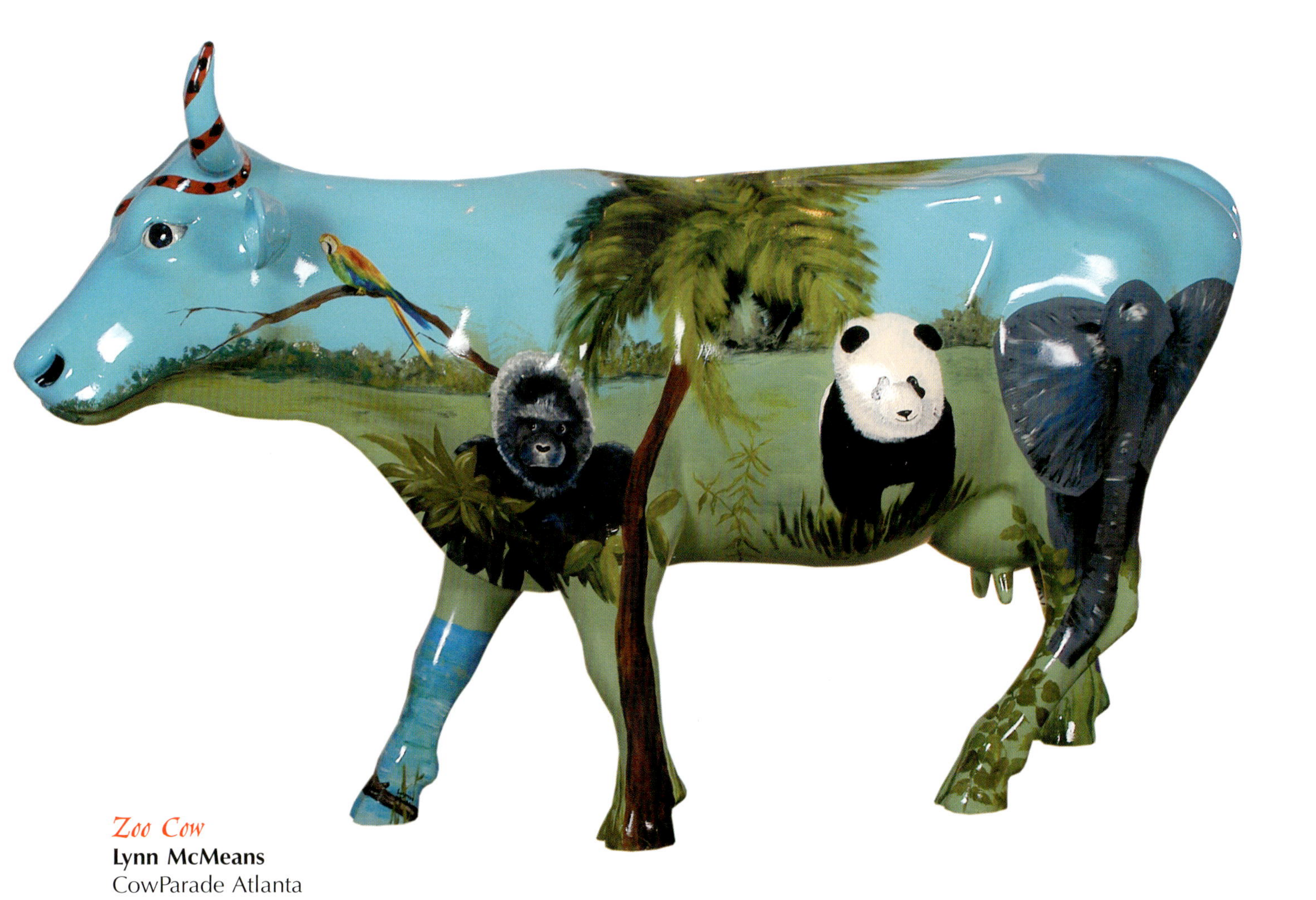

Zoo Cow
Lynn McMeans
CowParade Atlanta

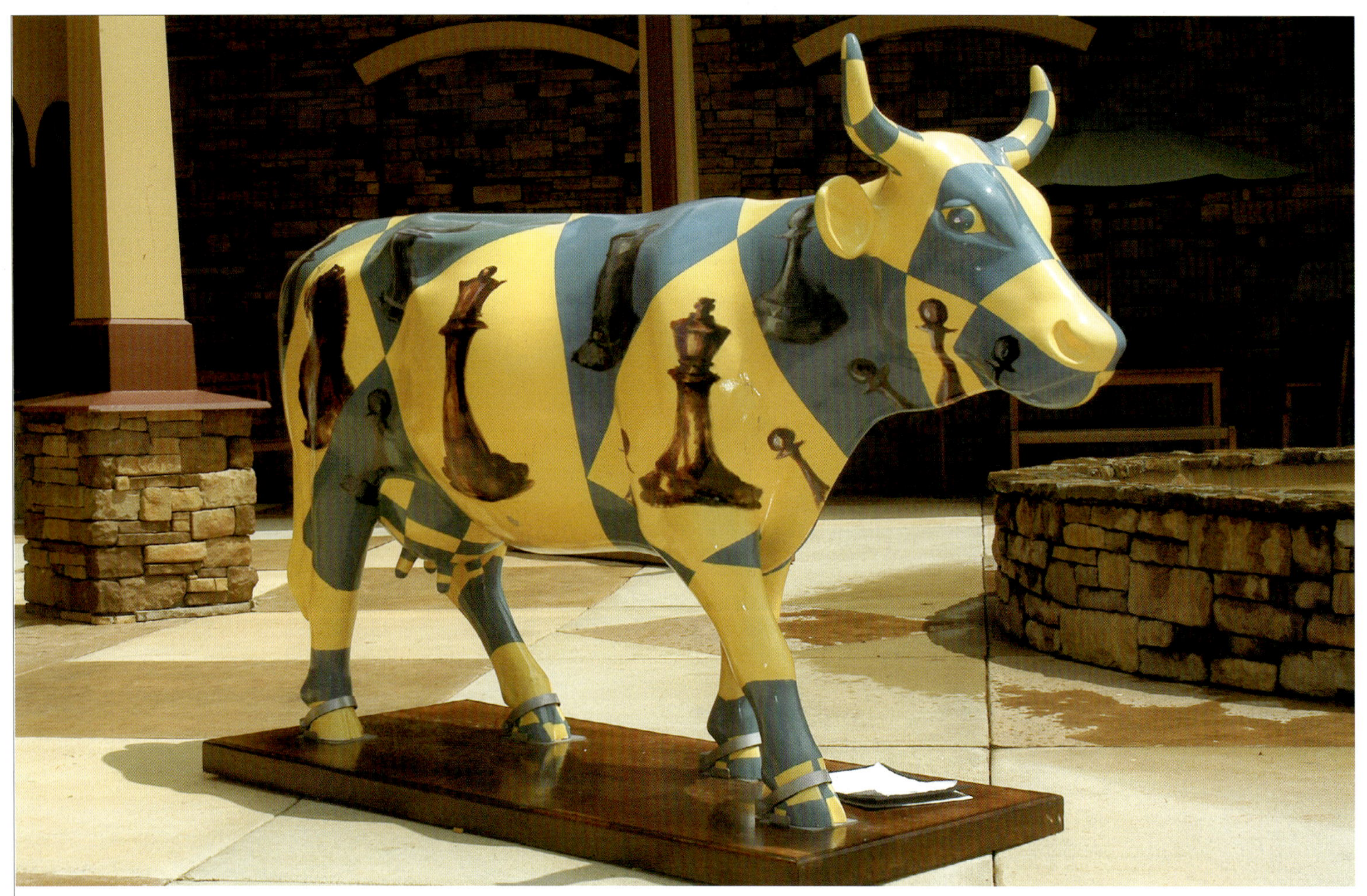

Color Chess Cow
Nikolay Lyutskanov
1st Stop Chevron

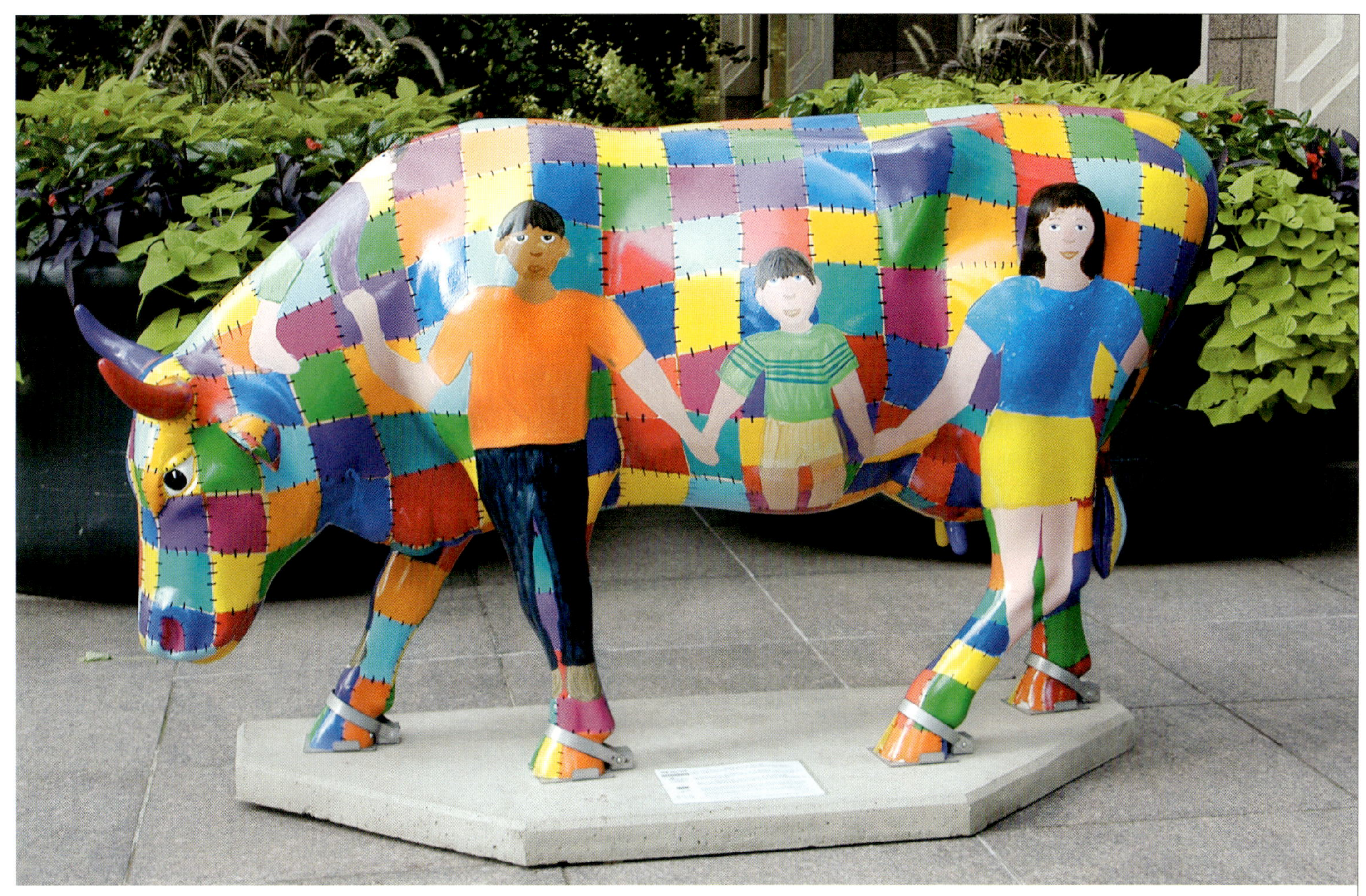

Kids in the South
Lacy Bedol
Accenture & BellSouth

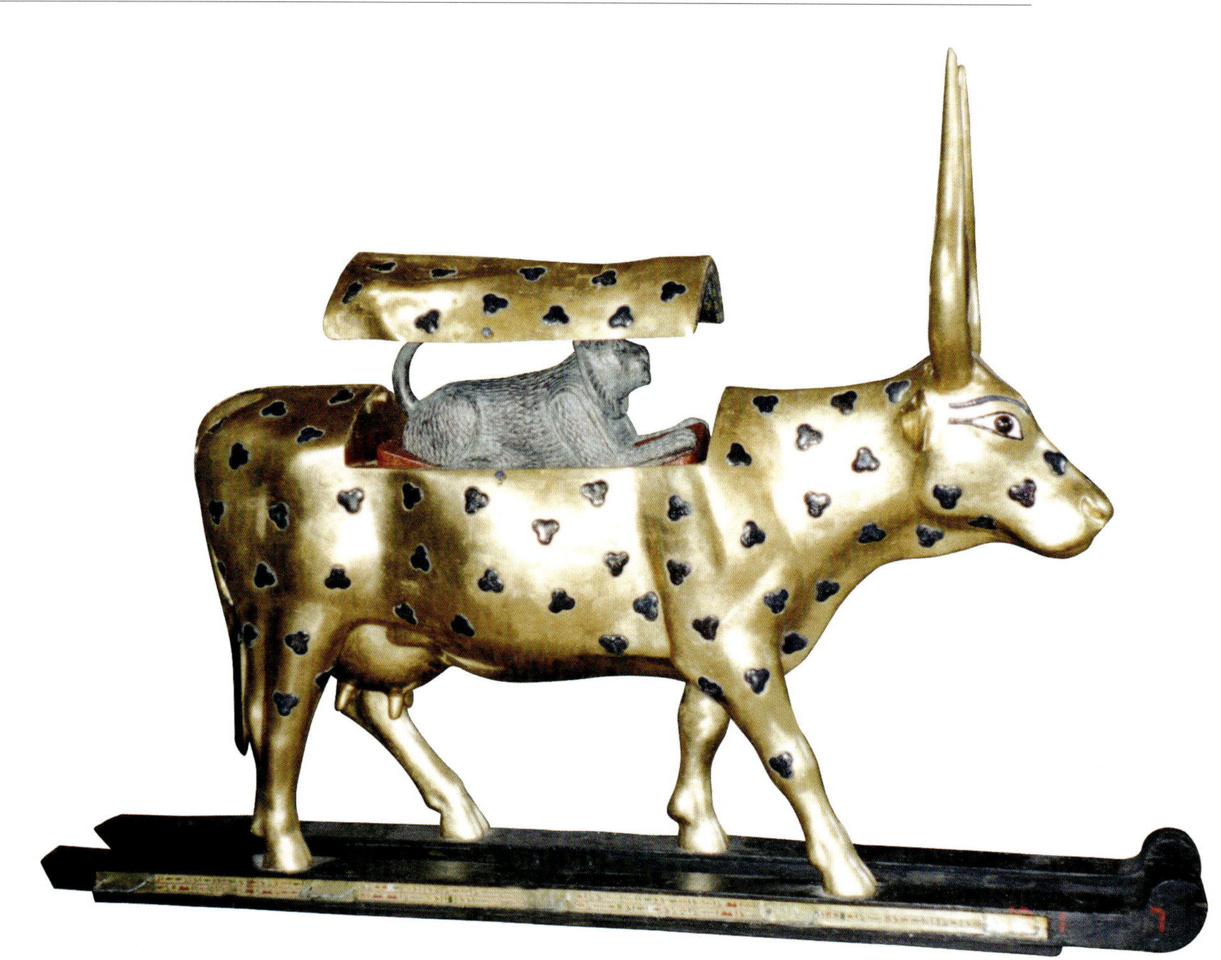

Hathor
Randy Gilman
CowParade Atlanta

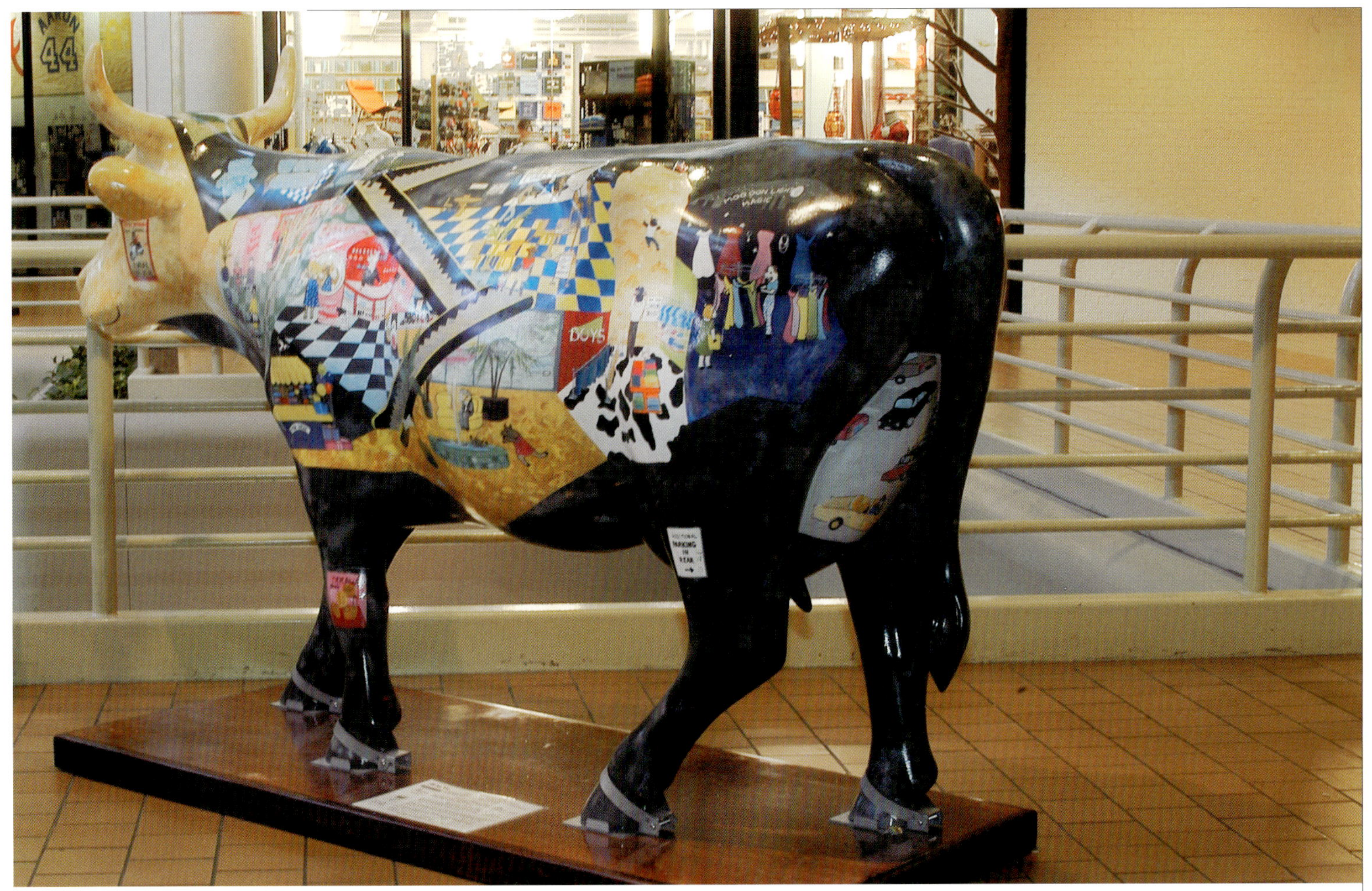

Shop 'til the Cows Come Home
Tim Maillet & Mary Jane Kenary
Rich's-Macy's

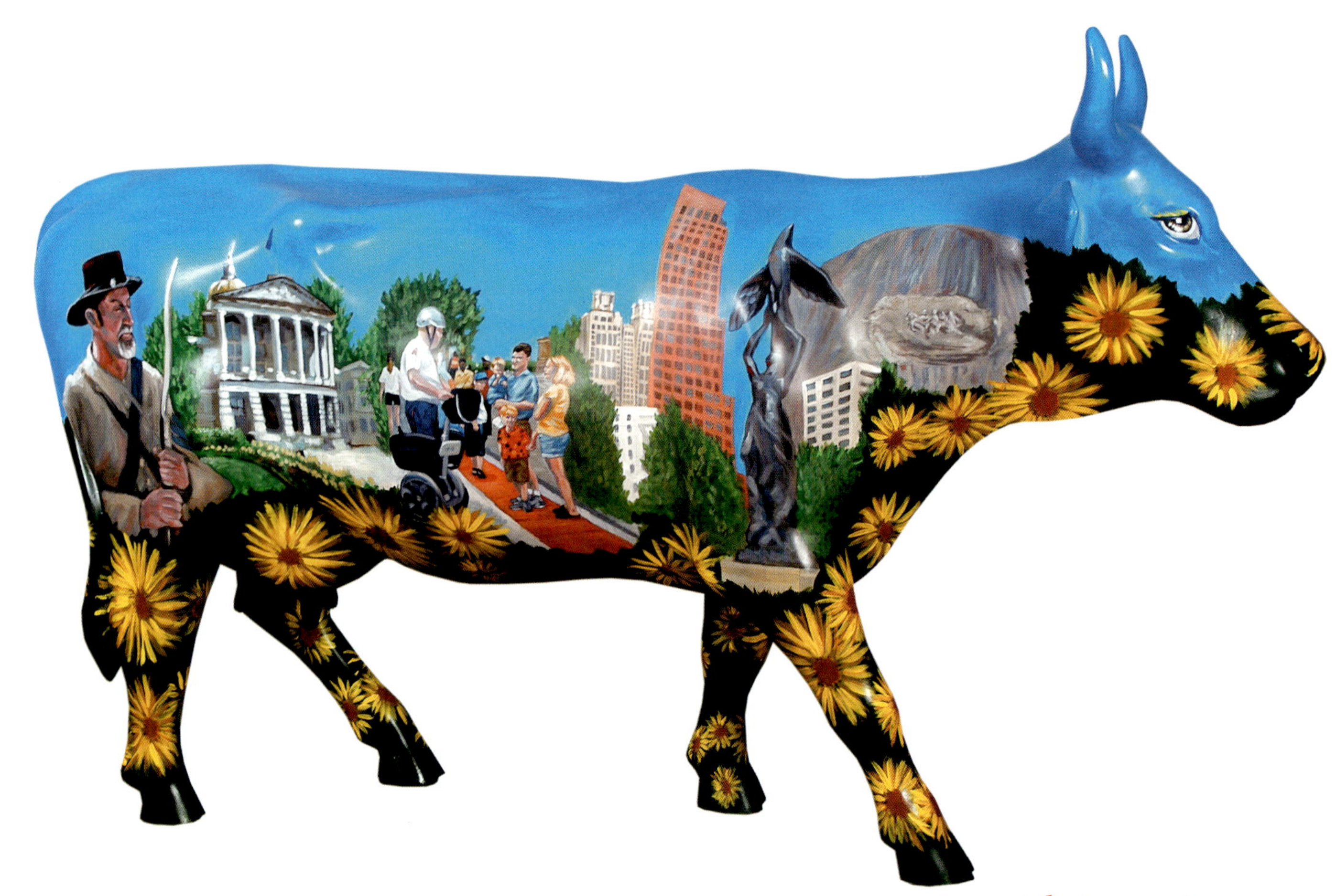

Sunny Atlanta Hometown Cow
Anthony Stewart
SunTrust

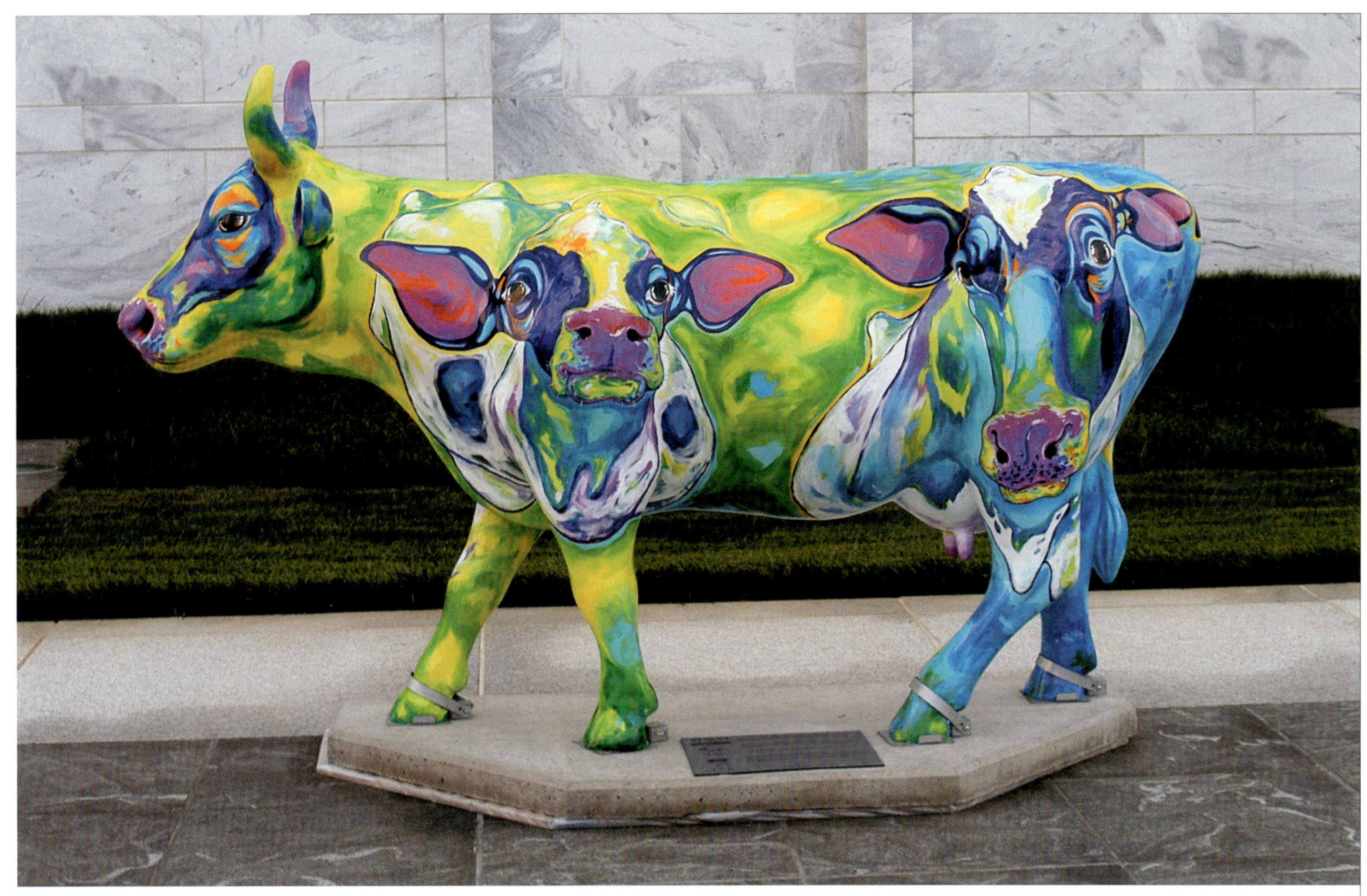

The Many Faces of Moo
Robert Marinich
Evelyn Ashley & Alan McKeon

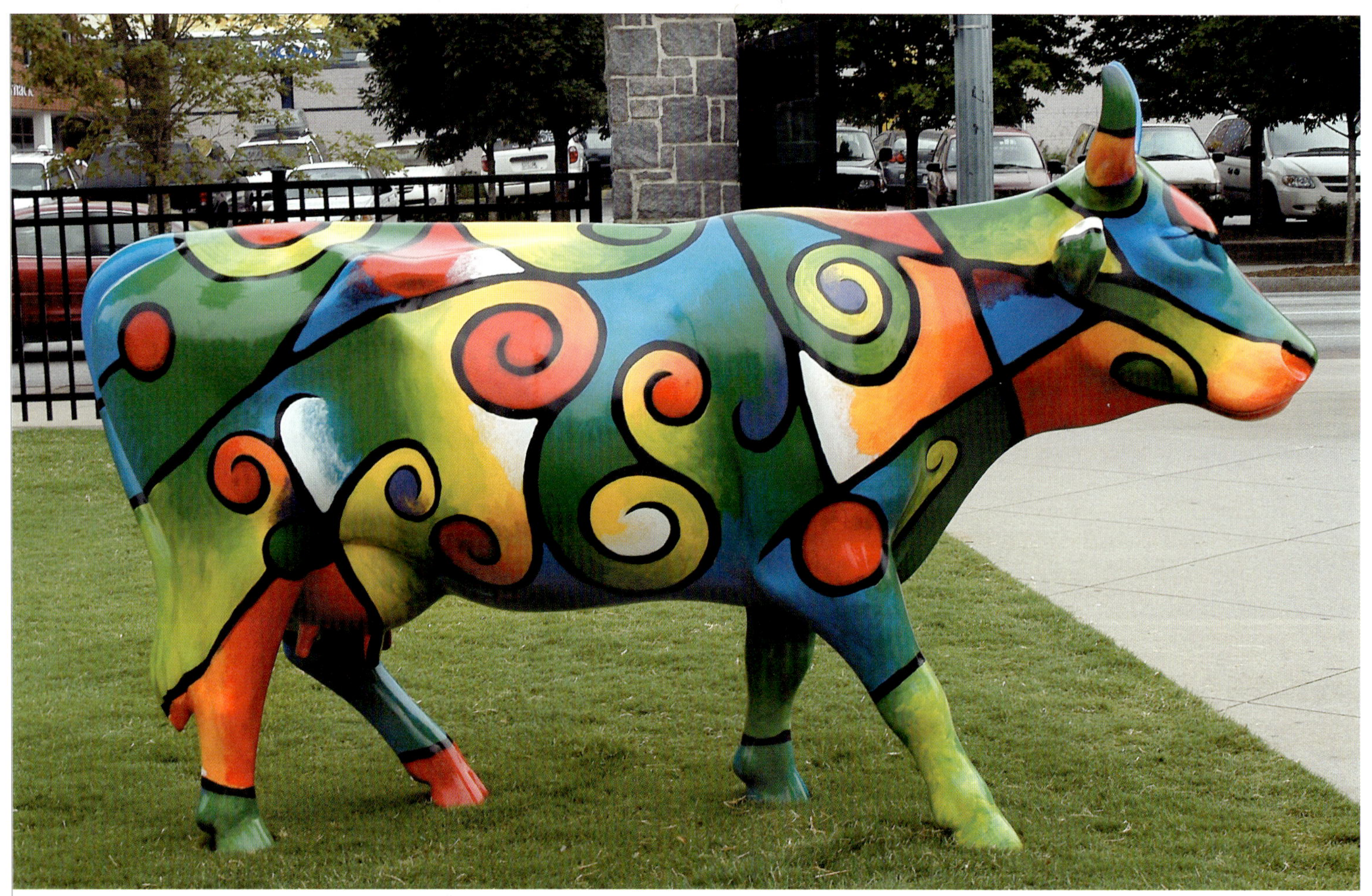

Cowposition of Color
David Boyd
Atlanta Gas Light Company

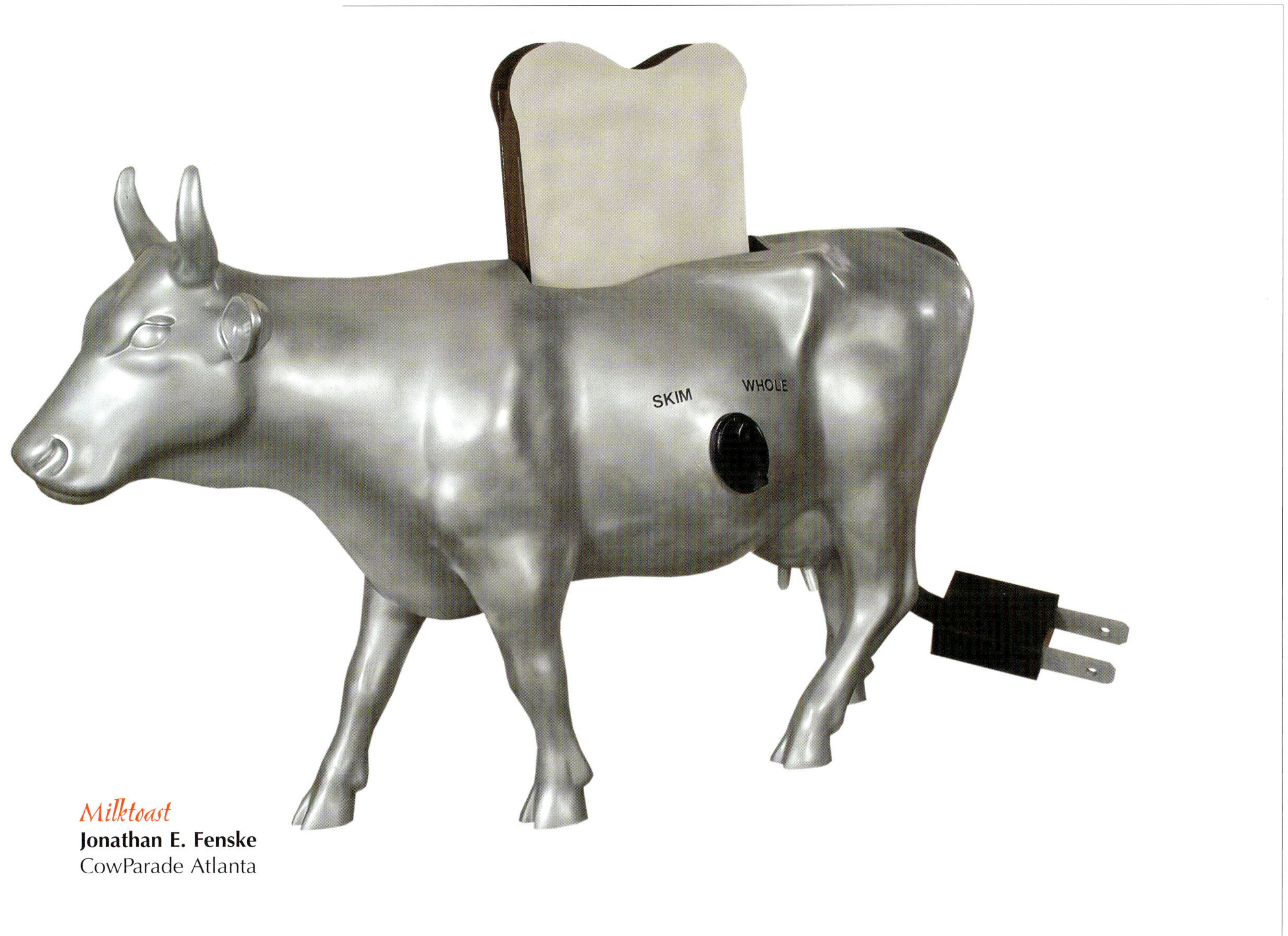

Milktoast
Jonathan E. Fenske
CowParade Atlanta

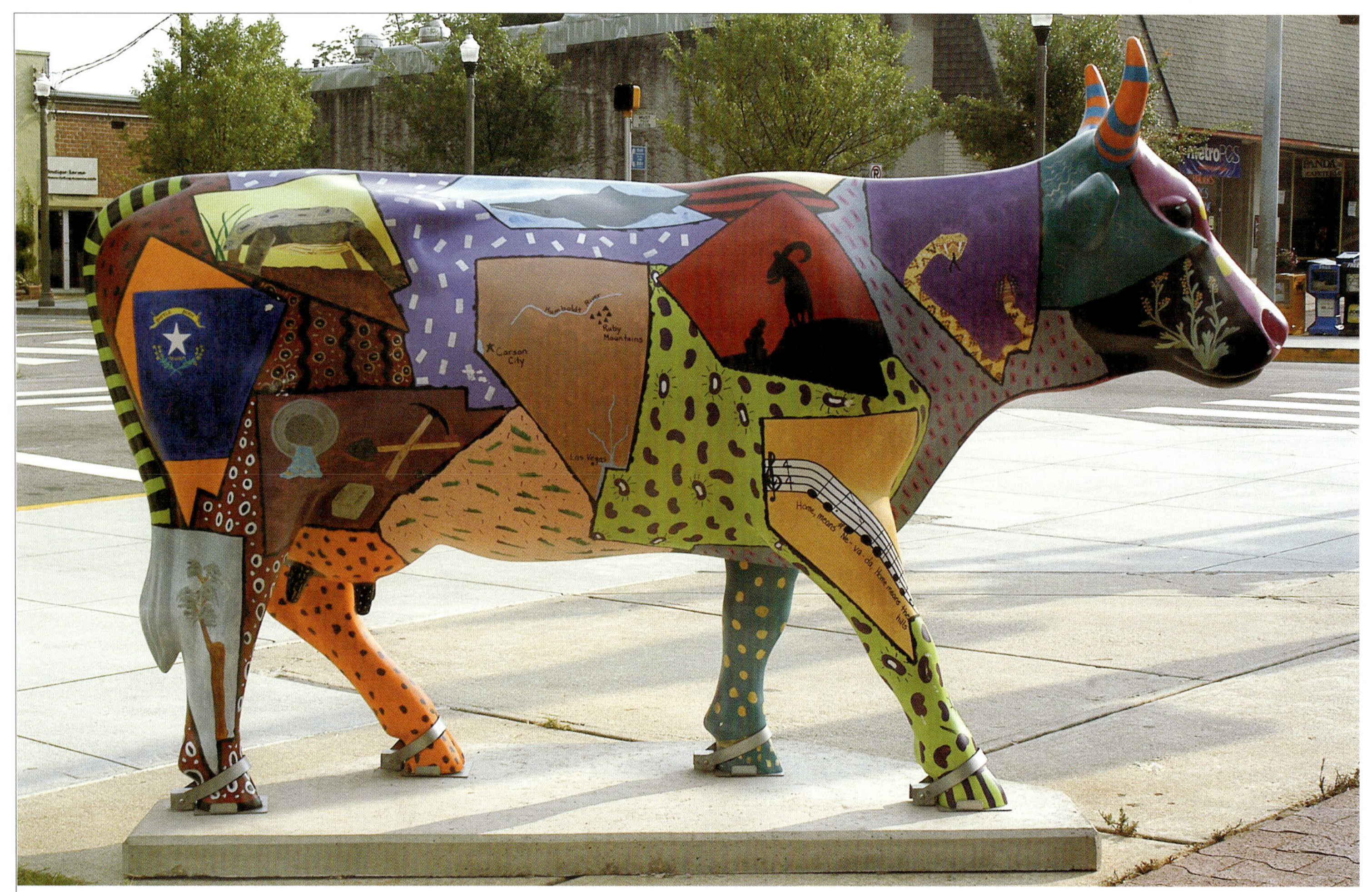

Miss Nevada
Phyllis Carbonaro
CowParade Atlanta

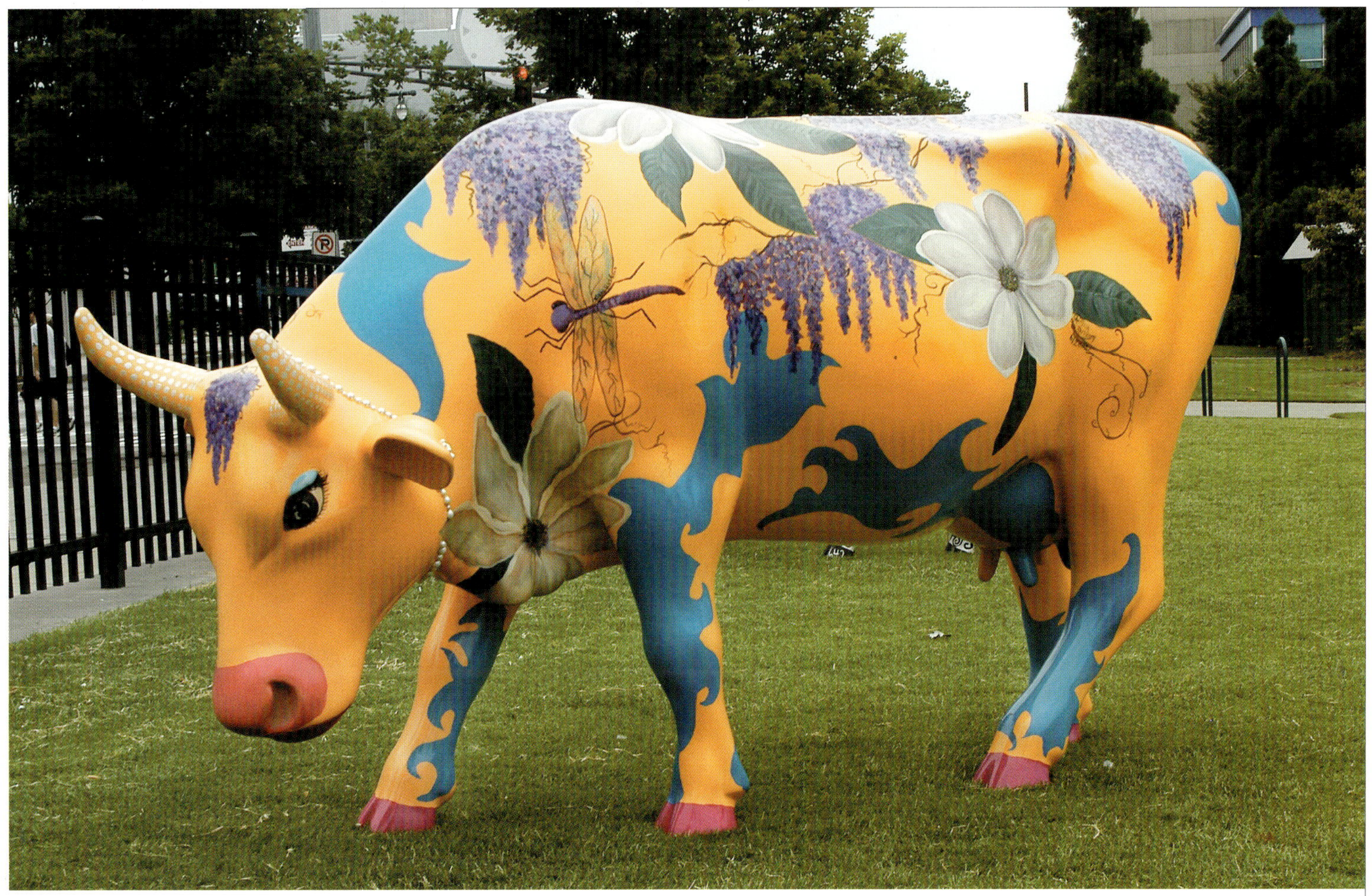

Magnolia, The Divine Bovine
Latrecia Raffety and Libby White
HRworks

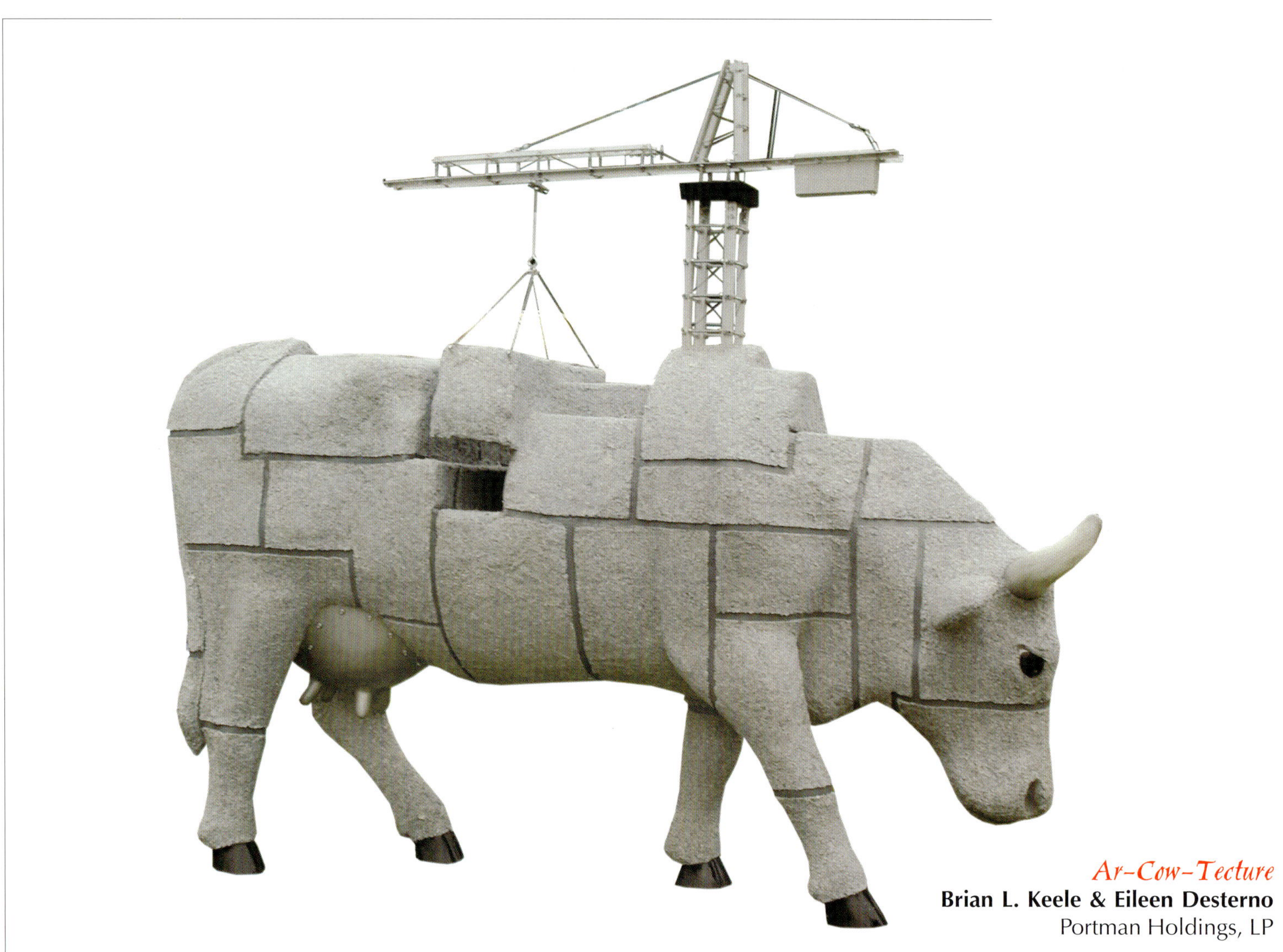

Ar-Cow-Tecture
Brian L. Keele & Eileen Desterno
Portman Holdings, LP

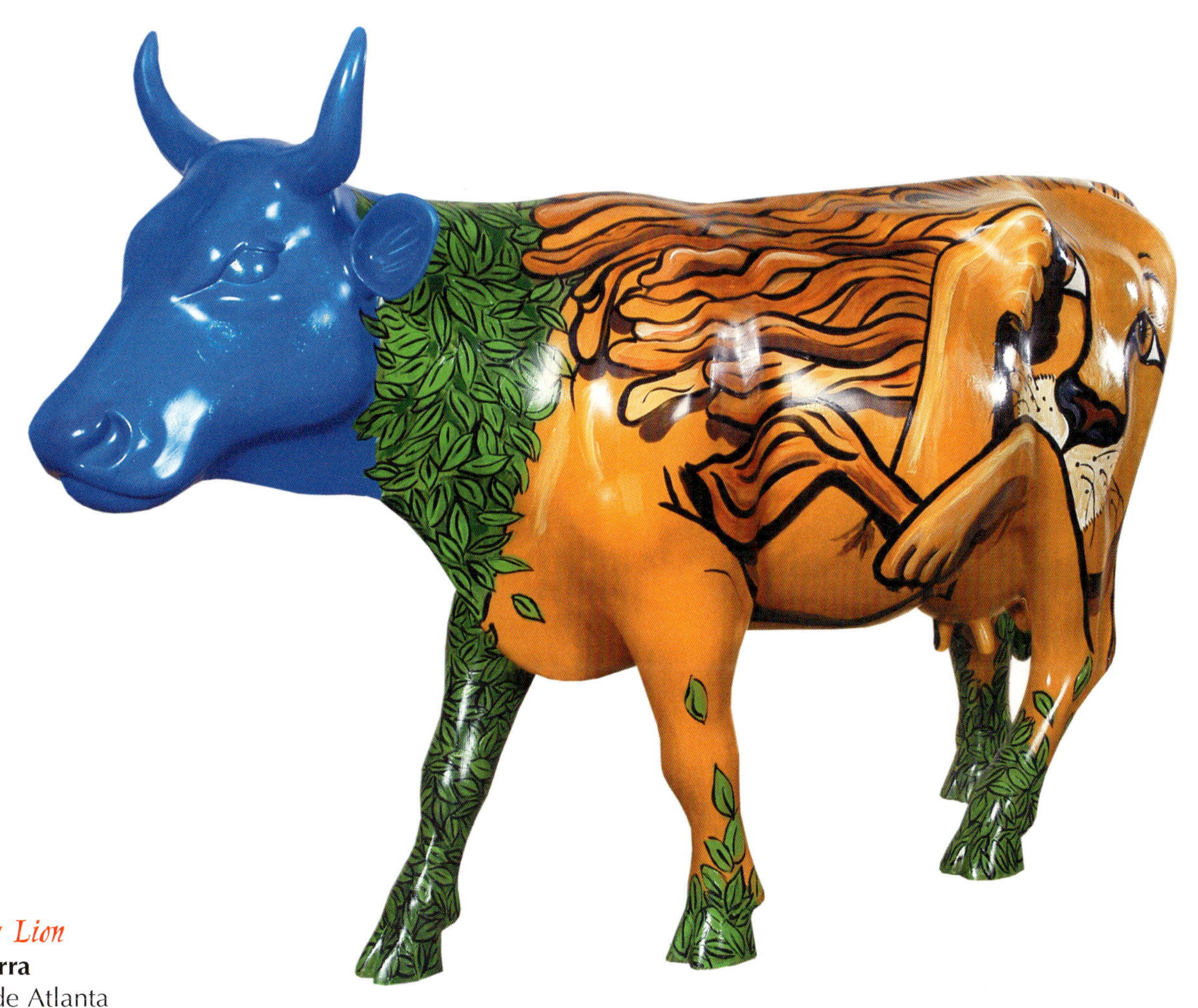

Cowardly Lion
Joni Segarra
CowParade Atlanta

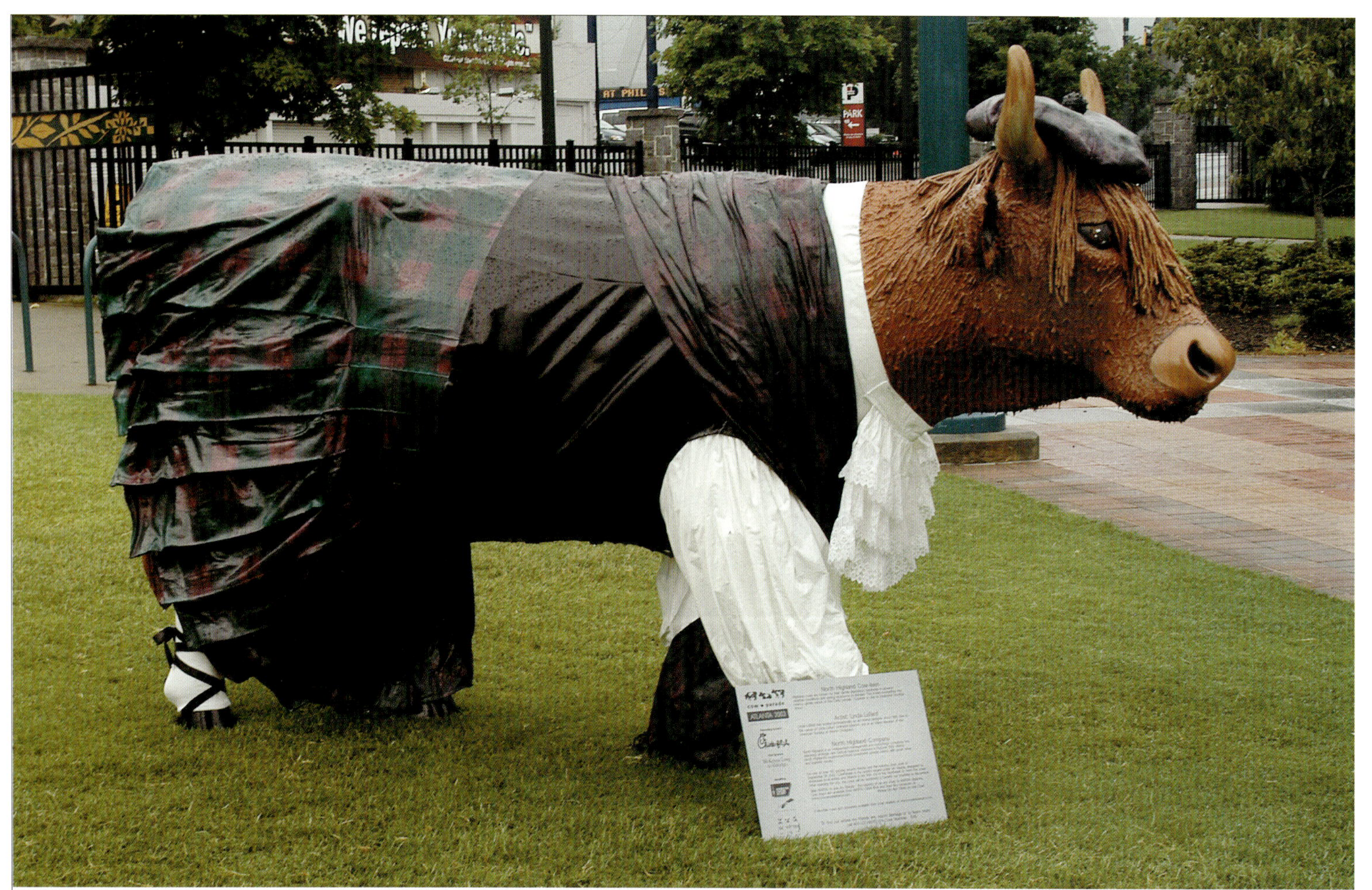

North Highland Cow-leen

Linda LeTard

The North Highland Company

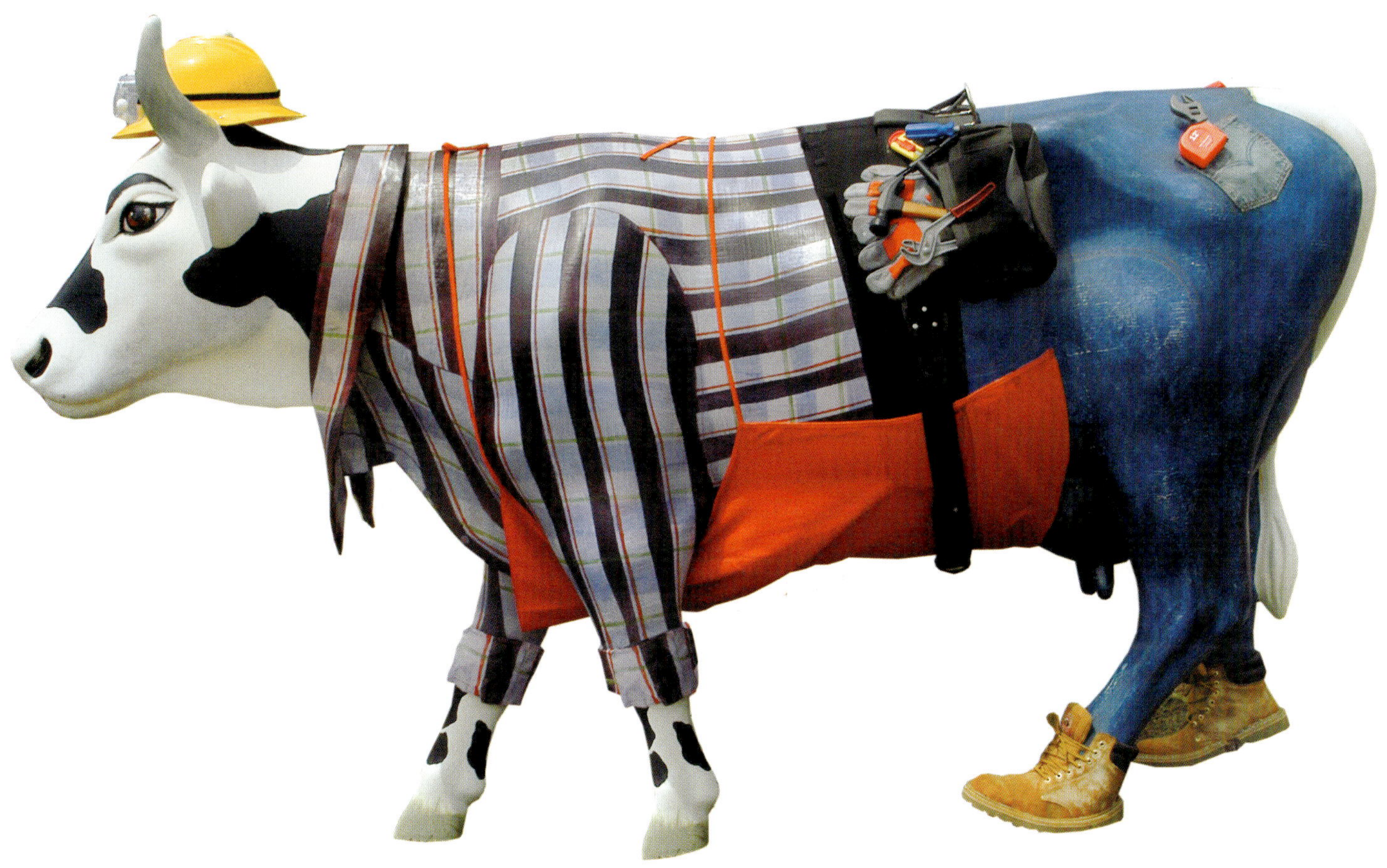

Handy Cow
Jaime Valero, Victoria Martin-Gilly, Waldo Vinces, Maria Lucia Sarmiento
Home Depot

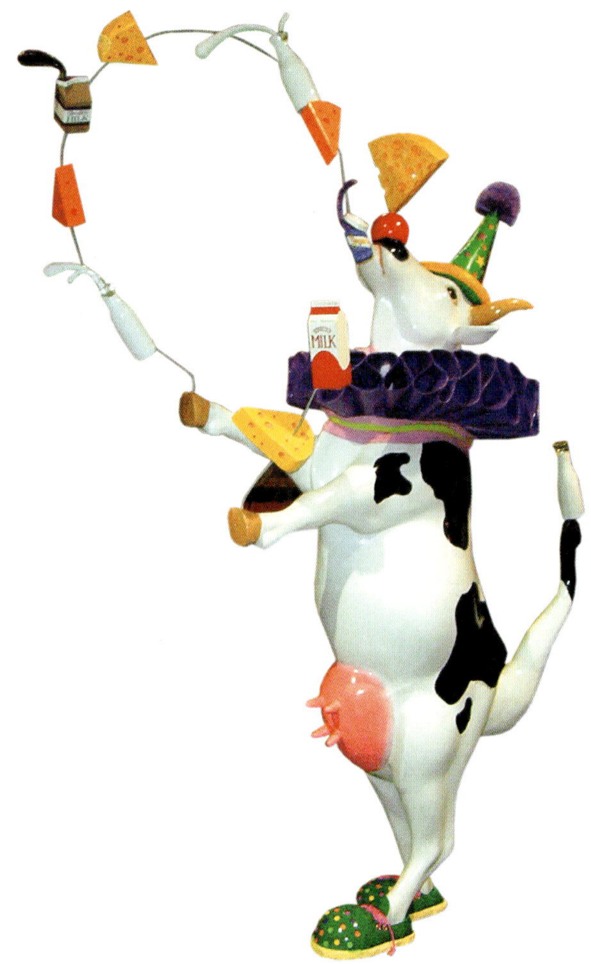

Circus Cown
Diane Yarbrough Sewell
Southeast United Dairy Association

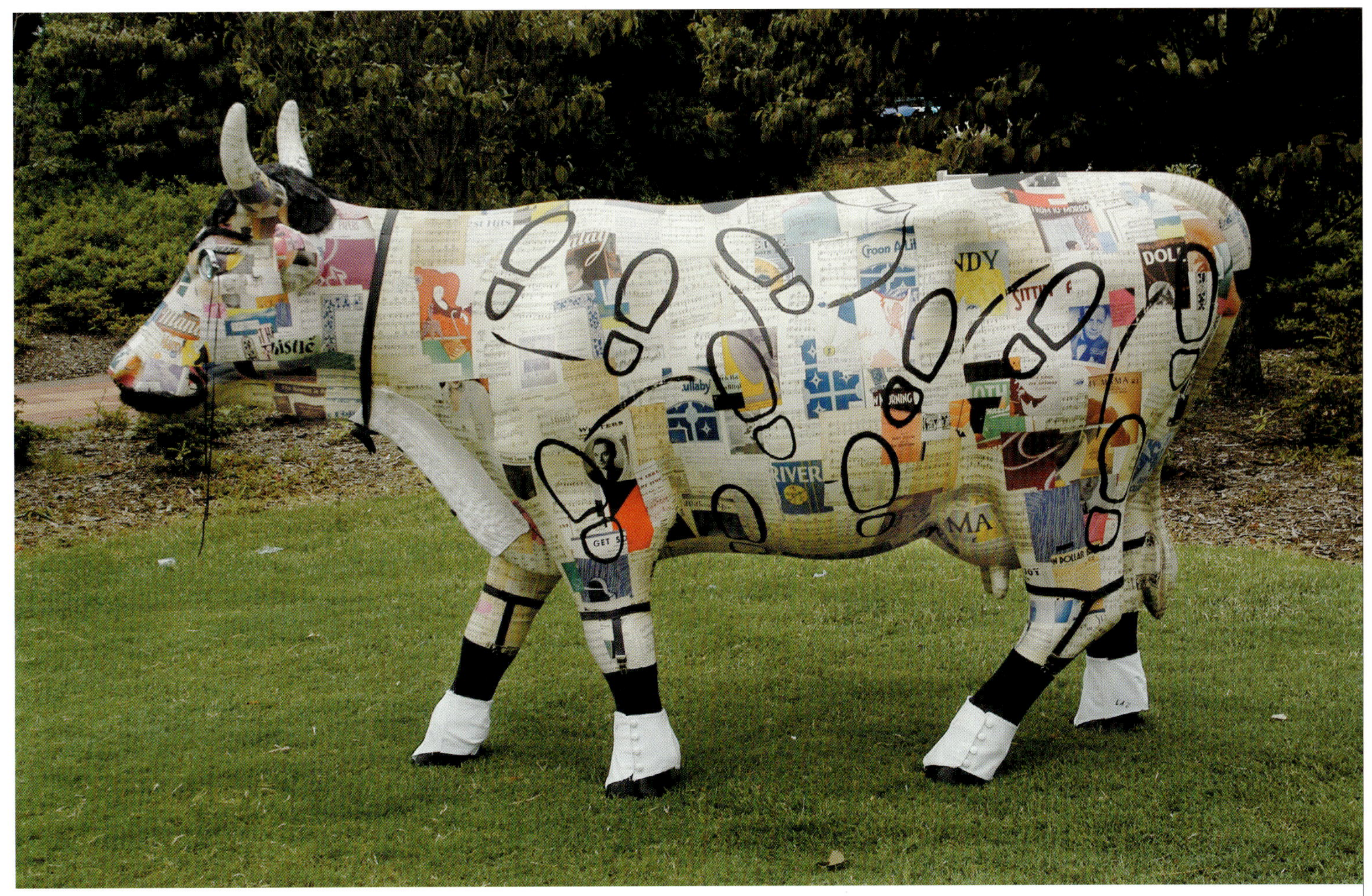

MOOnlight Serenade
Jeff Doud
The Biltmore

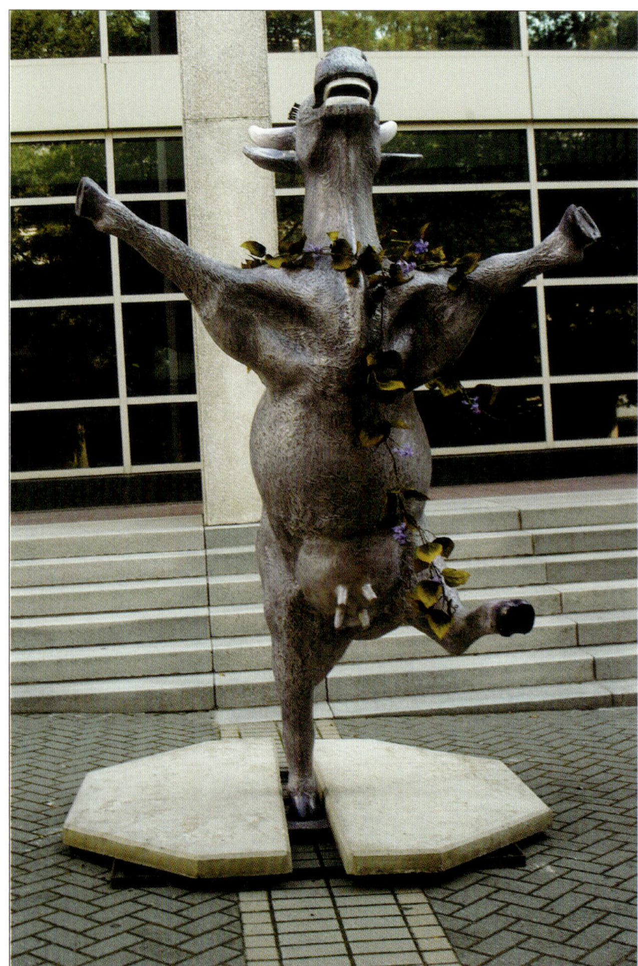

Kudzudora Duncown
Eileen Desterno
Harry Norman, Realtors

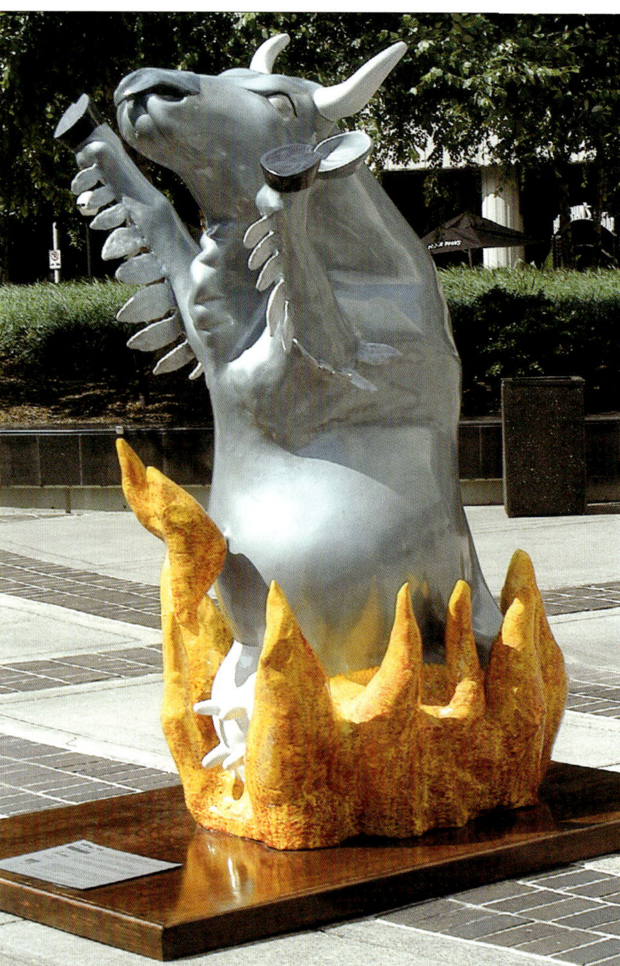

Transmoogrification
David Leedle
CowParade Atlanta, dedicated to its Volunteers

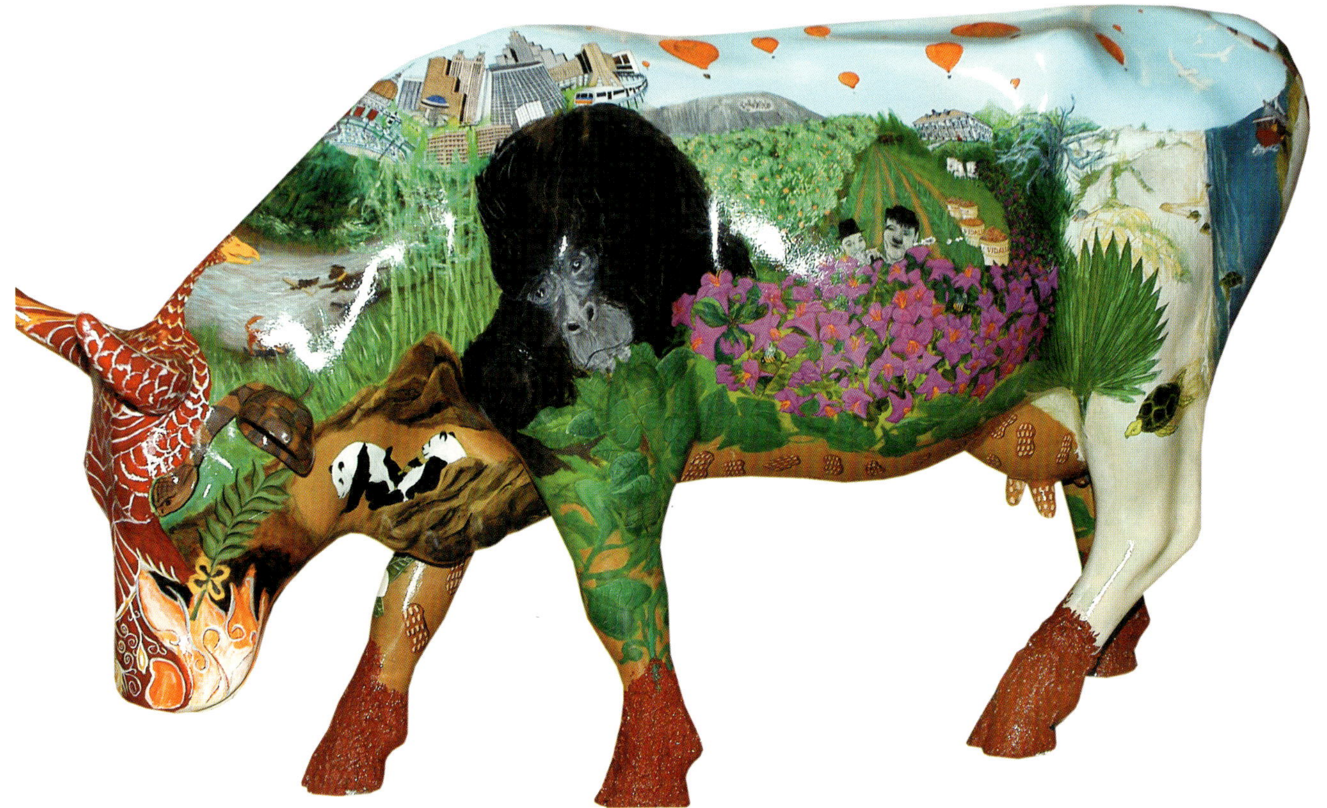

Georgia on Moo Mind
Robert DeLoach
Georgia Department of Industry Trade and Tourism

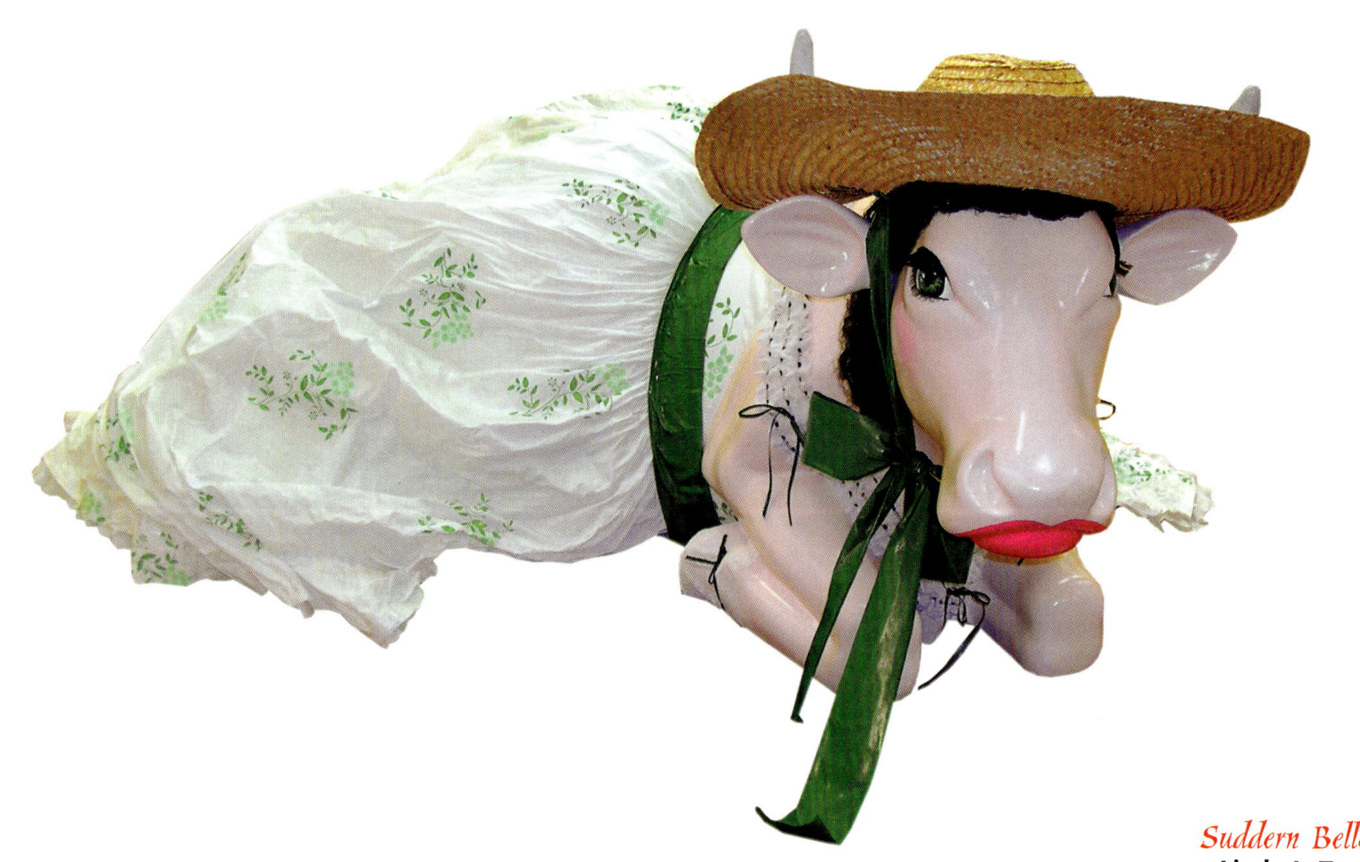

Suddern Belle
Linda LeTard
Atlanta Convention & Visitors Bureau

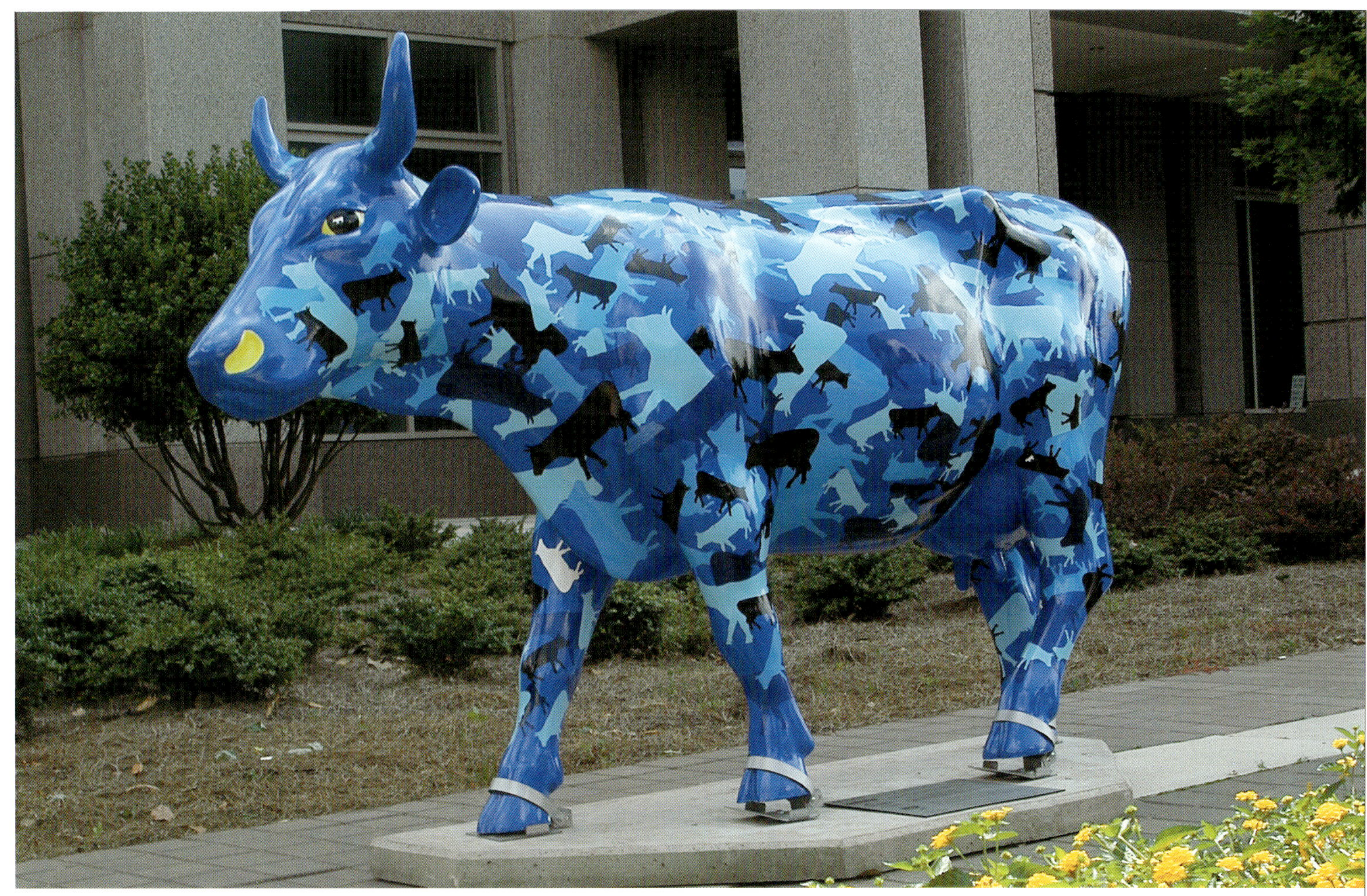

Cowmooflage

Wulf Kuehmstedt & Filipp Zyryanov

Fastsigns by Northlake Mall & Corporate Design, Inc.

Moo-Ha Da-Da & Paradise—A Southern Patchwork Quilt

FINSTER FEST IS AN ANNUAL EVENT in honor of America's most celebrated visionary/ folk artist the late Rev. Howard Finster. Artists and musicians gather at Finster's Paradise Gardens in tiny Summerville, Georgia, to pay tribute and continue the legacy of a respected friend and artist. At Finster Fest 2003, sixteen members of the Who-Ha Da-Da Artists Fellowship: Dr. Bob, Kim Clayton, Paul Flack, Ramona Hotel, Chris Hubbard, C.M. Laster, Grace Kelly Laster, Eric Legge, Joe Legge, Eric Pace, Mary Proctor, Robert Seven, j.d. Sipe, Miz Thang, Myrtice West and Willie Willie, collaborated to paint Moo-Ha-Da-Da; Paradise—A Southern Patchwork Quilt—and a tribute to Georgia's beloved Howard Finster.

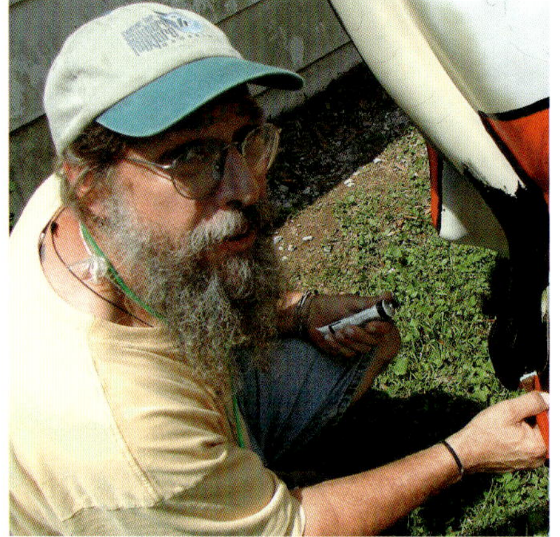

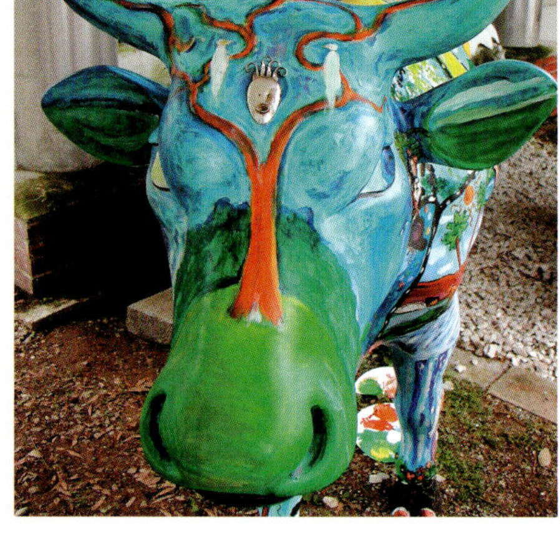

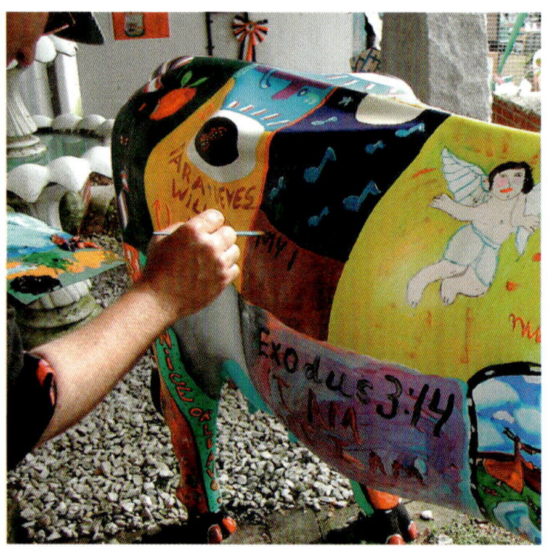

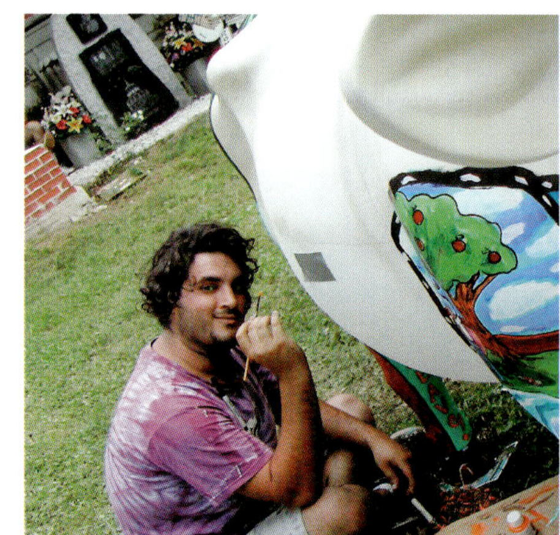

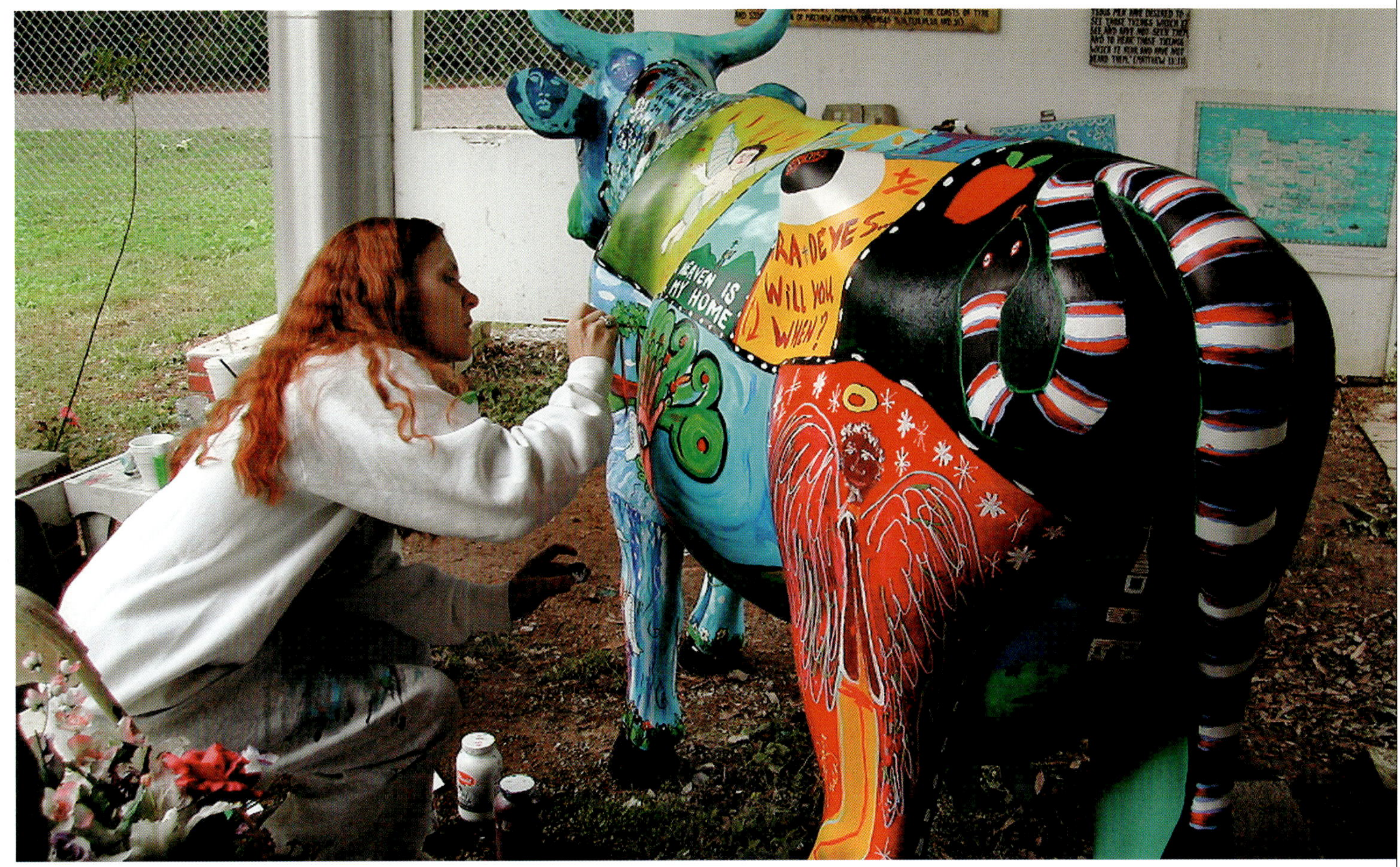
HEAVEN IS MY HOME
Will YOU WHEN?

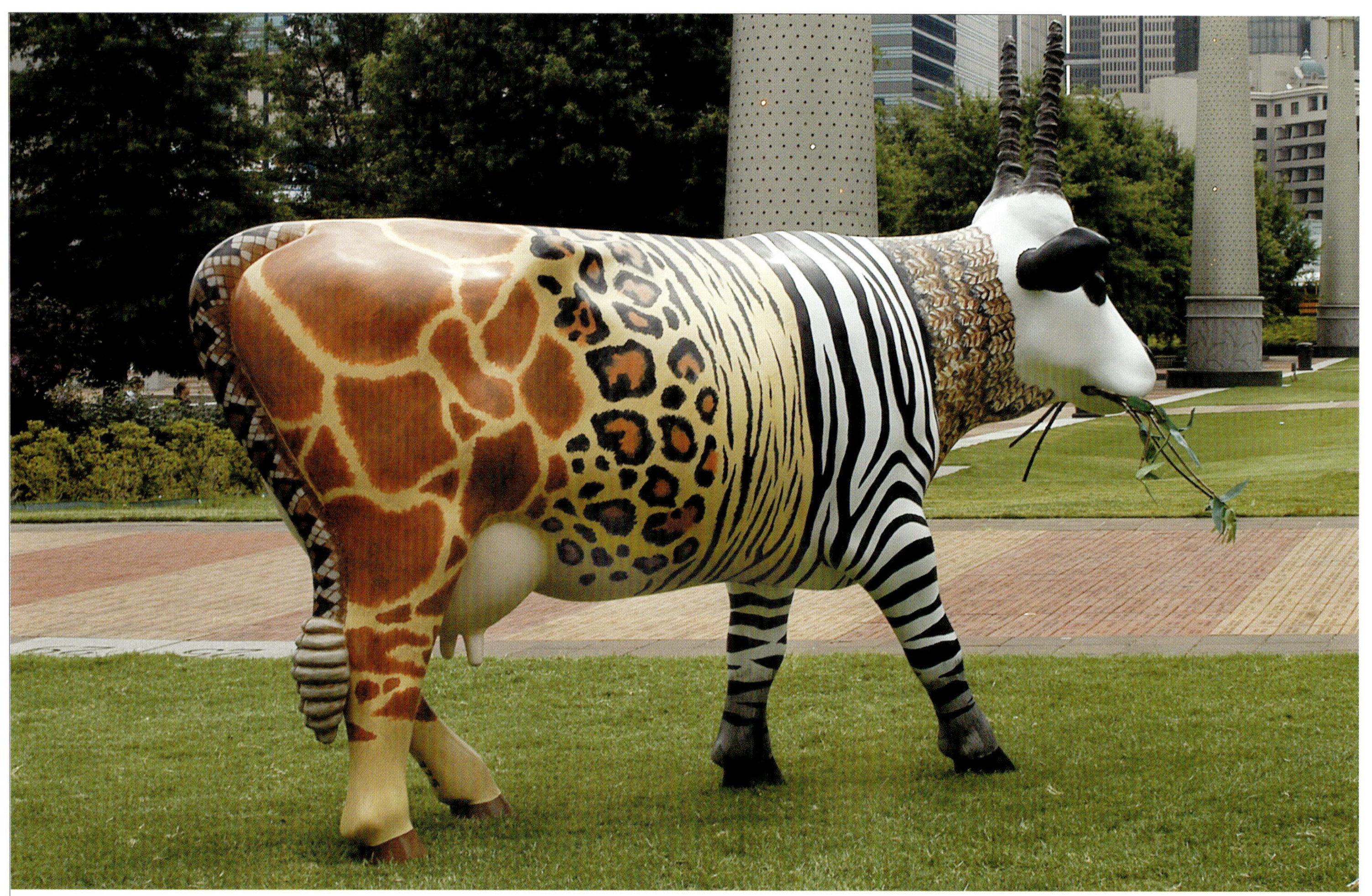

Moo Atlanta
Carol Askren-Armitage
GE Power Systems

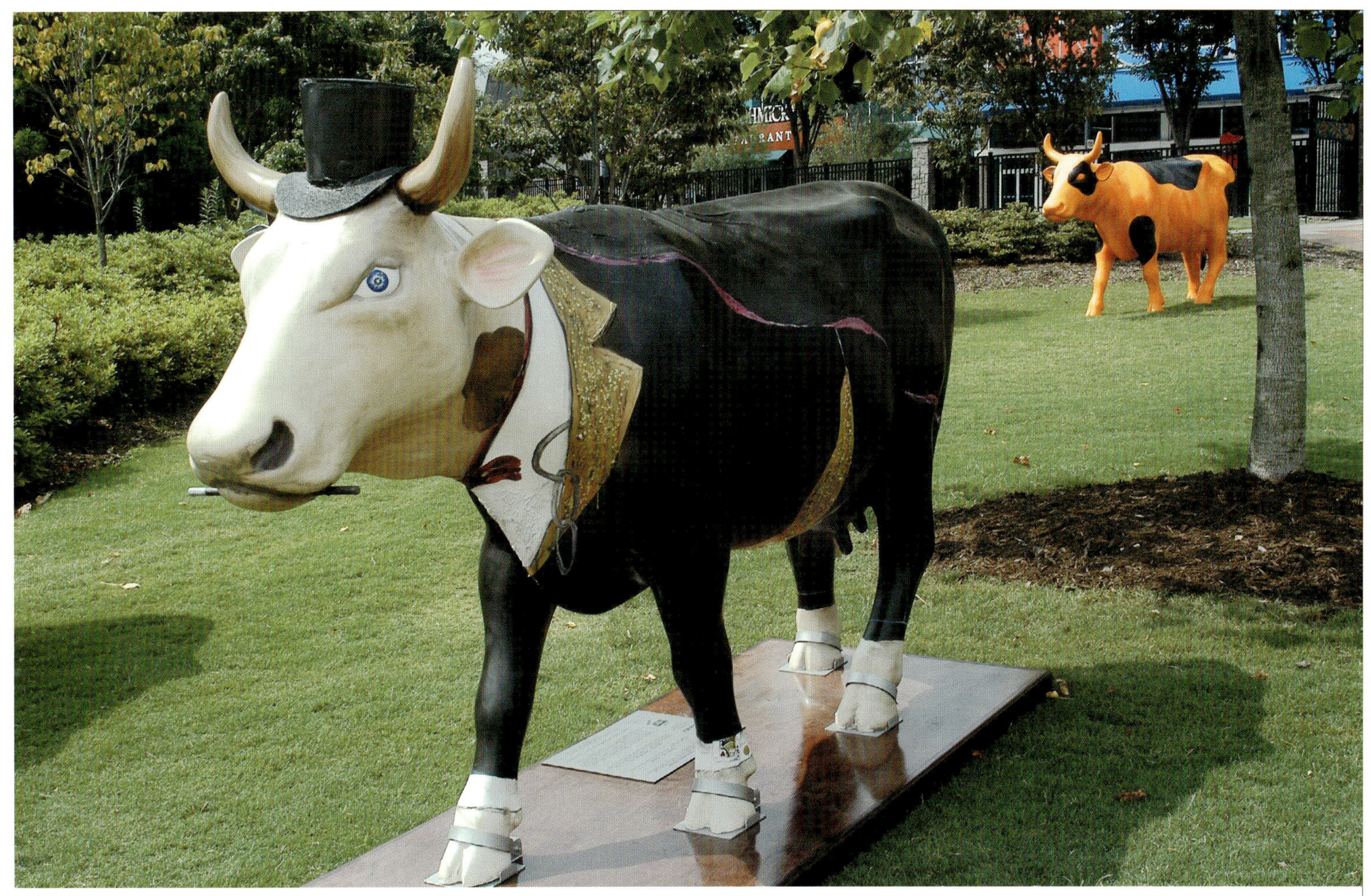

The Amazing Moodini
Udo Wooten
ChoicePoint

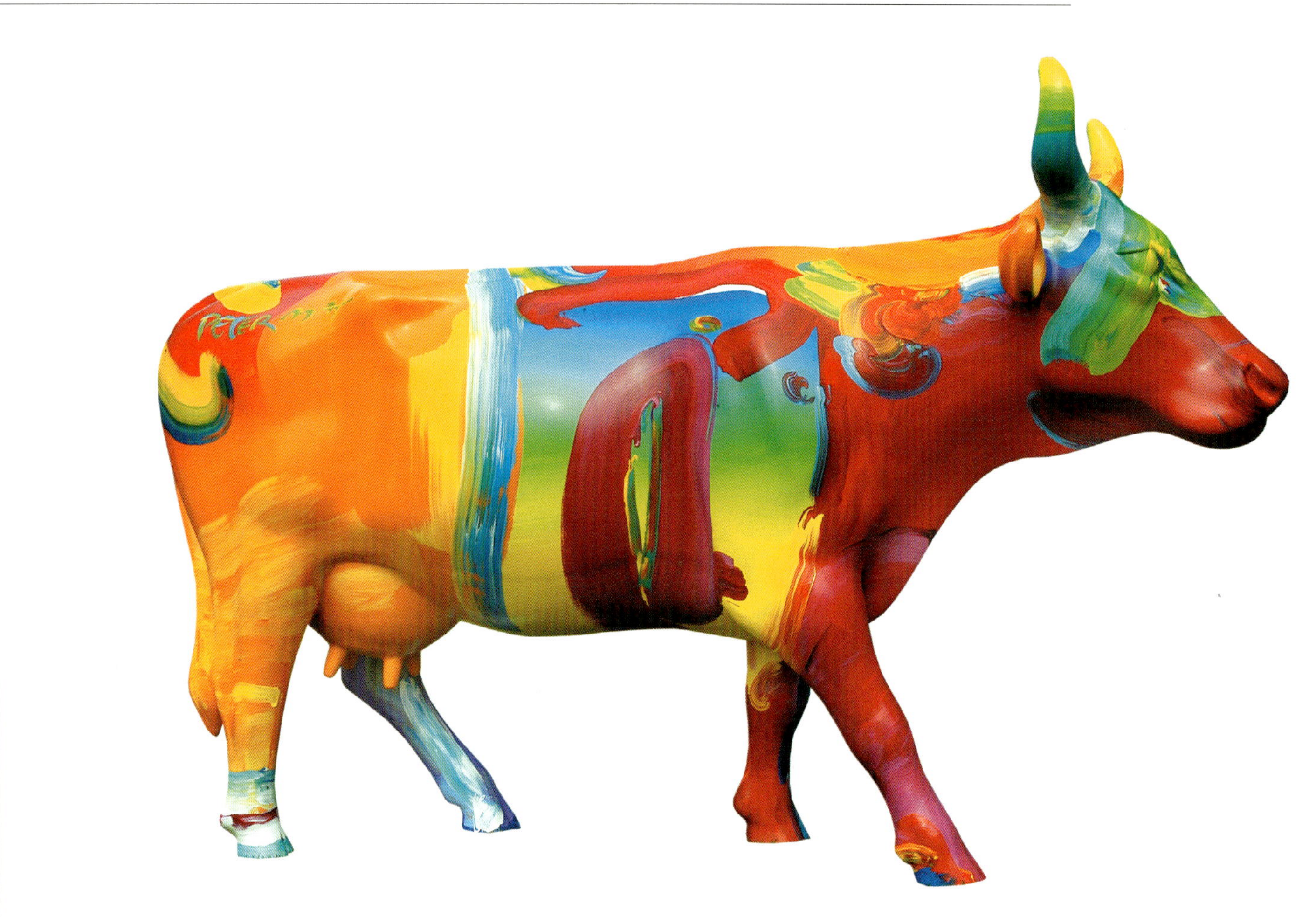

Cindy
Peter Max
The Coca-Cola Company

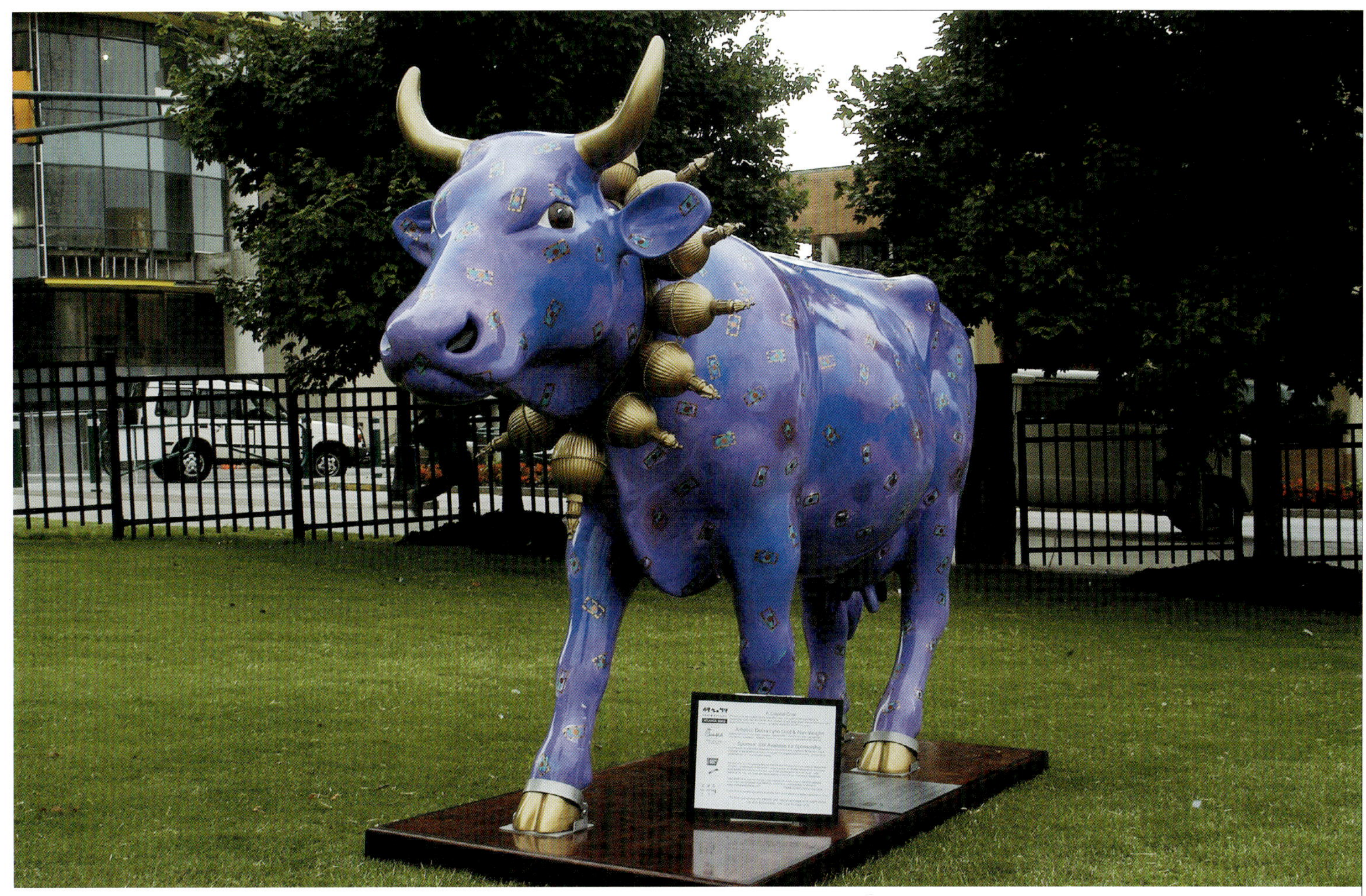

A Capital Cow
Debra Lynn Gold & Alan Vaughn
CowParade Atlanta

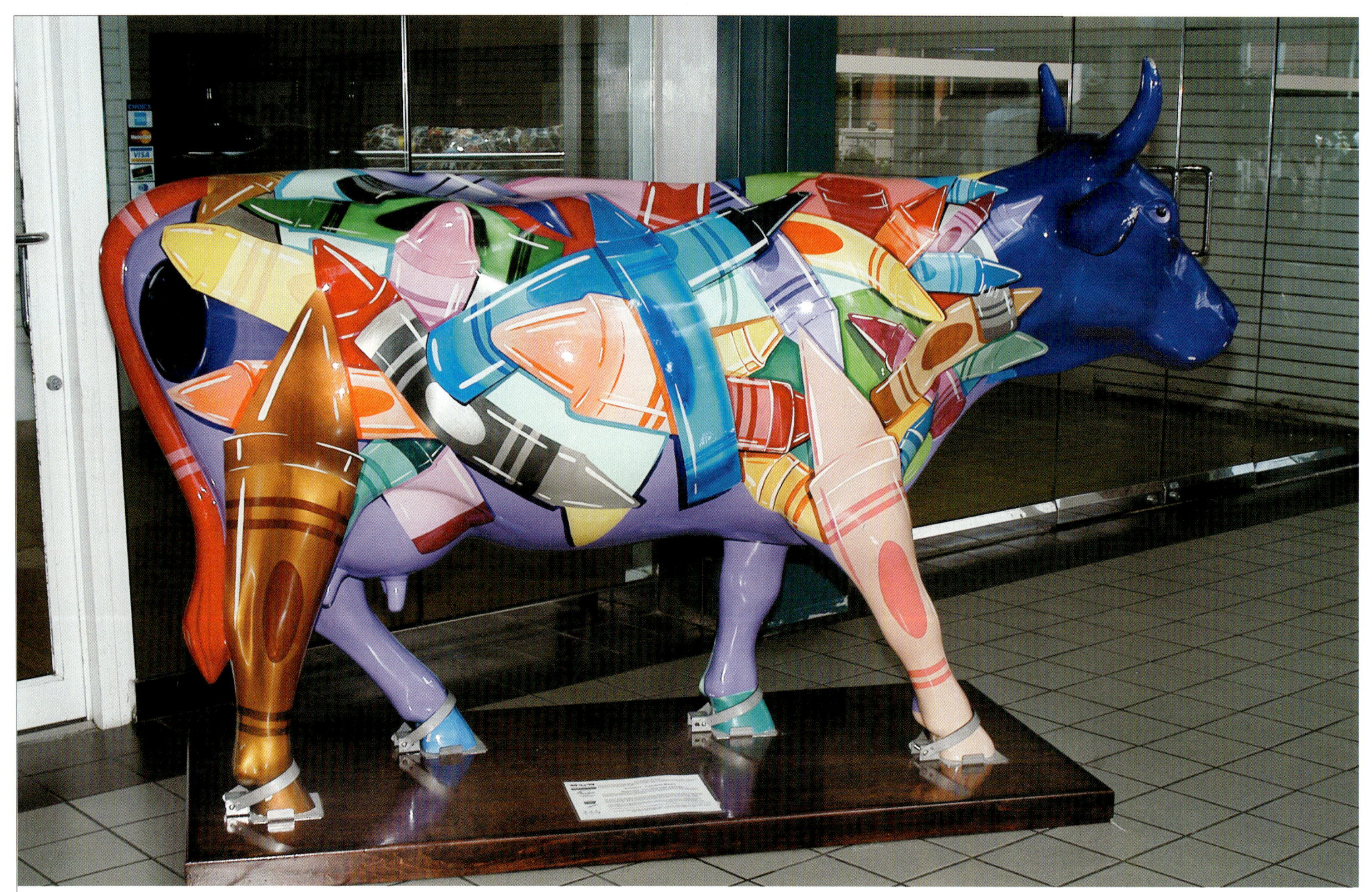

Crayon Cow
Candida Bayer
CowParade Atlanta

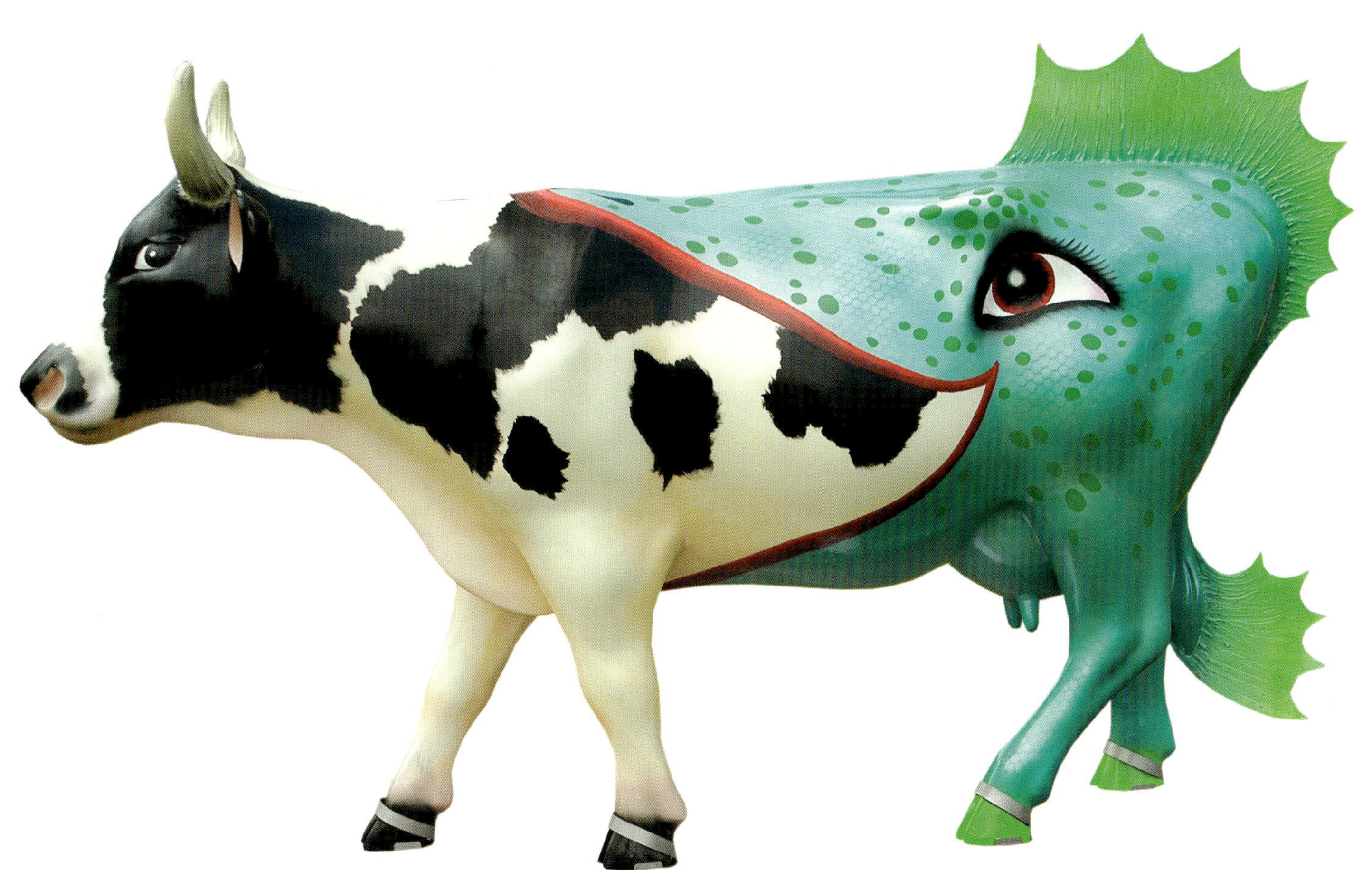

That's Cow It Goes
Justin Winslow
The Coca-Cola Company

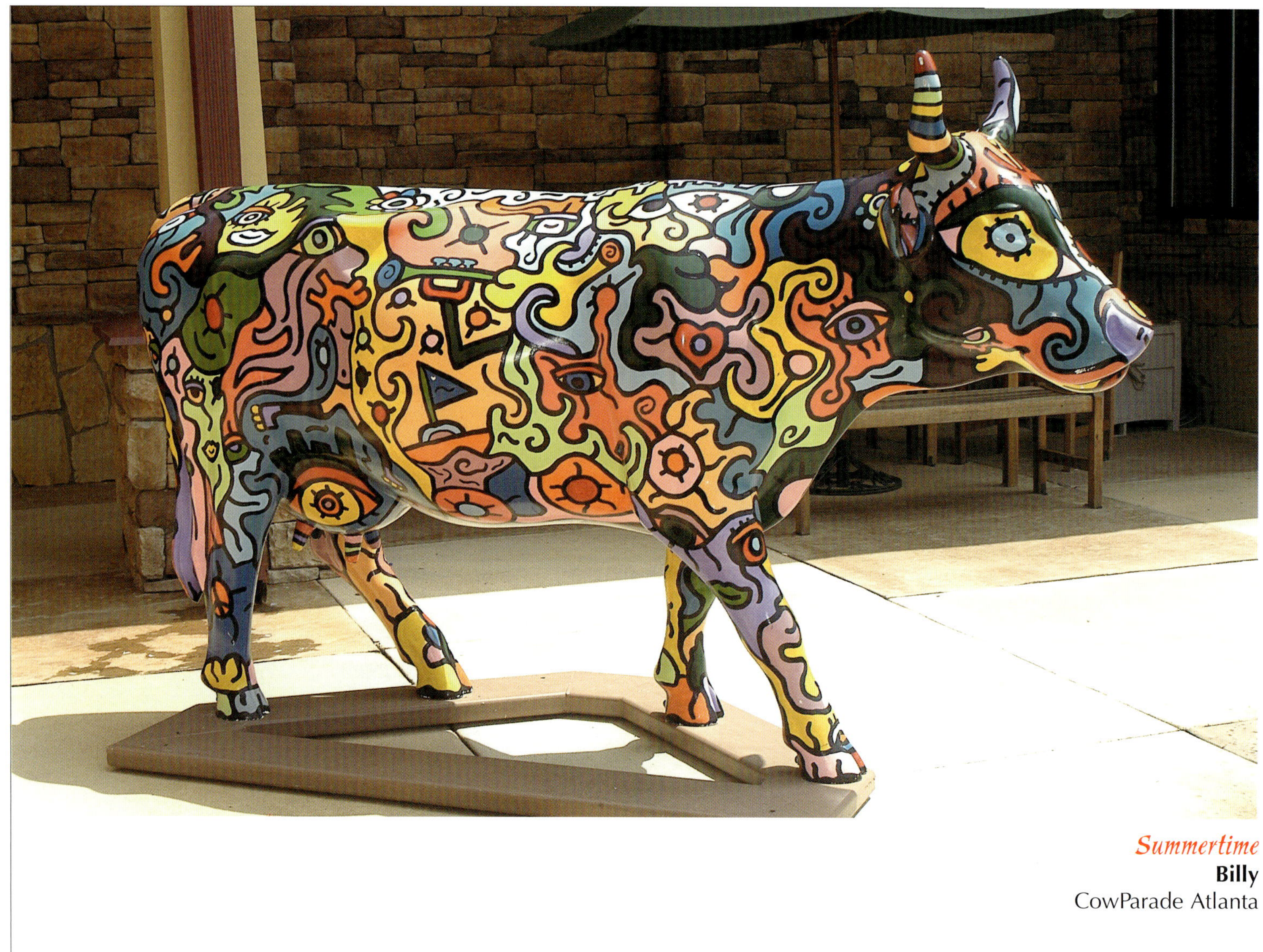

Summertime
Billy
CowParade Atlanta

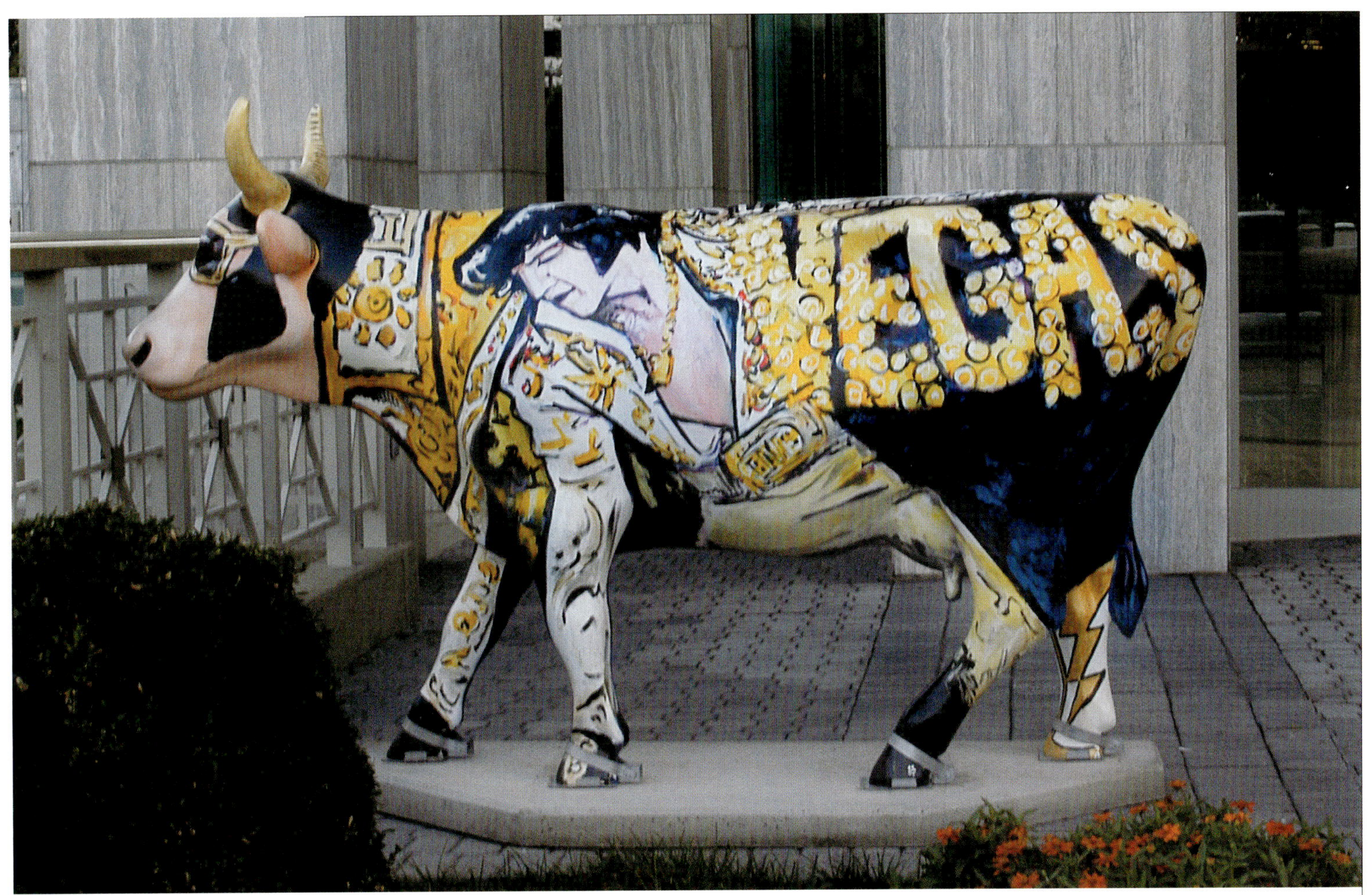

Can't Stop Loving Moo
Stan Mullins
Underground

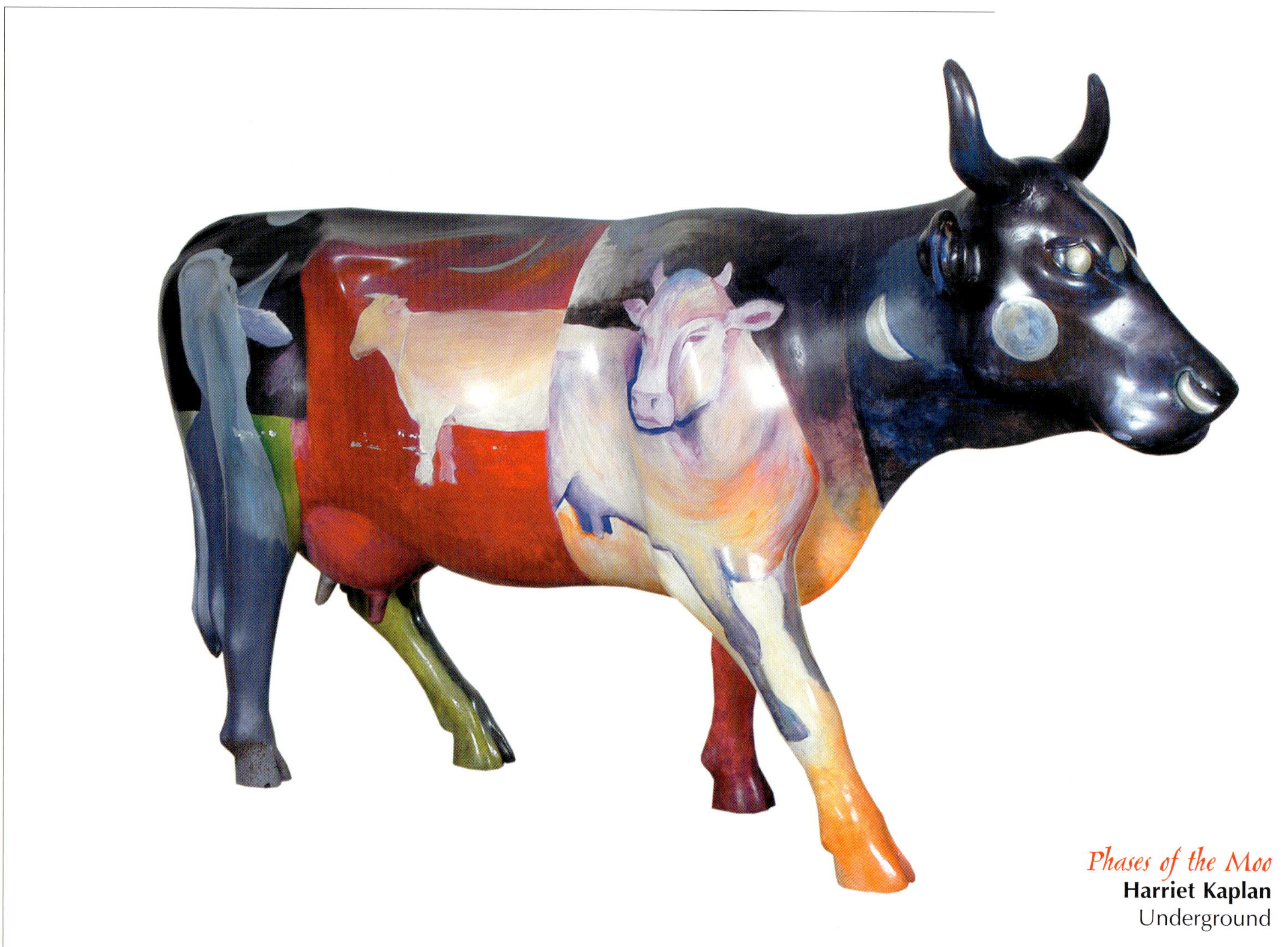

Phases of the Moo
Harriet Kaplan
Underground

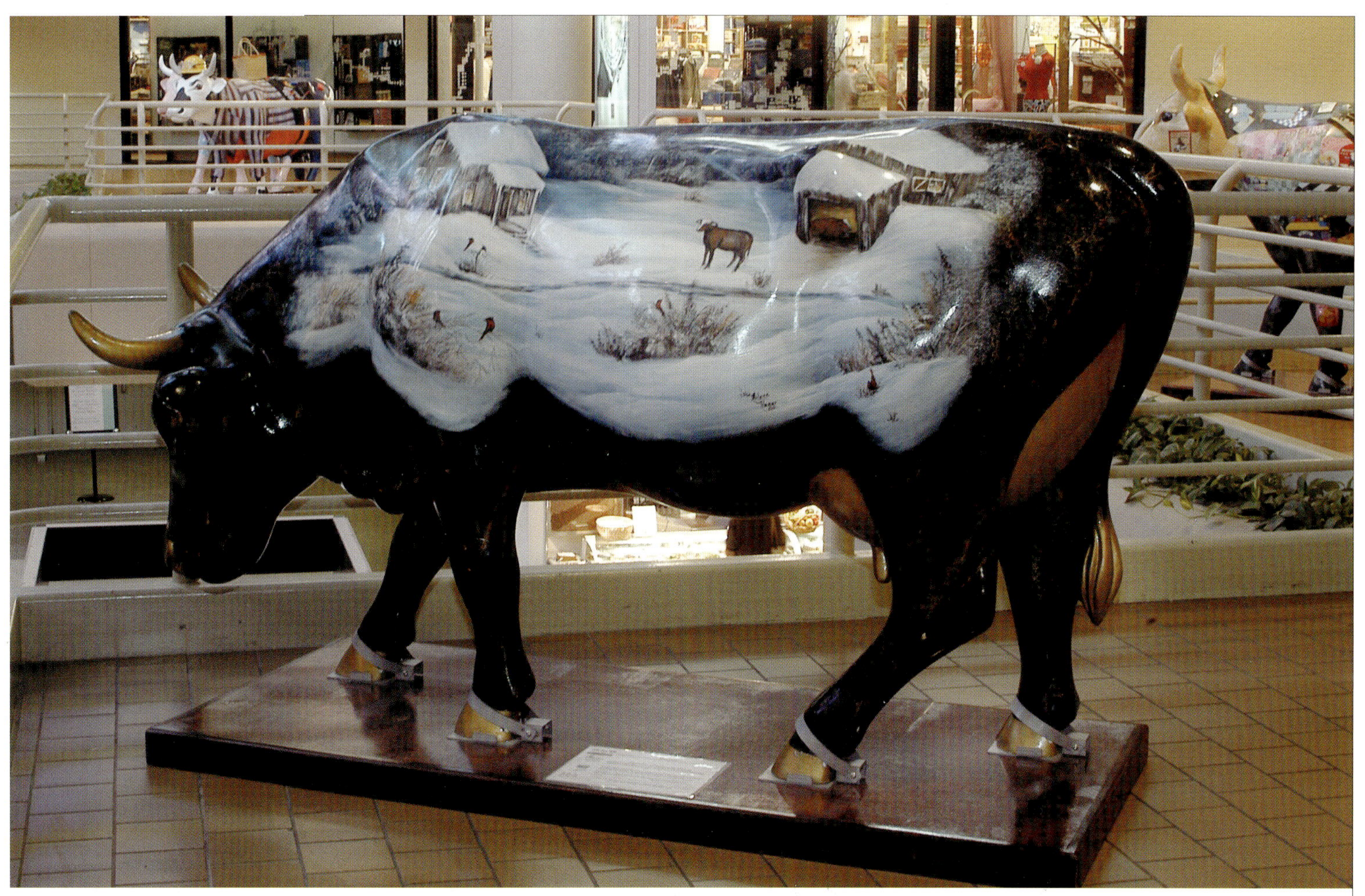

Udderly Moojestic
Arlene Haner
CowParade Atlanta

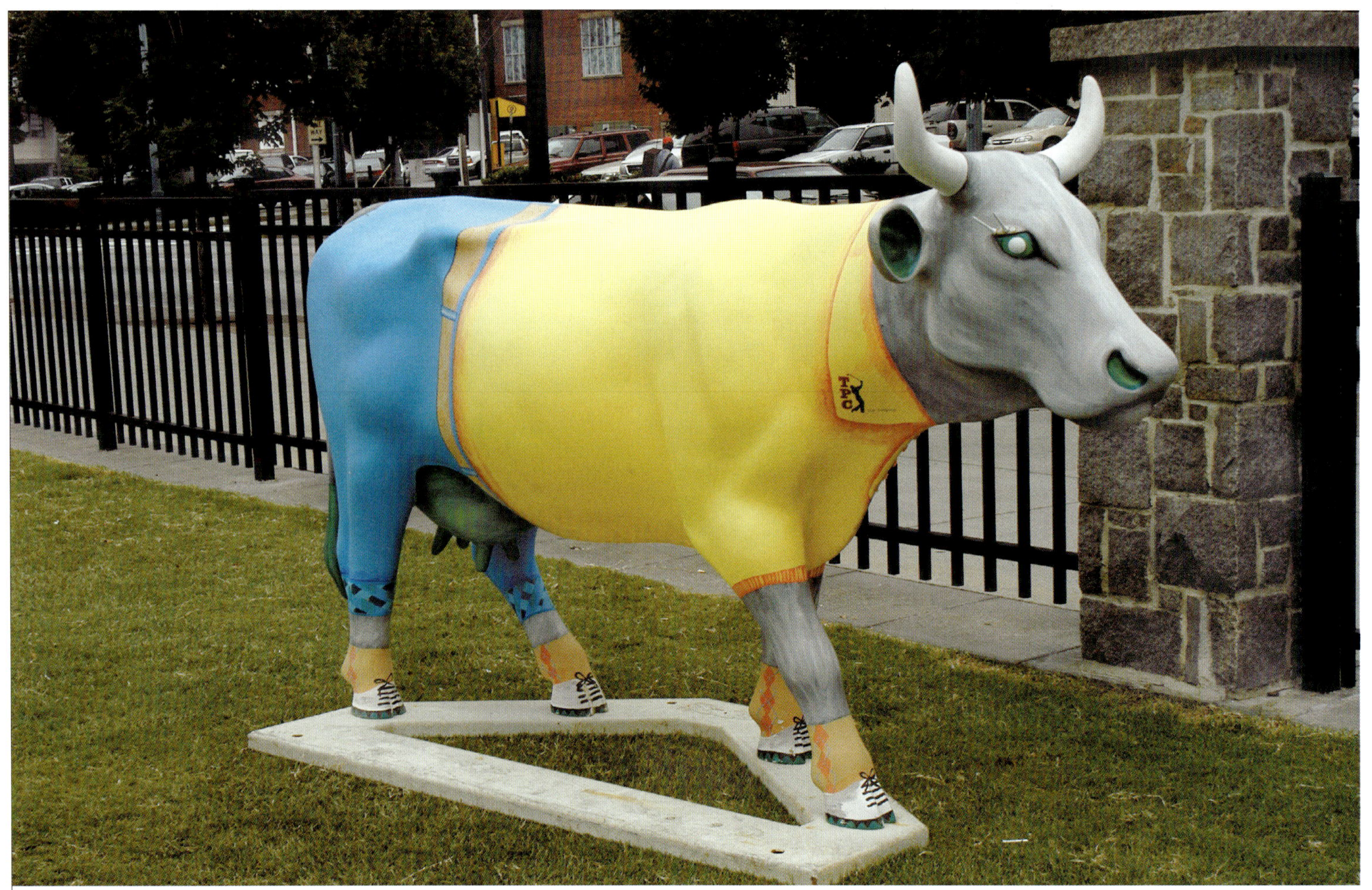

Home on the Range
Marybeth Butman
CowParade Atlanta

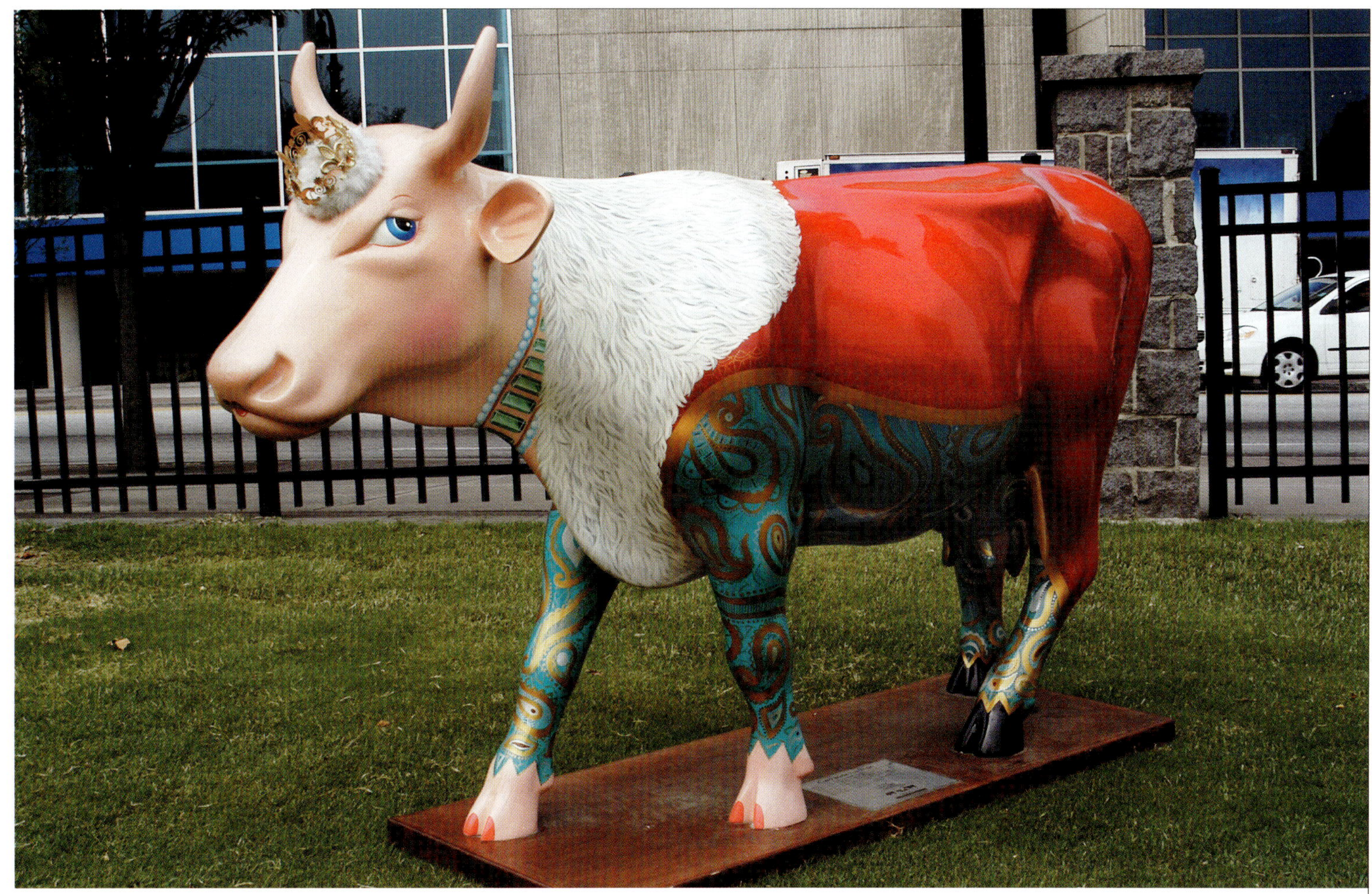

Queene
Mystery Artist
CowParade Atlanta

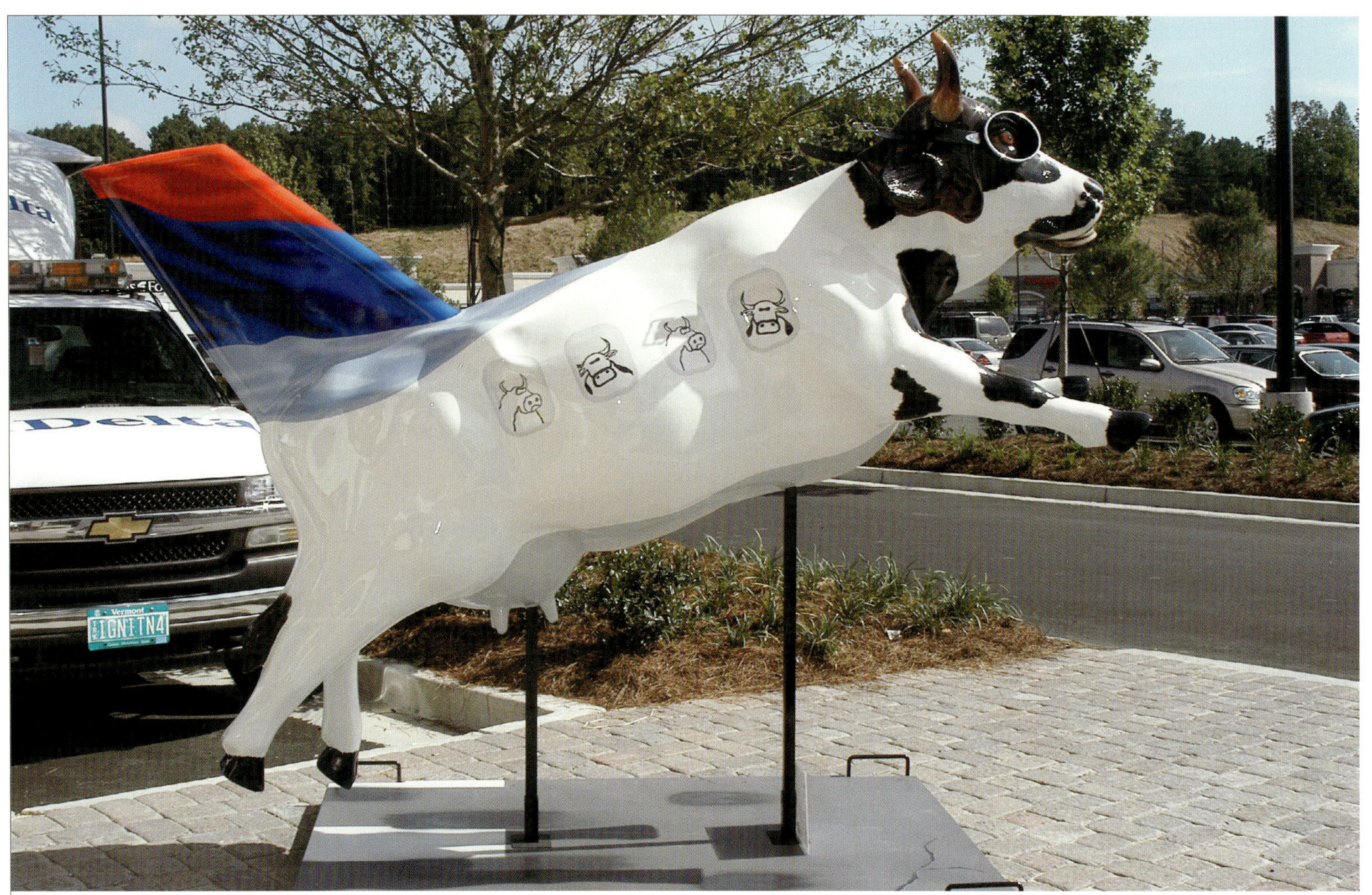

Platinum Moodallion

Delta Air Lines

Delta Air Lines

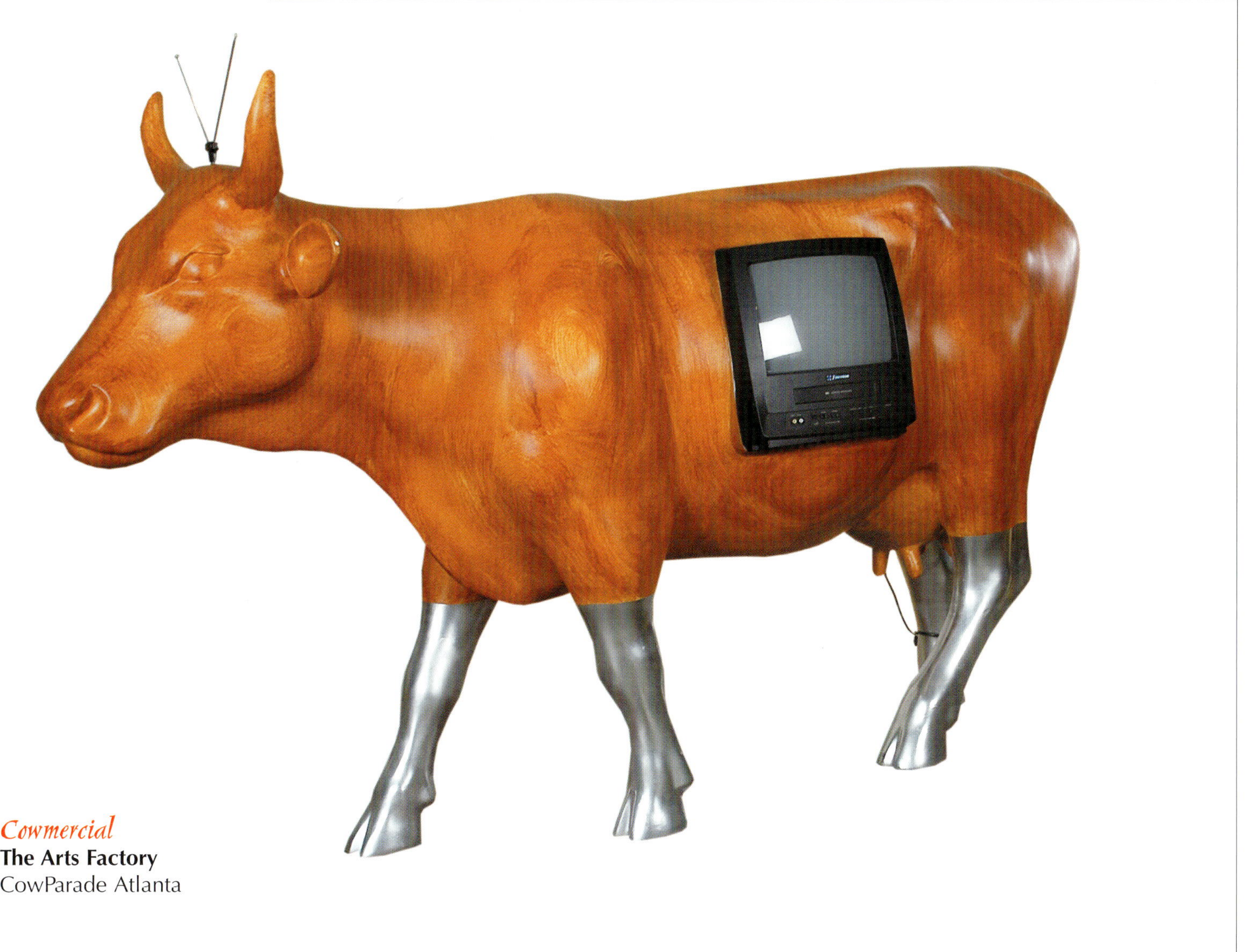

Cowmercial
The Arts Factory
CowParade Atlanta

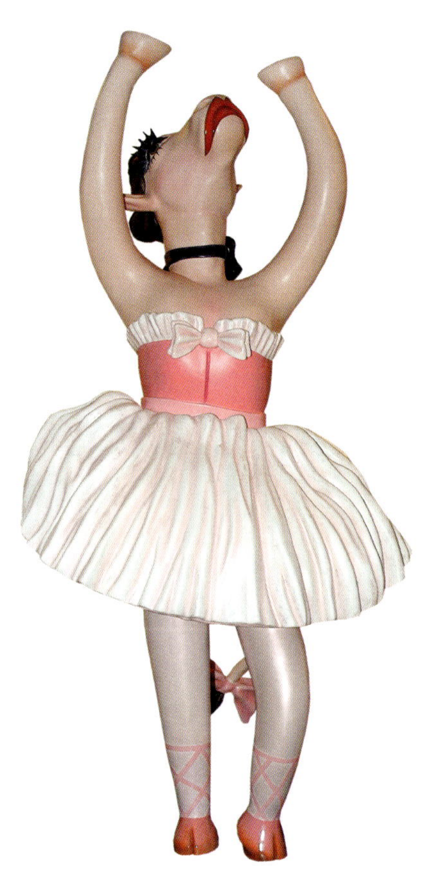

Moo Moo in a Tutu
Silvestri California
Westland Giftware & Museum Company

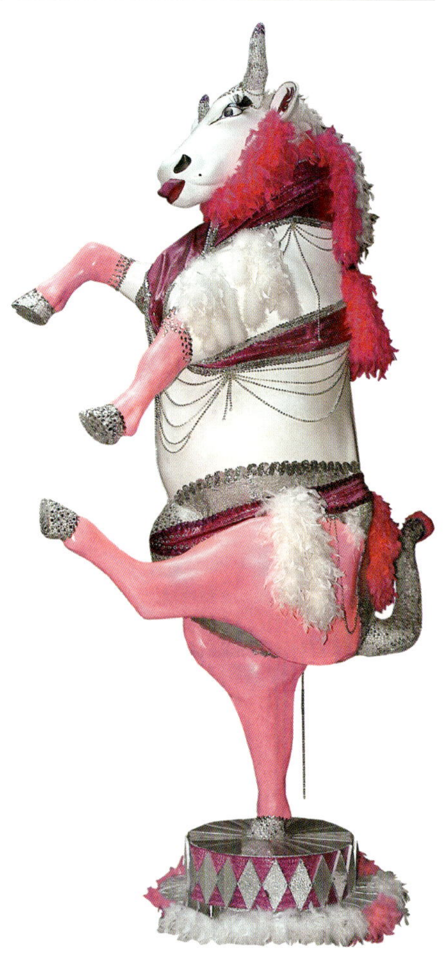

Bovina the Las Vegas Showgirl
Amber Felts
Czarnowski Exhibition Services

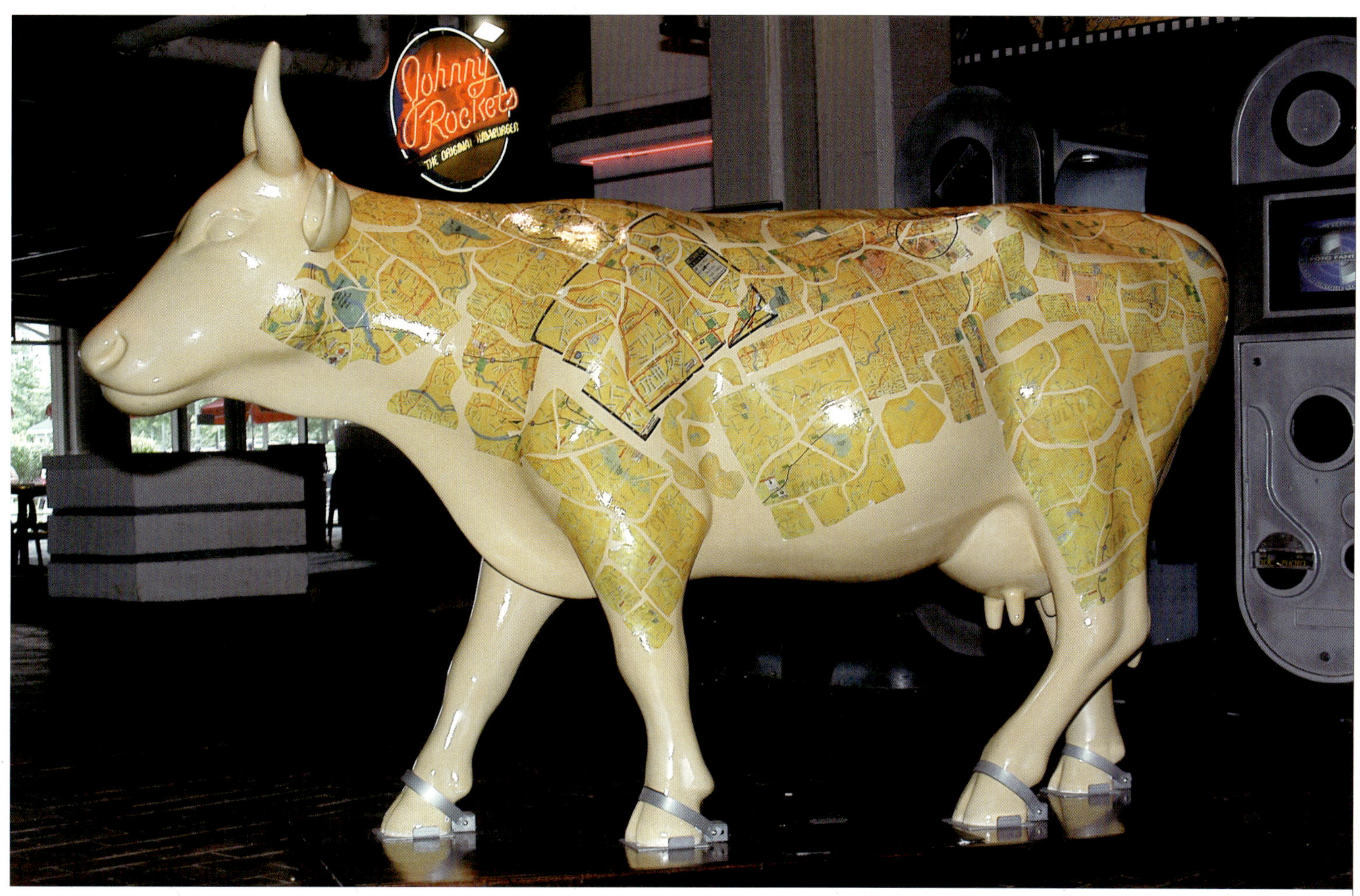

City Cow
Sheena Earl
BeavEx

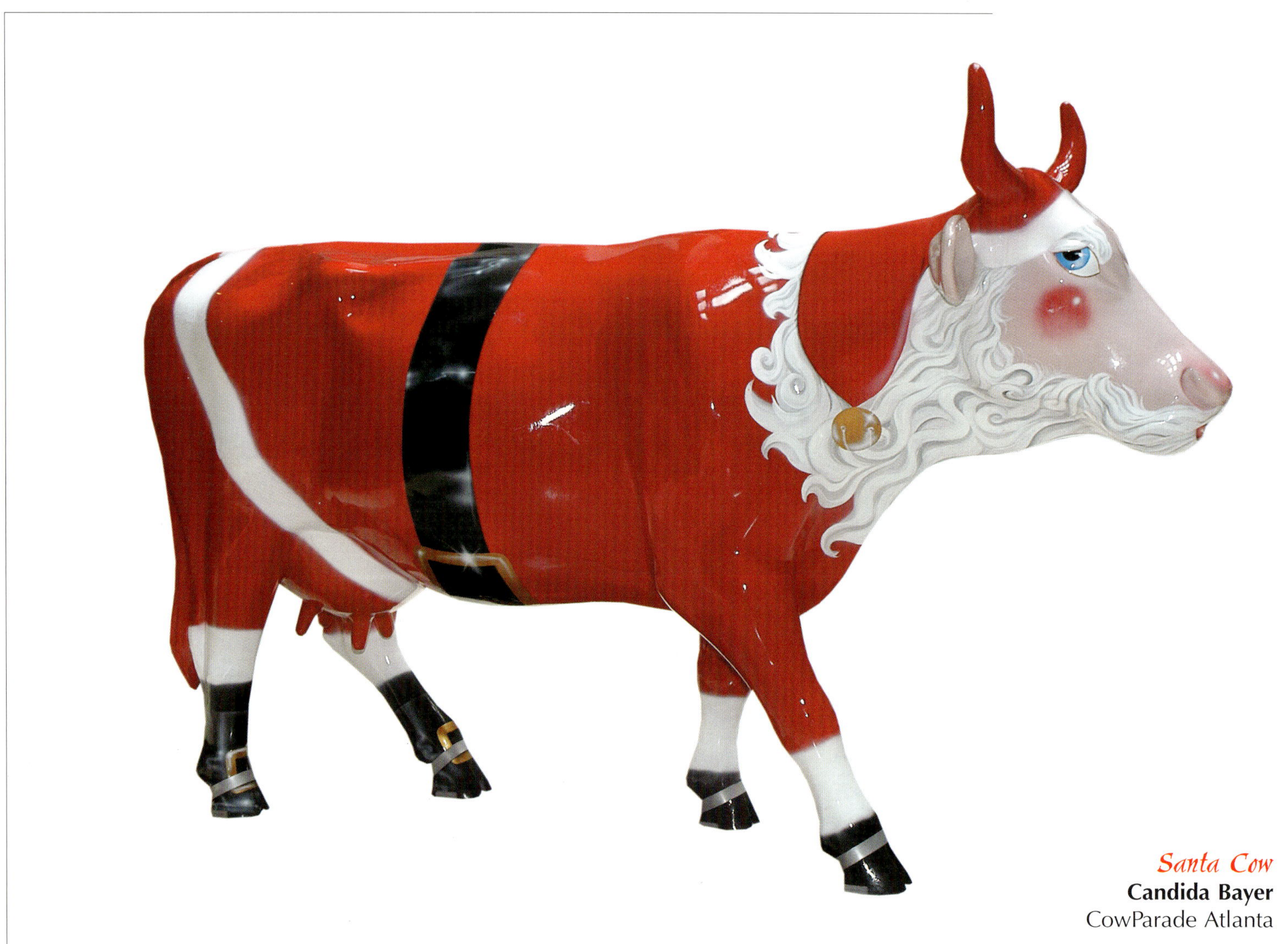

Santa Cow
Candida Bayer
CowParade Atlanta

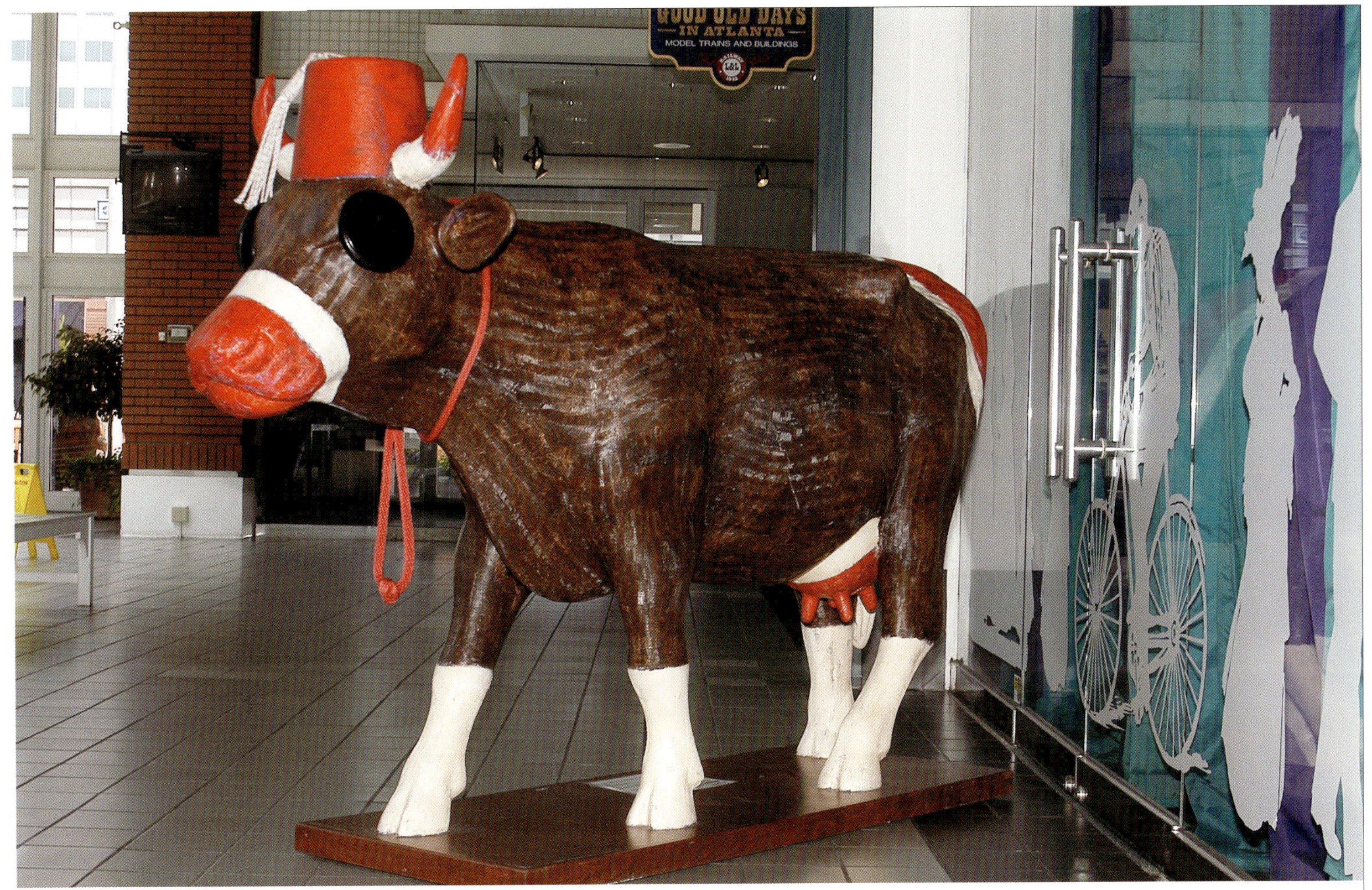

Sock Monkey
Sandra Spencer
CowParade Atlanta

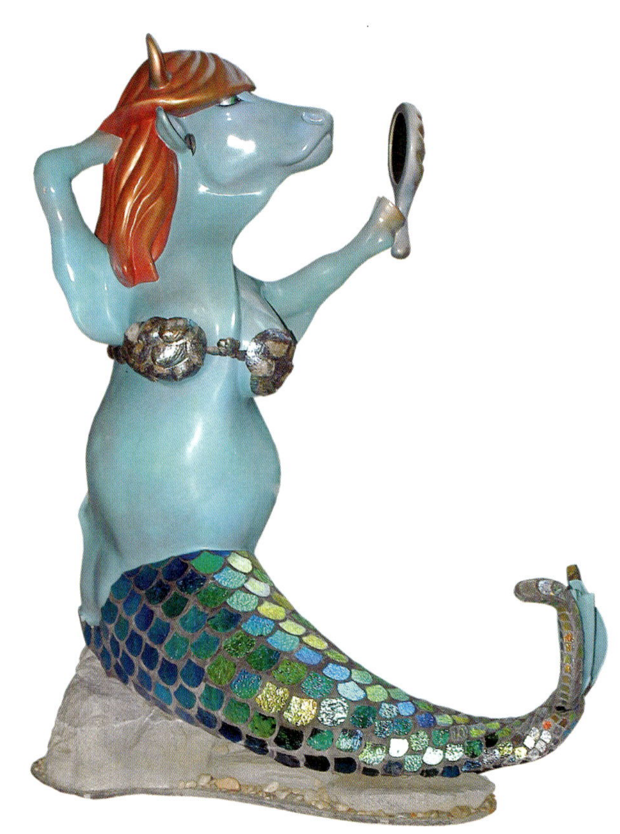

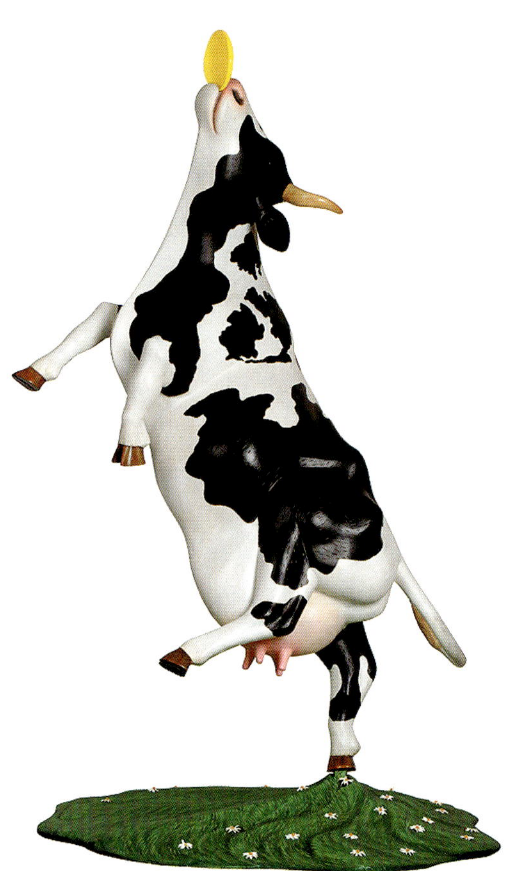

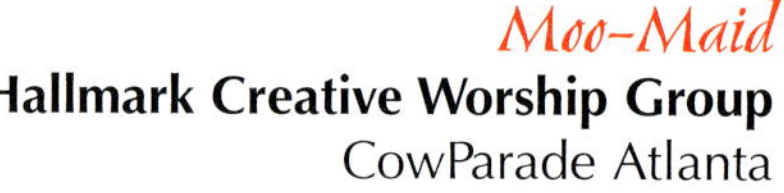

Moo-Maid
Hallmark Creative Worship Group
CowParade Atlanta

Daisy's Dream
Randy Gilman
CowParade Atlanta

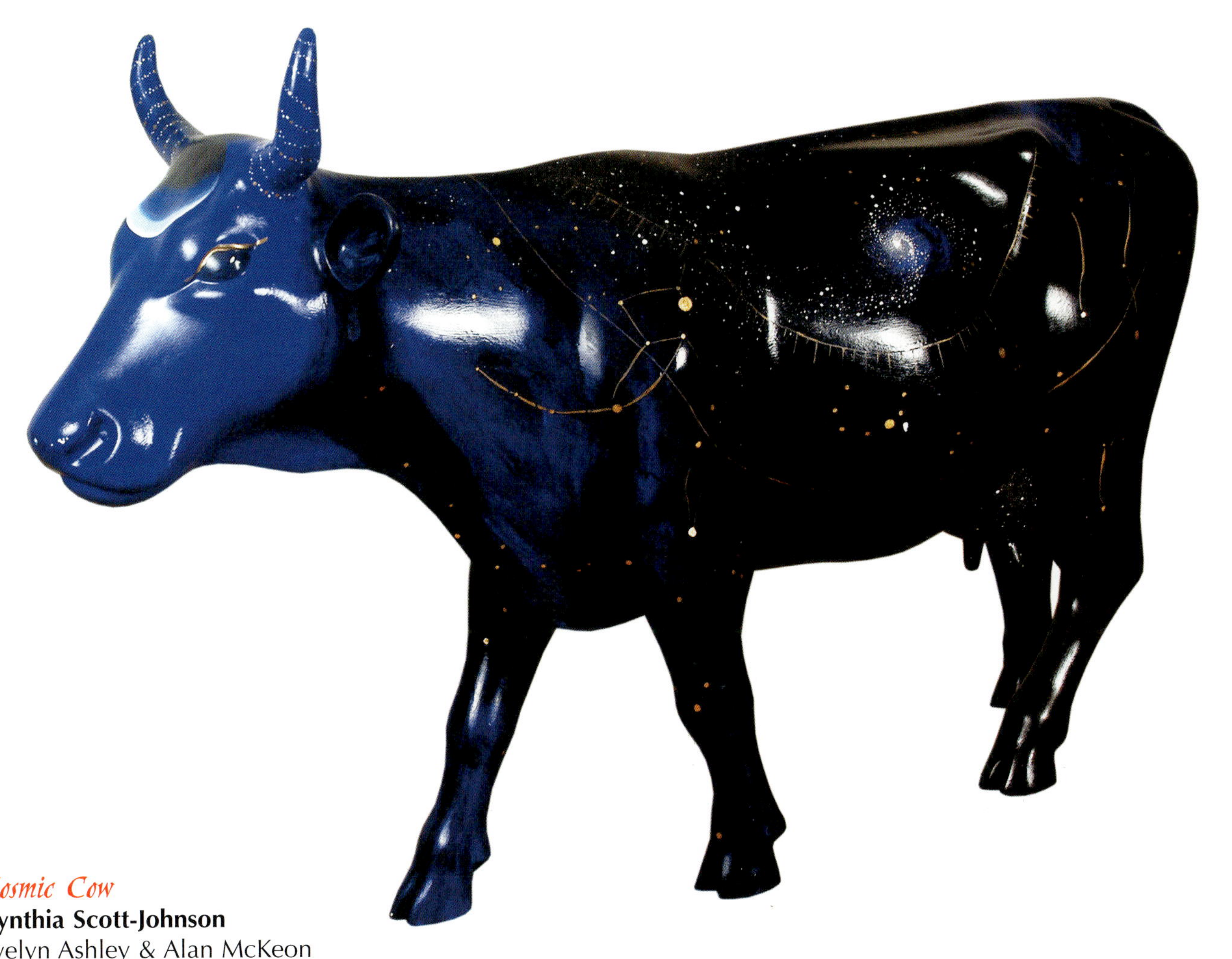

Cosmic Cow
Cynthia Scott-Johnson
Evelyn Ashley & Alan McKeon

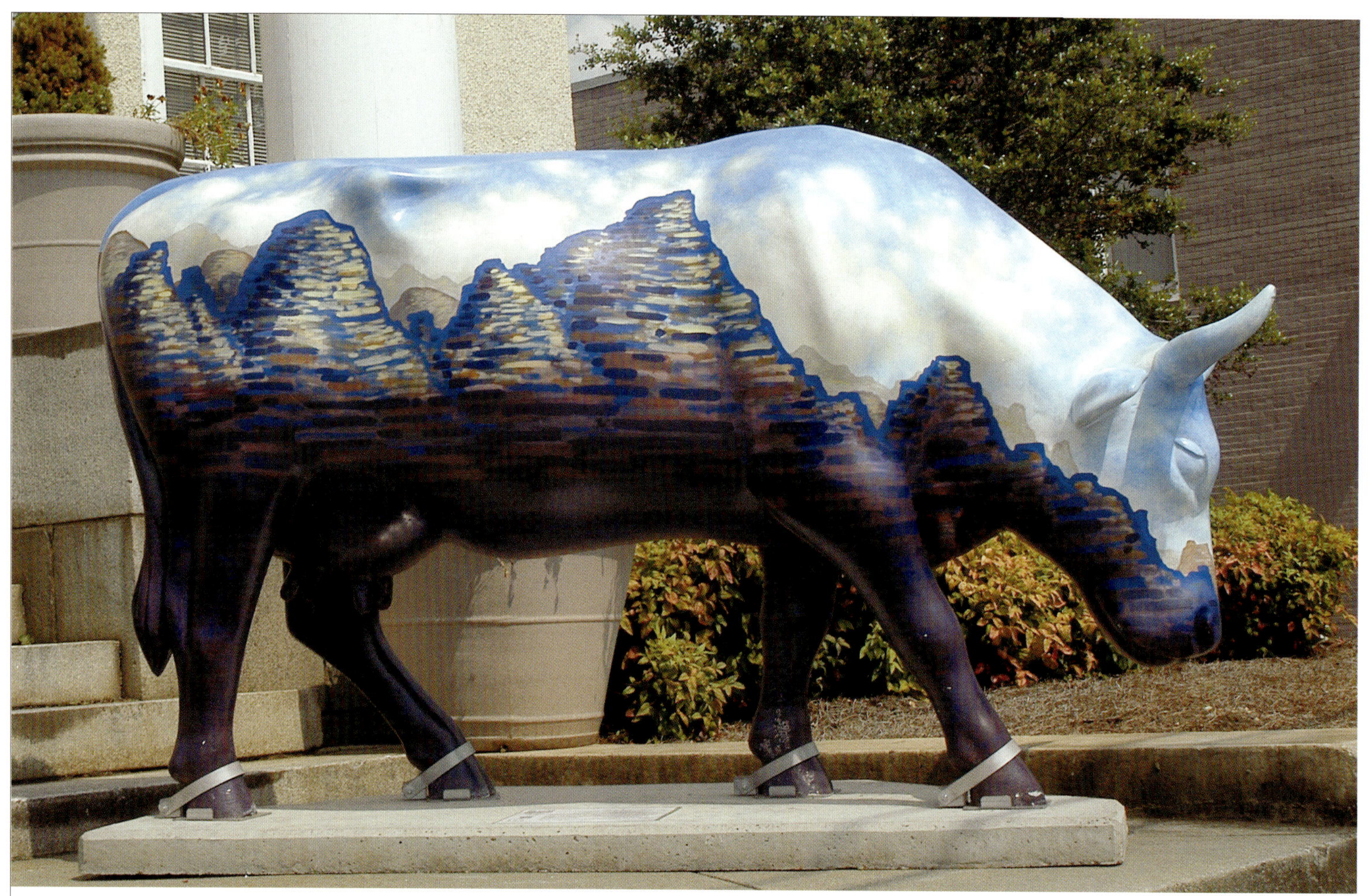

Hoofin' It
The Arts Factory
CowParade Atlanta

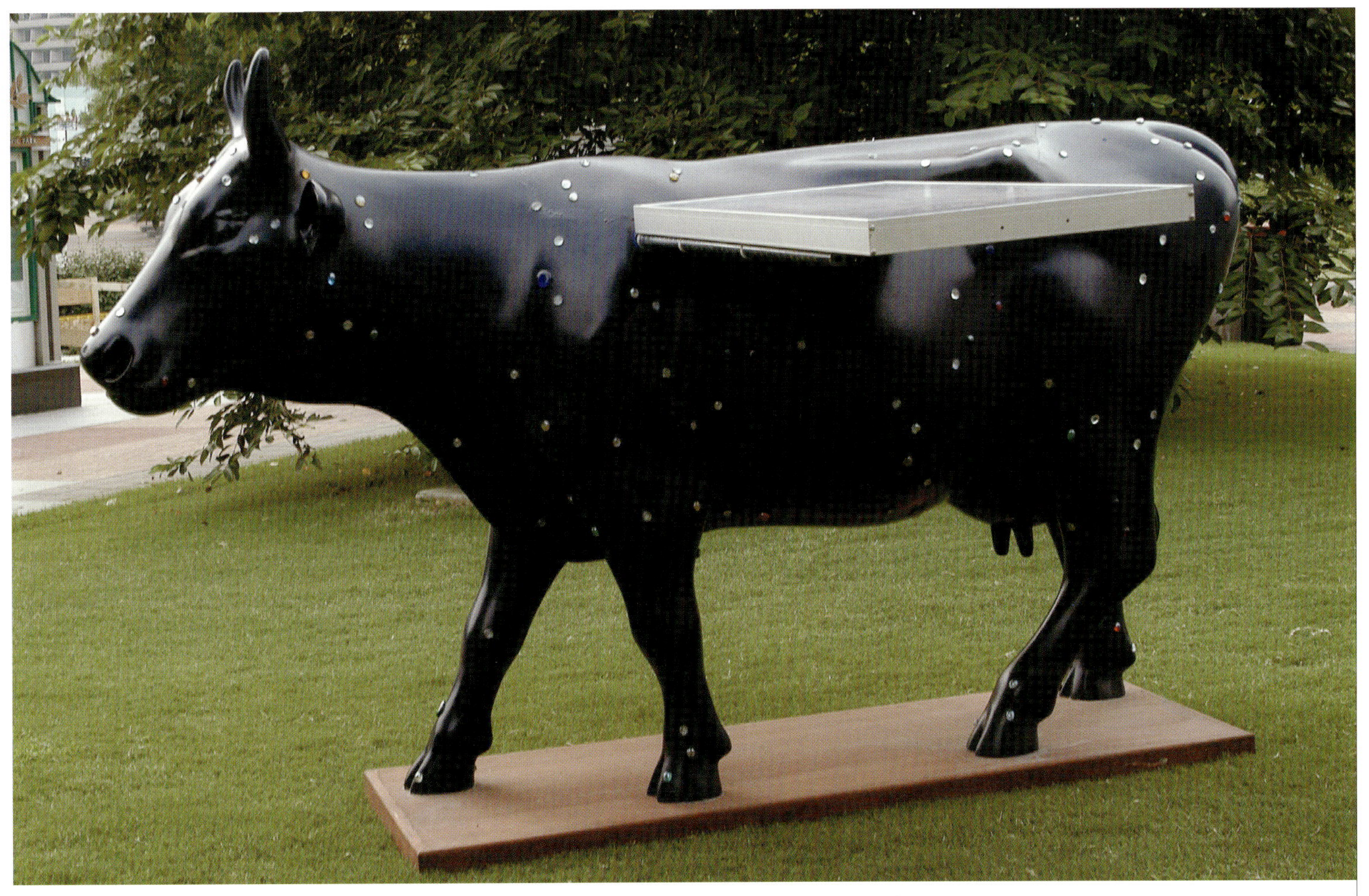

Power to MOOve
H. Kathleen Gresham
CowParade Atlanta

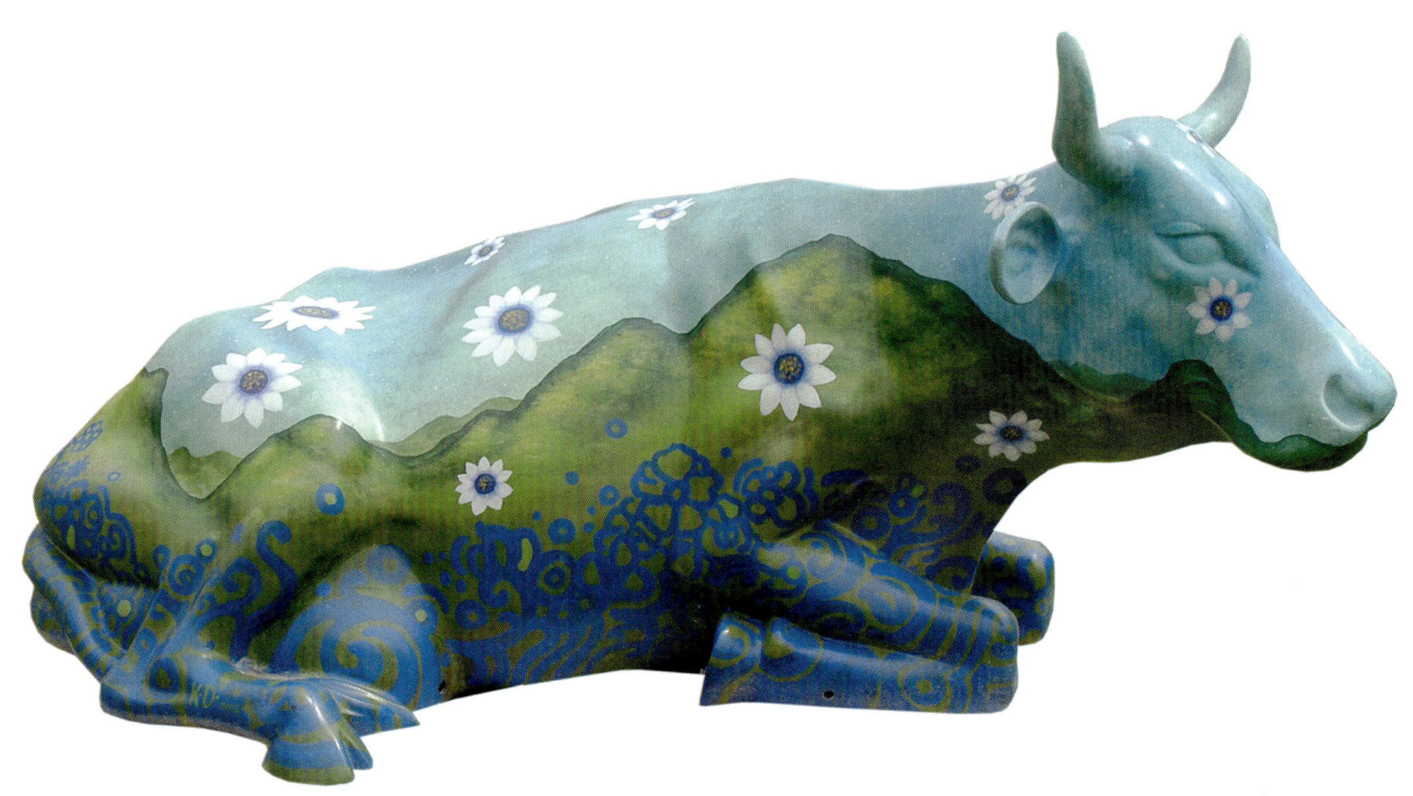

Greener Pastures
The Arts Factory
CowParade Atlanta

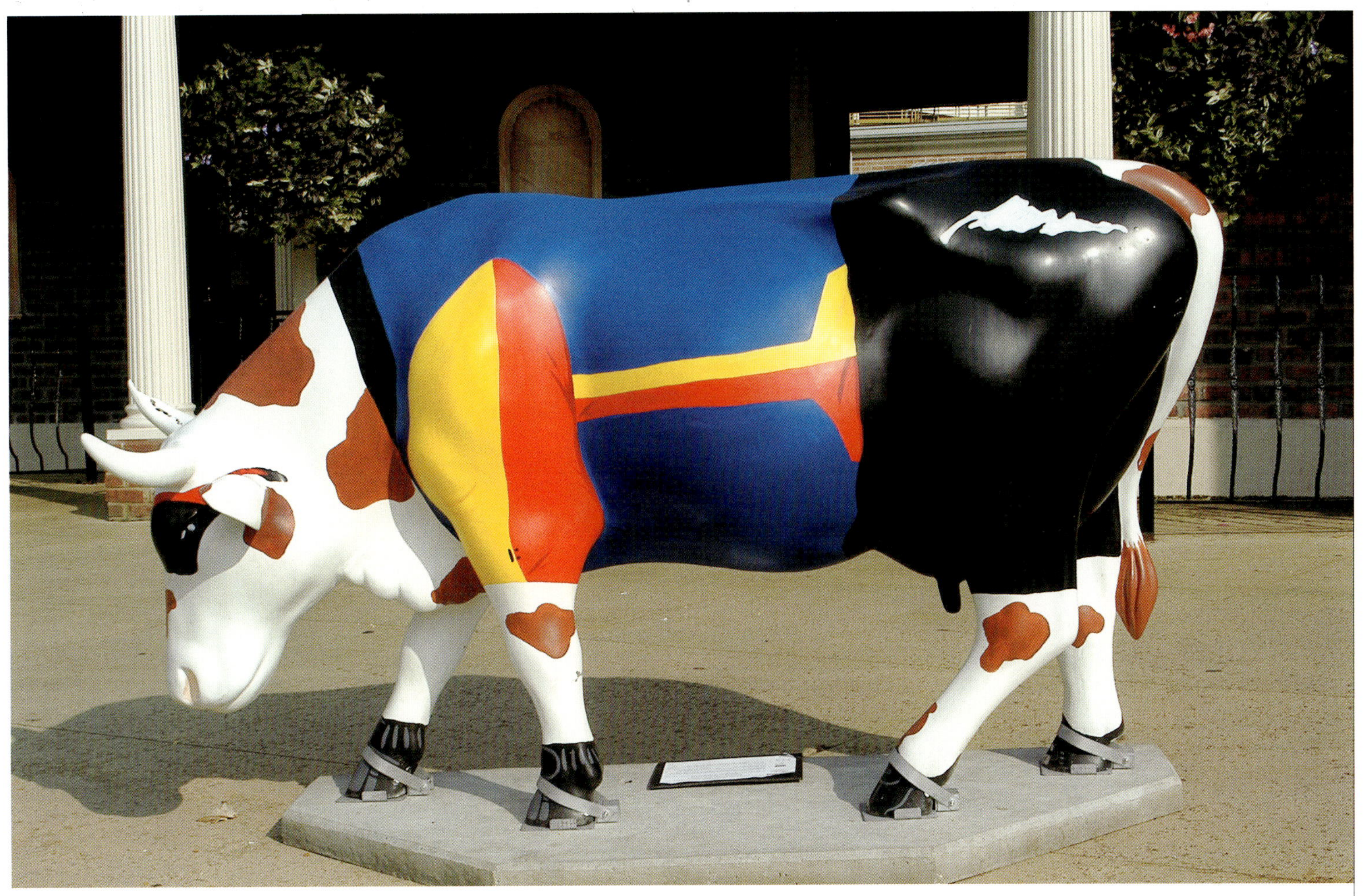

Bull Riders
The Arts Factory
Underground

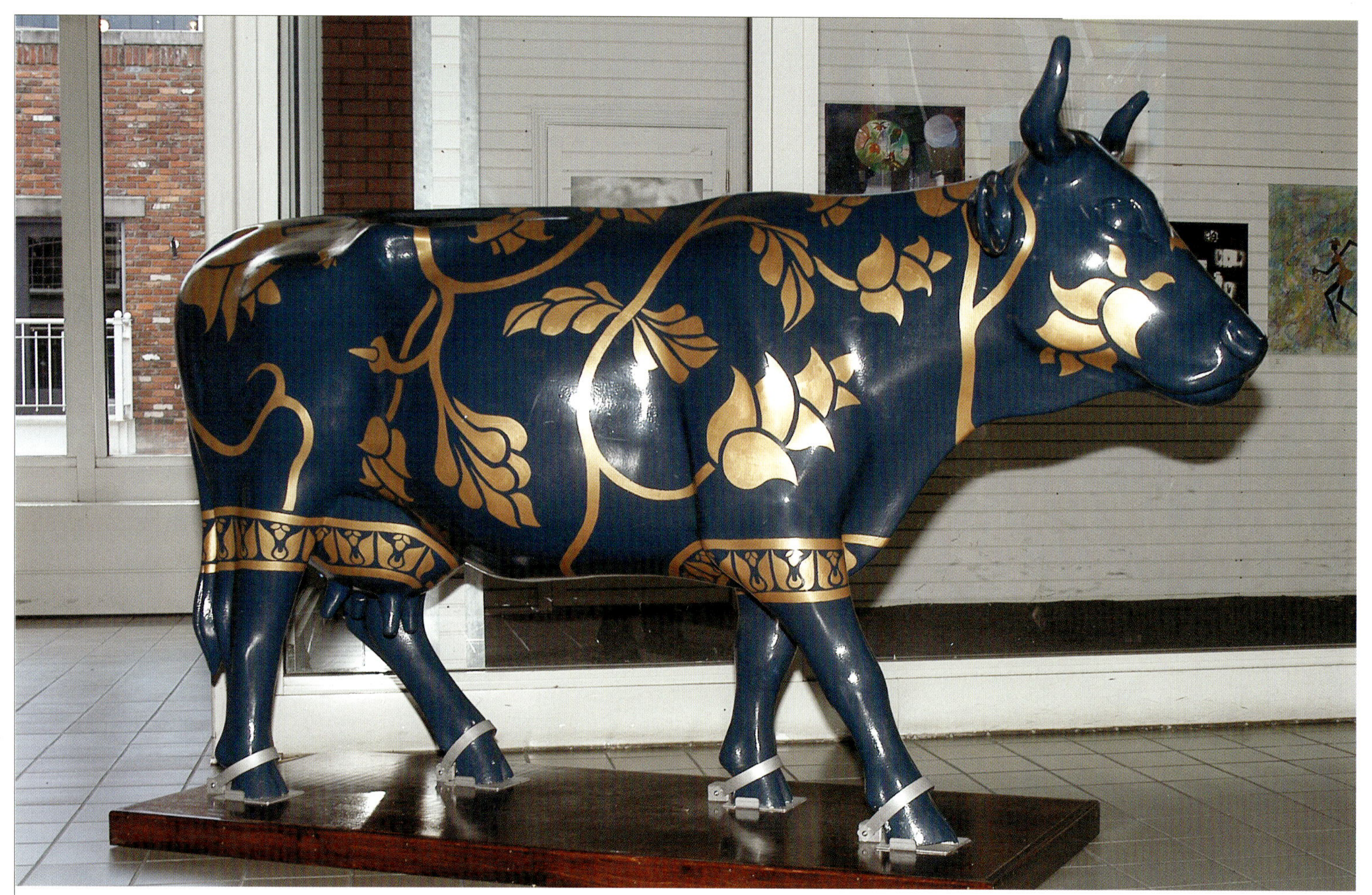

Moojestic
John Wanczyk
CowParade Atlanta

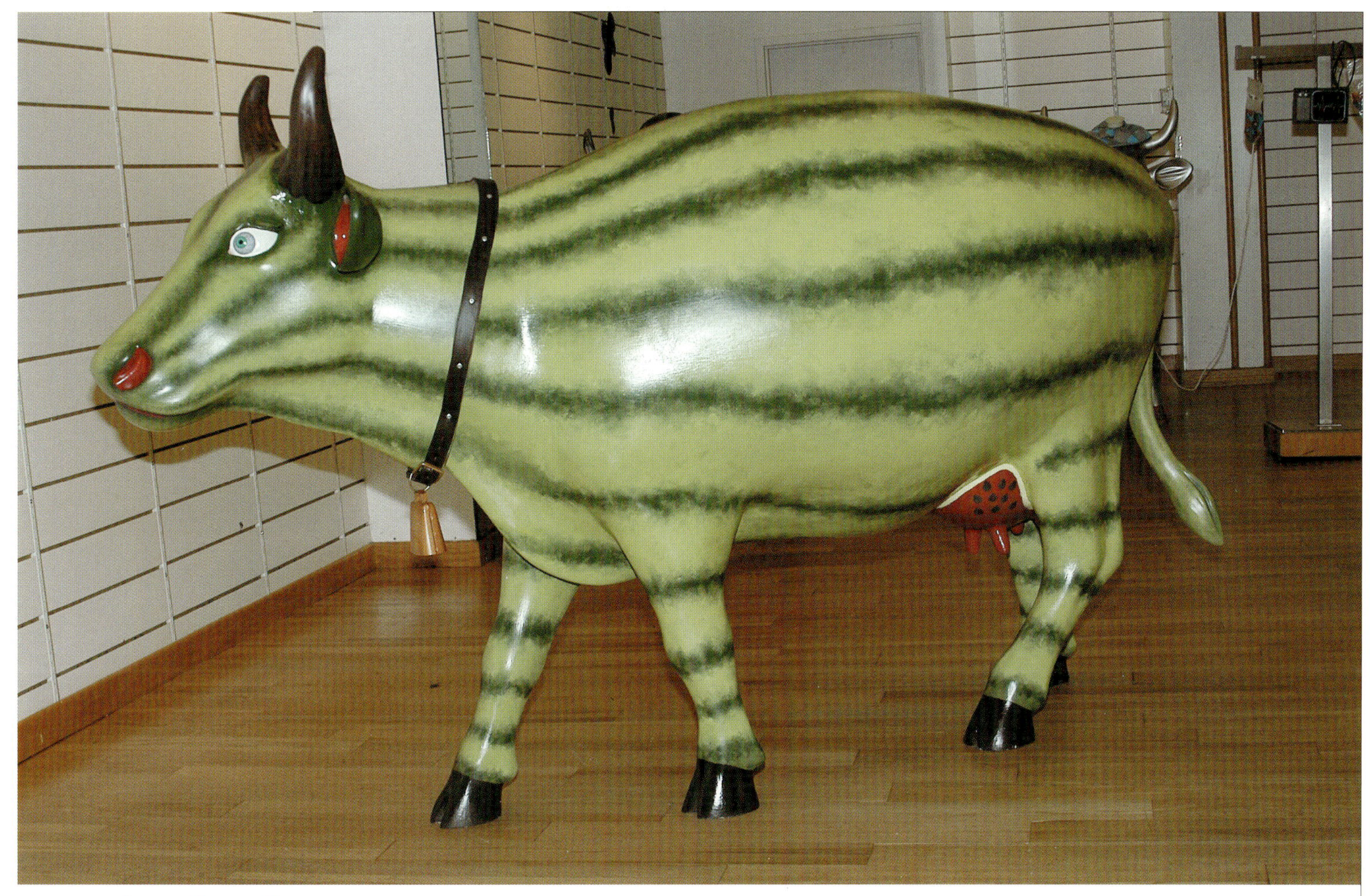

Watermelon Helen and Crazy Crow Cousins
Kate Royal
Resurgens Orthopedics

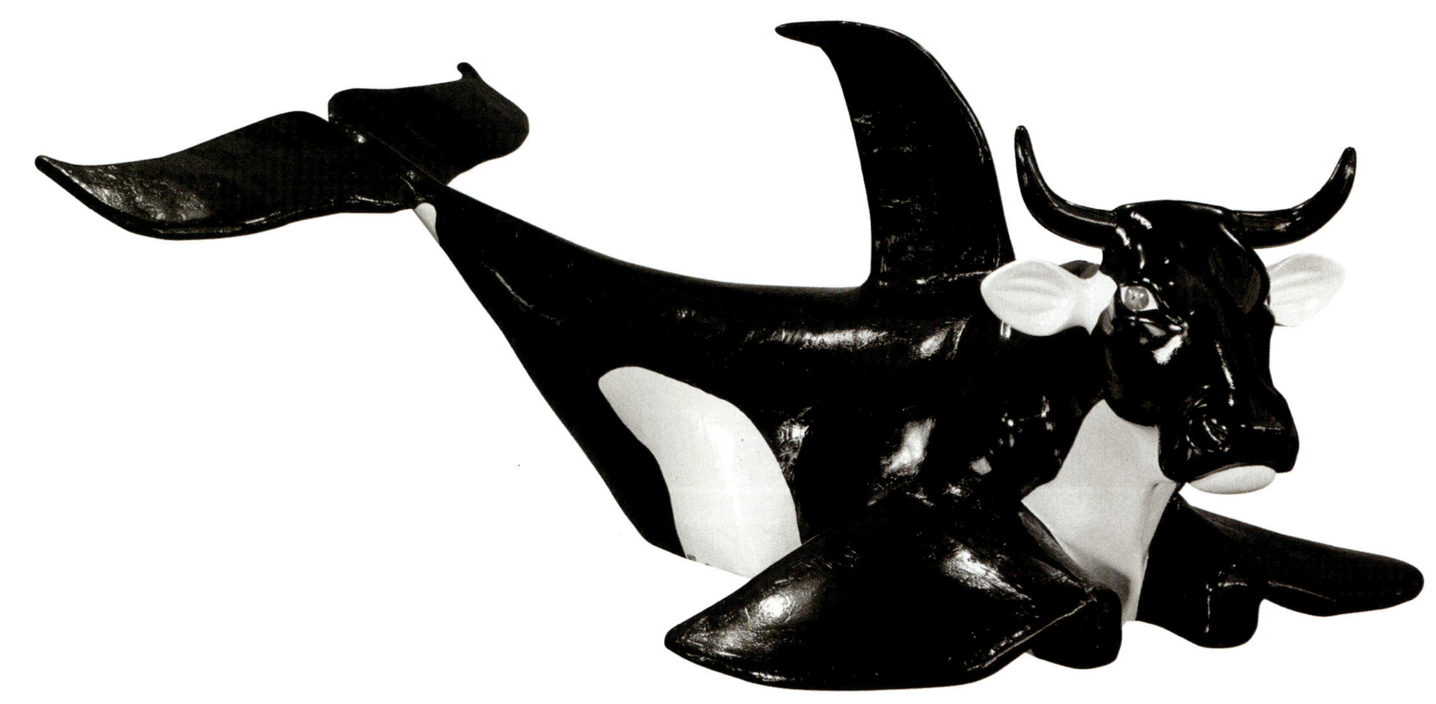

Shamoo
Harmony Middle School
CowParade Atlanta

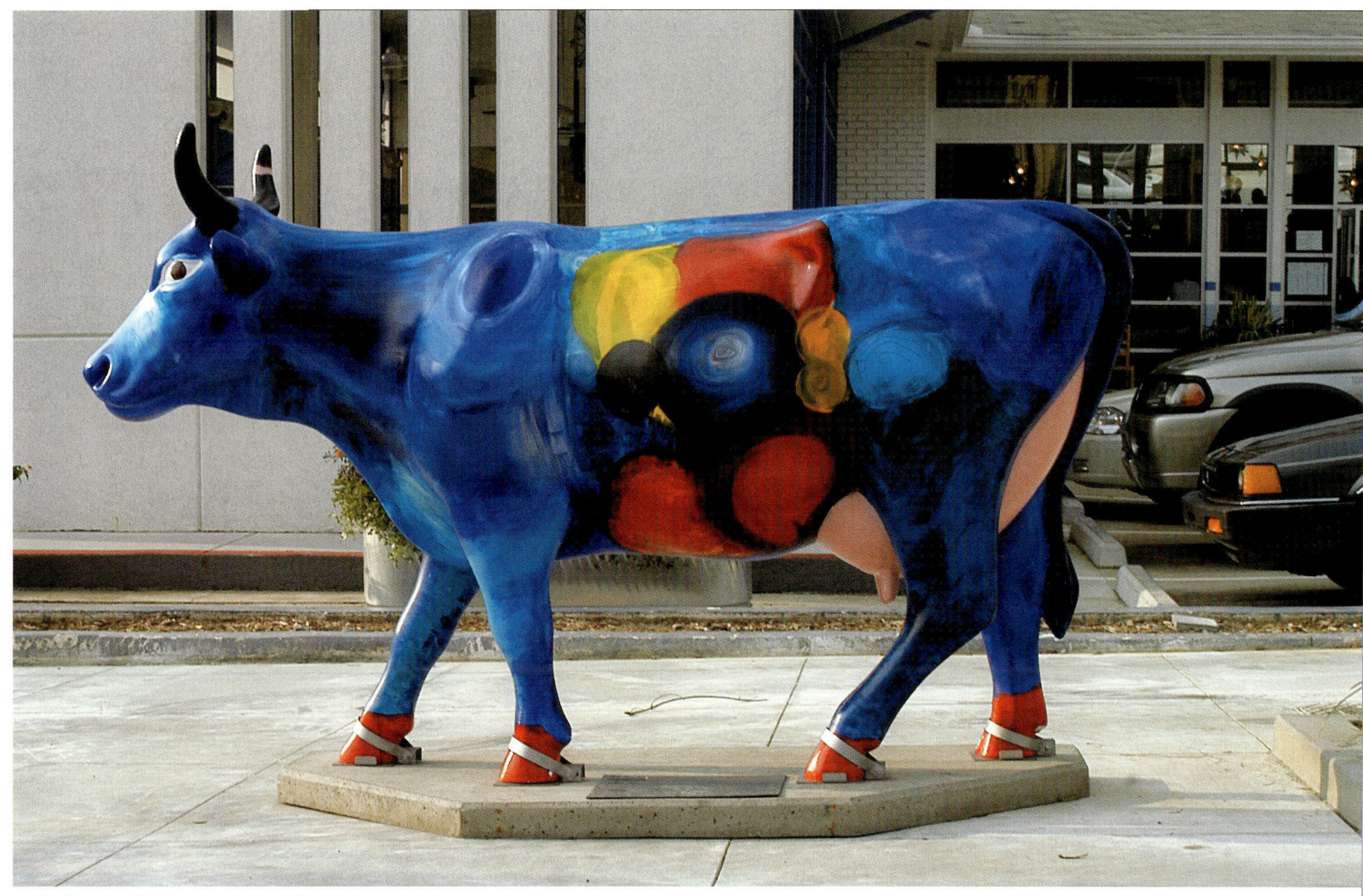

Rhythm & Blues Carnival
Anthony Liggins
Accenture

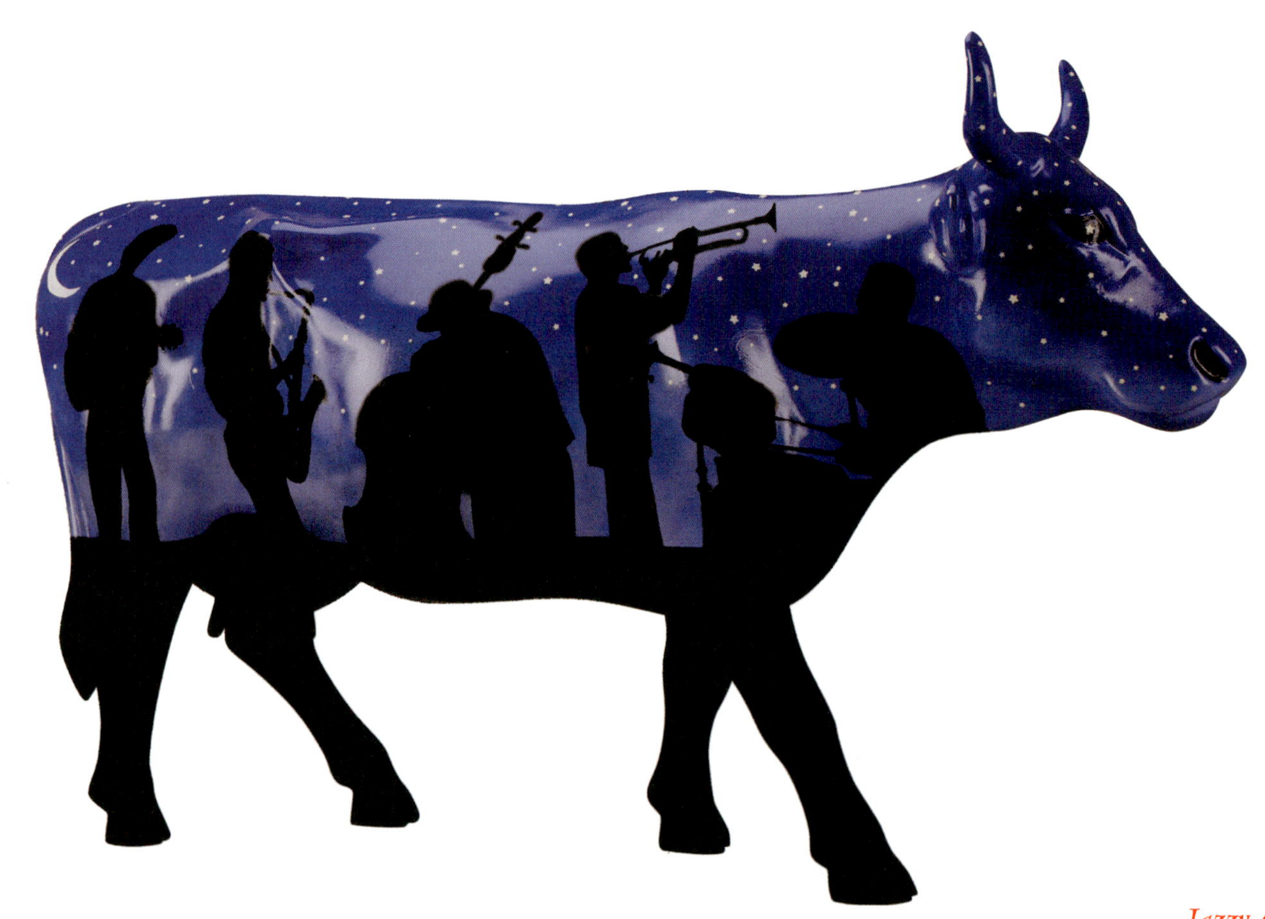

Jazzy Cow
Asher B. Johnson
CowParade Atlanta

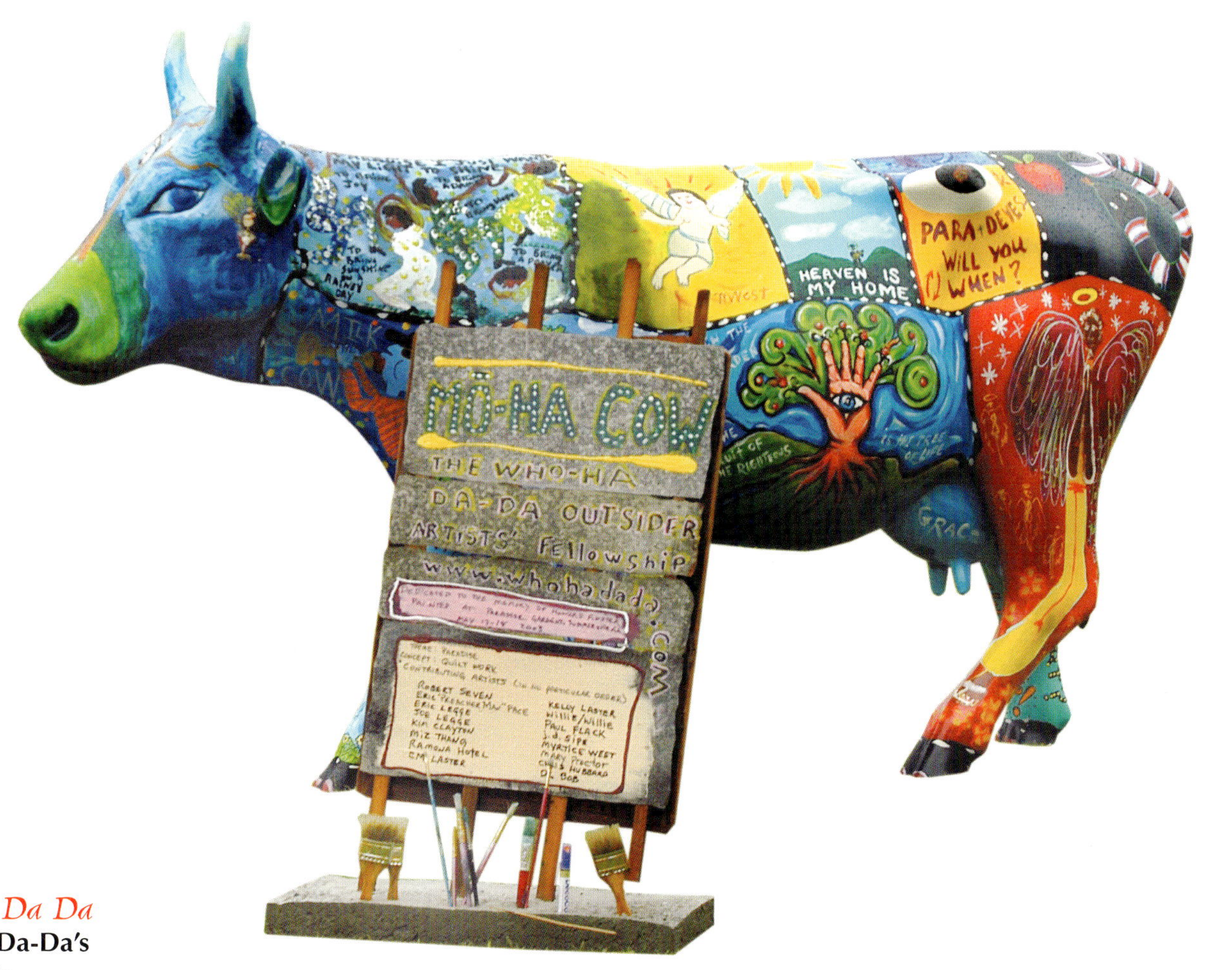

Moo Ha Da Da
Who-Ha-Da-Da's
Metropolis

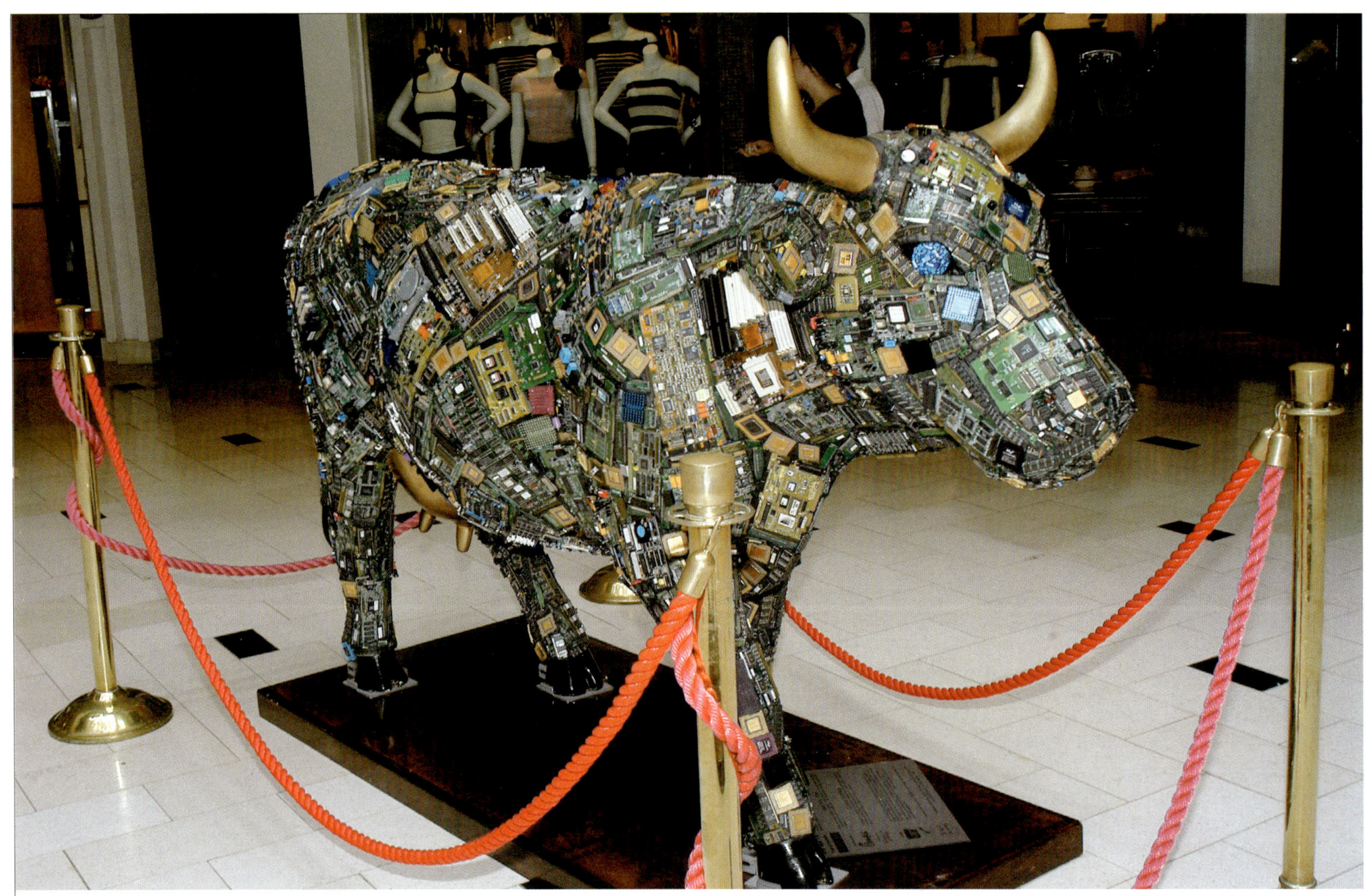

Chip
Mary Engel
Techbridge

“A discriminating palette is an udder necessity...”

—Mythic Art Cow Goddess

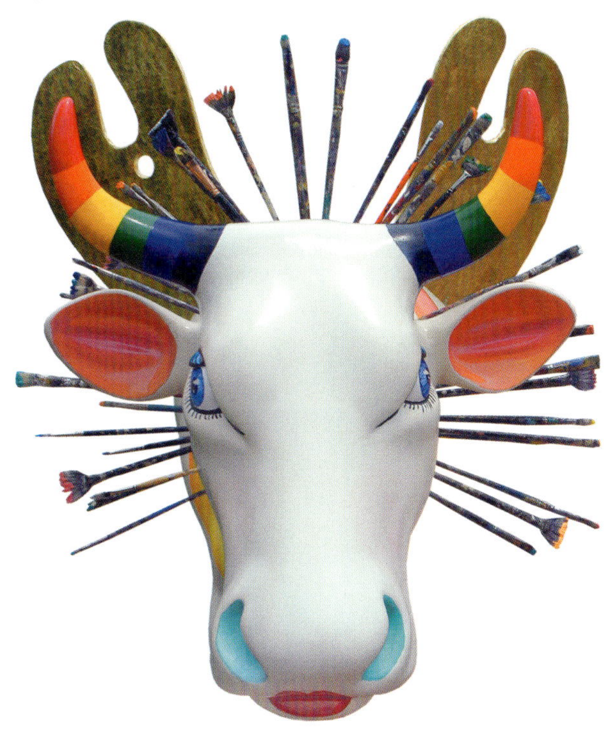

Acknowledgments

Event Production:

Chairman:
Evelyn A. Ashley
Chief Operating Officer:
Alan B. McKeon
Sponsorship Co-Chairs:
Alan B. McKeon, Dan Fernandez
Events & Communications Chairman:
Mary L. Sorrel
Arts Committee Chairman:
Laura Nix
Operations Co-Chairs:
John Coley, Gary R. Tilt
Non-Profit Liaison Chairs:
Janine Bowen, Henrietta (Henri) Barnes
Volunteer Chair:
Henrietta (Henri) Barnes
Government Affairs Chairman:
Sharon Gay
Event Coordinator & Artist Liasion:
Michelle M. Isom
Traffic Coordinators & Producers:
Dianne Atkins, Keith Fenton
CowMuseum Manager:
Monique (Moo-nique) Wilson
Assistant:
Corinne Shapiro
Summer Interns:
Jessica Cotton, Betsy Kulinski
Sponsorship Committee Members
Holly Bounds, Nicole Lipson

Arts Committee Members:

Dorothea Bozicolona-Volpe
Laurel Gross
Jillian Steinbrenner
Keith Duprey
Brett Lockwood
Emily Vorderbruegge
Sue (Moo) Davis
Lucia Duncan Harrison
Allison Wagner

Public Relations:

Sue Rodman
Hayslett Sorrel

Government Affairs Committee Members:

Steve Labovitz
Hakim Hillard
Tamera Alexander

Operations Committee Members:

Jeff Pierson
Deon Behrman
Brent Craig/Craig Graphics

CowParade Atlanta was the culmination of months of hard work by literally hundreds of volunteers and supporters. There are so many of these helping hands, there is just not enough space to thank each of them by name. But let it be known, it was their support, enthusiasm, introductions, and their smiles, that made this event a success.

Artist Index

Sponsor Index

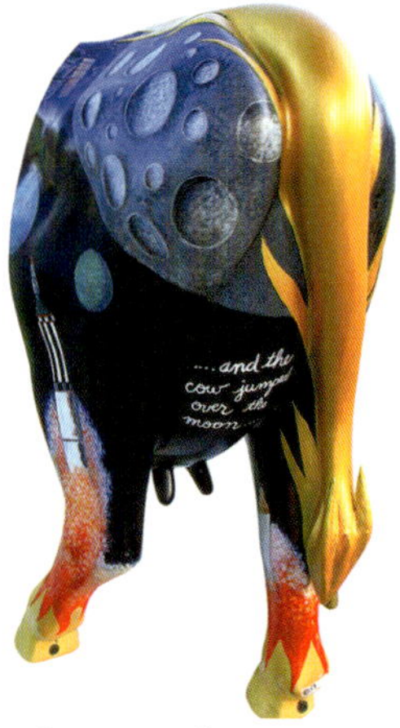

Great art picks up where nature ends.